OUR OCCULTED HISTORY

OUR
OCCULTED
HISTORY

DO THE GLOBAL ELITE CONCEAL ANCIENT ALIENS?

JIM MARRS

wm
WILLIAM MORROW
An Imprint of HarperCollins*Publishers*

ACKNOWLEDGMENTS

ACKNOWLEDGMENT MUST BE GIVEN TO THE MANY AUTHORS AND researchers who have dedicated themselves to the investigation of an early human history that differs from that in conventional textbooks. Special thanks go to the invaluable assistance of Maritha Gan, along with Tom Ruffner, Larry Sells, the editing skills of Henry Ferris and Danny Goldstein, and, of course, my wife, Carol, who nourishes my soul.

HarperCollins books may be purchased for educational, business, or sales promotional use. For information please e-mail the Special Markets Department at SPsales@harpercollins.com.

A hardcover edition of this book was published in 2013 by William Morrow, an imprint of HarperCollins Publishers.

FIRST WILLIAM MORROW PAPERBACK EDITION PUBLISHED 2013.

Designed by Jamie Lynn Kerner

Library of Congress Cataloging-in-Publication Data has been applied for.

ISBN 978-0-06-213032-7

13 14 15 16 17 OV/RRD 10 9 8 7 6 5 4 3 2 1

CONTENTS

PART III:
THE MIDDLE AGES

PART IV:
THE MODERN ERA

INTRODUCTION

The most merciful thing in the world, I think, is the inability of the human mind to correlate all its contents. We live on a placid island of ignorance in the midst of a black sea of infinity, and it was not meant that we should voyage far. The sciences, each straining in its own direction, have hitherto harmed us little; but some day the piecing together of disassociated knowledge will open up such terrifying vistas of reality, and of our frightful position therein, that we shall either go mad from the revelation or flee from the deadly light into the peace and safety of a new dark age.
—HOWARD PHILLIPS LOVECRAFT,
The Call of Cthulhu and
Other Weird Stories

LET'S GET SOMETHING STRAIGHT RIGHT OFF. THIS BOOK HAS nothing to do with stories of vampires, werewolves, devil worship, witchcraft, or anything else commonly thought to be of the occult, although there is an unearthly aspect.

Many believers choose to put their faith in such stories, but there is another narrative growing in the public consciousness that can no longer be written off as mere fable: the idea that aliens from outer space or other dimensions may have—or may be trying to—take control of the world.

The word *occult*, often misconstrued to mean supernatural or magical, actually is defined simply as hidden or concealed. Even so, the word also involves a connection to outer space or the heavens. In astronomical terms, the term *occulted* equates to an eclipse, in which one heavenly body is masked, or hidden, behind another.

What history is being hidden from us? It would appear that something nonhuman seeks to control the planet Earth and may even have contributed to the advent of modern humankind.

The field of entertainment is no stranger to this idea. The television series *V* presented benign humanlike aliens visiting Earth, who turn out to be a reptilian race set on conquering our world. Movies like *Invasion of the Body Snatchers* and books like Robert A. Heinlein's *The Puppet Masters* have depicted humans transformed into zombielike pod people after an alien invasion. But these seemingly outrageous concepts haven't always been the stuff of pulp fantasy novels or television scripts. Rather, they've been considered seriously by many people at different times throughout our history.

David Icke, author of the *The Biggest Secret*, has built a large worldwide following with his claims that certain world leaders, including the British royals, are shape-shifting reptilian aliens who have been on Earth since before written history. According to Icke, these leaders have descended from many generations of reptilian aliens. "A race of interbreeding [reptile-human hybrid] bloodlines . . . were centered in the Middle East and Near East in the ancient world," wrote Icke, "and, over the thousands of years since, have expanded their power across the globe . . . [through] a network of mystery schools and secret societies . . . creating institutions like religions to mentally and emotionally imprison the masses and set them at war with each other."

Lest one believe such talk comes only from loony fanatics, consider that none other than the famed scientist Carl Sagan wrote at length in his book *The Dragons of Eden* about the reptilian complex, which tops the brain stem, the oldest part of the human brain.

Sagan said this part is the "seat of aggression, ritual, territoriality and social hierarchy which evolved millions of years ago in our reptilian ancestors." He equated such characteristics with modern human bureaucratic and political behavior.

The idea that surreptitious space aliens want to take over the planet has been around since long before David Icke. A 1952 issue of *Weird Science*, a publication of the fabled Educational Comics (EC) that was shut down in the early 1950s due to the advent of the Comics Code, carried a story in which Allie Gator, a takeoff on the alligator character in the then-popular TV puppet program *Kukla, Fran and Ollie*, was elected president following a joke write-in campaign. Allie turned out to be the leading element of a reptilian alien force bent on taking over the Earth.

Much earlier and on a more somber note, journalist Charles Fort declared, "I think we're property." Fort was an American writer who from 1916 until his death in 1932 researched and wrote about a large number of "anomalous phenomena," a lofty term for artifacts and events that evade conventional explanation.

In his 1919 work, *The Book of the Damned*, Fort explained that by "damned" he meant that we, humans, have been excluded from certain knowledge. "I should say," he continued, "we belong to something. That once upon a time, this Earth was No-Man's Land, that other worlds explored and colonized here, and fought among themselves for possession, but that now it's owned by something: That something owns this Earth—all others warned off. . . . I suspect . . . that all of this has been known, perhaps for ages, to certain ones upon the earth, a cult or order, members of which function like bellwethers to the rest of us, or as superior slaves or overseers, directing us in accordance with instructions received—from Somewhere else—in our mysterious usefulness."

Fort compiled such a prodigious amount of data covering unusual events that his books are still in print. His followers founded the Fortean Society in 1931, which continues to exist and publishes

Fortean Times. The very words *Fortean* and *Forteana* have entered the English language, referring to the strange and unexplainable.

But it was Swiss journalist Erich von Däniken, with his 1968 book, *Chariots of the Gods*, who brought the concept of "ancient astronauts"—visitors who came to our world during the Stone Age to help perpetuate the human race—to a global audience.

Two questions arise from Fort's and von Däniken's writings. How warranted were their condemnations of the unwillingness of conventional science to investigate unconventional phenomena? And more important, how right were they about the concept of nonhuman control?

One of the most prominent websites for skeptics acknowledges ancient mysteries but shuns the idea of ancient astronauts, merely stating, "It is true that we still do not know how the ancients accomplished some of their more astounding physical and technological feats. We still wonder how the ancient Egyptians raised giant obelisks in the desert and how stone age men and women moved huge cut stones and placed them in position in dolmens and passage graves. We are amazed by the giant carved heads on Easter Island and wonder why they were done, who did them, and why they abandoned the place. We may someday have the answers to our questions, but they are most likely to come from scientific investigation not pseudoscientific speculation."

Others have concluded that standard science may not offer the right tools to figure out our past. Following a lifetime of research, author Philip Coppens concluded in his 2012 book, *The Ancient Alien Question*, that the manner in which science has considered the question of nonhuman contact in our distant past is "not the correct, or at least not the only, approach. When we look at reality the way it is, rather than within the reduced framework in which science prefers to operate, it becomes clear that there is only one answer. Were we alone? No."

William Bramley, in his 1990 book, *The Gods of Eden*, said

he began studying the causes of war but came to the conclusion that "Human beings appear to be a slave race languishing on an isolated planet in a small galaxy." He added that "the human race was once a source of labor for an extraterrestrial civilization and still remains a possession today. To keep control over its possession and to maintain Earth as something of a prison, that other civilization [Bramley called them Custodians] has bred never-ending conflict between human beings, has promoted human spiritual decay, and has erected on Earth conditions of unremitting physical hardship. This situation has lasted for thousands of years and it continues today."

After more than 360 pages cataloging evidence of possible ancient nonhuman visitation on Earth, author, psychologist, and ordained Baptist minister Paul Von Ward in his 2011 book, *We Have Never Been Alone*, concluded that "enough evidence of AB [Advanced Beings] involvement in human history exists that no responsible student of the human past and present can dismiss it in good conscience."

Australian researcher Paul White saw the involvement of non-humans as the basis of ancient legends and myths worldwide. "Just after the Deluge, at the dawn of the present time cycle, an era the Egyptians called ZEP TEPI, 'The First Times,' a mysterious group of 'gods' appeared, to initiate the survivors in the rudiments of ci-vilisation. From Thoth and Osiris in Egypt, to Quetzalcoatl and Viracocha in the Americas, traditions worldwide subscribe [*sic*] the origins of contemporary civilisation to this sophisticated group."

"Evidence from around the world, indicates these people were the hi-tech survivors of the previous civilisation of what we now refer to as Atlantis and Mu. Like the nuclear survival bunkers and secret research facilities of our own civilisation, there were those who arose from the underground 'cities of the Gods,' after the dust settled. These survivors are characterised in the Bible as the 'prediluvian patriarchs,' like Enoch and Methuselah, the 'giants and heroes of old,' mentioned in Genesis. These are the 'fabled gods' of ancient Summer [*sic*], Egypt and India."

Emmy Award–winning science journalist Linda Moulton Howe, after years of interviewing those who claim contact with nonhumans, also connected the ancient gods with human origins. "The perpetuation of the experiment through Noah's bloodline perhaps produced a human history which might be compared to stepchildren who had different parents, a difficult, confusing childhood, and who grew into rebellious teenagers resisting parental control," she wrote in her 1998 book *Glimpses of Other Realities.*

Is there any historical or archaeological evidence to support such beliefs? There is, and it's compelling, though it contradicts many of our conventional histories and beliefs. This is good. After all, at one time, conventional belief was that the earth was flat and the center of the universe.

If humankind's progress has been a long, slow climb from hunter-gatherers to modern empires, then the historical record should not describe much out of the ordinary. But the account introduced here—culled from ancient texts, tablets, and carvings found scattered throughout the world—tells a different story, one of visitors from the stars colonizing the Earth. From the flying sky gods of the Middle East to the destructive *vimanas* described in the Hindu Vedic texts, almost all ancient legends tell of flying objects under intelligent control. They also describe strange visitors who taught language, law, mathematics, agriculture, and building construction to primitive humans.

Strange and mysterious artifacts and structures abound throughout the world, from the Nasca lines etched in the dry plains of Peru to the pyramids found not only on the Giza Plateau but in Central and South America, China, eastern Europe, and even Arkansas. Odd-shaped skulls and ancient small statues of what appear to be aircraft are written off as mere anomalies. Researchers continually stumble over anomalies. By dictionary definition, an anomaly is a circumstance or thing that is irregular, a deviation from the rule, something abnormal—in computer slang, a giant scientific WTF! And the world is chock-full of them.

If any part of a thesis concerning extraterrestrials or even a prehistoric supercivilization could be proven true, why haven't academics and the mass media reported it? The mass media won't touch such deep subjects, except in a simplified version that can fill an hour of TV time for entertainment. Convention has viewed such speculation as the province of the occult. Even today, many thoughtful and well-documented books languish on the Occult or New Age shelf in your bookstore right alongside imaginative tomes on vampires, witches, and demons. Common assumptions about what is true are falling away in light of new and widespread information, primarily from the Internet.

So now the word *occulted* may be viewed in another way—one that reveals how conventional science, and perhaps even institutions administered by the federal government or funded by the wealthy elite, have worked to conceal our possible true heritage. This book will address many of the omissions and distortions in our history books, investigating the origins of our solar system and the Earth through the advent of humankind to our current ruling class. It will examine the history of not only our civilization and our culture, but also the science used to examine our history and the archaeologists and anthropologists who frame the conversations about our species.

And if indeed our universe has been populated by nonhumans since its beginning and if they were involved in creating our world and educating our species, then we must ask, Did these visitors leave at some point, or are they still among us? If they remain on or near our planet, then what is their agenda for the human race? These questions will take us deep into the quest to find our occulted history. So turn the page and join the search.

PART I

ORIGINS OF THE SOLAR SYSTEM

Science in its ideology sees itself as doing a fearless exploration of the unknown. Most of the time it is a fearful exploration of the almost known.
—RUPERT SHELDRAKE, BIOLOGIST AND ROYAL SOCIETY RESEARCH FELLOW

BEFORE WE TALK ABOUT WHO CONTROLS THE WORLD, WE FIRST need to understand how the world was created. Most people would agree that our universe was created by something, either a heavenly being such as God, Vishnu, Yahweh, Allah, the Great Spirit, the One or—as atheists might believe—by an accidental convergence of universal subatomic energy.

It is after this consensus that the trouble begins. Millennia of warfare and millions of deaths have resulted from religious disputes over exactly who God is and which people meet God's approval. There are also the Big Questions asked by humans down through the ages: Who are we? Where did we come from? Where are we going?

The answers to such questions may be found in the oldest known accounts of human history—the stone tablets from ancient Sumer, which predate the Bible by more than three thousand years. They tell of fantastic flying machines, trips to other worlds, destructive battles on Earth and elsewhere, and even the creation of a slave race. There are detailed accounts of gods, goddesses, and demigods, kings and queens, champions, tyrants, priests, holy men, wars, and insurrections. Beginning with the world's oldest known story—the quest of the great Sumerian king Gilgamesh, who claimed a nonhuman heritage—there exist enough tales of battles, court intrigues, jealousies, and adventures to rival any Hollywood blockbuster.

But to understand the reality of these recorded stories, one must start at the beginning.

BIG BANG QUESTIONED

Standard science tells us that our universe began with The Big Bang—a burst of energy that scientists estimate occurred about 13 billion years ago causing cosmic inflation milliseconds afterward.

Despite the scientific community's overall acceptance of the Big Bang, certain problems with the theory have come under scrutiny, leading some to question its validity. The cover story of the April 2011 edition of *Scientific American* included the article "Quantum Gaps in Big Bang Theory: Why Our Best Explanation of How the Universe Evolved Must Be Fixed—or Replaced." In the article Paul J. Steinhardt, director of Princeton University's Center for Theoretical Science, pointed out that astrophysicists have left a number of problems with the theory unresolved, stating that "the case against [the Big Bang theory] challenges the logical foundations of the theory. Does the theory really work as advertised? Are the predictions made in the early 1980s still the predictions of the inflationary model as we understand it today? There is an argument to be made that the answer to both questions is no."

But there have always been other theories, including our universe as a project of some superuniversal alien entities or the sudden appearance of Earth as an act of God. Anglican archbishop James Ussher, then Primate of All Ireland, set the tone for the next few centuries concerning the creation of Earth in his 1654 book modestly entitled *Annals of the World: The Origin of Time, and Continued to the Beginning of the Emperor Vespasian's Reign and the Total Destruction and Abolition of the Temple and Commonwealth of the Jews*. First published in Latin, this 1,600-page work traced the history of the world from the Garden of Eden to the fall of Jerusalem in AD 70. Ussher, a dedicated scholar of his time who traveled throughout Europe studying Church records, determined that ancient peoples, especially the Israelites, started their calendar at harvesttime, so he chose the first Sunday following the autumnal equinox to begin his history of the world. Ussher came to the startling conclusion that the world was created in the year 4004 BC. John Lightfoot, Master of St. Catherine's College, University of Cambridge, refined Ussher's calculations, declaring that the creation of the world occurred at exactly 9:00 a.m. on October 23, 4004 BC. Controversy over this date continues to this day between those who believe in the absolute inerrancy of the Bible—and hence Ussher's calculated date—and those who believe the geological record, which clearly indicates the Earth to be more than 4.5 billion years old, and with some evidence of human habitats dated prior to 10,000 BC.

More than two thousand years before the Bible was put into writing, the creation of the Earth was described on cuneiform tablets by the ancient Sumerians. Starting with the translations of ancient Sumerian tablets by Zecharia Sitchin in the 1970s, many authors have contributed to a more detailed understanding of the creation story as recorded by the Sumerians long before the Bible. Thanks to Sitchin's work, as well as that of Erich von Däniken, Michael Tellinger, Paul Von Ward, Alan F. Alford, R. A. Boulay, Neil Freer, Arthur David Horn, Joe Lewels, Joseph P. Farrell, David Hatcher Childress, C. L. Turnage, David Icke, Lloyd Pye, Laurence Gardner, and William Bramley, a novel and unconventional account of Earth's creation has been developing. The new account, based in part on ancient writings, deals with the recurring intrusion of a tenth planet into our solar system. Traditional science, wedded to its own texts and dogma, has dismissed these accounts as mere mythology, if not pseudoscience and pseudohistory.

SEARCH FOR THE TENTH PLANET

The search for an unknown planet (Planet X) in our solar system is nothing new. It has continued since at least 1843, when British astronomer John Couch Adams deduced through noticeable gravitational disturbances that another planet must lie beyond Uranus. His observations led to the discovery of Neptune. Scientists continued to use this method to deduce the existence of other solar bodies, such as Pluto, which was discovered in 1930 after gravitational perturbations in the orbit of Neptune were noticed. Initially Pluto was thought to be the long-sought Planet X. However, it has since been concluded that the combined mass of Pluto and its major moon, Charon, is too small to exert the observed effect on the orbit of Neptune. Poor Pluto was downgraded in 2006 from a full-fledged planet to a dwarf planet, although some astronomers continue to disagree. The hunt for Planet X continues.

In 1981, American scientists were theorizing the existence of a tenth planet in our system based on sightings by an orbiting telescope and studies of irregularities in the orbit of Pluto indicating an additional solar body. "If new evidence from the U.S. Naval Observatory of a 10th planet in the solar system is correct, it could prove that the Sumerians . . . were far ahead of modern man in astronomy," commented Hugh McCann, a writer for the *Detroit News*. Although the ancient Sumerians call it the twelfth planet, there is no inconsistency, as they counted the moon and the sun as planetary bodies, thus arriving at the number twelve, the same number as their pantheon of spacefaring overlords, whom they said arrived on Earth from Nibiru.

On December 30, 1983, the *Washington Post* reported on its front page, "A heavenly body possibly as large as the giant planet Jupiter and possibly so close to Earth that it would be part of this solar system has been found in the direction of the constellation Orion by an orbiting telescope aboard the U.S. Infrared Astronomical Satellite (IRAS). So mysterious is the object that astronomers do not know if it is a planet, a giant comet, a nearby 'protostar' that never got hot enough to become a star, a distant galaxy so young that it is still in the process of forming its first stars or a galaxy so shrouded in dust that none of the light cast by its stars ever gets through. . . ."

Gerry Neugebauer, IRAS chief scientist for California's Jet Propulsion Laboratory and director of the Palomar Observatory for the California Institute of Technology, was quoted saying, "All I can tell you is that we don't know what it is."

The Caltech scientists believed the large body was fifty billion miles away, a mere stone's throw in astronomical terms, and they speculated that it may be heading toward Earth. Others predicted that it could enter our inner solar system, wreaking havoc, in 2012. Perhaps giving an early indication as to how officialdom would treat such news, Neugebauer told the media, "I want to douse that idea with as much cold water as I can."

Recently traditional scientists have downplayed or dismissed the idea of Nibiru or any large body invading our solar system. Ian O'Neill, a science writer for *Universe Today* who specializes in astrophysics, in 2008 wrote that "any Neptune orbital perturbations have been put down to observational error and have since not been observed . . . so there doesn't appear to be any obvious object any bigger than the largest Kuiper Belt objects out there. . . . " The Kuiper Belt is an area of planetoids and asteroids that lies just outside the orbit of Neptune.

O'Neill maintained that IRAS never observed any astronomical body in the outer reaches of the solar system and concluded, "The story that Planet X will arrive [on December 21, 2012] is, in my view, total bunkum (but it helps to sell doomsday books and DVDs by scaring people). Nibiru will remain in the realms of Sumerian myth." O'Neill acknowledged that rumors have persisted that world governments, including NASA, were hiding the truth of an approaching world. "So why would governments want to hide a 'discovery' as historic as a doomsday planet approaching the inner Solar System anyway?" he asked, then provided his own facetious answer, "To avoid mass panic and pursue their own, greedy agendas (obviously)."

THE SUMERIAN ACCOUNT—MINGLING OF THE WATERS

The truly amazing fact remains that ancient Sumerians, whom traditional history tells us were just developing writing, accurately described the planets Uranus, Neptune, and Pluto, even though these three worlds cannot be seen without the aid of a telescope. Uranus was not known to modern man until it was discovered in 1781; Neptune, in 1846; and Pluto, in 1930.

Although they have long been considered fanciful myths, recent interpretations of Mesopotamian texts, particularly one entitled *Enuma Elish*, known as *The Creation Epic*, provided a most plausible explanation for the present composition of our solar system. "But why not take the epic at face value, as nothing more nor less than the statement of cosmological facts as known to the Sumerians, as told them by the Nefilim?" asked the late Zecharia Sitchin, a graduate of the London School of Economics who made a lifelong study of the Sumerian tablets and carvings. He died in October 2010, leaving behind a sizable following of devotees.

Sitchin's revisionist interpretation of the Sumerian texts asserts that more than four billion years ago, the planets Mercury, Venus, and Mars were closest to the sun. A large watery world called Tiamat was in orbit between Mars and Jupiter. Nibiru, a large rogue planet that theoretically travels an elliptical orbit, entering our system about every 3,600 years, arrived and narrowly missed Tiamat. Tiamat cracked under the gravitational stresses. In a subsequent pass by Nibiru—in Sitchin's early works, he refers to this orb by its Babylonian name, Marduk—Tiamat was cleaved in half when one of Nibiru's moons rammed into the planet.

The collision of Nibiru's moon and Tiamat knocked a large portion of Tiamat past Mars, ripping away its atmosphere and pieces of matter of various sizes. These fragments of Tiamat remained in its original orbit, becoming the familiar asteroid belt, or the Hammered Bracelet or Firmament, as it was called by the ancients. The greater portion of Tiamat was knocked into a new orbit closer to the sun. This larger chunk, retaining much of the planet's water and carrying material from Mars, coalesced, cooled, and began orbiting between Mars and Venus, becoming Earth. It was accompanied by one of Nibiru's moons (Kingu), which was captured by Earth's gravity and became our own satellite. Some say the huge gouge out of the Earth now encompassing the Pacific Ocean is where that portion of Tiamat broke apart.

The idea is that when Nibiru and Tiamat collided, many tons of sea water from both worlds were thrown into space—an event termed the "mingling of the waters" by the Sumerian scribes—along with dirt and debris, all of which became the erratic flying balls of "dirty" ice we call comets.

Interestingly enough, this theory could explain why the Earth is missing much of its crust, particularly on the half encompassing the Pacific Ocean, as well as the origin of the asteroid belt. This theory also offers an explanation for comets, which have caused so much speculation among scientists as to their origin.

This "War of the Worlds" concept has been strengthened by the recent discovery of meteorites in Antarctica containing the same gases known to compose the atmosphere of Mars and by the discovery by NASA scientists in 1996 of what appeared to be the remains of microorganisms in a Martian meteorite thought to be four billion years old.

MARTIAN LIFE

The concept of life on Mars got yet another boost when the results of the Viking Lander missions of the 1970s were reevaluated in

2009. Photos of the surrounding Martian landscape from Viking 2 showed a thin layer of frost on the ground. Many scientists now suspect that life-sustaining water might exist as close as ten inches under the Martian surface. Retired Viking scientist Patricia Straat told *Discover* magazine, "A lot of people think there isn't life on Mars because there wasn't any water on Mars. Our experiment was a definite positive response for life, but a lot of people have claimed that it was a false positive for a variety of reasons."

"The idea that all Earth life could be descended from Martian organisms may not be fully mainstream—but it's not too crazy to consider, either. While the Martian surface appears to be cold, dry and lifeless today, there is plenty of evidence that the planet was much warmer and wetter in the distant past, billions of years ago," stated Mike Wall, senior editor of Space.com. Apparently refuting the claim that Mars is a dead world devoid of life, scientists in 1996 announced they discovered evidence of fossilized microbial life in a meteorite from Mars called Allan Hills 84001. Although this claim continued to draw controversy, many saw this as evidence that humans are not the only living organisms in our universe.

Astrobiologist Chris McKay of NASA's Ames Research Center also has supported the concept that life on Earth might connect to Mars, stating, "It is not implausible that life on Mars will be related to life on Earth and therefore share a common genetics. In any case, it would be important to test this hypothesis."

Researchers in early 2011 were devising an instrument that could search through samples of Martian dirt and isolate any genetic material from microbes there. Scientists could then use standard biochemical techniques to compare such material with that found on Earth. "It's a long shot," admitted MIT researcher Chris Carr, one of those producing the device. "But if we go to Mars and find life that's related to us, we could have originated on Mars. Or if it started here, it could have been transferred to Mars."

Scientists have found that 97 percent of the DNA (deoxyribonucleic acid) in human cells does not code for proteins and appears to consist of meaningless and repeating sequences. They are puzzled as to the function of this "junk" DNA. Adding to this conundrum is the speculation of some that this mysterious DNA may be extra-terrestrial in origin.

The late Francis Harry Compton Crick, the English molecular biologist who jointly won the 1962 Nobel Prize in Physiology or Medicine for his codiscovery of the structure of the DNA molecule, once suggested that while the development of living systems from molecules may be a rare event in the universe, once it did develop, it may have been spread by spacefaring intelligent life forms in a process he called directed panspermia. He postulated, "Life did not evolve first on Earth; a highly advanced civilization became threatened so they devised a way to pass on their existence. They genetically-modified their DNA and sent it out from their planet on bacteria or meteorites with the hope that it would collide with an-other planet. It did, and that's why we're here. The DNA molecule is the most efficient information storage system in the entire uni-verse. The immensity of complex, coded and precisely sequenced information is absolutely staggering. The DNA evidence speaks of intelligent, information-bearing design."

Crick was not alone is his supposition that Earth may have been seeded with life by intelligent beings. "The likelihood of the forma-tion of life from inanimate matter is one to a number with 40,000 naughts after it. . . . It is big enough to bury Darwin and the whole theory of evolution. There was no primeval soup, neither on this planet nor on any other, and if the beginnings of life were not random, they must therefore have been the product of purposeful intelligence," stated British astronomer Sir Fred Hoyle.

Sitchin and many others view human DNA differences and de-fects as support for the theory that primitive man was genetically altered by nonhumans. If so, where would such beings originate? The ancient Sumerian tablets tell us they came from that other world they called Nibiru.

According to the followers of Sitchin, Nibiru is called the Planet of the Crossing, because its orbit crosses the solar system between Mars and Jupiter. It then proceeds on its elliptical orbit, which takes it far outside the solar system before being pulled back by gravitational force. Nibiru has been symbolized in numerous societies—particularly Egyptian—as a winged disc, a circle with wings stretching to either side.

Some scientists claim that a planet that far from a sun could not support life, but others say that if such a planet had a strong confining atmosphere and a molten core like the Earth, it might generate its own life-sustaining heat.

Life on Earth evolved based on its one-year orbit around the sun, the solar year. Researchers theorize that life on Nibiru developed based on its one-year orbit around the sun—3,600 years to us on Earth. It then stands to reason that life on Nibiru would have evolved somewhat sooner than on Earth. Its beings may also be long-lived compared to the normal life span of a human, which would seem to be immortal to many insects, with their weeklong lives.

STRANGE MOONS

IN ADDITION TO ALTERNATIVE VIEWS ON THE ORIGINS OF EARTH, several scientists and authors have speculated that as many as three moons in our solar system may not be natural objects.

In 1959, Russian astrophysicist Iosif Samuilovich Shklovsky calculated the orbital motion of the Martian satellite Phobos and concluded, based on several factors, including its changing speed, that the moon is artificial and hollow. He noted than none of the other moons in our solar system are as small as the two Martian moons—Phobos and Deimos—and that both orbit much too close to Mars. Shklovsky realized that Phobos's velocity and position no longer matched its mathematically predicted course. The combination of its odd and changing velocity, coupled with anomalies in its gravitational and magnetic fields, led Shklovsky to conclude that Phobos was nothing less than some sort of huge spacecraft.

At the time, the famous astronomer Carl Sagan, who coauthored the 1966 book *Intelligent Life in the Universe* with Shklovsky, agreed, stating, "A natural satellite cannot be a hollow object." Sagan argued for serious consideration of paleocontact—that is, extraterrestrials in early Earth history—and called for reexamination of myths and religious literature for evidence of such contact. In 1960, Sagan was joined by S. Fred Singer, a special adviser on space developments to President Dwight D. Eisenhower, who speculated that Phobos might be an orbiting space station. The chief of applied mathematics at NASA, Raymond H. Wilson Jr., joined Shklovsky and Singer, saying that "Phobos might be a colossal base orbiting Mars."

Although in later years Sagan backpedaled from his belief in early extraterrestrial contact, he wrote then that "it seems possible that the Earth has been visited by various Galactic civilizations many times (possibly every 10,000 years) during geological time. It is not out of the question that artifacts of these visits still exist— although none have been found to date—or even that some kind of base is maintained within the solar system to provide continuity for successive expeditions." He added that such visits would require a base in proximity to Earth and suggested the back side of the moon.

Both then and now, conventional scientists have publicly scoffed at the notion of ETs on Earth. But author and publisher Dirk Vander Ploeg has since pointed out that the United States Naval Observatory verified Shklovsky's calculations. Ploeg interpreted this verification as a concession that mysterious alien ships might be orbiting Mars for purposes unknown. "Speculations over what the giant artificial spaceships might be have ranged from massive Martian space observatories, to half-completed generational interstellar spaceships, or even gargantuan planet-killing space bombs left over from an interplanetary war waged millions of years ago," he wrote.

IAPETUS

One of the moons of Saturn also has been suspected of containing something alien, if not being an artificial spacecraft itself. Iapetus, the planet's third largest moon, has puzzled researchers since its discovery by Italian astronomer Giovanni Domenico Cassini in 1671. Like our own moon, Iapetus is in a near-perfect circular orbit and one side always faces its planetary host. But even more puzzling are square and hexagonal craters that, according to one former NASA employee, appear to be gigantic artificial plates holding the moon together, making Iapetus resemble nothing so much as the Death Star in George Lucas's film *Star Wars*.

Because of its swirling two-tone coloration—a distinctly dark side and a light or white side, due to differences in surface reflectivity—Iapetus has been called the yin-yang moon, referring to the Chinese symbol indicating a connectedness even between opposites in the natural world.

But the most astonishing aspect of Iapetus is the strange mountainous ridge which encircles the equator of the entire moon. Some of the peaks reach nearly thirteen miles in height, making this oddity the tallest mountain range in our solar system. Despite a number of theories, no one can adequately explain how the ridge was formed or why it is confined to the equator. The cause of this moon's unusual inclined orbital plane is also unknown.

Richard C. Hoagland, a former consultant to NASA and science adviser to Walter Cronkite and CBS News, stated that " 'the

Great Wall of Iapetus' now forces serious reconsideration of a range of staggering possibilities that some will most *certainly* find . . . upsetting: That, it could really *be* a 'wall' . . . a vast, planet spanning, *artificial* construct!!" (emphasis in the original). Hoagland went so far as to speculate that the entire moon might be an artificial nine-hundred-mile-wide "spacecraft."

Hoagland does not stand alone in this assessment. Tobias Owen and Donald Goldsmith, authors of *The Search for Life in the Universe*, wrote, "This unusual moon is the only object in the solar system which we might seriously regard as an alien signpost—a natural object deliberately modified by an advanced civilization to attract our attention. . . ."

Could the clues to Iapetus's purpose in the solar system be hidden in the mythology surrounding its name? In Greek mythology, Iapetus was the Titan son of Uranus, who was the god of the heavens and who was married to Gaia, mother of the Earth. Iapetus was the father of Atlas, a Titan who held up the Earth, and Prometheus, a god who brought knowledge in the form of fire and light to humankind. Robert Graves, British mythologist and author of *I, Claudius*, cited old Jewish traditions that equated the name Iapetus (Iapetós in Greek) with Japheth, a son of Noah. These Greek gods were all considered progenitors of the human race, and they fit quite neatly into the Sumerian accounts of extraterrestrial visitors creating a worker race. Only the names change through succeeding languages and cultures.

MOON ANOMALIES

Even our own moon, long the object of both human fear and reverence, continues to be enmeshed in controversies. Lights, moving shadows, unexplained structures, and even the moon's unnatural orbit might be explained by intelligent design, but such an idea would exclude this being done by human beings from Earth, at least those in our recorded history.

After six moon landings between 1969 and 1972 and the return of some 842 pounds of rocks and soil samples plus the placement of five nuclear-powered scientific stations on the lunar surface, there still have been no clear-cut answers to the moon's mysteries.

The moon is far older than previously imagined, perhaps even much older than the Earth and sun. By examining tracks burned into moon rocks by cosmic rays, scientists have dated them to 5.3 billion years ago, making them almost a billion years older than our planet. This puzzle was compounded by the fact that the lunar dust in which the rocks were found proved to be a billion years older than the rocks themselves, indicating that it may have come from somewhere else, perhaps as a result of traveling through space. The heavier moon rocks are found on the surface and do not match the surrounding soil.

The moon is extremely dry and does not appear to have ever had water in any substantial amounts, as none of the moon rocks, regardless of location found, contained free water or even water molecules bound into the minerals. Yet instruments left behind by Apollo missions sent a signal to Earth on March 7, 1971, indicating that a "wind" of water had crossed the moon's surface and lasted for fourteen hours. Although NASA officials attempted to explain this cloud of water as water vapor escaping from tanks on two separate Apollo descent stages, many declined to accept this theory, pointing out that the two tanks—from Apollo 12 and 14—were some 108 miles apart, yet the water vapor was detected at the same flow rate at both sites, although the instruments faced in opposite directions.

The presence of maria, or large seas of smooth solidified molten rock, on the moon indicates nothing less than a vast outpouring of lava at some distant time. It has now been confirmed that some of the moon's craters are of internal origin. In comparison to the rest of the moon, the maria are relatively free of craters, suggesting that craters were covered by lava flow. Yet scientists have found no evidence of volcanic activity on the moon. Some have associated this lava flow with mascons, large dense circular masses that lie twenty to forty miles below the center of the moon's maria. They were discovered because their denseness distorted the orbits of spacecraft flying over or near them. One scientist proposed that the mascons are heavy iron meteorites that plunged deep into the moon while it was in a soft, formable stage. This theory has been discounted because meteorites strike with such high velocities that they would vaporize on contact. Another mundane explanation is that the mascons are nothing more than lava-filled caverns, but skeptics say there isn't enough lava present, nor is lava dense enough, to accomplish this. "What they are is a major moon mystery," wrote author Don Wilson. "It now appears that the mascons are broad disk-shaped objects that could be possibly some kind of artificial construction. For huge circular disks are not likely to be beneath each huge maria, centered like bull-eyes in the middle of each, by coincidence or accident."

Almost three thousand seismic disturbances termed *moonquakes* were recorded between 1969 and 1977 after Apollo missions placed seismographic equipment at six separate sites on the moon. Most of the vibrations were quite small and perhaps were caused by meteorite strikes or falling booster rockets. But many other quakes were detected deep inside the moon. This internal creaking is believed to be caused by rocks settling due to the gravitational pull of our planet, as most moonquakes occur when the moon is closest to Earth. But in November 1958, Soviet astronomer Nikolai A. Kozyrev of the Crimean Astrophysical Observatory photographed the first recorded gaseous eruption on the moon. He attributed this to escaping fluorescent gases. Some scientists refused to accept Kozyrev's findings until astronomers at the Lowell Observatory also saw reddish glows on the crests of ridges in the Aristarchus region in 1963. Days later colored lights lasting more than an hour were reported at two separate observatories. Something was going on inside the volcanically dead moon.

Perhaps strangest of all the anomalies are the many indications that the moon may be hollow. Studies of moon rocks indicate that the moon's interior differs from the Earth's mantle in ways suggesting a very small core or none at all. A 1962 study found the interior of the moon to be less dense than the exterior. "Indeed, it would seem that the moon is more like a hollow than a homogeneous sphere," concluded NASA scientist Gordon MacDonald.

MIT's Sean C. Solomon noted, "The Lunar Orbiter experiments vastly improved our knowledge of the moon's gravitational field . . . indicating the frightening possibility that the moon might be hollow."

The most startling evidence that the moon could be hollow came on November 20, 1969, when the Apollo 12 crew, after returning to their command ship, sent the lunar module (LM) ascent stage crashing back onto the moon, creating an artificial moonquake. The LM struck the surface about forty miles from the Apollo 12 landing site, where ultrasensitive seismic equipment recorded something both unexpected and astounding—the moon reverberated like a bell for more than an hour. Frank Press of MIT stated, " . . . none of us have seen anything like this on Earth. In all our experience, it is quite an extraordinary event. That this rather small impact . . . produced a signal which lasted 30 minutes is quite beyond the range of our experience."

Undoubtedly the greatest mystery concerning our moon is how it came to be there in the first place. Prior to the Apollo missions, one serious theory as to the moon's origin was that it broke away from Earth eons ago. This idea was discarded when it was found that there is little similarity between the composition of our world and the moon. A more recent theory had the moon created out of space debris left over from the creation of Earth. This concept proved untenable in light of current gravitational theory, which predicts that one large object will accumulate all loose material, leaving none for the formation of another large body. Mainstream science now accepts the theory that the moon originated elsewhere and entered the Earth's gravitational field at some point in ancient times. But how the body came to orbit our planet is the subject of two theories: one states that the moon was formed from debris after a space object smashed into Earth, while the second states that the Earth captured the moon in its gravitational field while it was wandering through the solar system.

Neither of these theories is especially compelling because of the lack of evidence that either Earth or Luna has been physically disrupted by a past close encounter. There is no debris in space indicating a past collision, and it does not appear that the Earth and the moon developed during the same time period. As for the capture theory, even scientist Isaac Asimov wrote, "It's too big to have been captured by the Earth. The chances of such a capture having been effected and the moon then having taken up nearly circular orbit around our Earth are too small to make such an eventuality credible."

Asimov was right to consider the moon's orbit: not only is it nearly a perfect circle, but the moon's rotation is synchronized with its period of revolution, so one side always faces Earth, with only the slightest variation. This circular orbit is especially odd, considering that the moon's center of mass lies more than a mile closer to the Earth than its geometric center. This fact alone should produce an unstable, wobbly orbit, much as a ball with its mass off-center will not roll in a straight line.

THE BIG WHACK

In the late 1960s, the Planetary Science Institute's senior scientist, William Kenneth Hartmann, conjectured that the moon's creation resulted from a collision between Earth and another body at least as large as Mars. By 2000, computer models seemed to bring further support to what became known as the Big Whack theory. If this theory sounds familiar, it should—it's basically the story told in the ancient Sumerian tablets.

The Big Whack did not adequately explain why such an impact did not increase the Earth's orbital speed, so it was suggested that a second collision occurred by an object coming from the opposite direction and thus canceling out the increased spin celestial mechanics demanded by the first strike. Researchers theorized that the second orb striking the Earth must have been a giant—at least three times the size of Mars. This, of course, lends scientific support to the story of Nibiru's large moon Kingu striking the watery world called Tiamat, as recounted in the ancient Sumerian tablets.

The Big Whack theory has been tentatively accepted by conventional science for the simple reason that it seems to be the least impossible explanation currently available, yet it still does not explain how our moon ended up exactly one four-hundredth the size of the sun and in an orbit exactly one four-hundredth the distance between the sun and Earth while traveling at just the correct orbital speed to maintain that distance.

As science writer William Roy Shelton wrote, "It is important to remember that something had to put the moon at or near its present circular pattern around the Earth. Just as an Apollo spacecraft circling the Earth every 90 minutes while 100 miles high has to have a velocity of roughly 18,000 miles per hour to stay in orbit, so something had to give the moon the precisely required velocity for its weight and altitude. . . . The point—and it is one seldom noted in considering the origin of the moon—is that it is extremely unlikely that any object would just stumble into the right combination of factors required to stay in orbit. 'Something' had to put the moon at its altitude, on its course and at its speed. The question is: what was that 'something'?"

If the precise and stationary orbit of the moon is seen as sheer coincidence, is it also coincidence that the moon is at just the right distance from Earth to completely cover the sun during an eclipse? While the diameter of the moon is a mere 2,160 miles against the sun's gigantic 864,000 miles, it is nevertheless in just the proper position to block out all but the sun's flaming corona when it moves between the sun and Earth. Asimov explains, "There is no astronomical reason why the moon and the sun should fit so well. It is the sheerest of coincidences, and only the Earth among all the planets is blessed in this fashion."

SPACESHIP MOON?

The idea of coincidence being involved in the configuration of the Earth, moon, and sun pales at the odds involved, but the concept of intelligent design raises more questions than answers. In July 1970, two Russian scientists offered a bizarre theory of the origin of the moon—but one that provided an answer to all the mysteries. Michael Vasin and Alexander Shcherbakov published an article in the Soviet journal *Sputnik* entitled "Is the Moon the Creation of Alien Intelligence?"

The Russians advanced the theory that the moon is not a completely natural world, but a planetoid that was hollowed out eons ago in the far reaches of space by intelligent beings possessing a technology far superior to ours. Huge machines were used to melt rock and form large cavities within the moon (the mascons?), spewing the molten refuse onto the surface (the maria?). Protected by a hull-like inner shell plus a reconstructed outer shell of metallic rocky junk, this gigantic craft was steered through the cosmos and finally parked in orbit around Earth. This ship could be compared to the Death Star in the *Star Wars* films. "Many things so far considered to be lunar enigmas are explainable in the light of this new hypothesis," they wrote. In fact, supporters of the spaceship-moon theory believe that the moon may be a hollowed-out asteroid once used to transport the space travelers mentioned in the ancient Sumerian tablets.

In fact, the spaceship-moon theory may come closer than any other in reconciling the contradictions inherent in the origin and amazing orbit of the moon. However, such a consideration is supposed to be outside the discussion of educated and rational people. The circular logic of conventional science regarding the origins of the moon runs something like this: We know that extraterrestrials don't exist, but we do know that the moon exists and has been mentioned throughout human history. We humans did not create it nor place it in orbit around Earth, so it must have been done by extraterrestrials. But because we know they don't exist, we will simply call it an anomaly and will not publicly say any more about it.

NONHUMANS ON THE MOON

The evidence of life on Mars and speculation concerning a lunar spaceship has raised the question whether someone may still be residing on the moon. Such thinking stems from the numerous reports of activity and structures seen on the moon during the past decade. Actually, the accounts of lights seen moving about on the moon go back centuries.

On July 29, 1953, *New York Herald Tribune* science editor John J. O'Neill claimed to have seen a twelve-mile-long "bridge" straddling the Mare Crisium crater. A month later, the structure was confirmed by British astronomer H. P. Wilkens, who told the BBC, "It looks artificial. It's almost incredible that such a thing could have been formed in the first instance, or if it was formed, could have lasted during the ages in which the moon has been in existence." Sometime later this bridge was no longer observed.

Another most amazing structure is known as the Shard. Located in the Ukert area of the moon, which is at the point nearest Earth, the Shard was photographed by Orbiter 3 in preparation for the Apollo missions. This odd monument towers a mile and a half from the moon's surface. Bruce Cornet, an independent geologist who has studied photos of the Shard at length, said, "No known natural process can explain such a structure."

Perhaps even more amazing is a huge upright structure in the Sinus Medii region dubbed the Tower. Cornet said, "The Tower represents an enigma of the highest magnitude, because it rises more than five miles above the surface of the moon, and has been photographed from five different angles and two different altitudes. In all four photographs the same structure is visible and can be viewed from two different sides. The Tower exists in front of and to the left of the Shard in the Lunar Orbiter III-84M photograph. The top of the Tower has a very cubic geometry and appears to be composed of regular cubes joined together to form a very large cube with an estimated width of over one mile!"

In November 1966, Lunar Orbiter 2 took photos from twenty-nine miles above the Sea of Tranquility in the Moon's northeastern quadrant, showing what appear to be several slender pyramids or obelisks similar to Central Park's Cleopatra's Needle, some as high as a fifteen-story building. Predictably, NASA denied that that Orbiter photos disclosed anything unusual on the moon, even as they released the pictures. Because there was no official confirmation, most news outlets did not cover the story. However, the *Washington Post* carried the story on the front page with the headline, "Six Mysterious Statuesque Shadows Photographed on the Moon by Orbiter." In this article, staff writer Thomas O'Toole wrote that scientists had no idea what was casting the tall shadows but that the "largest shadow is just the sort that would be cast by something resembling the Washington Monument."

Russian space engineer Alexander Abramov added to the mystery by stating, "The distribution of these lunar objects is similar to the plan of the Egyptian pyramids constructed by Pharaohs Cheops, Chephren and Menkaura at Gizeh, near Cairo. The centers of the spires in this lunar 'abaka' are arranged in precisely the same way as the apices of the three great pyramids."

If these structures are pyramids and if they do match the layout of the Egyptian pyramids, they might connect to the pyramid-shaped structures photographed by a Viking probe of Mars in 1976. Objects that appear to be pyramids, along with the controversial "face on Mars" were seen in photos taken of the Cydonia area. Some researchers have wondered if these monuments might represent some grand design.

"It is the eerie similarity between the pyramidal structures that have come to stand for 'Egypt' and those lying—empty and abandoned—at Cydonia, that almost scream of some 'connection,'" wrote former NASA consultant Hoagland, who has advanced the theory of artificial structures on both Mars and the moon.

Hoagland suggested that perhaps the Apollo missions had an unstated agenda of seeking the truth of these anomalies. He and other suspicious-minded UFO researchers have publicly wondered if the destinations of some of the Apollo moon missions—such as the Sea of Tranquility for Apollo 11 and the Taurus-Littrow area for Apollo 17—were selected because of the high incidence of abnormal sightings in those locations. If they were, nobody in NASA officially is talking about it.

Private researcher and author George H. Leonard came to a startling conclusion regarding activity and structures on the moon. In 1977, after years of "haunting" NASA photo files, Leonard claimed to have found enough evidence to convince him that "the moon is occupied by an intelligent race or races which probably moved in from outside the solar system." He added, "The moon is firmly in the possession of these occupants. Evidence of their presence is everywhere: on the surface, on the near side and the hidden side,

in the craters, on the maria, and in the highlands. They are changing its face. Suspicion or recognition of that triggered the U.S. and
Soviet moon programs—which may not really be so much a race as
a desperate cooperation."

Leonard in 1977 wrote *Somebody Else Is on the Moon*, in which
he discussed more than two dozen NASA photos. While many of
these photos were indistinct to the untrained eye and might have
shown almost anything, some were indeed curious. Some seem to
show "bridges" across lunar chasms similar to the one reported in
the *New York Herald Tribune*, "stitching" with some sort of material
connecting surface splits, domed-shaped objects in the center of lit
craters, and lengthy "tracks" in the moon dust. "The professionals
choose to ignore these signs. They do not fit into the orthodoxy,"
wrote Leonard, adding that an unnamed NASA scientist confided
to him that "discoveries" had been made but not announced to the
public.

After studying hundreds of lunar photos, Leonard concluded
that whoever is on the moon is doing at least two things: mining
for minerals, or perhaps water and oxygen, and repairing damage
to the moon's surface. Leonard was not alone in his beliefs. Some
researchers claim that moon photos show a series of transparent
domes under which can be seen orderly lines indicating the possible
ruins of cities or large stations. Ingo Swann, who helped develop the
U.S. Army's remote-viewing techniques, has stated that he psychi-
cally viewed humanlike figures working on the surface of the moon.
Since man has made such a tremendous effort to send astronauts to
the moon—thought by most to be a lifeless world—someone might
have made a similar effort to send their astronauts to Earth. This
could have taken place in man's dim early history, leaving behind
only tantalizing evidence leading to the present widespread belief in
ancient astronauts.

LOST PROBES

It should be noted that past attempts to make a close-up study of both Mars and particularly Phobos have been disastrous. The unmanned Russian probe Phobos I was lost en route to Mars, reportedly due to a command communication failure. Phobos II disappeared in March 1989 as it approached orbit around Mars; communication was lost as the craft passed into the vicinity of Phobos. The Soviets suggested that it had spun out of control due to an erroneous ground command.

In mid-1991, six former U.S. Army remote viewers were commissioned by officials within the Russian space program to study the cause of Phobos II's disappearance. Remote viewing is the term given to a controlled psychic ability that allows one to perceive persons, places, and things at a distance without the use of the normal five senses. Such techniques were studied by both academic and government scientists before the creation of a remote-viewing unit within the U.S. Army's Intelligence and Security Command (INSCOM) in the early 1970s.

On September 29, 1991, the remote viewers issued a final report, entitled "Enigma Penetration: Soviet Phobos II Space Craft Images Anomaly." The report stated that a disc-shaped object rose from the Martian surface toward Phobos II while a second object moved into even closer proximity and scanned the probe with a penetrating particle beam device, which disrupted the communication and guidance equipment. The out-of-control Soviet craft was then struck by a "micrometeorite" that delivered the coup de grâce. The remote viewers said this may have been no accident, as it seems that all of the technology put into space from Earth is scrutinized closely by nonhumans. If it would reveal alien activities, then it is decommissioned. After being struck, Phobos II spiraled down, crashing onto the Martian surface.

Amazing as this account appears, there was supporting feedback from the Soviets themselves. It first came from Alexander Dunayev, chairman of the Soviet space organization responsible for the Phobos II project. Dunayev announced that the doomed probe had photographed the image of a small odd-shaped object between itself and Mars. He speculated that the object might have been "debris in the orbit of Phobos" or even jettisoned parts from the spacecraft. His tone was anything but certain.

More astounding feedback came in December 1991, when Soviet cosmonauts visited the United States. Retired Soviet Air Force colonel and cosmonaut trainee Marina Popovich displayed to newsmen in San Francisco one of the last photographs received from the Phobos II. The photo showed the silhouette of an odd-shaped object approaching the spacecraft. Popovich said the picture was taken on March 25, 1989, in deep space near Phobos shortly before contact with the craft was lost. She said the object very well may have been an alien spacecraft.

The photographed object bore an uncanny resemblance to the object drawn in sketches by the remote viewers. If their account of the demise of Phobos II is correct, then serious attention must be given their statement that the same fate befell the Mars Observer.

The Mars Observer, launched by the United States, vanished on August 20, 1993, just as it was about to go into orbit around Mars. Both scientists and laymen had high hopes that the Mars Observer would transmit photographs back to Earth which might solve some of the Martian mysteries—such as the human "face on Mars" and the three symmetrical pyramids seen in NASA photographs.

The 5,672-pound Mars Observer spent eleven months traveling to our neighboring planet and was scheduled to go into orbit around Mars on August 24. NASA officials initially theorized that the probe's timing clock malfunctioned, making the onboard computer unable to process commands being radioed from the Jet Propulsion Lab. But as days passed and communication was never resumed with the craft, hopes dimmed of ever knowing precisely what happened to it.

The military-trained remote viewers, however, said they saw Mars Observer meeting the same fate as Phobos II as well as another, secret space launch that same month in 1993. They noted the similarity of fates between the Phobos missions and Mars Observer.

This pattern may have continued in another failed Russian attempt to probe the secrets of Phobos. In the fall of 2011, control over Phobos Grunt (literally, Phobos Soil) was lost, and fears grew that its ten-ton load of toxic fuel and oxidizer might wreak havoc when the failed craft reentered Earth's atmosphere. The stricken craft reportedly crashed into the Pacific Ocean on Sunday, January 15, 2012, with no reported consequences. Why would all these probes be failing? Could it be that something on Mars doesn't want us observing the planet? One thing seems clear—someone or something continues to operate far outside Earth.

HUMANKIND: THE ANOMALIES CONTINUE

BEFORE TAKING UP THE CONCEPT OF ANCIENT ASTRONAUTS, ONE must consider the origins of humankind. What is conventional science holding back regarding the beginnings of our species, and what might this mean to our future?

DARWINISM UNDER FIRE

The squabble over how the world was created or whether some moons are artificial appears puny compared to the ongoing fight over the origins of humankind. The focus of this argument centers around the English naturalist Charles Darwin's theories in his 1859 book *On the Origin of Species*. In this work, Darwin proposed a simple explanation for life on Earth—that life evolved through a series of biological changes deriving from random genetic mutations in conjunction with a process known as natural selection. This supposes that those species best adapted to environmental change are best suited to survive. Although Darwin never explicitly stated that man descended from the ape, his devotees advocated that conclusion, drawing criticism from religious fundamentalists. The idea of survival of the fittest is perhaps the best known of Darwin's principles and has been taught in schools for several generations.

The evolution account is familiar—fish evolved into amphibians, which changed into reptiles, which became birds and mammals, which eventually evolved into humans. "However, it is far easier to explain this to schoolchildren—with cute illustrations and pictures of a lineup of apes (beginning with those having slumped shoulders, transitioning to those that are standing upright)—than it is to prove," cautioned Will Hart, author of *The Genesis Race*. In fact, Darwin's theory continues to generate controversy because, as Hart pointed out, it "is the only scientific theory taught worldwide that has yet to be proved by the rigorous standards of science."

Even after a hundred years of effort, no one has been able to fully substantiate Darwin's theories through documented fossil exhibits. Yet Darwin's theory of evolution continues to be taught in most schools and continues to generate controversy. The late Harvard biologist Stephen Jay Gould noted, "All paleontologists know that the fossil record contains precious little in the way of intermediate forms; transitions between major groups [of species] are characteristically lacking."

Darwin never actually insisted that man descended from the ape. This was a conclusion of his followers. Darwin himself admitted to giant holes in his own theory. "If it could be demonstrated that any complex organ existed, which could not possibly have been formed by numerous, successive slight modifications, my theory would absolutely break down," he wrote in *On the Origin of Species*.

No such indisputable linkage to complex organs has yet been found, and some respected scientists use this as evidence against the theory of human evolution. Lehigh University biochemistry professor Michael Behe, after studiously researching blood clotting, cilia, the human immune system, transfer of materials between cells, and nucleotides, concluded that these aspects of human physiology are too "irreducibly complex" to have evolved from "less complete" predecessors through natural selection. Proponents of the intelligent-design theory of life seized upon Behe's work as justification for their beliefs.

In 2005, Behe presented his theory of "irreducible complexity" in a Pennsylvania court case challenging a school district mandate that a statement about intelligent design be included with evolution in science classes. U.S. District Court Judge John E. Jones III, a conservative Republican appointed in 2002 by President George W. Bush, ruled that the required statement was unconstitutional because Professor Behe's claim was not science but a form of creationism, a religious belief that had been "rejected by the scientific community at large."

HUMAN CHRONOLOGY REVISED

Although Behe's ideas were rejected by the court, could he have been on to something about human development and the way it fits in with the theory of evolution? After all, we have every reason to doubt the timeline of our development, as it continually is being revised. For example, fishhooks and fishbones dating back 42,000 years were discovered in a limestone cave in East Timor in early 2012. This finding indicated that humans were capable of skilled, deep-sea fishing 30,000 years earlier than previously thought. One of the discoverers, Sue O'Connor of the Australian National University's Department of Archaeology and Natural History, told the media, "There was never any hint of [what] maritime technology people might have had in terms of fishing gear 42,000 years ago."

Alan Butler and Christopher Knight, best-selling authors of the alternative history *Civilization One*, have pointed to further evidence that the human race developed far earlier than believed. Butler and Knight described a large-scale gene-mapping program by researchers at deCODE Genetics in Reykjavik, Iceland, which found that it was possible to date the origin of a genetic difference among nearly thirty thousand Icelandic women. This was accomplished by counting the number of DNA differences from normal DNA. This study indicated that the differences began about three million years ago, long before modern humans were thought to have evolved.

The study of DNA also supports the idea that genetic connections can be found in a wide diversity of the human population, indicating widespread early migration and genetic mingling. Author Gavin Menzies found support for such far-flung travel in an unexpected place. In the study of human DNA, mitochondrial DNA carries a rare genetic marker, or haplogroup, called haplogroup X. Even rarer is haplogroup X2, which has been found in the Caucasus Mountain region, the Mediterranean, and, surprisingly, among the Ojibwa Native Americans living primarily around Lake Superior.

Analyzing blood gave credence to the idea of an island in the mid-Atlantic. In his 1978 book, *Our Ancestors Came from Outer Space*, aerospace engineer Maurice Chatelain, who helped conceive and design the Apollo spacecraft that journeyed to the moon, reported that five Incan mummies in the British Museum contained a blood type unlike that of their American neighbors but identical to the Basque population found on the Atlantic coasts of Spain and France. One even had an Rh factor not found elsewhere on Earth. Unfortunately, this intriguing study, conducted by a British scientist in 1952, cannot now be duplicated, as the mummies were destroyed when a water pipe burst in the basement of the British Museum. It is unclear if this was sheer accident. Chatelain also noted that the mummification processes of the Mayans and the Incas were the same as those of the Egyptians and Sumerians.

Fossilized bones found in China have been carbon-dated to more than 11,500 years ago and indicate that a previously unknown type of humanoid was living at the same time as modern humans. Termed the Red Deer Cave people because of the now-extinct red deer they cooked and ate, these fossils exhibit an unusual mixture of features both from modern humans and something else. Stone artifacts found at the site also suggest they were toolmakers.

The Red Deer Cave people fossils exhibited long, broad, and tall frontal lobes like modern humans. But they differed from modern *Homo sapiens* in having prominent brow ridges, thick skull bones, flat upper faces with a broad nose, jutting jaws lacking a humanlike chin, brains moderate in size by ice-age human standards, large molars, and primitively short parietal lobes, brain lobes at the top of the head associated with sensory data. "These are primitive features seen in our ancestors hundreds of thousands of years ago," commented Darren Curnoe, a paleoanthropologist with the University of New South Wales in Australia. Scientists said the mixture of features made them difficult to classify either as a new species or an unusual type of modern human. "In short, they're anatomically unique among all members of the human evolutionary tree," said Curnoe.

In 2010, archaeologists found evidence in the Buttermilk Creek complex forty miles northwest of Austin, Texas, that proved humans were in the Americas as early as 15,500 years ago—around 1,500 years earlier than previously believed. "This is the oldest credible archaeological site in North America," said team leader Michael R. Waters, director of the Center for the Study of the First Americans at Texas A&M University.

The squabble over Darwinism is not confined to religious fundamentalists. However, any mainstream scientists and academics who challenge evolution orthodoxy are often excluded from the debate and even find themselves unemployed, a grim reminder of the unforgiving nature of the status quo.

MAVERICK SCIENTISTS QUELLED

There is even controversy concerning the Ice Age, the most recent (Pleistocene) glaciation, an event recently popularized by three 20th Century Fox animated films. Author and computer scientist Kurt Johmann has noted that the conventional concept of the Ice Age is that a layer of ice up to two miles thick in places extended all the way from the North Pole down to where London and New York are located today and peaked about twenty thousand years ago. So much water was locked up as ice that the sea level worldwide was about 450 feet lower than it is now, and this lowering opened up land bridges, which made it possible for prehistoric humans to spread around the world.

"One may call these three beliefs—the alleged giant ice sheets, the alleged greatly lowered sea level, and the alleged Bering Strait land-bridge by which the Indians came—the holy trinity of the Ice Age," Johmann wrote. "For the average educated American the truthfulness of this holy trinity goes unquestioned. After all, not only is one brainwashed with it in school, but that brainwashing is reinforced by the many books and magazines, and TV shows (including both fiction shows such as movies, and so-called science shows), that take the reality of the Ice Age for granted.

"Up until my recent reading of the book *Cataclysm!* [by D. S. Allan and J. B. Delair], I had assumed there were ice sheets, just as the Ice Age belief system teaches, and just as I had been brainwashed to believe. However, the authors of *Cataclysm!* say that the imagined ice sheets are a fiction, because the drift deposits and scratch marks, which constitute the primary physical evidence for the ice sheets, are better explained as the result of moving water (in effect, a great flood), rather than moving ice."

Johmann suggested that the idea of moving ice was chosen over moving water because a great flood meant catastrophism, while moving ice sheets means gradualism. "The doctrine of gradualism better served the interests of the establishment than catastrophism," he wrote. Likewise, the idea of a "missing link" between primates and modern man also has created a number of problems for modern science, which suggest that our entire understanding of the timing and origins of the human race could be flawed. Could conventional science be hiding a stranger truth to the story of the human race?

In their popular 1993 book, *Forbidden Archeology: The Hidden History of the Human Race*, Michael A. Cremo and Richard L. Thompson argued that the scientific community could be suppressing shocking evidence. Both Cremo, a U.S. Navy veteran who attended George Washington University, and Thompson, who received a PhD in mathematics from Cornell University in 1974, became involved in the topic of creationism from the perspective of Hindu Vedic writings. Based on the study of these ancient works coupled with a multitude of archaeological anomalies found worldwide in the past two centuries, they concluded humans have existed on Earth for millions, perhaps billions, of years. But they claimed such evidence has been suppressed. Needless to say, traditionalists have called their work pseudoscience based on specimens and artifacts that no longer can be produced.

However, such scientific arrogance was also noted by scientists Giorgio de Santillana and Hertha von Dechend. In the introduction to their 1969 seminal work, *Hamlet's Mill*, they commented that "the experts now are benighted by the current folk fantasy, which is the belief that they are beyond all this—critics without nonsense and extremely wise."

Cremo and Thompson provided an example of scientific suppression of evidence, recounting the discovery of sophisticated stone tools at Hueyatlaco, seventy-five miles southeast of Mexico City, in the 1960s. The tools rivaled the best work of Cro-Magnon man in Europe. More tools were found at the nearby site of El Horno. Both sets of tools seem to undoubtedly have come from layers of rock that are the same age. But what made the tools controversial was their age—they were dated to about 250,000 years ago.

A U.S. Geological Survey team headed by archaeologist Virginia Steen-McIntyre had established this age through the use of four separate dating methods, including uranium series dating, fission track dating, tephra hydration dating, and the study of mineral weathering, and their findings were confirmed by multiple peer-reviewed studies. If the dating had been accepted, "it would have revolutionized not only New World anthropology but the whole picture of human origins," Cremo and Thompson noted. "Human beings capable of making the sophisticated tools found at Hueyatlaco are not thought to have come into existence until about 100,000 years ago in Africa."

Steen-McIntyre was both blocked and ridiculed when she tried to get her team's conclusions published. In a note written in 1976, she stated, "I had found out through back fence gossip that [team members] Hal, Roald, and I are considered opportunists and publicity seekers in some circles, because of Hueyatlaco, and I am still smarting from the blow." She also soon found that she could not find more work in her chosen profession.

Writing to one editor of a scientific publication, H. J. Fullbright of the Los Alamos Scientific Laboratory, Steen-McIntyre argued her case thusly: "Our joint article on the Hueyatlaco site is a real bombshell. It would place man in the New World 10 times earlier than many archaeologists would like to believe. Worse, the bifacial tools that were found in situ are thought by most to be a sign of H[omo] sapiens. According to present theory, H.s. had not even evolved at that time, and certainly not in the New World.

"Archaeologists are in a considerable uproar over Hueyatlaco. They refuse even to consider it. I've learned from second-hand sources that I'm considered by various members of the profession to be 1) incompetent; 2) a news monger; 3) an opportunist; 4) dishonest; 5) a fool. Obviously, none of these opinions is helping my professional reputation! My only hope to clear my name is to get the Hueyatlaco article into print so that folks can judge the evidence for themselves." Steen-McIntyre received no reply. Her article was not published, nor was it even returned to her.

Although her group was finally able to present a paper at an anthropological conference in 1975, it was not until 1981 that a paper on Hueyatlaco was published in the scientific journal *Quaternary Research* (Number 16, pp. 1–17).

Sometime later, Steen-McIntyre offered her article to another scientific publication but warned that if the findings were accepted, all anthropology textbooks would require rewriting. The editor responded by stating that while he would consider her article for publication, he believed it would be difficult to obtain objective reviews from most archaeologists. The editor's reasoning was circular: because everyone knew that *Homo sapiens* evolved in Eurasia between 30,000 and 50,000 years ago, any tools or artifacts dated to 250,000 years ago were impossible, since everyone knew that humans evolved in Eurasia 30,000 to 50,000 years ago.

Cremo and Thompson commented on Virginia Steen-McIntyre's case, writing that it "opens a rare window into the actual social processes of data suppression in paleoanthropology, processes that involve a great deal of conflict and hurt." Even Cremo and Thompson faced hardship due to their involvement in the case.

"We ourselves once tried to secure permission to reproduce photographs of the Hueyatlaco artifacts in a publication," they wrote. "We were informed that permission would be denied if we intended to mention the lunatic fringe date of 250,000 years."

In a 1997 interview intended for *Harper's* magazine but only published later in the *Midwestern Epigraphic Journal*, Steen-McIntyre was asked why respectable scientists and even governments would resist anything at odds with the current scientific worldview. "Because it's interwoven with the Theory of Evolution: accept one, you have to accept the other," she responded, adding that Darwin's theory is just a theory and "a shaky one at that."

Steen-McIntyre added, "When the Theory of Evolution is taken to its logical conclusion, the only moral imperative demanded is 'survival of the fittest.' I don't like it, for scientific reasons: it goes against the Second Law of Thermodynamics for one thing. I don't like it for philosophical and religious reasons. I especially don't like it because it helped ruin my career. . . . The archaeologist in charge of the Hueyatlaco dig rejected our geologic dates of a quarter-million years because, according to her belief, modern man, the maker of those tools, had not yet evolved 250,000 years ago. . . . A classic case of arguing from theory to data, then tossing out the data that don't fit."

Steen-McIntyre believed that her data was rejected by a superior due to "a matter of influence on her part and lack of it on mine. She was an anthropologist, a graduate of Radcliffe and Harvard with powerful friends; I was a geologist with a new PhD from the University of Idaho, looking for a job." That superior was Cynthia Irwin-Williams, who led the initial digs at Hueyatlaco. Though she had argued with Steen-McIntyre and called her "irresponsible," she has never published a final report on the findings.

SUPPRESSION BY THE SMITHSONIAN

The suppression of the geologists' data from Mexico may be an unfortunate example of dogma getting in the way of discovery, but what happens when such discoveries are hijacked? Researcher and historian Martin Doutré related a conversation he had with a former National Park Service employee about an incident that took place at Arizona's Canyon de Chelly National Monument in 1999. "A big washout had occurred in the canyon after torrential rains, and a number of skeletons were exposed at a few sites. All of the Park Service personnel were pressed into service to gather up and box up the newly revealed bones. However, in a somewhat sinister twist, all of the work was overseen by personnel from both the Smithsonian Institution and the FBI. The Parks Service workers were forbidden to bring cameras to the site and were subjected to full body searches by the FBI when arriving in the morning or leaving at night. All of the skeletal remains and artifacts were carefully boxed up and taken away by the Smithsonian Institute. The Park's Service workers were forced to sign secrecy agreements of non-disclosure of information related to their activities in the canyon."

In a follow-up e-mail, the former Park Service employee offered further details of the find. She said in one grave was a "male, approximately seven-foot in height, [with] six fingers and six toes . . . the teeth were like human, except they had no canine (eye) teeth, and [had] extra-large molars and incisors. The skull was large—heavy jaw [with a] long, large cranium. Large eye sockets. Finger bones [were] extra-long, but small hands. Buried with beautiful pottery and baskets of fine weave—never seen anything similar. A necklace of fiber and feathers. He looked rather fresh for 6,000 years old, as the Smith [Smithsonian] people claimed. Clean bones-but not brittle . . . " Her description is especially interesting in light of a biblical passage, II Samuel 21:18–22, telling of giants related to Goliath with six fingers and toes.

Some believe the Smithsonian has a huge underground warehouse in New York City, filled with thousands of skeletons, objects, and information that might prove embarrassing to conventional history.

"It's appalling that the American people are so blatantly denied access to very important archaeological evidence, which would quickly clarify mysteries related to long-term regional history," said Doutré. "Whereas North American archaeology has been stagnated or has gone backwards for 130 years, all of the essential evidence is in the hands of the authorities to rectify that abysmal situation, but is kept permanently under wraps and beyond the reach of the socially-engineered American public."

The late Vine Deloria, an activist historian and author of the 1969 book *Custer Died for Your Sins: An Indian Manifesto*, also charged the Smithsonian with suppression of valuable historical information. "It's probably better that so few of the ruins and remains were tied in with the Smithsonian because they give good reason to believe the ending of the Indiana Jones movie—a great warehouse where the real secrets of earth history are buried," he wrote. "Modern day archaeology and anthropology have nearly sealed the door on our imaginations, broadly interpreting the North American past as devoid of anything unusual in the way of great cultures characterized by a people of unusual demeanor. The great interloper of ancient burial grounds, the nineteenth century Smithsonian Institution, created a one-way portal, through which uncounted bones have been spirited. This door and the contents of its vault are virtually sealed off to anyone but government officials. Among these bones may lay answers not even sought by these officials concerning the deep past."

British scientist James Smithson first founded the Smithsonian Institution and then bequeathed it to the United States despite having never visited there. Since the U.S. Government started funding and administrating the Smithsonian in 1836, the institution has been involved in several disputes over odd discoveries. In the early 1800s, pioneers moving into the Ohio and Mississippi valleys discovered vast numbers of abandoned earthworks, generally termed *mounds*. The pioneers attributed these mounds to a sophisticated race of long-vanished builders. In 1848, the new Smithsonian Institution drew attention to the mystery of the mounds' creation in its first published book *Ancient Monuments of the Mississippi Valley*. The book's authors concluded that the builders could not have been the ancestors of the supposedly savage Native American groups still living in those regions.

According to David Hatcher Childress, an author and a world-traveling researcher on ancient cities and cultures, the contents of many ancient mounds and pyramids of the Midwest show that an ancient and sophisticated culture once populated the Mississippi River watershed. Not only had this culture been in contact with Europe and other areas, but, according to Childress, many mounds revealed burials of giants seven to eight feet tall, dressed in full armor, sometimes buried with huge treasures.

This was not the only time oddly large bodies have been found or that amazing discoveries have been proverbially swept under the rug by the Smithsonian. Certain reports say that in the 1880s, skulls with horns protruding from them were pulled from a burial mound at Sayre, Bradford County, Pennsylvania, by a group of antiquarians. The odd horned skulls were part of skeletons measuring seven feet tall. It was estimated that the bodies had been buried around AD 1200. According to this account, the bones were sent to the American Investigating Museum in Philadelphia, where like so many finds that question conventional anthropology, they were stolen and never seen again.

In 1924, a paleontologist discovered skeletons of red-haired giants in the Lovelock Cave of Nevada, confirming Indian legends that a race of red-haired giants lived there about fifteen thousand years ago. According to legend, the giants were already in the area when the first Indians arrived. These giants were reputed to be vicious and unapproachable cannibals. During ensuing wars, the giants were decimated and finally cornered in the cave. When they refused to surrender, the Indians filled the entrance with brush and set it afire. The giants who tried to escape were shot with arrows and the others suffocated in the cave.

Beginning in 1911, the cave was worked for its bat guano to be used in making gunpowder, and most of the remains were destroyed. But an expedition in 1924 did recover the mummified remains of two giants—a female six and a half feet tall and a male more than eight feet tall. Reportedly, artifacts from the cave, but not the mummies, may be viewed at a small natural history museum in Winnemucca, Nevada.

How strongly are we to believe that races before our own were actually much larger than we are today, especially when supporting evidence has been wiped from textbooks? Another episode illustrates Smithsonian suppression of historical artifacts. The late naturalist and author Ivan T. Sanderson told of an incident during World War II on the Aleutian island of Shemya in which engineers building an airstrip uncovered the remains of gigantic humans. One cranium measured almost twenty-four inches from base to crown, compared to the normal eight inches. Oddly, all the skulls showed evidence of trepanning (poking holes in the skull with crude tools to release evil spirits). The remains were reportedly sent to the Smithsonian, which, despite the seeming importance of such a find, never released any further information. Sanderson asked, "Is it that these people cannot face rewriting all the textbooks?"

The Smithsonian has been involved in several other controversies over eyebrow-raising discoveries, such as the objects found in 1944 by German hardware merchant Waldemar Julsrud at Acámbaro, Mexico, located about 175 miles northwest of Mexico City. In 1923, Waldemar was a codiscoverer of an archaeological site first thought to be of the Tarascan culture. This discovery brought worldwide attention after it was found to actually be a whole new Indian culture—the Chupicauro civilization, which flourished in Mexico about a thousand years before the Tarascans.

Julsrud's 1944 find consisted of more than thirty-three thousand ceramic and stone objects, including statues and obsidian knives. The amazing aspect of the statuary was the fact that the carvings depicted humans in association with large reptiles resembling dinosaurs. Along with other weird creatures, there were representations of Sumerian and Egyptian motifs, as well as bearded Caucasians, Africans, and Polynesians.

Although radiocarbon and thermoluminescence testing indicated that the objects could be dated as far back as 6,500 years, Smithsonian officials quickly proclaimed the entire episode a hoax. In recent years, when researcher John H. Tierney filed a Freedom of Information Act request, it was learned that all of the Julsrud case files at the Smithsonian were missing.

Dennis Swift, on his website Dinosaursandman.com, has written of visiting Acámbaro. He noted, "Waldemar, in print [his book was published in 1947], theorized that the colossal collection of ceramic and stone artifacts had been buried by a people who had experienced catastrophes. He conjectured that there had been a period of catastrophes that had changed the face of the earth, and that there must have been ancient civilizations wiped out by the catastrophes. His most radical suggestion that clashed violently with scientists was that man had existed contemporaneously with the dinosaurs. Although there was sound evidence that Julsrud was on to something of major scientific importance, he was ridiculed by the authorities when his book was published."

In 1955, Charles Hapgood, then professor of history and anthropology at Keene State College of the University of New Hampshire and author of *Earth's Shifting Crust* and *Maps of the Ancient Sea Kings*, spent several months in Acámbaro studying the Julsrud collection. To eliminate the possibility the collection was merely a modern hoax, Hapgood located a house that had been built at the same location in 1930.

According to Dennis Swift, "They found a house directly over the site owned by the Chief of Police and asked permission to dig beneath the floor of his house. Permission was granted, and they dug a six-foot-deep pit beneath the hard concrete floor of the living room, unearthing dozens of the controversial objects. Since the house had been built twenty-five years previously, it exonerated Julsrud, eliminated the hoax theory, and negated [two reports alleging fakery] at all the important points."

One enduring mystery—or conspiracy—stems from reports of the discovery of ancient Egyptian artifacts in the north end of the Grand Canyon at the beginning of the last century. According to a front-page article in the *Phoenix Gazette* of April 5, 1909, an expedition funded by the Smithsonian Institution had begun work following the discovery of a "great underground citadel" in a cave "some 42 miles up the [Colorado] river from the El Tovar Crystal canyon."

The article stated that a thirty-year employee of the Smithsonian, identified as G. E. Kinkaid, had discovered the cave a few months earlier while boating on the Colorado River. The cavern was nearly inaccessible: the entrance was 1,486 feet below a sheer canyon wall.

Once inside, Kinkaid found mummies and relics that he shipped to Washington, D.C. Quoting from a report by Kinkaid, the *Gazette* wrote, "On all the urns, or walls over doorways, and tablets of stone which were found by the image are the mysterious hieroglyphics, the key to which the Smithsonian Institute [*sic*] hopes yet to discover. The engraving on the tablets probably has something to do with the religion of the people. Similar hieroglyphics have been found in southern Arizona. Among the pictorial writings, only two animals are found. One is of prehistoric type." Kinkaid's report also noted that in one large room were mummies, all male and all wrapped in a "bark fabric."

Other rooms contained cooking vessels and storage places, and one room that smelled "snaky" seemed to be filled with gas or chemicals. It was estimated that as many as fifty thousand people could have lived in the caverns comfortably. According Kinkaid's report, "The whole underground installation gives one of shaky nerves the creeps."

The *Gazette* article also related that another Smithsonian archaeologist, S. A. Jordan, was making additional searches of the cave and had discovered evidence strongly indicating that the cavern had once been inhabited by a race "of oriental origin, possibly from Egypt, tracing back to Ramses." The scientists had discovered several hundred rooms, linked by passageways running from the main passage. Some of these rooms included "articles which have never been known as native to this country, and doubtless they had their origin in the orient. War weapons, copper instruments, sharp-edged and hard as steel, indicate the high state of civilization reached by these strange people."

The article's conclusion was shocking. It argued that if the archaeologists' theories were "borne out by the translation of the tablets engraved with hieroglyphics, the mystery of the prehistoric peoples of North America, their ancient arts, who they were and whence they came, [would] be solved. Egypt and the Nile, and Arizona and the Colorado [would] be linked by a historical chain running back to ages which staggers the wildest fancy of the fictionist." Unfortunately, the century-old *Phoenix Gazette* article seems to be the only real evidence that this discovery ever took place. Some have called the story a planted hoax, and officials at the Smithsonian continue to deny involvement in any such expedition or that Egyptian artifacts have ever been recovered in the canyon.

But the mystery lingers. One young man, who did not want his name involved in this matter, related in the late 1990s that he was backpacking in the north end of the Grand Canyon when he came across concrete platforms. Knowing of the Egyptian artifacts story, he surmised that the platforms may have been the base for cranes to lower heavy artifacts from the cave on the sheer rock face. David Hatcher Childress, who founded the World Explorers Club, looked into the matter. After obtaining a map of the Grand Canyon, Childress and club members reported:

Poring over the map, we were amazed to see that much of the area on the north side of the canyon has Egyptian names. The area around Ninety-four Mile Creek and Trinity Creek had areas (rock formations, apparently) with names like Tower of Set, Tower of Ra, Horus Temple, Osiris Temple, and Isis Temple. In the Haunted Canyon area were such names as the Cheops Pyramid, the Buddha Cloister, Buddha Temple, Manu Temple and Shiva Temple. Was there any relationship between these places and the alleged Egyptian discoveries in the Grand Canyon?

We called a state archaeologist at the Grand Canyon, and were told that the early explorers had just liked Egyptian and Hindu names, but that it was true that this area was off limits to hikers or other visitors, because of dangerous caves. Indeed, this entire area with the Egyptian and Hindu place names in the Grand Canyon is a forbidden zone—no one is allowed into this large area. We could only conclude that this was the area where the vaults were located. Yet today, this area is curiously off-limits to all hikers and even, in large part, park personnel.

The Vatican has been long accused of keeping artifacts and ancient books in their vast cellars, without allowing the outside world access to them. These secret treasures, often of a controversial historical or religious nature, are allegedly suppressed by the Catholic Church because they might damage the church's credibility, or perhaps cast their official texts in doubt. Sadly, there is overwhelming evidence

that something very similar is happening with the Smithso-
nian Institution.

HOAXES AND FORGERIES

In addition to the problems of inconsistency that plague Darwin's
theory of evolution, efforts to solve the "missing link" problem have
been hampered by false discoveries.

In 1887, for example, the Dutch anatomist Marie Eugène Fran-
çois Thomas DuBois moved to the Dutch East Indies and joined
the Dutch Army as a medical officer. Aided by two army engineers
and some forced laborers, in 1890 DuBois moved his search for
fossils to the island of Java, where two years previously a human
skull had been found. Once there, DuBois's workers found an incomplete skull and, upon widening the search, a partial jawbone
with three teeth attached, on the banks of the Solo River. Further
searches uncovered a molar, an intact skullcap, and a thighbone. In
1894, DuBois published a description of his fossils, claiming that
they came from one creature and that, when put together, they represented a link between ape and human that he called *Pithecanthro-
pus erectus,* "ape-human that stands upright." Informally, the fossils
were known as Java Man.

DuBois's theory was never fully accepted even after his return
to Europe in 1895. Some scientists charged that the thighbone and
skullcap were unrelated and represented two separate individuals.
Others merely argued against DuBois's claim that the specimen represented an intermediate primate, or missing link. Stung by the controversy, DuBois had stopped discussing Java Man all together by the
turn of the century and hid the fossils away from the public in his
home. Today, Java Man has been lumped in with other fossil discoveries, classified as a large, prehistoric hominid called *Homo erectus.*

Certain "missing link" discoveries have turned out to be outright hoaxes. One of the most famous of these was the Piltdown Man, based on a large skull and jawbone found in a gravel pit at Piltdown, East Sussex, England, in 1912. The artifact was given the impressive-sounding name *Eoanthropus dawsoni* or Dawson's dawn-man, after British amateur archaeologist Charles Dawson, who claimed to have collected the remains from pit workmen.

But instead of being the missing link everyone was hoping for, Piltdown Man actually was revealed to be a gigantic hoax in 1953. Dawson and others, including even the famous Sherlock Holmes novelist Arthur Conan Doyle, were suspected of forging the missing link by combining a modern human skull with the jawbone of an orangutan. Many suspect that whoever fabricated the Piltdown Man, and it may have consisted of more than one person, did so in a shortsighted effort to support the theories of Darwin.

The Piltdown Man hoax succeeded for so long because at the time of its presentation, the scientific establishment had long supposed that the large modern human brain preceded the modern omnivorous diet. The forgery had provided exactly the evidence that suited the theory.

Public acceptance of anthropology increased in 1974 with the discovery of the skeleton of a hominid australopithecine female in the Afar Triangle region of Hadar, Ethiopia. American paleoanthropologist Donald Johanson, assisted by Maurice Taieb and Yves Coppens, suggested the name Lucy after the Beatles' tune "Lucy in the Sky with Diamonds," which was heard on a tape the night of the discovery. Lucy, a three-and-a-half-foot-tall biped, initially was considered merely another *Australopithecus africanus*, a previously known hominid from the late Pliocene epoch. It was sometime later, following other finds, that she was recognized as a separate species.

In the months following Lucy's discovery, Johanson's team found prehistoric hominid teeth and bones from at least thirteen individuals, collectively called *Australopithecus* 333. The fossils are estimated to be about 3.2 million years old and represent a species now known as *Australopithecus afarensis*. Because this species may be even older than the Neanderthals and even *Homo erectus*, Johanson's group of fossils is sometimes known as humankind's first family.

Scholars Colin P. Groves, Charles E. Oxnard, and Louis Leakey have agreed that *Australopithecus* was totally different in morphology from humans. Groves commented that "non-Darwinian" principles would be required to explain any connection between Lucy and modern humans.

Conventional science now accepts that Neanderthals were also a completely separate race from humans as well. Following the first analysis of mitochondrial DNA (mtDNA) taken from the fossils from the Neander Valley, Germany, in 1997, *National Geographic* concluded that Neanderthals did not contribute substantially to the modern human genome.

If the empirical evidence doesn't support Darwin's theory of evolution, what can account for our existence? Hominids, a term used to describe humans as well as closely related apes, evolved at a slow and steady pace until about 450,000 years ago, when the primate family tree began to divide, creating many separate branches of species during the late Pleistocene epoch. Interestingly enough, this period of change coincides with dates during which the Sumerian tablets described extraterrestrials manipulating the human DNA.

THE WEALTHY CONTROL RESEARCH

Woe be to those who attempt to argue against conventional thinking. According to many independent researchers, there appears to be a conspiracy against any discovery that conflicts with prevailing wisdom. Consider the fate of Thomas E. Lee of the National Museum of Canada. In the early 1950s, Lee discovered sophisticated stone tools caught in ice on Manitoulin Island in Lake Huron. These tools were proven to be at least 65,000 years old and perhaps as old as 125,000 years, totally contradicting conventional theories concerning the date that such well-fashioned stone tools were first created. Following his discovery, Lee claimed he was "hounded" from his position, his work was misrepresented, and no one would publish his findings. Most of the artifacts he found "vanished" into storage bins, and the museum director was fired for refusing to discharge Lee.

"The treatment of Lee was not an isolated case," noted Cremo and Thompson in *Forbidden Archeology*. "There exists in the scientific community a knowledge filter that screens out unwelcome evidence. This process of knowledge filtration has been going on for well over a century and continues right up to the present day." One particularly exasperated researcher recently wrote, "Realize, that scientific institutions, such as the Smithsonian and the National Geographic Society, are set up by the world's elite factions in the first place to either debunk, distort or simply ignore any scientific data that tends to enlighten people about their true origins."

Michael Cremo said he saw in science evidence of both misfeasance and malpractice. "You can find many cases where it's just an automatic process. It's just human nature that a person will tend to reject things that don't fit in with his particular world view," he said. Cremo cited the words of a young paleontologist and expert on ancient whale bones at the Museum of Natural History in San Diego. Asked if he ever found signs of human markings on any of the bones, the scientist responded, "I tend to stay away from anything that has to do with humans because it's just too controversial."

Cremo was suspicious of activities by the Rockefeller Foundation in its funding of Canadian paleoanthropologist Davidson Black, who conducted research in China and came to the conclusion that humankind originated in Asia, specifically China and Tibet. Correspondence between Black and his superiors with the foundation indicated that Black's work was part of a broader agenda. One letter stated, " . . . thus we may gain information about our [human] behavior of the sort that can lead to wide and beneficial control." Cremo saw this as meaning that the research was being funded with the specific goal of control. "Control by whom?" Cremo wondered.

"The motive to manipulate is not so hard to understand," explained J. Douglas Kenyon, publisher of the magazine *Atlantis Rising*. "There's a lot of social power connected with explaining who we are and what we are," he says. "Somebody once said knowledge is power. You could also say power is knowledge. Some people have particular power and prestige that enables them to dictate the agenda of our society. I think it's not surprising that they are resistant to any change."

Kenyon believes that scientists today have become a virtual priest class, exercising many of the rights and prerogatives that their forebears in the industrial-scientific revolution sought to wrest from an entrenched religious establishment. They set the tone and the direction for our civilization on a worldwide basis, he says. "If you want to know something today you usually don't go to a priest or a spiritually inclined person, you go to one of these people because they've convinced us that our world is a very mechanistic place, and everything can be explained mechanically by the laws of physics and chemistry which are currently accepted by the establishment. . . . I think many people are starting to see that the world view they are presenting, just doesn't account for everything in human experience."

Brad Steiger, author of *Worlds Before Our Own*, wrote, "Archaeologists, anthropologists, and various academicians who play the 'origins of Man' game, reluctantly and only occasionally acknowledge instances where unique skeletal and cultural evidence from the prehistoric record suddenly appear long before they should and in places where they should not. These irritating artifacts destroy the orderly evolutionary line that academia has for so long presented to the public. Consequently, such data have been largely left buried in site reports, forgotten storage rooms, and dusty archives where one suspects that there is a great deal of suppressed, ignored, and misplaced pre-historical cultural evidence that would alter the established interpretations of human origins and provide us with a much clearer definition of what it means to be human."

By the early twentieth century, the intellectual community had cemented its support around Darwin's theories. Instead of challenging the status quo, it soon became much more prudent for the aspiring archaeologist or anthropologist to simply ignore or dismiss any unorthodox data. Such attitudes are in full force today.

Did such distortion in the sciences come about by some flaw in the natural evolution of scientific inquiry? The record indicates a conscious effort to derail true scientific investigation by a clique of wealthy and powerful people. "For a brief period during the late 1920s and early 1930s, Rockefeller philanthropies flirted with, and ultimately abandoned, the field of anthropology," notes anthropologist Kevin Jones-Kern of Bowling Green State University. "During those crucial years and through their modest grants, however, they dramatically affected the course of anthropology."

The Rockefellers, along with other wealthy and elite American families, such as the Mellons, Carnegies, and Gettys, gained unequaled control over many of the nation's largest universities both through direct grants and through their foundations. But with the approach of World War II, these funds began to dry up, and certain types of scientists, such as anthropologists, found no jobs available upon graduation. There were few teacher openings and even fewer funded opportunities for fieldwork. Those who did find work with colleges and corporations were limited in what and how they investigated. "Relatively munificent funding for the social sciences continued after this point, but in a more controlled and directed manner. One of the casualties of this restructuring was the already limited Rockefeller support for anthropology," stated Jones-Kern.

"Although the Rockefeller Foundation gave only half-hearted

attention to the field of anthropology, the repercussions of its relatively modest involvement were profound and long-lasting. From sponsorship and publication of classic research studies, to the training of a generation of ethnologists, to the solidification of sturdy university departments that trained future generations of anthropologists, the Rockefeller Foundation greatly affected the course of the field spurned in 1934," wrote Jones-Kern. "Thus, while Beardsley Ruml, Edmund Day, Sydnor Walker and their peers quietly working at the New York offices of the Rockefeller Foundation are not generally recognized as important figures in the history of the anthropology, perhaps they should be," he concluded. Of course, if one helps create something, than one has some degree of control over that thing.

Some indication of the power of these families in scientific investigation may be found in the list of founding members and presidents of the National Science Board, the governing board of the National Science Foundation, whose members serve as policy advisers to the U.S. Congress and the president: Chester I. Barnard (Rockefeller Foundation), Detlev W. Bronk (Rockefeller University), Charles Dollard (Carnegie Corporation of New York), and H. Guyford Stever (Carnegie Mellon University).

One example of subtle control over research is the fact that even as the study of human DNA was becoming more established and accepted, there was in academia a subtle persuasion away from incorporating deep DNA research in archaeological studies. Instead, emphasis was placed on using carbon dating and the conventional categorization of artifacts into a predefined evolutionary line, usually beginning two million years or earlier.

In addition, institutions have limited paleoanthropology to the study of hominids at least a million years old. At least two proposals, from Berkeley and Southern Methodist University, for study of more recent fossils were rejected by the National Science Foundation for "lack of adequate scientific merit" due to the paucity of relatively recent fossil hominids.

In 1971, when as an undergraduate Donald Johanson found the bones of Lucy, he announced a split in the evolutional chain of ancestors, much to the chagrin of conventional anthropologists, who lambasted him for even offering such a hypothesis at such a young age. This set the stage for more restrained hypotheses in ancient hominid studies, prompting the media to describe any unorthodox ideas on evolution as exotic. Was this by design? Thus the funding of pure science was controlled, and the general public and academia were distracted from any non-Darwinian theories.

It should be noted that in 1974 Johanson graduated from the University of Chicago, a recipient of Rockefeller largesse, with a scholarship from the National Institute of Dental Research that directed him to write a thesis on teeth. It was through grants from the National Science Foundation, the L.S.B. Leakey Foundation and the National Geographic Society that Johanson was able to carry out his research in Ethiopia, Yemen, Saudi Arabia, Egypt, Jordan, and Tanzania.

In the 1800s, huge sphinx-like statues, such as winged bulls and a lion with a human head, were excavated in what was once the palace of the Assyrian king Sargon II, who ruled Mesopotamia from 721 to 705 BC. John D. Rockefeller purchased much of the recovered art and transported it to New York.

The Rockefellers' interest in art and the social sciences in North America reflect similar interests by the Rothschilds in Europe and the Middle East. An Israeli foundation called Yad Hanadiv, which means "benefactor" in Hebrew, was established in 1958 in honor of Baron Edmond de Rothschild. According to its website, Yad Hanadiv acts "on behalf of a number of Rothschild family philanthropic trusts, continuing a tradition of support for Jewish revival in Palestine begun by Baron Edmond de Rothschild in the second half of the 19th century." Since the organization's creation, it has been guided by an advisory committee comprised of members of the Rothschild family. As many as twelve Rothschild Fellowships are awarded each year in the natural, exact, or life sciences and engineering, and up to eight in the humanities and social sciences.

During the past century, the Rothschilds were the largest financial supporters of archaeological digs in Palestine, and the famous Masada excavation of the 1950s was actually called the Edmond de Rothschild Masada Dig. It has been reported from several sources that the Rothschilds believe themselves descended from the Sumerian king Nimrod, the biblical great-grandson of Noah. According to the prestigious genealogical publication *Burke's Peerage*, one Rothschild child born in 1922 was named Albert Anselm Salomon Nimrod Rothschild.

In 1947, a Bedouin shepherd exploring a cave in Palestine found jars that contained seven scrolls. He sold a few parchments to an antiques dealer for the equivalent of a few dollars. Eventually word of the discovery reached the ears of Hebrew University archaeologist Yigael Yadin, who mortgaged his home and traveled into dangerous Arab areas seeking the scrolls. He managed to secure seven of them for his university, which promptly published them.

Between 1947 and 1960, archaeologists pulled 972 ancient biblical and nonbiblical texts from twelve caves in modern-day Palestine. What many don't know, however, is that these texts, known together as the Dead Sea Scrolls, reveal the dominating influence of the Rockefellers. Although many of the scrolls have found their way to publications, "not so for the remaining scrolls," Bible scholar and former intelligence analyst Patricia Eddy has reported. "The Rockefeller Archaeological Museum in Palestine soon became involved and managed to acquire the rest of the scrolls from the government of Jordan . . . who stipulated that no Jewish scholars be allowed access to the ancient Jewish texts. Today, Israel controls the scrolls as a result of overrunning the place where they were stored during the Six Day War of 1967 . . . these scrolls are largely unpublished today (and) no one knows if all of them have been obtained. There is the possibility that others are in the possession of, or have been destroyed by, the Bedouins."

Other members of the wealthy elite have exerted their influence over archaeology. For example, Donald Johanson was involved in strange entanglements with the wealthy Getty family. Jon Kalb, a Texas paleontologist who had studied geological depressions in Ethiopia for years and helped acquire funding for Johanson's research, wrote in his 2001 book, *Adventures in the Bone Trade*, that Ann Getty, who was married to Gordon Getty, heir to the Getty family's oil fortune, was involved in Johanson's work. Kalb reported:

> *Mrs. Getty was then taking courses from [Tim] White [a University of California–Berkeley paleoanthropologist associate of Johanson] at UCB and soon joined [Johanson's excavation] team. She became an outspoken supporter of White and, during trips to Ethiopia (in her private Boeing 727), was in a position to make large donations to the National Museum, winning influence in the Ethiopian government. Worse for Johanson, Mr. Getty was the IHO's [The Institute of Human Origins, which funded the majority of Johanson's project] largest financial donor and a member of its board. In April 1994, Getty abruptly withdrew his support from the institute, charging Johanson with mismanagement of funds and personnel. Because Getty was responsible for half of IHO's nearly $2 million annual budget, his defection was widely reported in the press, from the* Wall Street Journal *to the* London Times.

Archaeologists and anthropologists are not the only ones subjected to intense pressure to toe the official science line. In January 2012, the *Wall Street Journal* published a letter from sixteen scientists, including Nobel Prize–winning physicist Ivar Giaever, who resigned from the American Physical Society over its warning that the evidence of global warming is "incontrovertible." The scientists wrote that "stubborn scientific facts" argue against warming being a man-made phenomenon. They said a growing number of dissenting scientists have serious doubts about the much-publicized and alarmist global-warming message being used to argue for new carbon taxes on the public but are afraid to speak up because of "fear of not being promoted—or worse."

"They have good reason to worry," stated the letter. "In 2003, Dr. Chris de Freitas, the editor of the journal *Climate Research*, dared to publish a peer-reviewed article with the politically incorrect (but factually correct) conclusion that the recent warming is not unusual in the context of climate changes over the past thousand years. The international warming establishment quickly mounted a determined campaign to have Dr. de Freitas removed from his editorial job and fired from his university position. Fortunately, Dr. de Freitas was able to keep his university job."

CIA INVOLVEMENT

When Donald Johanson and his team arrived in Ethiopia to set out on his famous archaeological dig, he came merely days after a military coup that ousted Ethiopia's ruler, Emperor Haile Selassie. When Johanson arrived, he demanded a permit for field investigation from Ethiopian Antiquities Administration director Bekele Negussie, who had previously declined Johanson's authorization due to politics.

According to Jon Kalb, who later became a competitor of Johanson, Negussie came to his office one day at lunchtime and told him that Johanson had accused Kalb of being a CIA agent and receiving covert money from a CIA front organization known as FORGE. Negussi said Johanson had also alleged that Kalb was connected to the U.S. embassy somehow. The accusations against Kalb plagued him for years, and they eventually led to his expulsion from Ethiopia. He has since discussed how other scientists suffered similar charges. Johanson said Kalb's charges were baseless although he admitted that he, as well as many other scientists in foreign lands, was sometimes questioned about the national affairs of other countries by officials of the U.S. Government.

Was Kalb actually a CIA agent, as per Johanson's accusation? Or were any other members covertly working for the agency? It is possible the CIA somehow was involved with the archaeological community to gain access to many otherwise impenetrable parts of the world. In fact, accusations of CIA involvement among archaeologists and anthropologists were not totally without merit, according to a government committee. The circuitously named Select Committee to Study Governmental Operations with Respect to Intelligence Activities, called the Church Committee after its chairman, Democratic senator Frank Church, stated in a 1976 report that the CIA had penetrated a large contingent of American academia:

> The CIA is now using several hundred American academics, who in addition to providing leads and, on occasion, making introductions for intelligence purposes, occasionally write books and other material to be used for propaganda purposes abroad." These academics are located in over 100 American colleges, universities, and related institutes. At the majority of institutions, no one other than the individual concerned is aware of the CIA link. At the others, at least one university official is aware of the operational use made of academics on his campus. In addition, there are several American academics abroad who serve operational purposes, primarily the collection of intelligence. . . . Although the numbers are not as great today as in 1966, there are no prohibitions to prevent an increase in the operational use of academics.

The report went on to state that the Church Committee was "disturbed" by the CIA's lack of appreciation for the dangers it caused for the academics and institutions involved in its operations.

Such collusion between human sciences, the National Science Foundation, and the CIA continues even today. In 2004, as a result of a Freedom of Information Act request, the Electronic Privacy Information Center (EPIC) obtained a memorandum of understanding between the NSF and the CIA discussing joint funding in mathematics and the physical sciences. This was placed under the rubric of combating terrorism.

It can be rationalized that the CIA might involve itself in scientific activities in order to enhance national security. But could its involvement with science have a more controlling purpose, such as protecting the official narrative of our species's genesis?

Several researchers place the CIA in the center of a money merry-go-round that begins with institutions of higher learning and foundations, then spins off into conferences, charitable and educational associations, and student groups and on into journalism and the mass media.

If someone knew of extraterrestrial intervention in human development in the past and did not want that information made public, they would certainly try to limit archaeological and paleontological investigations to only the earliest time periods of two million years or more. Could it be that those at the top are controlling science in order to blunt our discovery of our true human origins?

HUMAN ORIGINS CONTROVERSY

Since the release of the Darwin's books, the public has been told that humans slowly evolved from apes between fifteen and thirty million years ago. Yet in 1967, when molecular biologists Allan Wilson and Vincent Sarich of the University of California used an immunological study to compare protein reactions in the blood of African apes and humans, their experiment indicated that humans and apes began evolving apart from each other only five million years ago. Naturally, they were roundly booed by anthropologists.

In the early 1980s, Wilson again incensed his conventional associates by submitting a mitochondrial Eve thesis, which proposed that all modern human races diverged recently from a single population while older human species, such as Neanderthal and *Homo erectus*, became extinct. Mitochondrial DNA (mtDNA) are genes that sit in the mitochondria, the energy-producing organelles within each cell, not in the nucleus, and are passed from mother to child. After comparing people of different racial backgrounds, Wilson and his coworkers concluded that all modern humans evolved from one "lucky mother" in Africa about 150,000 years ago. Some wits have suggested that perhaps her name was Lucy. This finding may prove most significant in light of the ancient Sumerian tale of the creation of man.

The implications of Wilson's proposal were extreme: that modern humans suddenly evolved from a single African population roughly two hundred thousand to three hundred thousand years ago. According to geneticist Mark Stoneking, one of Wilson's former students, the theory then posits that we "spread across and out of Africa between 50,000 and 100,000 years ago and replaced completely, without any interbreeding, the archaic populations from earlier migrations from Africa. The evidence in favor of this hypothesis is the fact that the earliest fossils of anatomically modern humans come from Africa, and that early modern human fossils from regions outside Africa tend to be more similar to those from Africa than to archaic human fossils from the same region."

There were attacks and recriminations among the scientists, but eventually Wilson and Sarich's evolutionary worldview prevailed. Stoneking has since explained the underlying causes for science's concurrence on the issue.

Ultimately, the controversy was resolved not through rhet-
oric but, of course, through additional data and analyses.
The resulting view of our relationship to other apes, which is
widely accepted today . . . is remarkably similar to the results
that Sarich and Wilson published more than 40 years ago:
namely, that we share a close relationship with African apes,
having diverged from them only approximately 5–7 million
years ago. . . . One can see the same logic at work here as
with the early incorrect views about our relationships with
apes: namely, the desire to see "us" as special—where "us"
now refers to Europeans—compared with other groups, be-
cause it took a long time for us to become so special.

Despite the mitochondrial Eve's attack on our preconceptions
of widespread human evolution, Stoneking has suggested that nothing has contradicted the thesis since it was presented. "All analyses
of mtDNA variation in contemporary human populations basically
agree: she lived in Africa roughly 150,000–200,000 years ago, and
modern humans then began spreading across and out of Africa between 50,000 and 100,000 years ago, with no evidence that any archaic, non-African populations contributed their mtDNA to us—a
view that is remarkably similar to that which we published more
than 20 years ago."

In a 2011 article, Stoneking reminded readers how conventional
science treats unwelcome evidence. "The idealized view of science
and scientists holds that when data contradict theory, no matter
how long or how well that theory has performed, scientists must
reject the old theory and come up with a new explanation to account for the new data. The reality, as any scientist knows, is that
it is difficult to overcome ideas that have dominated a field for a
long time; instead, there is a tendency to reject the data—and the
scientists—which do not fit the theory," he wrote.

REMOTE VIEWING HUMAN ORIGINS

The idea of early intervention from off planet is not relegated to academics and book writers. U.S. military intelligence officers, trained in the psychic methodology called remote viewing, saw Earth originally seeded with protohumans.

From the late 1970s to 1995, the U.S. Army utilized about two dozen remote viewers to successfully conduct psychic spying on the old Soviet Union and other nations. There are those who even claim that since the psychic spying used by both sides pierced all secrecy, it ended the Cold War.

One of the most successful of the Army-trained remote viewers was Joseph McMoneagle, one of the original members of the military unit eventually called Project Stargate. In 1984, McMoneagle was awarded the Legion of Merit for "producing crucial and vital intelligence unavailable from any other source" to the intelligence community.

In 1983, working with Robert A. Monroe, founder of the Monroe Institute in Faber, Virginia, which provided basic out-of-body orientation for many of the military remote viewers, McMoneagle conducted a session seeking to discover the origin of humans. During the 129-minute session, he described a shoreline on what appeared to him to be a primitive Earth. He later estimated a time of about thirty million to fifty million years after the time of the dinosaurs. Cavorting on this shoreline was a large family of protohumans—hairy animals about four feet in height, walking upright and possessing eyes exhibiting a spark of intelligence despite a somewhat smaller cranial capacity.

Two things surprised McMoneagle in this session. These creatures appeared to be aware of his psychic presence, and they did not originate at that location. McMoneagle described his experience thus in his 1998 book, *The Ultimate Time Machine*:

This particular species of animal is put . . . specifically in that barrier place . . . called the meeting of the land and the sea. . . . I also get the impression that they're . . . ah . . . they were put there. They mysteriously appeared. They are not descended from an earlier species, they were put there . . . [by a] seed ship . . . no, that's not right. Keep wanting to say ship, but it's not a ship. I keep seeing a . . . myself . . . I keep seeing . . . oh, hell, for lack of a better word, let's call it a laboratory, where they are actually inventing these creatures. They are actually constructing animals from genes. Why would they be doing that? Can we do this yet . . . here and now? Like cutting up genes and then pasting them back together. You know, sort of like splicing plants . . . or grafting them, one to another. . . . Interesting, it's like they are building eggs by injecting stuff into them with a mixture of DNA or gene parts or pieces.

As to who "they" might have been, he could only describe what he suspected was an "implanted picture" of a delicate-looking, aquiline-featured humanoid unclothed and possessing a prehensile tail and large "doe-like" eyes. This strange being seemed to be using a flashing light that produced frequencies of energy. Searching his mind for a corollary, McMoneagle blurted out, "It's a grow light, for Christ's sake."

McMoneagle said he was disturbed by the impression that this was like someone tending a garden and planting seeds, but "there isn't any concern about the seeds after they are planted." He added, "It's simply like . . . well . . . put these seeds here and on to better and bigger business. No concern about backtracking and checking on the condition of the seeds. They can live or die, survive or perish."

He said the session ended with him moving closer in time and seeing dramatic changes as the small hairy creatures grew both in size and abilities into herding humans. He also cautioned against attempting to make public any information that disturbs people's preconceived ideas.

Additional evidence for surveillance over humans in the past can be found in *The Book of Enoch the Prophet*, a compilation of fragments of a Judaic book written by a variety of authors contemporary with biblical scribes. An Ethiopic edition of this book survived and was discovered in 1768 in Ethiopia by Scotsman James Bruce. Although considered a book of the Bible for five centuries, *The Book of Enoch* eventually was excluded from orthodox versions in favor of the book of Revelation. Both books contain some of the most puzzling and controversial passages in the Bible.

Chapter 12 of *The Book of Enoch* states, "Before all these things Enoch was concealed; nor did any one of the sons of men know where he was concealed, where he had been, and what had happened. He was wholly engaged with the holy ones, and with the Watchers in his days. . . . And behold the Watchers called me Enoch the scribe. Then *the Lord* said to me: Enoch, scribe of righteousness, go tell the Watchers of heaven, who have deserted the lofty sky, and their holy everlasting station, *who* have been polluted with women. And have done as the sons of men do, by taking to themselves wives, and who have been greatly corrupted on the earth. . . ."

Throughout *The Book of Enoch*, it is made clear that the Watchers were not human but came from the heavens and that humans were their "offspring" to whom they imparted knowledge. "Destroy all the souls addicted to dalliance, and the offspring of the Watchers, for they have tyrannized over mankind," the writer commands in chapter 10, verse 18. This same theme is found in Genesis 6:4 (New International Version): "The Nefilim were on the earth in those days—and also afterward—when the sons of God went to the daughters of men and had children by them. They were the heroes of old, men of renown." The Holman Bible Dictionary defines the Old Testament Nefilim as "ancient heroes who, according to most interpreters, are the products of sexual union of heavenly beings and human women."

In his 1978 book, NASA engineer Maurice Chatelain concluded, "Can anyone really think that all the fantastic knowledge in astronomy, mathematics, geodesy, and many other sciences was acquired by mankind without outside help? Frankly, is it not much more logical to accept the idea that all this knowledge was brought by astronauts who came from a another world, just as many legends and the Bible tell us, or that the advancement of mankind was stimulated by some very highly developed cultures located in the Land of Mu or Atlantis, which were visited even earlier by outside civilizations from within the solar system or even distant galaxies?"

ANCIENT EVIDENCE—WORLDWIDE ANOMALIES

EVIDENCE OF PREHISTORIC CIVILIZATIONS ABOUND THROUGHOUT the planet but are usually sloughed off as anomalies, especially because such accounts usually include myths of sky-traveling visitors. Unexplained manufactured sites, such as Stonehenge and Silbury Hill in Britain, the huge heads of Easter Island, the Peruvian Nazca lines, the Great Serpent Mound of Ohio, and the controversial prehistoric "rock wall" east of Dallas, Texas, seem to indicate a technology lost in prehistory.

The roster of strange anomalies around the world includes about sixty unusually small ancient Chinese porcelain "seals" discovered all over Ireland in the eighteenth and nineteenth centuries, a time when there was no known commerce between the Emerald Isle and China. Today these artifacts have been identified as porcelain seals originating in the Dehua kilns in the Fujian Province of China from the earliest Qing Dynasty (221–207 BC). It has been speculated that the seals were brought from China by the seafaring Phoenicians, by ancient Irish tribes traveling as far as China, or by far-ranging medieval Irish monks.

Further evidence connecting cultures from opposite sides of the Earth came in September 1996, when Han Ping Chen, an authority on the ancient Chinese Shang dynasty, confirmed that markings found on Central American figures dated to more than three thousand years ago were clearly Chinese characters. The figures were from the Olmecs, forerunners of the Aztec and Mayan civilizations, and were discovered in Mexico in 1955. Smithsonian archaeologist Betty Meggers supported Chen's analysis, stating, "Writing systems are too arbitrary and complex. They cannot be independently reinvented."

Evidence of human activity (tools, fireplaces, etc.) at Monte Verde in Llanquihue Province in southern Chile has been dated to around 14,800 BC, thus predating Noah's Flood by three thousand years, as many researchers, based on the obvious water erosion on the Sphinx plus other evidence in Mesopotamia, believe the flood occurred about 11,500 BC. The findings at this site, now considered the oldest human settlement in the Americas, initially were dismissed by the scientific community but today gradually have found some acceptance, even though it destroys long-held beliefs about the occupation of both North and South America, as the date 14,800 BC places it into the last ice age, which would have made a Siberian land bridge impassible.

Mysterious life-size crystal skulls dated to at least 3,600 years ago have been recovered in South America. A study published in the May 2008 edition of the *Journal of Archaeological Science* detailed how a team of British and American researchers, using electron microscopy and X-ray crystallography, found that a crystal skull in the British Museum had been worked and shaped using tools not available to the ancient Aztecs or Mayans. So they concluded that the museum's skull may have been produced in the 1950s or later. "Some of them are quite good, but some of them look like they were produced with a Black & Decker in someone's garage," remarked Cardiff University professor Ian Freestone. Despite such efforts to explain away the crystal skulls, their true manufacture remains a mystery. The fact remains that many of the existent skulls are made from milky or clear rock crystal found in suitably large deposits only in Brazil, Madagascar, and even the Alps. Both the dating and locations in which the clear rock crystal skulls were found argue against simple forgery.

In Cuzco, Peru, long holes bored in ancient stone blocks exhibit score marks that show the use of some sort of high-speed rotary or vibrational drill, indicating that someone may have had access to such equipment, rather than the holes being simply modern hoaxes.

Throughout England, France, and Germany today stand many ancient stone forts constructed in defensible positions—there are at least fifty just in Scotland—built with large rocks that at some point were vitrified, melted from such heat as to become fused and glassy. The heat necessary to produce such an effect—up to 1,100 degrees Celsius (1,980 degrees Fahrenheit)—ruled out the possibility that the stones were melted by conventional fires. Due to the fact that the vitrification took place at the weakest point in the walls, many believe the fire was brought on by attackers, although no one can imagine how they generated such sustained heat.

Dr. E. W. Matvegeva with the Central Scientific Research Department of Geology and Exploitation of Precious Metals in Moscow reported in 1992 that tiny spirals of tungsten and copper were found by Russian geologists in the Ural Mountains. These particles were studied at four scientific institutions and were found to measure between .0003 millimeters and 3 centimeters (from about one one-hundred-thousandth of an inch to a little over one inch). They were dated to between three hundred thousand and one hundred thousand years ago, yet the proportions of their spirals were so regular that they could have been produced only by mechanical means. No one knows what purpose the spirals served. Today nanotechnology is commonplace, but such advances only began in the 1970s.

What appeared to be a computer dated almost a hundred years before Jesus was discovered in 1900 off the island of Antikythera near Crete. Known as the Antikythera mechanism, the device contained a system of differential gears not known to have been used until the 1700s. Many believe it is an artifact predating Greek culture that was looted and then lost while being shipped to Rome. Some think the mechanism may have been an early personal computer, as its door contained at least two thousand characters, composing what researchers have referred to as an instruction manual. Its attachment to the mechanism implied that it was designed for ease of transport and personal use. Studies in 2011 determined that the mechanism is an astronomical calculator whose tiny gears can track celestial bodies. A system of thirty-seven hand-cranked interlocking dials keep track of the day of the year, the positions of the sun and the moon and perhaps other planets, as well as predicting eclipses. Cardiff University professor Michael Edmunds, who headed a recent study of the mechanism, stated, "This device is just extraordinary, the only thing of its kind. The design is beautiful, the astronomy is exactly right. The way the mechanics are designed just makes your jaw drop. Whoever has done this has done it extremely carefully . . . in terms of historic and scarcity value, I have to regard this mechanism as being more valuable than the Mona Lisa."

A five-inch-tall terra-cotta vessel containing a copper cylinder with an iron rod inside, discovered in an Iraqi village and dating from at least 220 BC turned out to be nothing less than a battery. When grape juice, lemon juice, or vinegar was added to this and other similar objects, which have become known as the Baghdad batteries, it became an acidic electrolyte solution that produced a half volt of electricity that may have been used for electroplating gold and silver. Since to acknowledge the battery's use for electro-plating at so early a time would upset conventional history, this theory has been largely dismissed by modern scientists. Paul Crad-dock of the British Museum explained, "The examples we see from this region and era are conventional gild plating and mercury gild-ing. There's never been any untouchable evidence to support the electroplating theory." But as pointed out by Marjorie Senechal, a professor of the history of science and technology at Smith College, "I don't think anyone can say for sure what they were used for, but they may have been batteries because they do work."

Carvings located twenty-five feet above the floor in the ancient Temple of Seti I in Abydos, Egypt, resemble nothing less than two jet airplanes, possibly a submarine, and an Apache attack helicopter. Their presence has been noted by recent travelers and reportedly was mentioned in an 1842 report, yet no one knows what they truly represent. Researchers have wondered if the carvings in Seti's temple might be connected to small delta-wing "jet planes" still on display in the Gold Museum in Bogotá, Colombia. The diminu-tive models, estimated to be at least 1,500 years old, have been ex-plained away as stylized bees or flying fish, but no one has explained the presence of both horizontal and vertical tail fins, not found on any animal.

In August 1997, two German researchers, Peter Belting and Conrad Lübbers, tested a scale model of one of the gold Bogotá "jets" to determine whether it demonstrated true flight characteristics. Dub-bing their 1:16 scale model Goldflyer II, they attached a jet engine at the rear, which theoretically allowed room for three passengers in the front. Did it fly? According to journalist Philip Coppens, a frequent contributor to *Nexus* and *Atlantis Rising* magazines,

> *The proof is in the demonstration, and in this case, the proof is there: Goldflyer II behaved impeccably, its landings being a thing of beauty. It is impressive to see enthusiasts take this ap-*

proach and demonstrate their case—no one can argue with the flight capabilities of the "insect" as it is. This is what the model looks like, and this is how it flies. But the definitive answer is still in the future. In my opinion, [the German experimenters] have been able to demonstrate that the artifact is not an insect. At the moment, they have only been able to prove it is an anomaly, an "item" that has all the characteristics of an airplane. But is it one? Or is it something else? Only new evidence, or comparisons with other findings of a similar nature, might give us the final answer.

Cuneiform Babylonian tablets in the British Museum describe the phases of Venus, the four largest moons of Jupiter, and the seven largest satellites of Saturn, none of which could have been seen in ancient Babylon without the aid of telescopes.

Many other artifacts indicate advanced knowledge in the far distant past, and not only in the Western world. One example is what seems to be an X-ray machine possessed by China's emperor Qin Shi Huang, who lived from 259 to 210 BC. This device was described by contemporary scribes as a rectangular mirror about four feet wide and five feet nine inches in height that "illuminates the bones of the body." It was said that when a person stood before this device, medical practitioners could detect any hidden malady within the organs.

An ancient Brahman medical text compiled about 1500 BC called the *Sactya Grantham* described what appeared to be an early vaccination technique. It stated, "Take on the tip of a knife the contents of the inflammation, inject it into the arm of a man, mixing it with his blood. A fever will follow but the malady will pass very easily and will create no complications." This was some 3,500 years before British scientist Edward Jenner was credited with developing the smallpox vaccination in the 1800s.

Maps by Turkish admiral Piri Reis dating from 1513 and still available at the library of the Topkapi Palace in Istanbul, though not usually displayed for the public, are said to be based on earlier maps predating Alexander the Great. The Piri Reis map and his other charts accurately depict the Amazon basin of South America and the northern coastline of Antarctica, neither of which was surveyed until after the advent of aircraft in the twentieth century. The accuracy of these maps regarding Antarctica is especially puzzling because it has been under an ice cap for at least four thousand years. Piri Reis wrote that he made use of charts and maps dating back to ancient Greece, whose intellectuals acknowledged that they drew from even older Egyptian and Mesopotamian sources. In a letter dated July 6, 1960, Air Force colonel Harold Z. Ohlmeyer of the Eighth Reconnaissance Tactical Squadron of the Strategic Air Command stated, "The geographic detail shown in the lower part of the [Piri Reis] map agrees very remarkably with the results of the seismic profile made across the top of the ice-cap by the Swedish-British Antarctic Expedition of 1949. This indicates the coastline had been mapped before it was covered by the ice-cap." The discovery of ice-encased Cenozoic unicellular algae in 1983 indicated that Antarctica may have been at least partly free of ice as late as three million years ago.

The late professor Charles Hapgood, who taught the history of science at Keene College in New Hampshire, advanced the theory in 1953 that Antarctica may have moved farther south by some two thousand miles due to "Earth-crust displacement" and therefore could have been partially free of ice until as late as 4000 BC. This is still a thousand years before traditional academics believe that the first true civilizations of Egypt and Sumer with their seafaring explorers began. The idea that someone had accurately mapped an ice-free Antarctica in prehistoric times paled beside the fact that Piri Reis's 1513 map also depicted the correct position of the Falkland Islands, not discovered until 1592, and the rivers of South America—the Orinoco, Amazon, Paraná, Uruguay, and others not fully charted until the advent of satellites. The Piri Reis maps were not flukes. Another Turkish map from 1559 depicts Alaska and Siberia joined together, indicating that, unless the Bering Strait was intentionally omitted, this was a copy of a map made more than twelve thousand years ago.

Author Erich von Däniken saw evidence of slight distortions of the South American coast on the Piri Reis map. He claimed this same type of distortion is noticeable on satellite photos in which corners of pictures warp due to the curve of the Earth's surface. Von Däniken concluded that Piri Reis's source documents may have been drawn from aerial photographs. Of course, the thought that someone may have flown over Antarctica and South America prior to 4000 BC cannot be seriously considered within the context of traditional history. Such evidence drove both Hapgood and his student, author Graham Hancock, to speculate that a previously unknown and very advanced civilization existed in prehistoric times. Neither man appeared willing to publicly postulate that such a civilization might have been the result of extraterrestrial contact, yet the evidence for this supposition continues to grow.

HOARY STRUCTURES

Many ancient monuments attest civilizations existing long before accepted history. For example, a rectangular ziggurat recently was discovered under about seventy-five feet of water off the island of Yonaguni, southwest of Okinawa. This structure is six hundred feet long and ninety feet high and is said to be about more than eight thousand years old, meaning it would be comparable (by unconventional dating) to the pyramids of Egypt and predate the ziggurats of the Babylonians. The structure includes two closely spaced eight-foot pillars, a wide wedge called the Loop Road, a straight wall named the Dividing Wall, an L-shaped "stage," and a depressed "pool" with two large holes at its edge. Those who believe that it is artificial argue that this number of regular-shaped objects in one small area make natural formation highly unlikely. Boston University geologist Robert M. Schoch, who has claimed that the Sphinx is about ten thousand years old, was impressed by the regularity of the structure's steps. Although retaining the belief that its regularities are most probably the work of repeated scoring by the tides, he has written that if it is indeed an artificial structure, "the Yonaguni Monument appears to bear testimony to a previously unknown, yet very early and highly sophisticated civilization."

The purposes of some such structures have changed over the years. The world-famous stone circles at Stonehenge, begun in 3100 BC, a date comparable with the Early Dynastic period of ancient Egypt, were considered only monuments for pagan rituals until the 1700s, when British antiquarian William Stukeley, considered by many to be a forerunner of archaeology, proposed that the builders of Stonehenge knew about magnetism and had aligned the stone circles with magnetic north. Then, in 1962, Gerald Hawkins of Boston University provoked an outcry in the scientific community by using computer technology to prove that Stonehenge was nothing less than a giant observatory that could be used to predict both solar and lunar eclipses.

Again the status quo weighed in, this time against Hawkins's new ideas. British archaeologist Richard J. C. Atkinson, who directed excavations at Stonehenge for the Ministry of Works from 1950 and 1964, remained adamant that the builders of Stonehenge were merely "howling barbarians" and that Hawkins's theory was "tendentious, arrogant, slipshod and unconvincing."

The scientific outcry became muted after the much-respected British astronomer Sir Fred Hoyle agreed with Hawkins and went even further, stating that Stonehenge was a model of our solar system and could predict the date of a lunar eclipse nineteen years into the future.

Hawkins and Hoyle had merely added to the growing evidence

that the ancients had much more sophisticated knowledge about the solar system and the stars than previously believed. This concept was further support by the recent discoveries of Stonehenge-type ruins in South Africa and Brazil.

In 2006, the BBC announced the discovery of a similar ancient stone structure in the state of Amapa, in northern Brazil. The structure is comprised of 127 large blocks of stone, each well preserved and weighing several tons, driven into the ground on top of a hill. The stones are evenly spaced and placed upright.

Judging from pottery found nearby, the site, thought to have been an observatory or place of worship, was built about two thousand years ago and thus long predates European colonization. It evinces a sophisticated knowledge of astronomy and has been compared to Stonehenge, although the latter is much older, dated to about 3000 to 1600 BC.

The South African circular ruin, called Adam's Calendar, is perched on the rim of the Transvaal Escarpment and is believed to be more than two hundred thousand years old. African shaman Sanusi Credo Mutwa described the site as the most sacred place on Earth. Based on the descriptions of the African home of the Sumerian overlord Enki, researcher Michael Tellinger believed the site might well have been the laboratory of the Enki, who, according to ancient tablets, created a hybrid there by genetically engineering human and alien DNA.

In addition, Tellinger and his associates noted that none of the thousands of such circular ruins have openings, although modern archaeologists have called the South African structures *kraals*, corrals for cattle. The only gateways in these *kraals* are those that have been knocked out recently. However, there were channels leading into the center of the structure and connecting to other circles. It has been theorized by Tellinger and others that these were used for moving energy out of the circle.

Similar circular stone ruins, with spokes radiating outward but visible only from the air, have been found stretching from Syria to Saudi Arabia. New satellite-mapping technologies coupled with an aerial photography program in Jordan have revealed thousands of these giant ancient circles termed *geolyphs*. Researchers believe that they date to prehistoric times.

One example is the Monastery of Saint Moses the Abyssinian, or Deir Mar Musa, located fifty miles north of Damascus in Syria. Termed Syria's Stonehenge by archaeologist Robert Mason of the Royal Ontario Museum, who happened upon the site in 2009, the area contains stone tools dating back as far as ten thousand years, as well as stone circles. The stone circles were described as "corral-like" and were said to be used as traps for gazelles and other animals. Mason said much work is needed to decipher the mysteries of Deir Mar Musa, but such effort is uncertain due to the violence and political upheaval in that country.

"In Jordan alone we've got stone-built structures that are far more numerous than [the] Nazca Lines, far more extensive in the area that they cover, and far older," said David Kennedy, a professor of classics and ancient history at the University of Western Australia. The purpose of the stone "wheels" is unknown. Kennedy said theories that they were houses or cemeteries are unsatisfactory.

Tellinger believed that the African circular structures were created on ley lines—theoretical lines on the ground that intensify or carry the electromagnetic energy of Earth, similar to the popular Chinese concept of feng shui—and were used to channel Earth's energy. Along with a satellite communications technician, Tellinger used an electromagnetic flow meter to measure the temperature gradient per foot from more than six hundred feet belowground to the surface. They found the average temperature outside the stones circles to be about 42 degrees Fahrenheit while inside the circles it rose to more than 136 degrees. "It was extraordinary!" exclaimed Tellinger. "Our measurements in sound frequency, heat signature and electromagnetic intensity were infinitely higher inside the circles than on the outside. In fact, the maximum energy could not be measured on our instruments. It went beyond 375 gigahertz."

"Now that we understand the energy-generating principle, it seems that this is a good example of an early diagram of an energy-generating complex. The energy is channeled via the channels that connect them all together, they create a continuous energy grid. The simple non-polar, or radiant energy would have been used for everything as we imagine it today—and more. It is not a dangerous form of energy like the polar energy we use today," said Tellinger, referring to the AC/DC-generated electricity commonly in use today.

Found within the circular ruins were several carvings of a serpent in the same horseshoe shape of the Greek letter omega, Ω, long used to symbolize the unit of electrical resistance, the ohm. The identically shaped snake image can be found on ancient Greek coins.

THE CORAL CASTLE

The Earth-drawn energy mentioned by Tellinger may be comparable to that of the Serbian-born inventor Nikola Tesla, who in 1900 constructed Wardenclyffe Tower on Long Island to establish intercontinental wireless transmission of electrical energy. Initially funded for $150,000, the majority of which came from American financier J. P. Morgan, the project was scrapped after Morgan realized that wireless energy would eliminate the profit from his investments in copper wiring. Tesla had successfully demonstrated wireless energy transfer in 1891 and claimed that he could draw abundant energy from the earth.

This same energy manipulation may be behind Florida's curious Coral Castle, a collection of stone carvings and monoliths assembled by Latvian immigrant Edward Leedskalnin. Standing no

more than five feet tall and never weighing more than 120 pounds,
Leedskalnin moved to Florida about 1919 and, working primarily at night, constructed his coral rock collection during the next
twenty years. In the mid-1930s, Leedskalnin moved his entire collection to Homestead, Florida. Some say this move came following
an altercation with vandals, while others contend it was to locate on
better aligned ley lines.

The site includes more than 1,500 tons of dense coral blocks,
some weighing up to 30 tons. Yet there was no evidence of modern
machinery being used, and Leedskalnin would offer only polite
but cryptic responses to questions concerning his method of construction. On more than one occasion he did state, "I have discovered the secrets of the pyramids, and have found out how the
Egyptians and the ancient builders in Peru, Yucatan and Asia,
with only primitive tools, raised and set in place blocks of stone
weighing many tons!"

Leedskalnin explained that science had an incorrect knowledge
of atomic structure and electricity. He said all forms of existence are
made up of three components—north and south poles and neutral
particles of matter. Leedskalnin said he understood the laws involved in the relationship of the Earth to celestial alignments. He
also said he had an intimate understanding of magnetism and even
claimed to have cured himself of tuberculosis through the use of
magnets. Leedskalnin died of kidney failure in 1951 after checking himself into a hospital. Coral Castle was added to the National
Register of Historic Places in 1984.

One account of Leedskalnin's methods came from Tellinger,
who related, "The truck drivers used to deliver the rocks and stand
around the corner as he single-handedly offloaded these huge stones.
And then he would come round the corner and tell them they could
take the truck and go. Nobody knows how he did it, but there were
reports of these eerie sounds and high frequency pitch noises and
so forth but two school kids reported seeing him from the bushes

nearby offloading these rocks with ice cream cones in his hands. We are dealing with sound and the focusing of sound frequencies. This is what I refer to as the ice cream cone phenomenon." He added that in San Jose, California, there is a museum which houses "beautiful cones that were extracted from temples in [ancient Sumer] that commemorate the building of the temples." Tellinger theorized that such conelike objects were used to somehow channel natural energy through the energy of the individual user.

In contemplating the idea of moving objects by sonic energy, one cannot help but recall the biblical story of Joshua and the battle of Jericho in which ram's horns were sounded, the Israelites were exhorted to shout, and the city walls crumbled. Yet another account of the levitation of giant stones by sonic frequency came from retired New Zealand airline pilot and author Bruce Cathie, who related an account of Tibetan monks lifting huge boulders up a mountainside by the use of sound frequencies. This feat was observed by a Swedish doctor who had traveled deep into Tibet in 1939. Using a collection of drums and trumpets, the chanting monks were able to levitate a large stone some 250 meters (820 feet) upward to a ledge in only three minutes.

Interestingly, a cache of cone-shaped stone tools made of basalt has been found on Easter Island, the site of the huge monolithic stone giants. Researchers have long wondered how the people were able to lift the massive statues into position. Perhaps the stone cones provide the answer.

STRANGE ARTIFACTS

Also in South Africa can be found the Klerksdorp spheres, small round objects collected near Ottosdal, South Africa, by miners and locals from three-billion-year-old pyrophyllite deposits. Ranging in size from one-half to four inches in diameter, the spheres are found in the Klerksdorp Museum, located about seventy miles from Ottosdal. Described by some as "out-of-place artifacts" possibly manufactured by nonhumans, the spheres reveal well-defined and parallel latitudinal grooves or ridges when cut open and are balanced to near perfection, an impossible feat even with today's technology. Naturally, there is controversy over both the nature and creation of the spheres. One, for example, has three parallel grooves around its equator.

Conventional geologists, such as Paul V. Heinrich, say the strange structure of the hematite spheres indicates they are "natural concretions that are pseudomorphs after original pyrite concretions." He concluded that the spheres are entirely natural and added, "The misidentification of natural objects as the by-products of 'intelligent design' is an important lesson that needs to be learned by many fringe group members."

Others are not as certain as Heinrich of the spheres' natural origins. Roelf Marx, curator of the Klerksdorp Museum, has stated, "The spheres are a complete mystery. They look man-made, yet at the time in Earth's history when they came to rest in this rock no intelligent life existed. They're nothing like I have ever seen before."

Even stranger was the explanation of Douglas James Cottrell, a trance psychic similar to the famous Edgar Cayce. During one session, he was asked about the Klerksdorp spheres. He stated that they are "sighting instruments," similar to tape recorders, created by extraterrestrials to pass along information from one world to another via subtle energy vibrations. His explanation for such ancient cell phones sounded eerily similar to that of the accounts of Tellinger, Cathie, and Leedskalnin.

Other ancient artifacts are equally intriguing. One such was found by author Sitchin in Turkey's Istanbul Archaeology Museum. The carving, which measures about six inches long by four inches wide, was described by Sitchin as "a sculpted scale model of what, to modern eyes, looks like a cone-nosed rocket-ship . . . powered by a cluster of four exhaust engines in the back surrounding a larger exhaust engine, the rocket-ship has room for a sole pilot, actually shown and included in the sculpture."

A figure described as the pilot was sitting with legs folded toward his chest and appeared to be wearing a one-piece ribbed pressure suit with boots and gloves. As the head is missing, it is impossible to know if the figure wore a helmet, goggles, or other headgear.

The carving was excavated at Toprakkale, a city known in ancient times as Tuspa. Curators had not put the carving on display; they had concluded that it was a fake because it differed from other objects of its era and mostly because it resembled a space capsule. Sitchin convinced them to display the artifact and let the public decide. Most observers do see the figure as a person sitting in some sort of cockpit.

Austrian researcher Klaus Dona, who presented a well-received public exhibit at the Vienna Art Center Schottenstift in 2001, displayed many amazing artifacts that gave indication that our history is not as we have been taught.

A small tool called the Hammer of Texas was one exhibit indicating intelligent life before that accepted by conventional science. This hammer was made of almost pure iron but showed no signs of rusting. It was placed within a wooden handle and was obviously a manufactured tool. The tool was found encased in limestone dated to more than 140 million years ago, when no humans were thought to exist. Adding to this puzzle are several humanlike handprints and footprints found in the same geological stratum with dinosaur tracks. Humans and dinosaurs are not supposed to have coexisted, according to conventional science.

One of Dona's most fascinating exhibits was a stone pyramid embedded with precious stones, including one placed near the top. The artifact eerily resembled the "all-seeing eye" atop a pyramid that is imprinted on every dollar bill. But this ancient artifact was found in Ecuador.

Dona's many quaint and curious artifacts included statues and carvings of prehistoric animals thought to have been extinct long before the advent of humankind, art depicting strange humanoids wearing helmets, replicas of flying machines, and engravings of the planets and stars. Several ancient carvings depict saucer-shaped craft and beings with large slanted eyes identical to modern depictions of alien "grays" as described by persons who claim to have experience of them.

ELONGATED SKULLS AND THE STARCHILD

Evidence from the exhibition of Klaus Dona indicating that nonhumans may have lived on Earth in the past included skulls brought from Central and South America with features that may not be human.

Many such skulls are termed *elongated,* as they extend up and beyond normal human length, similar to the skull of an interdimensional alien depicted in the film *Indiana Jones and the Kingdom of the Crystal Skull.* Like so many legends and fables, this film may have contained a modicum of truth.

Archaeologists, operating under the narrow constraints of science, claim a conventional explanation for the misshapen skulls. They say young Inca children's heads were bound so as to produce the elongated effect. A more far-reaching view is that this was done to emulate their elder creator gods, and it has been noted that the practice was confined to the ruling and religious class.

But this explanation fails to address other issues. Brien Foerster, author of *A Brief History of the Incas*, while studying the Paracas culture in Peru, found one elongated skull with no molar teeth or even sockets for them. The skull also exhibited exceptionally large eye sockets and two small identical holes in the back of the skull which could not be explained by the ancient practice of trepanning. Other skulls exhibited strangeness with the normal three suture lines that connect the parietal, sagittal, and lambda portions of the human skull. Some had only two lines, while others had four, and one skull was completely smooth with no suture lines. Foerster, while remarking on the oddity of the skulls, only hinted that they might represent ancient aliens viewed as gods by the Incas.

Researcher and author Lloyd Pye has been more forthright. Pye has spent countless dollars and many years of his life attempting to determine that his Starchild, a strange and misshapen skull found last century in Mexico, is not of human origin. The skull, dated to about nine hundred years ago, was found in Mexico in the 1930s and subsequently ended up in the hands of Ray and Melanie Young, who asked Pye to head efforts to identify the origin of the skull. In 1999, Pye formed the Starchild Project, an informal group of researchers and scientists, who soon ruled out all known natural deformities and initially found that the skull presented a genetic and physical profile never before seen on Earth. X-rays of the teeth indicated the skull belonged to someone about five or six years old. Yet degradation of the teeth's enamel indicated the skull was that of an adult. X-rays also revealed natural convolutions of the unusually flattened back of the skull, proving that it had not been cradleboarded, an explanation offered by skeptics. Cradleboarding was a common Native American practice of binding a babe to a board on the mother's back while moving about.

Pye and his Starchild team have now documented at least twenty-two physical abnormalities on the small skull. Such anomalies, unheard of in any one subject, have been brushed off by conventional scientists as mere deformities. Pye commented:

> *Mainstream science has consistently failed to explain—or even explain away—any of the Starchild's anomalies, much less the complex combination that somehow created a functioning being. Why? Because science has collectively agreed*

to set its BS detector to go off if anything passes by it that
is not already understood or does not fit accepted theories.
. . . Peer pressure is crushing relative to subjects deemed
"off limits" for serious discussion and analysis. Things like
UFO's, aliens, hominoids (bigfoot, etc.), and cold fusion
are "forbidden" because their proof would utterly transform
"reality" as it is today. No scientist wants to be on the hot
seat when a paradigm overturns, so they work diligently to
keep these various genies corked up in bottles of ignorance
and intimidation fueled by their "credentialed" ridicule
and disdain.

In 1999, Pye asked six laboratories equipped to test ancient DNA to examine the Starchild, but all six demurred, citing the "professional stigma" involved. Finally, DNA tests in 2003 demonstrated that the Starchild's mother was human but its father was less than 100 percent human, as the nuclear DNA was viable but not recoverable by human testing methods. Further DNA tests on the Starchild languished due to the prohibitive costs.

Early in 2011, a geneticist identified several fragments of the Starchild skull which, while matching human mitochondrial DNA, presented many more nucleotide differences than are normally found among humans. Pye said the new DNA findings indicate that the Starchild skull may well be alien. "Now all that remains is to determine whether alien means foreign to normal human genetics within the framework of that subject as it is currently understood or definitely not from planet Earth . . . or something in between," he said.

Such determination came later in 2011. One lab, using newly developed techniques, agreed to test the DNA on the condition that the lab's name not be made public. The result was astounding. It was reported that "no significant similarity" was found between the Starchild DNA and a genetic database that, though limited, nevertheless contained millions of DNA samples representing thousands of species including humans. This indicated that at least some of the Starchild's nuclear DNA is not found on Earth.

More striking was a study of the Starchild's mitochondrial DNA in which was reported a total of ninety-three variations different from human mtDNA. Pye believes this high level of variation could mean that the DNA in different parts of Starchild's skull could differ even further from normal human DNA.

In early 2012, a fragment of the Starchild's skull containing a special protein called FOXP2, was shown to exhibit fifty-six variations from the same type of protein in humans. "To put this in perspective, let's imagine that when alive, the Starchild was indeed some unknown humanoid. No matter how different from humans it might have been, to be in the humanoid family, its FOXP2 gene would have to be in the range of 1 or 2 or at most 3 base pair variations from a normal human. To go past 5 or 10 would put it into another class of species; 20 to 25 would put it in the range of mice and elephants, and dogs and frogs. To have 56 is to put it in another realm, another dimension entirely. It is utterly unique," said Pye. "This is the real deal," he added. "We simply lack the funding to complete a DNA study which we hope will prove the Starchild is not human."

Lack of funds and interest also stopped Zecharia Sitchin from conducting a DNA analysis on the skeleton of Nin Puabi, also called Queen Shubad, a Mesopotamian royal who was buried at Ur about 4,500 years ago and thought to be related to the Anunnaki. The queen's skeletal remains are still in London's Natural History Museum. But when Sitchin suggested a DNA study, Margaret Clegg of the museum's Human Remains Unit replied, "No DNA analysis has ever been conducted on these remains . . . the museum does not routinely conduct DNA analysis on remains in the collection, and there are no plans to do so in the near future."

Despite the lack of DNA studies and a seeming lack of desire on the part of archaeological authorities to test the thesis, evidence continues to pile up indicating an extraterrestrial presence in our solar system and on Earth, lending strong support to the ancient legends of long-lost civilizations and extraterrestrial visitations.

SACRED SITES

THE ANCIENT EGYPTIANS HAVE ALWAYS BEEN THOUGHT OF AS being strangely advanced for their time. René Adolphe Schwaller de Lubicz, a philosopher who studied the temples at modern Luxor (ancient Thebes) for fifteen years, found that the early Egyptians had implemented a mathematical constant called the golden section, or golden ratio. Though the golden ratio was originally attributed to the Greeks, it seems that at Thebes the Egyptians applied it with great complexity and sophistication. The golden ratio is a mathematical ratio between two components such that the larger is the same proportion of the whole as the smaller is of the larger. In art and architecture, it creates an eye-pleasing proportion. Artists, architects, engineers, and others have used it through the years. The fact that ancient Egyptians used it demonstrates knowledge of mathematics long before the Greeks and Pythagoras. What prompted this ancient knowledge and technical prowess?

THE OSIRION

About fifty miles down the Nile from Thebes, in Abydos, the early capital of dynastic Egypt, sits the New Kingdom temple of Seti I, where the golden ratio was applied. The temple is perhaps the finest built during Egypt's Nineteenth Dynasty (1298–1197 BC). Behind the temple and far below, an amazing megalithic structure called the Osirion (sometimes spelled Osireion) protrudes into the desert. The structure, with its gigantic posts and lintel stone blocks, looks for all the world like a better-constructed Stonehenge, as its stones are smooth and wonderfully aligned in comparison to the worn and partially collapsed English landmark.

The Osirion was discovered in 1902 by the British team of archaeologist William Flinders Petrie and Egyptologist and anthropologist Margaret Alice Murray. Some conventional Egyptologists argued that the Osirion was just another part of Seti's temple, but Murray knew better. In a 1903 report, she stated that "we had found a building which has no known counterpart in Egypt." Because a number of the cartouches of Merneptah, who succeeded Ramses II, were found at the site, one hypothesis offered up was that the Osirion was the pharaoh's tomb, despite the fact that no funerary materials nor body were found. Murray countered this idea by stating, "There is no tomb even among the Tombs of the Kings that is like it in plan, none having the side chamber leading off the Great Hall. Then, again, no tomb has ever been found attached to a temple; the converse is often the case, I mean a temple attached to a tomb . . ." Some thought Merneptah had merely taken possession of a structure there long before him.

"The other hypothesis was that this was the building for the special worship of Osiris and the celebration of the Mysteries and this appears to me to be the true explanation, for many reasons," Murray wrote. "Each reason may not be convincing in itself, but the accumulation of evidence goes to prove the case." As its name suggests, the Osirion may indeed have been built to worship Osiris, the Egyptian god of the underworld, death, and rebirth. According to the ancient mythologies, the Egyptian god Osiris had roughly the same description as the Sumerian god Enki.

There are several credible arguments against the Osirion being built by early Egyptians. Virtually all New Kingdom temples are constructed at ground level from stone blocks weighing no more than two tons, and every available space is filled with carving, hiero-glyphics, or painted walls. Not so the Osirion. The floor is located forty feet below present ground level, while the stone blocks, often weighing sixty tons or more, were put into place without mortar, and even a piece of paper cannot be slipped between them. And with the exception of a few hieroglyphic images, which obviously appear to have been placed there long after the structure was built, the exquisitely cut stone walls are bare. Geologists have found that the layer of earth above the Osirion gives the structure a minimum age of eighteen thousand years.

It is worthwhile to note that Abydos was the center of the cult of Osiris, the god of death and rebirth. Nearly all researchers agree that the Osirion is dedicated to Osiris. Some researchers have noted that the only two structures found in Egypt that resemble the Osirion are the Sphinx Temple and the Valley Temple, both found beside the Sphinx. The two Sphinx temples also display the same water erosion as the Sphinx itself and therefore must have sat out under heavy rains, which only took place more than ten thousand years ago. Since they are known to have been built from stone removed from the base of the Sphinx during its construction, this would mean their construction took place several thousand years before the arrival of Seti.

Yet another hypothesis is that Seti, in constructing his temple, discovered the Osirion and in deference to the god Osiris, actu-ally turned his uncompleted temple toward the ancient site, thus making it the only temple in Egypt with an L-shaped turn.

It is interesting to note that a pyramidal structure with a flat-tened top or platform is found at the sacred Mayan site of Chichen Itza in the Mexican state of Yucatán. It is called the Ossario. In the center of a temple atop the Ossario is an opening that leads to a cave in which was found skeletons and various ornaments, leading some archaeologists to conjecture that this was the home of the Mayan high priests, a theory that has come under some dispute. Some believe this structure demonstrated some connection to the energy-generating pyramids of Egypt and Sumer.

According to certain researchers, it is at the Osirion at Abydos where the first mention was made of the Djed Pillar or Tet Pillar, known as the Pillar of Osiris. For the Egyptians, the Djed Pillar, depicted as a tall cylindrical object divided by four parallel bars, represented a source of power as well as the backbone of Osiris. Controversy continues over whether the Dejd was merely a representation or a functional device. Several ancient Egyptian reliefs depict men holding what appear to be elongated glass objects attached to a Djed Pillar as though to a power source. Interestingly, on at least one of these reliefs, the men holding the device are outlined with double lines as though to indicate they were being shaken by the power of the Djed.

This object of power also may be a metaphysical symbol. As one website explained, "The Djed is the supreme unifying symbol of all polarities, connecting us to the transcendent reality of the whole, the One. It symbolizes the macro and microcosmic 'axis.' As the cosmic axis the Djed is the 'cylinder,' the column of light linking the Earth to the pole star."

Also within the Osirion, a geometric design of multiple evenly spaced and overlapping circles known to those interested in "sacred geometry" as the Flower of Life can be found.

It's interesting that this same design, a flowerlike circle, can be found in the temples, art, and carvings of cultures all over the world, including Stonehenge, the Masada, China's Forbidden City, the ancient Bulgarian city of Preslav, Mayan and Incan sites in South America, and even some crop circles.

If the Osirion wasn't in fact created by Seti and the Djed really contained such incredible power, then it's possible that an undiscovered yet technologically advanced civilization existed in Egypt long before the rise of the dynasties of the Pharaohs and that the Flower of Life was a common motif.

According to Egyptologist John Anthony West, "The Greeks themselves acknowledged the great fount and source of the wisdom that came later. In other words, civilization has been on a downhill slide since ancient Egypt. In fact, ancient Egypt itself was on a downhill trip from its very beginnings, because, strangely enough, it reached its absolute peak—the height of its prowess and sophistication—fairly early in the Old Kingdom around 2500 B.C. . . . and pretty much everything thereafter was a lesser accomplishment, even the fabulous temples of the New Kingdom."

Other ancient structures continue to baffle researchers who dare to look beyond their conventional textbooks.

CARNAC

Thousands of monolithic stones, including pillars, erected near the coast of Brittany in northwestern France prior to the arrival of the Celts attest the skills of Neolithic people living there more than 4,000 years ago. Carnac, as it is called, is regarded by locals as a Neolithic cathedral, and it is considered a sacred site by many. Unnoticed until the seventeenth century, Carnac is composed of more than three thousand stones spread out in multiple rows. One row measures more than five miles in length. During World War II, Carnac was almost obliterated by the Allies, who thought the pillars were a German defense line.

Some of the larger stones weigh more than twenty tons, and their true age is hard to determine. Carnac is a mystery, because no one knows how the builders managed to balance these mighty stones in such shallow ground. After all, ten inches below the present ground level lies impenetrable granite. No one knows for certain why the ancients went to the trouble to construct Carnac, but one man has presented compelling evidence that again such a prehistoric site is connected to the stars.

Howard Crowhurst, a longtime Carnac researcher, determined that the builders of Carnac used sophisticated geometry and mathematics to mark solar and lunar eclipses. The pillars also seem to be designed to match ley lines in that location.

Philip Coppens wrote that Carnac "involved careful alignments to astronomical phenomena, but also played with the energies of the Earth—which is likely one of the reasons why the stones of Carnac were placed on top of a granite surface. Certain energies were harnessed here, but how and why remains a question that can only be answered in the future. What we *can* say is that the site shows that the builders of Carnac—in 4500 B.C.—possessed knowledge with which official archeology refuses to credit them."

GÖBEKLI TEPE

Göbekli Tepe is a hilltop complex of megaliths erected on the highest point of a mountain ridge about five hundred miles from Istanbul in southeastern Turkey. Hunter-gatherers reportedly used the site for religious purposes some twelve thousand years ago during the Neolithic period. Its discovery in 1964 was the most astonishing archaeological find in modern times, and today it is considered the oldest advanced civilization on Earth. Prior to the discovery and dating of Göbekli Tepe, structures in Malta dating back to 3500 BC were considered the most ancient megalithic site known. The complex consists of twenty round structures, most still buried, measuring thirty-three to one hundred feet in diameter. Only four have been excavated to date. Each structure is decorated with massive T-shaped limestone pillars.

The most extraordinary thing about Göbekli Tepe is the fact

that the entire complex was buried under sand, not through some natural disaster but intentionally. Much damage has occurred over the centuries due to farming and construction by locals who had no idea of the antiquity of the site. With the discovery of Göbekli Tepe, archaeologists have had to completely revise their timetable of history, as it was not thought possible for Neolithic people using primitive quarrying tools to build such a complex.

Archaeologist Klaus Schmidt of the German Archaeological Institute, who is in charge of the Göbekli Tepe excavation, believes its creators came from far distant places. The various strata at the site suggest several millennia of work, perhaps reaching back to the Mesolithic period. Considering that only about 5 percent of Göbekli Tepe's total area has been excavated, Schmidt said the dig might well continue for another fifty years and still "barely scratch the surface."

British journalist Sean Thomas, who visited the site, noted, "That early Neolithic hunter-gatherers could have built something like Göbekli—is world-changing. Hitherto, it was presumed that agriculture necessarily preceded civilization, and that complex art, society and architecture depended on the reliable food supplies derived from farming. Göbekli Tepe shows that the old hunter-gatherer life, at least in this region of Turkey, was far more advanced than was ever conceived."

But why would so-called primitive people use so much time and energy to construct something like Göbekli Tepe and then bury it? After finding human bones in portions of the complex, Schmidt opined, "Göbekli Tepe is not a house or a domestic building. Evidence of any domestic use is entirely lacking. No remains of settled human habitation have been found nearby. That leaves one purpose: religion. Göbekli Tepe is the oldest temple in the world. And it isn't just a temple; I think it is probably a funerary complex." Schmidt viewed the site as a place of veneration and perhaps communication with supernatural entities or domains.

Schmidt's interpretation has been challenged in late 2011. In an article published by *Current Anthropology*, archaeologist Ted Banning argued that based on evidence of daily food preparation and flint working, the structures at Göbekli Tepe were living quarters for a large population.

Termed by some the Turkish Stonehenge, the Göbekli Tepe complex predates its more famous British namesake by seven thousand years. Hassan Karabulut, associate curator of the nearby Urfa Museum, has called Göbekli Tepe "one of the most important monuments in the world." Some have even claimed the site may have been the basis for the Bible's Garden of Eden. One factor leading to this belief is the number of pillars there covered with elaborate animal figure reliefs. Archaeologists also have found a statue of a human and sculptures of a vulture's head and a boar. Reptiles and vultures are commonly depicted. Most of these carvings are found on the older pillars.

As in Egypt, the older columns at Göbekli Tepe are oddly more elaborate and finely detailed than the later ones, evincing a deterioration of the culture. After visiting Göbekli Tepe in 2008, Andrew Curry, a reporter for *Smithsonian* magazine, wrote, "Predating Stonehenge by 6,000 years, Turkey's stunning Göbekli Tepe upends the conventional view of the rise of civilization. . . . What was so important to these early people that they gathered to build (and bury) the stone rings? The gulf that separates us from Göbekli Tepe's builders is almost unimaginable. Indeed, though I stood among the looming megaliths eager to take in their meaning, they didn't speak to me. They were utterly foreign, placed there by people who saw the world in a way I will never comprehend. There are no sources to explain what the symbols might mean. Schmidt agrees, 'We're 6,000 years before the invention of writing here.' "

A series of complete circles have been located buried within the Göbekli Tepe complex reminiscent of reports by Michael Tellinger of the stone circles in South Africa. "As we walk around the recently excavated pillars, the site seems at once familiar and exotic. I have seen stone circles before, but none like these," commented Sandra Scham, a fellow of the American Association for the Advancement of Science. She added, "Scholars thought that the earliest monumental architecture was possible only after agriculture provided Neolithic people with food surpluses, freeing them from a constant focus on day-to-day survival. A site of unbelievable artistry and intricate detail, Göbekli Tepe has turned this theory on its head."

British author and explorer Andrew Collins stated, "There is no obvious explanation for a high culture existing in Upper Mesopotamia at the end of the last Ice Age, when the rest of the world was still populated by hunter-gathering communities concerned with day-to-day survival, and little more. However, these faceless individuals, known to archaeologists as the Pre-Pottery Neolithic (PPN) peoples, created some of the most mesmeric art in the ancient world, which would not be bettered for thousands of years."

Collins pointed out that the similarities between this account of Göbekli Tepe's formation and the mythology from the *Book of Enoch* are striking.

It is my belief that the trafficking between the suspected ruling elite and the peoples of Upper Mesopotamia is the story found in the Book of Enoch, where beings called Watchers are said to have gone amongst mortal kind giving them the forbidden arts and sciences of heaven. These were said to have included the use of herbs and plants, metallurgy, the fashioning of weapons, female beautification, and astronomy, many of the firsts accredited to the Early Neolithic world in Upper Mesopotamia.

Similar stories exist in the myths and legends of Sumeria, which speak of gods called Anunnaki coming among mortal kind and providing them with the rudiments of civilization. I believe there is strong evidence to suggest that the Watchers, and their offspring the Nephilim, were indeed the shamanic elite that founded the early Neolithic cult centres of Upper Mesopotamia. They are repeatedly referred to in pseudepigraphical literature as birdmen, and we know that the Neolithic period's highly prominent cult of the dead was focused around excarnation, and the use of the vulture as a symbol of both astral flight and the transmigration of the soul in death. Clear carvings and depictions of vultures, as well as representations of birdmen, have been found at Göbekli Tepe and other PPN sites in SE Turkey and North Syria.

Klaus Schmidt agreed that the T-shaped pillars of Göbekli Tepe may represent mythical creatures or even ancient gods. Such speculation supports the Sumerian tablets, which state that agriculture, animal husbandry, and weaving were brought to mankind by ancient Sumerian deities. Göbekli Tepe sits at the heart of places from biblical mythology, and many nearby locations are clearly mentioned in Genesis. Turkey borders northern Iraq, placing it in proximity to the source of the Mesopotamian legends of the Anunnaki, visitors who came from the heavens. The Turkish town Sanliurfa, which is close to Göbekli Tepe, was once known as the city of Ur Kaśdim. Some believe it may be mentioned in the Old Testament as the hometown of the patriarch Abraham.

It is fascinating to note that Göbekli Tepe was not lost in the sands of time, but deliberately buried, hidden from succeeding generations. But buried by whom and why? No one knows. And if Klaus Schmidt is correct in believing that the builders of Göbekli Tepe came from elsewhere, where could that have been? They could not have come from the world's oldest known civilization, Sumer, as that culture has been dated back only to 3300 BC, more than six thousand years too late to have built Göbekli Tepe.

Researcher and author Wayne Herschel stated, "Göbekli Tepe's layout plan and even its builders' motives are decoded. They had the same secret knowledge . . . hidden records of their star ancestors matching the same blueprint secret knowledge of a star of their ancestors like the empires of ancient Egypt, the Maya, the Inca and at Stonehenge." As with structures in ancient Egypt and even carvings of the Dogon tribe in Africa, Herschel found that the layout of Göbekli Tepe is a match for the star systems of Orion and the Pleiades.

Strangely enough, the carvings and depictions of bird-headed figures at Göbekli Tepe are also depicted in carvings on the mysterious buried statues on Easter Island in the Pacific. Herschel found more amazing similarities between the two sites. "The thin arms art style [of Easter Island] is exactly like the . . . unearthed megaliths at Göbekli Tepe in Turkey. This alone speaks volumes and if this isn't convincing enough, the two large symbols on the back of the Moai [Easter Island head statues] are of the same theme and style too," he noted after visiting the island.

Herschel found it odd that the statues on Easter Island, which was originally called Rapa Nui, were excavated in 1915 but then reburied. "What could have been so shocking for them to have been completely covered up again?" After comparing much evidence at Easter Island with other ancient cultures, Herschel concluded, "Scholars hate this obvious but impossible-to-avoid theory and its simple . . . [sentence incomplete in source] Almost all ancient civilisations carry the same star visitor claim . . . show celestial ships and mostly bird head deities . . . built unique megalith structures . . . [and] show pieces of the same star map.

"All ancient civilizations had exactly the same obsession with star visitors . . . people who are most likely our ancestors returning to try and teach us who we are and where we come from. But what did our people do . . . they worshipped them as Gods."

BAALBEK

Herschel's theories are astounding because they force us to reconsider our history in a new way. Did our ancestors descend from the heavens? How close to the truth was Herschel?

Years of war and terrorism have kept tourists away from the ancient ruins at Baalbek in Lebanon. The site was once known as the Roman city of Heliopolis and is one of the largest and best-preserved Roman ruins. Baalbek may also present some of the most significant evidence of prehistoric space flight.

While attention has been directed mostly to the wondrous Roman towers and columns, the puzzling aspect of Baalbek concerns the massive, multi-ton stone block undergirding the Baalbek acropolis, larger than the one that is the site of the Parthenon in Athens. Below the Roman Temple of Jupiter, a wonder in itself, lies a wall of some two dozen stone blocks, each weighing 300 tons. In one corner are three massive blocks, known as the trilithon, each more than sixty-two feet long and weighing an estimated 800 tons. Nearby is yet another stone block almost eighty feet in length and weighing 1,100 tons. A former curator at Baalbek, Michel Alouf, said of these blocks, "In spite of their immense size, they are so accurately placed in position and so carefully joined, that it is almost impossible to insert a needle between them. No description will give an exact idea of the bewildering and stupefying effect of these tremendous blocks on the spectator."

Since it has become apparent that the gigantic stone blocks under Baalbek far predate Roman Heliopolis, the question arises of how could a primitive people move such weight? Conventional authorities have suggested the blocks were all moved with wooden rollers. Some have even demonstrated how this might be done. Steel rollers—it seems more than eight hundred tons will crush wooden rollers—and levers have been used to move a five-thousand- to six-thousand-pound stone on a concrete platform. Other researchers, straining to find an explanation, announced that they could move stone blocks by flipping them. They first pried up a two-and-a-half-ton block and placed shims under it. By repeating the process, they could flip stones up to about three fourths of a ton with only four or five men. In 1996, author Alan F. Alford asked representatives of Baldwins Industrial Services, a leading construction company, if they could move the thousand-ton Baalbek stone and place it at the same height as the trilithon.

"Although it is sometimes claimed that modern cranes cannot lift stones as heavy as 800 tons, this is actually incorrect," Alford discovered. "Bob MacGrain, the technical director of Baldwins, confirmed that there were several mobile cranes that could lift and place the 1,000-ton stone on a support structure 20 feet high. . . . Unfortunately, however, these cranes do not have the capability to actually move whilst carrying such heavy loads." Such a crane, fitted with crawler tracks, would require massive ground preparation to move such a block, including a level and sturdy roadway.

After hearing other plausible explanations as to how Baldwins might achieve the movement and placement of such a massive stone block, Alford noted, "This is all very interesting, and gives us some feel for the scale of the engineering challenge, but there is, of course, one slight problem with the Baldwins scenario, namely that none of this twentieth century technology was supposedly available when Baalbek was built."

Noting that not one Roman emperor ever claimed credit for the Baalbek temple complex or for the construction of its massive foundations, Alford said, "What we do find instead are legends which suggest that Baalbek was built by super-human powers in an epoch long before human civilization began."

According to local legend, Baalbek was once ruled by the legendary Nimrod, that Sumerian ruler who led the attack on the gods by building the fabled Tower of Babel. Nimrod was said to have been the great-grandson of Utnapishtim, Sumerian equivalent of the Biblical Noah. This suggests a sacred aspect to Baalbek.

Searching for perhaps a religious meaning in the artifacts at Baalbek, Alford suggested that "the Roman gods are only part of the answer to the sanctity of Baalbek, for the town was in fact named after Baal, the Storm-God of the Canaanites/Phoenicians. And the legends of the god Baal provide numerous fascinating parallels to the gods of the ancient Mesopotamian exploded planet cults. . . . Indeed, my own private research suggests that the Canaanite/Phoenician religion could itself be described as an exploded planet cult."

Matest Agrest, a Russian-born ethnologist and mathematician, once proposed that the giant stone foundation at Baalbek was at one time used as a launch site for space vehicles and that the destruction of the biblical Sodom and Gomorrah was caused by a nuclear blast. Agrest, who in 1970 became head of Leningrad University's laboratory and in the early 1990s immigrated to the United States, came to believe that the monuments of early cultures resulted from contact with extraterrestrials.

Zecharia Sitchin, in his copious works concerning ancient Sumerian texts, also asserted that the massive stones of Baalbek constituted an antediluvian landing pad for the shuttle craft of ancient astronauts. Could its builders have been ancient astronauts, or might they have been from some prehistoric civilization?

And Baalbek is not the sole site of massive stone blocks whose size and weight would seem to be beyond the ability of primitive people to move and lift. The megalithic ruins of Tiahuanaco lie twelve miles south of Lake Titicaca in western Bolivia. Amazingly, the immense stones are joined with modular fittings and complex breach-locking levels not found in any other ancient culture. Many of these blocks are joined together with T-shaped metal clamps that were poured into place from a portable forge. Some of these blocks weigh between 100 and 150 tons. One stone weighs about 800 tons!

Known variously as the Baalbek of the New World or an American Stonehenge, Tiahuanaco's huge stoneworks are considered by some to be the oldest ruins in the world. In fact, the recent discovery of underwater structures indicates that Tiahuanaco was built, not as a port on the lake, but prior to Lake Titicaca's existence. Legends in the area say that the city was a gift of the ancient sky gods but was drowned in a flood long ago. It is also said that at the time that Tiahuanaco flourished, the moon was not in its present orbit.

Near Tiahuanaco are ruins known as the Puma Punku, which is strewn with giant, precisely shaped blocks, many of which appear machine-made. The stones, composed of granite and diorite, are harder than any other material except diamonds. The ruins at both Tiahuanaco and Puma Punku lie scattered about as if destroyed by a catastrophic event.

PYRAMID POWER

Structures throughout the world give evidence of ancient man's fixation on the heavens and his fascination with harnessing the powers of the Earth, none more so than the Great Pyramid of Egypt—the only survivor of the original Seven Wonders of the Ancient World. Mysteries and questions abound regarding this pyramid, even as to who constructed it.

Many geologists now agree that water erosion on the Great Pyramid and the Sphinx indicates that both structures sat under heavy rains, which have not occurred on the Giza Plateau for more than ten thousand years. In other words, the Egyptian civilization, which is dated to the beginning of the Early Dynastic Period of King Menes about 3100 BC, could not have built the Great Pyramid. It had to have been created much earlier.

Though characterized as a burial place for the Fourth Dynasty pharaoh Cheops (alternately called Khufu), no hieroglyphics adorn the walls of the Great Pyramid, unlike every other ancient Egyptian structure. Furthermore, no evidence of a burial has been found, except one cartouche, which has been called into question as a possible modern addition, reportedly found in 1837 by British Egyptologist Colonel Howard Vyse, who was haunted by suspicions of fabrications as he was desperately in need of justification for his Egyptian expedition expenditures.

After viewing evidence from German robotics engineer Rudolf Gantenbrink, British engineer Christopher Dunn believes that the Great Pyramid might be a giant power generator based on harmonic resonance. In 1993, Gantenbrink sent a remote-controlled robot named Upuaut II (Upuaut, or Wepwawet, was a deity whose name means Opener of the Ways, probably in the sense of Scout) to explore the southern shaft in the Queen's Chamber. The robot traveled up the shaft and revealed what Dunn interpreted as electrical terminals, cables, and even ancient wiring diagrams etched on the walls.

"The discovery of electrical contacts and wiring inside the Great Pyramid, along with markings that show how to connect them, do not fit anywhere in conventional Egyptology but confirm the theory first published in my book, *The Giza Power Plant: Technologies of Ancient Egypt*, in 1998," said Dunn. In his book, Dunn proposed that the Queen's Chamber "served as a reaction chamber and the shafts leading to this chamber supplied two chemicals that when mixed together created hydrogen." Dunn has pointed out that at the end of the pyramid's southern shaft, in what is now known as Gantenbrink's door, there are two metal pins.

While the metal pins have been described as ornaments or door handles by some, no one has explained why ornamental metal pins would have been placed out of sight in small shafts within the pyramid. It is possible that they are actually electrodes.

In May 2011, *New Scientist* magazine published new images of these shafts, including a stone block in one—possibly a door—near the outside of the pyramid. The two small shafts have been described as "the last great mystery of the pyramid" by Zahi Hawass, Egypt's former minister of state for antiquities affairs. The latest exploration also revealed abnormal hieroglyphs in red paint and odd carvings thought to be marks made by the original builders. "If these hieroglyphs could be deciphered they could help Egyptologists work out why these mysterious shafts were built," said Rob Richardson of the University of Leeds.

Christopher Dunn has produced a compelling argument that the Great Pyramid, far from being simply a tomb, was instead a giant power source.

> *There was no immediate explanation for what these red symbols mean, but they are a significant discovery and have the potential to open up an entirely new area of research in gaining an understanding of ancient Egyptian symbolism. When considered along with the metal pins the symbols provide all the evidence necessary to prove the electrical use of the pins and also give us a roadmap for exploration into the future. Not only did the ancient Egyptians leave us with the physical evidence that proves this to be so, they also provided us with an electrical schematic that showed how the pins were wired!*

COSMIC WAR

Joseph P. Farrell also believes the pyramids were power sources, and he has even taken Dunn's conclusions a step further. In a series of books, Farrell postulated that in the remote past, the power of the Great Pyramid was used as a weapon in a great cosmic war that encompassed our entire solar system. After calling attention to a huge gouge on Mars, Farrell stated, "Certainly impacts from comets and meteors have occurred and can wreak untold destruction on the planetary bodies that endure them. But so can wars fought with weapons of sufficient power to scar whole regions. . . ."

Farrell's thesis received strong support in 2011 with the publication of *Life and Death on Mars* by John Brandenburg, senior propulsion scientist at the Orbital Technologies Corporation and one of the early researchers on the Cydonia project, a private study of the strange monuments on Mars. Brandenburg states that Mars was actually earthlike for most of its geologic history. It contained a massive and evolving biosphere but experienced a mysterious and astonishing nuclear catastrophe.

Hoagland also saw the asteroid belt as an exploded planet, a notion entertained by many. "What mechanism can explain why planets should suddenly explode? The problem is not a small one, nor will it go away," said Hoagland.

Farrell's scenario is not as implausible as it may sound on the surface. The notable astronomer Tom Van Flandern, referring to the possibility of an exploded planet, stated, "This speculative possibility might result from magnetic separation and storage of the antimatter in a planet over billions of years before the explosion; or from some sort of chain-reaction high-energy antimatter generation process; or from the intervention of intelligent beings. In my opinion, the last possibility should not be dismissed out of hand." Farrell noted, "Van Flandern is gingerly and delicately implying that his exploded planets might have been blown up in deliberate acts of war. Yet . . . it is precisely this model that the abundance of ancient texts actually supports!"

After listing the previously mentioned strange formations on the moon, Mars, and elsewhere, Farrell has stated that these anomalies are "very real, very artificial structures that are no mere metaphors. This implies, however unbelievable it may seem, that the war was also real, that it was interplanetary, and that it happened millennia ago."

Farrell went on to theorize that this war devastated the Earth, reducing the population to a primitive state, produced bomb craters on the moon, and left Mars a desolated world. A small group survived, according to Farrell, and throughout our history has attempted to manipulate humanity into re-creating the super science of this former age so that this remnant can dominate and subjugate the Earth. Again he is supported by Brandenburg, who wrote that in the distant past, survivors on Mars fled to Earth and that we are the "children of Mars," both culturally and biologically.

PYRAMIDS AS STAR MAPS

Symbologist Wayne Herschel believes that the Great Pyramid, among other monuments, provides a map to the stars. Proceeding from the conclusions of Robert Bauval and Adrian Gilbert's 1994 work, *The Orion Mystery,* Herschel believes that the Giza Plateau pyramids reflected the constellation Orion, which was said to be the home of reborn pharaohs. Bauval had determined that the configuration of the three Giza pyramids—two in line while the third is offset—indeed matched the configuration of Orion's stars and that a small tunnel or air shaft inside the Great Pyramid aligned with the star cluster of Orion's belt. Shockingly, Bauval and Gilbert realized that the arrangement of the Giza pyramids reflected the position of Orion as it would have appeared about the year 10,450 BC—a date that is consistent with the growing body of evidence suggesting that the Great Pyramid was built thousands of years before we originally thought.

In his graphics-laden 2003 book, *The Hidden Records,* Herschel presented seven years of research, which showed that a wide variety of pyramids, temples, and ancient texts worldwide all represented maps of the stars that served as the original homes of our progenitors. Studying a number of primary sources, including fifty star maps found around the world, Herschel concluded that the "gods" of early humans originated from other solar systems and their sun was depicted on star maps left on Earth.

British author Colin Andrews has offered an alternate explanation for Bauval, Gilbert, and Herschel's pyramid configurations. Andrews has argued that while the three Giza pyramids do resemble Orion's Belt, they don't match it exactly. However, the constellation Cygnus *does* precisely match the Giza Plateau's layout. In fact, every star of the Cygnus constellation matched an Egyptian structure on the overlay map, except for the star Deneb. He speculated that something heretofore unknown must be at that location.

Supporting each of these researchers' hypotheses, a new tomb with a nine-foot-long sarcophagus was discovered in Egypt in 1999, considered by Egyptian antiquities minister Zahi Hawass to be the "symbolic" tomb of the ancient god Osiris. "It is at least interesting that the tomb of Osiris was located directly under where the star Deneb . . . strikes the Giza Plateau," noted UFO radio commentator Kevin Smith. "It is interesting because it rather indicates that the fact that the Giza Plateau and the constellation Cygnus match is not an accident. Not only does the constellation Cygnus match the layout of the pyramids, but it marks the precise spot where Osiris' tomb lay deep under the ground."

Though the discovery of Osiris's tomb was an incredible find, Smith noted that there was something odd about its retrieval. There are numerous photos showing the workers lifting the sarcophagus from its resting place in the tomb's lower pit to the workers' level. In addition, there are photos of the workers preparing to lift the sarcophagus's lid. Yet oddly enough, there isn't a single released photo showing the inside of the sarcophagus at the instant when the lid was removed.

Smith noted that Hawass later said the sarcophagus was empty when the lid came off. "But was it?" he asked. "This is not to imply that Hawass was lying, but it does seem more than odd that there are photos of all the work leading up to taking the lid off the sarcophagus, but no concurrent photo of what was seen inside the instant the lid came off." Smith believes that what Hawass may have been covering up was that the mummy of Osiris was inside. If so, this would mean that Osiris was in fact an extraterrestrial— after all.

In addition to Colin Andrews, conventional academia also rejected the idea that the three pyramids at Giza fully align with the three stars of Orion's Belt because the Giza pyramids and the Sphinx do not match up with every star in the Orion constellation. Wayne Herschel believes there is an explanation for this, however—that the ancient Egyptians intended to encompass much more than just the system of Orion. Near the pyramids are piles of ruins that may have been pyramids long ago. With these ruins, Herschel devised a match between pyramids at not only Giza but also at Abu Rawash, Zawyet el-Aryan, and Abusir with the star systems of Sirius, Aldebaran, the Pleiades, and Orion, including Rigel and Betelgeuse. He explained that the ruin to the south of the Sphinx had been slightly offset to avoid protruding into the Nile. Other than that, the positions of the pyramids were a perfect representation of the star systems.

"It can be said with a certain amount of finality that all the pyramid star maps you have evidenced around the globe and even on another planet—Mars—marked the start of something utterly monumental in our solar system. *They were probably built in celebration of the epoch of the genesis of the human species in our solar system . . . as an 'arrival' scenario from the 'ak,' the star of the 'gods'* [emphasis in the original]," wrote Herschel, explaining that Ak is the name of the sun from which the sun god Ra originated.

He elaborated: "The ancient Egyptians revered a Sun . . . but it was not our Sun! Astronomers can confirm that the Solar Temple obelisk is the only monument in the entire pyramid field to emulate a 'Sun-like' star . . . and it is relatively nearby. The correlation occurred only at its most precise position 17,250 years ago, perhaps documenting the dawning of humanity. All the other pyramids match bright stars that are nothing like our Sun." Herschel suggests that the Sun Temple was named after a sunlike star (HD 283271 in the Pleiades) and has nothing to do with Sol, our sun, at all.

FORGOTTEN PYRAMIDS

Other pyramids also have generated controversy. An ongoing dispute was generated in late 2005 when it was announced that the world's largest pyramid had been found near the town of Visoko (literally, High), northwest of the Bosnian city of Sarajevo. Semir "Sam" Osmanagić, a Houston, Texas, manufacturer who was born in Bosnia and a foreign member of the Russian Academy of Natural Sciences in Moscow, said he first found two pyramids earlier in 2005 when he noticed that what had been thought to be merely hills had triangular faces and obvious edges.

After his creation of the nonprofit Archaeological Park: Bosnian Pyramid of the Sun Foundation, Osmanagić said a team of international scientists found five pyramids at the site, the largest of them rising 722 feet, which makes it higher than the Great Pyramid, which is 481 feet tall. He also said radiocarbon dating conducted by the Institute of Physics of the Silesian Institute of Technology in Gliwice, Poland, indicated the pyramid was constructed more than ten thousand years ago, making it the oldest pyramid in the world by conventional standards. This date could mean its construction was contemporary with what some people believe was the construction of the Great Pyramid. Most astonishing of all were Osmanagić's further claims:

A team of physicists detected an energy beam coming through the top of the Bosnian Pyramid of the Sun. The radius of the beam is 4.5 meters with a frequency of 28 kHz [kilo-

*hertz]. The beam is continuous and its strength grows as it
moves up and away from the pyramid. This phenomenon
contradicts the known laws of physics and technology. This
is the first proof of non-herzian technology on the planet. It
seems that the pyramid-builders created a perpetual motion
machine a long time ago and this "energy machine" is still
working.*

*Almost everything they teach us about the ancient history
is wrong: origin of men, civilizations and pyramids. Homo
sapiens is not a result of evolution and biologists will never
find a "missing link," because intelligent man is the product
of genetic engineering. Sumerians are not the beginning of
the civilized men, but rather the beginning of another cycle of
humanity. And finally, original pyramids, most superior and
oldest, were made by advanced builders who knew energy,
astronomy and construction better than we do.*

Mainstream scientists were quick to deny anything unusual
about the mounds in Bosnia, describing them merely as natural
geologic formations—hills. Anthony Harding, president of the European Association of Archaeologists and holder of the anniversary
chair in archaeology at Exeter University in England, was encouraged to verify the find. "Since such claims obviously belonged to a
fantasy world, I was inclined to ignore the affair, . . . " he later wrote.
"I called in at the hill of Visocica, on the edge of the town of Visoko,
and looked at the excavation trenches that had been opened. We did
this solely in order to avoid the charge, already laid at our door, that
we had condemned the project without seeing it for ourselves. As
we expected, we saw areas of natural stone (a breccia), with fissures
and cracks; but no sign of anything that looked like archaeology,"
said Harding. However, he and other scoffers failed to explain the
accounts and photos of Osmanagić and others depicting tunnels
and chambers within this "natural geologic formation."

"Mainstream scientists, archaeologists, historians and anthropologists, are often the main obstacle for scientific progress," argued Osmanagić. And the controversy continued.

Yet there is another non-Egyptian pyramid, dated to more than ten thousand years ago by scientists in China, found in the western province of Qinghai. It has been compared to pyramids photographed on Mars. The Xianyang pyramid rises almost two hundred feet above the surrounding countryside and has a flat top thought by some to accommodate landing craft. "Local villagers claim their distant ancestors spoke of great sky ships that navigated the heavens and used the pyramid as a landing, refueling and resupply site. The hypothesis regarding extra-terrestrials is 'understandable and worth looking into' Yang Ji, one of the scientists and a researcher at the Chinese Academy of Social Sciences, explained to reporters," wrote retired major George Filer of the National UFO Center, which published photos of the pyramid and strange pipelike tubes found there.

According to a Chinese news agency report, the pyramid has three caves with openings shaped like triangles on its facade and is filled with red-hued pipes leading into the mountain and the nearby saltwater lake. Above the caves are dozens of pipes of various diameters running into the mountainside beneath the towering pyramid. Filer suggested that the pipes, more than simply carrying water, may have been used to channel and transport energy from the earth.

The Toltec Mounds near Scott, Arkansas, are similar to the mysterious Indian mounds in Ohio and have been compared to the Egyptian pyramids by the state's Department of Parks and Tourism. One of the largest and most complex sites in the Lower Mississippi Valley, the numerous Toltec Mounds have been a National Historic Landmark since 1978. They are thought to have been built by the Plum Bayou culture as early as AD 700. According to state literature, "The mound locations were apparently planned using principles based on alignment with important solar positions. . . .

This alignment can still be witnessed at the site on the spring and fall equinoxes."

Another large North American pyramid is located near St. Louis. Called the City of Cahokia, the pyramid and surrounding mounds are described as one of the greatest cities of the world, for in AD 1250 it was home to more people than London at that time. Built by Native Americans along the Mississippi, its creators were craftsmen who erected palisaded villages, a wide variety of structures, and a social hierarchy led by the Great Sun.

PART II

THE ANCIENTS

"De t'ings dat yo' li'ble / To read in de Bible, / It ain't necessarily so."
—"It Ain't Necessarily So," *Porgy and Bess,*
lyrics by Ira Gershwin

FROM THE GEOLOGICAL AND ARCHAEOLOGICAL DATA, IT WOULD seem that Earth has been home to several civilizations—human or otherwise—long before recorded history.

In a book little known in America entitled *Gods of the New Millennium: Scientific Proof of Flesh & Blood Gods*, British author Alan F. Alford wrote, "A shadowy pre-history seems to exist as a legacy in the form of stone, maps and mythology, which our 20th century technology has only just allowed us to recognize."

Scholars have always faced at least two choices in dealing with ancient texts and legends—to either assume that the texts are allegorical fantasy or to take them literally. For too long, they wrote off the old stories as fables. But in the modern world, with recent advances in geology, archaeology, and even spaceflight, a whole new view of our past is taking shape, one that ties together the stories of our path to reveal an underlying truth about our heritage.

It was once thought that the Greek poet Homer's account of the Trojan War was sheer fiction until Troy's ruins were located by Charles Maclaren in 1822. Even then, it was not until the extensive excavations of Heinrich Schliemann in 1870 that the reality of Troy was accepted. Likewise, the ancient Mesopotamian city of Ur was thought to be largely myth until it was discovered and excavated by Leonard Woolley following World War I.

Much of the Bible simply recasts narratives from ancient Sumer, which, for example, include a nearly identical account of the Great Flood. Sumerian culture was the wellspring for much of ancient Middle Eastern mythology.

The very foundation of Egyptian culture may well have been passed down by immigrants from devastated lands of Sumer. One of these later migrants was the Biblical patriarch Abraham, a ranking Sumerian who came from the city of Ur to Egypt with the "Tables of Destiny." These objects were thought by many to be the original "tables of testimony" mentioned in Exodus 31:18. According to genealogical expert and author Laurence Gardner, the name Abraham actually was a title (like the name David) and could have referred to any number of persons. Ab-ram—or Av-ram—which means "exalted father" in Hebrew, can also be translated as "he who possesses Ram," an expression used in India, Tibet, Egypt, and in the Celtic world to denote a high degree of universal knowledge.

Abraham crossed the whole of the Near East and built an army, all the while guided by his god, who had provided weapons that allowed him to defeat much larger forces. Abraham arrived in Egypt carrying the wisdom of Sumer in cleverly worded codes found within the Torah and other old Hebraic texts such as the *Sefer Yezirah* (Book of Creation), the *Sefer ha-Zohar* (Book of Light), and the *Ha Qabala*.

Paracelsus, the Swiss-German Renaissance alchemist who reflected his family's knowledge of Greco-Roman history, gave an account of how Adam predicted the destruction of the world by water and how his successors engraved ancient knowledge on two tablets of stone, which were found by Noah following the Great Flood. "At length this universal knowledge was divided into several parts, and lessened in its vigor and power," wrote Paracelsus. "Abraham . . . a consummate astrologer and arithmetician, carried the Ark [containing the tablets] out of the land of Canaan into Egypt, whereupon the Egyptians rose to so great a height and dignity that this wisdom was derived from them by other nations."

Evidence of flooding around the world lends credence to tales of the Great Flood. The same time frame encompassing the flood is also cited as the time that fabled Atlantis sank into the waters.

WHERE WAS ATLANTIS?

Our planet looked much different 250 million years ago. Instead of a world of seven distinct continents, Earth was two things—a mass of ocean and a mass of land. This giant landmass was a supercontinent called Pangaea. But some researchers believe Pangaea was not the first, and that other supercontinents had existed before Pangaea but simply broke apart and then recombined.

There are also many tales of fabulous cities, nations, and cultures lost to cataclysm. Mu, Lemuria, Agartha, Thule, Shambhala, Shangri-La, and Cibola are just a few of the names tossed out referring to ancient lost civilizations.

But the most famous of these is Atlantis, a name revered by students of the metaphysical and reviled by those predisposed to conventional science. The two men most connected to the legend of Atlantis are the Greek philosopher Plato, a student of Socrates who lived four hundred years before Christ, and Ignatius Donnelly, a populist congressman and a student of catastrophism in general and Atlantis in particular.

The story of Atlantis has continued to fire the imagination for centuries. Sir Francis Bacon, a leading member of England's Invisible College, which claimed access to the "Underground Stream of Knowledge," referred to newly found America as the New Atlantis. In recent years, theorists have devised all sorts of hypotheses as to how Atlantis came to be and where it ended up, but the famous philosopher Plato was the first to introduce the concept of the lost city. He claimed to have obtained his knowledge passed down through his family from his ancestor Solon, who in turn had obtained it while living in Egypt. In the dialogue *Timaeus* in 360 BC, Plato wrote of a great war between ancient Greeks and Atlantis, "a mighty power" spanning the globe "which was aggressing wantonly against the whole of Europe and Asia. . . ."

This power had landed on the Atlantic coast, for in those days the Atlantic was navigable from an island situated to the west of the straits which you call Pillars of Hercules: the island was larger than Libya and Asia [Asia meaning the Middle East] put together, and from it could be reached other islands, and from the islands you might pass through to the opposite continent, which surrounded the true ocean; for this sea which is within the columns of Hercules is only a harbour, having a narrow entrance, but that other is a real sea, and the surrounding land may be most truly called a continent. Now, the island was called Atlantis and was the heart of a great and wonderful empire, which had rule over the whole island and several others, as well as over parts of the continent; and besides these, they subjected the parts of Libya as far as Egypt and of Europe as far as Tyrrhenia [an ancient kingdom centered in the Alps above Italy]. . . . But afterward there occurred violent earthquakes and floods, and in a single day and night of rain all your warlike men in a body sank into the earth, and the island of Atlantis in like manner disappeared beneath the sea. And that is the reason why the sea in those parts is impassable and impenetrable, because there is such a quantity of shallow mud in the way; and this was caused by the subsidence of the island.

Notice that Plato referred to a continent opposite Africa and Europe. This is clear evidence that the American continents were known as far back as Plato's time, four centuries before the birth of Jesus and way before conventional history has stated that they were discovered by Leif Eriksson and Christopher Columbus.

How did Atlantis come to be? Plato, writing through the words of Critias, offered this explanation, "I have before remarked in speaking of the allotments of the gods, that they distributed the whole earth into portions differing in extent, and made for themselves temples and instituted sacrifices. And Poseidon [comparable to the Anunnaki Enki, known as the lord of waters], receiving for his lot the island of Atlantis, begat children by a mortal woman, and settled them in a part of the island, which I will describe."

While most people today still consider Atlantis a myth, others, including nineteenth-century American congressman Ignatius Donnelly, took Plato's words as "veritable history," claiming Atlantis was the place where humankind first rose from barbarism to civilization. Donnelly considered that the "gods and goddesses of the ancient Greeks, the Phoenicians, the Hindus, and the Scandinavians were simply the kings, queens, and heroes of Atlantis, and the acts attributed to them in mythology, a confused recollection of real historical events." He also said Egypt was the oldest colony of Atlantis and its civilization, which along with that of the Mayans of Central America represented a primitive reproduction of the Atlantean culture. Both in Atlantis and in Central and South America, gold was extensively mined and treasured, not for any intrinsic value, but for its association with elder "gods."

But many even today dismiss Atlantis as mere myth and legend sparked by Plato's writings. Apparently, they failed to notice that many authors of classical literature, such as Proclus, Diodorus, Plutarch, Posidonius, Strabo, and Pliny, all made references to Atlantis.

In recent years, a variety of other theories as to the location of Atlantis have been advanced. Based on Plato's description, and assuming the "Pillars of Heracles" refers to the Strait of Gibraltar, most researchers believe Atlantis was located in the middle of the Atlantic Ocean between Africa and the Americas. In the 1920s, the "sleeping prophet," Edgar Cayce, saw Atlantis as a continent-size region extending from the Azores to the Bahamas, with ships and aircraft powered by a mysterious form of energy crystal. Cayce predicted that portions of Atlantis would be found in modern times.

In 2010, geologists working with seismic data collected by oil companies discovered buried deep beneath the sediment of the

North Atlantic Ocean west of the Orkney and Shetland islands an ancient landscape with furrows cut by rivers and mountain peaks. Researchers traced eight major rivers and took core samples from the rock beneath the ocean floor, which revealed pollen and coal, evidence of land-dwelling life.

"It looks for all the world like a map of a bit of a country on-shore," said Nicky White, the senior researcher. The submerged landscape, described as "reminiscent of the mythical lost Atlantis," covers about 3,861 square miles, could have held a population of tens of thousands, and may be part of a larger region that merged with present-day Scotland and may have extended toward Norway in a world before recorded history.

THE BIMINI ROAD

It was in 1969, within prophet Cayce's predicted time frame, that researchers Robert Ferro and Michael Grumley set out from Rome to the Caribbean and claimed to have discovered underwater formations off the Bimini Islands in the Bahamas that are now known as the Bimini Road. In 1970, they published a book entitled *Atlantis: The Autobiography of a Search* concerning their adventure aboard their boat, the *Tana*.

Initial investigations indicated that the huge stone blocks and pavement stones were man-made, but as the name Atlantis began to be batted about in the media and corporate America became involved, the tone changed to disbelief.

R. Cedric Leonard, author of *Quest for Atlantis*, along with J. Manson Valentine of the Science Museum of Miami, in 1970 studied a structure near the Bahamas island of Andros called the Andros Temple. This structure measured approximately sixty feet wide and a hundred feet in length with crumbling stone walls roughly three feet thick. "This is clearly an edifice of importance built by a mathematically sophisticated civilization," he wrote. Leonard soon learned that the North American Rockwell Corporation, which had substantial land holdings on Bimini, had been granted exclusive excavation rights on all the underwater ruins in the area of Bimini Island. "Soon after, they hired a geologist with previous experience in the area. . . ." According to Leonard, [journalist Robert Marx reported] "that the investigation was 'brief,' and that the geologist didn't even go into the water for the 'scientific' inspection. . . . The hired geologist announced shortly after that the walls were not man-made and that the columns were nothing more than 'ballast' from a shipwreck."

The National Geographic Society eventually entered the picture, sponsoring an investigation by University of Miami geologist John Gifford, who carbon-dated the age of the giant stones as fifteen thousand years old. Marine engineer Dimitri Rebikoff, as far back as 1969, had stated that the Bimini Road is identical to numerous ancient man-made harbors discovered throughout the Mediterranean. Rebikoff, who spent much time and energy diving at the site, firmly disagreed with the skeptics who claimed that the site was all natural formations because there were no leveling stones underneath the large stone blocks at Bimini.

Could these Caribbean ruins be the site of Atlantis? It's hard to tell, mainly because so many professional archaeologists and geologists have backed away from the project. "Once speculation concerning Atlantis enters the picture, professionals begin to back away (and the way they were treated by their own colleagues, who could blame them)," Leonard stated. Those who involved themselves with projects related to the site were ostracized, and due to the reluctance of qualified scientists within this academic environment, "the scientific community is overlooking significant and sound evidence."

THE MINOAN EMPIRE AND SANTORINI

More recent theories have placed Atlantis at various Mediterranean locations, including Crete, Cyprus, and the island of Santorini (ancient Thera). In his 2011 book, *The Lost Empire of Atlantis*, author Gavin Menzies presented a cogent argument for the legend of Atlantis being simply a vague and garbled recollection of the Minoan Empire, a Bronze Age seafaring civilization centered on the island of Crete and named for its line of kings, collectively named Minos. According to Menzies's studies, Minoan ships ranged from the Americas to India. Their empire ended about 1500 BC with the gigantic eruption of the volcano on the island of Santorini, which sent millions of tons of volcanic ash into the atmosphere, produced intense atmospheric shock waves, and generated disastrous tsunamis.

Menzies wrote of ingots of nearly pure copper found in a sunken Minoan ship near Thera. Because copper of this quality is found only near Lake Superior in North America, the Minoans clearly had amazing range with their fleet of ships. Menzies also noted that the tobacco beetle, *Lasioderma serricorne*, was found in volcanic ash in the Minoan town of Akrotiri. This beetle is only indigenous to the Americas.

Because Menzies has equated the Minoan civilization with the Atlantean Empire, he believes that the great volcanic eruption on Santorini helped create the legend of Atlantis. Much like the myth of Atlantis's destruction taken from Plato, the resulting tidal waves, deadly gaseous clouds, famine due to destroyed crops, and opportunistic pirate clans finished off the great Minoan Empire, leaving remarkably little behind.

Yet there are others who disagree with Menzies's position. R. Cedric Leonard said that Menzies and others who believe Minoan Empire and Atlantis were one and the same have mistakenly traced Atlantis back to the Bronze Age instead of the Ice Age as described by Plato, who placed the time of Atlantis at about 9600 BC. "By thus 'miniaturizing' it (both size-wise and time-wise), it has been made more palatable for modern scientists and scholars to accept," said Leonard. "Plato describes Atlantis as having 'subjected the parts of Libya within the columns of Heracles as far as Egypt, and of Europe as far as Tyrrhenia.' The Minoan kings never conquered neither Europe nor North Africa. But archeological evidence is abundant indicating that a cohesive 'megalithic culture' occupied those very same areas of Europe and North Africa in Mesolithic times (5,000–6,000 years before the Minoan empire began)." Moreover, the area of Atlantis as described by Plato was far larger than that ascribed to the Minoan culture.

THE SOUTH CHINA SEA

Physicist James M. McCanney, who has studied exotic energy sources reaching back to antiquity, placed Atlantis at the opposite end of the Earth. He came to believe that Atlantis was located in the South China Sea prior to a shifting of the poles: "The South China Sea, before the rotation of the pole shift, was about five degrees south of the Equator. If you take a globe and you put your finger where the old North Pole used to be—north of the state of Michigan—and you put your other finger on the globe in the South Indian Ocean—diametrically opposed—and you rotate this Earth, you'll find that the South China Sea, where Atlantis was, ends-up just a few degrees south of the old Equator." McCanney was heavily influenced by the Brazilian professor Arysio Nunes dos Santos, author of *Atlantis: The Lost Continent Finally Found*. Explaining their theories, McCanney stated, "In ancient times, there was no Pacific Ocean by name, and the waterways were quite a bit different than they are now because of the tilt of the Earth. It was before a pole shift. What we call the Laurentian Ice Shield was actually the old North Pole. At the time, Siberia had a tropical climate with large herds of Mastodons and vast tropical plains and forests. . . . Basically, the mantle, the layer beneath the Earth's crust, shifted by about 40 degrees." He claimed that Plato's reference to a "real sea" was to the Ocean of the Atlanteans, or the Atlantic Ocean, which, in precataclysmic times, stretched unimpeded by northern ice from the South China Sea eastward across the Pacific to the present Atlantic. And the Pillars of Hercules did not refer to the Strait of Gibraltar but to the island of Krakatoa and its sister volcano that sits now in the Strait of Sunda, between Sumatra and Java, the entrance into the channel leading to the main continent of Atlantis. "The ancient Greeks didn't know that there was all of this—the North American continent and what we now call the Pacific, which was, in ancient days, simply one vast ocean called the Atlantic Ocean," explained McCanney.

OUT OF THIS WORLD

But McCanney went much further than simply naming a location for Atlantis. He added spaceflight to the puzzle by describing Atlantis as

> . . . a very advanced culture that we hear about in legends that had directed energy beams, big mirrors, big lasers, had the ability to fly, and I believe, space flight. I believe that they were landing on Mars. They had regular movement between Earth and Mars, when Mars was a water planet. When Mars came very close in its orbit to Earth, it was a very simple shuttle trip to go to Mars, and you did not have to take any provisions with you because Mars was a water planet, just like Earth. So, basically, there were civilizations on Mars, on Earth, and once every 5 years or so, when

*the planets aligned, you could make a trip back and forth,
which was quite commonplace at that time. . . . They knew
about atmospheric electricity. They were able to tap into it.
They had unlimited electrical power. They had been around
for thousands of years, as opposed to, say, our civilization of
modern, Western man in the United States, of the last 100
years. In a 10,000-year period they would have been quite
advanced, and learned how to live with the environment
without destroying themselves and the environment.*

Austrian-born researcher and writer Rich Anders had an even
stranger take on the story of Atlantis. Noting that Solon stated that
Atlantis "disappeared" rather than sank into the sea, Anders postulated that Atlantis vanished into a parallel world, another dimension, thus explaining the lack of evidence for its existence.

"Greek paintings show the sun in different positions. For
thousands of years this planet has been revolving around an axis.
Clearly, this is an indication that in the world before the planet did
not revolve around an axis," explained Anders. "Furthermore, the
predecessors of the Greek, the Hellenic people, knew of a place in
the Atlantic called Aea. According to legend, its inhabitants were
technologically very advanced and they did not fear death. Either
they were immortals or they knew enough about death not to fear
it. Most importantly, though, it was told that over Aea the sun was
always in the midday position. This is yet another indication that as
long as the parallel world, the paradise, existed, this planet did not
revolve around an axis."

Much like Ignatius Donnelly, Anders believed the Atlanteans
were gods, except that they "did not make it into the present world.
. . . Atlantis and everything that belonged to it remained in the parallel world, the paradise, which disappeared about 3,500 years ago."

POLE SHIFT AND ANTARCTICA

The pole shift described by James McCanney may explain some of the world's mysterious history. The 1513 maps of Admiral Piri Reis depicted an ancient Earth because the map's coastlines had been handed down from the Phoenicians, who had obtained them from even older maps. Reportedly, Columbus carried these maps on his expeditions, and made notes indicating what is now Queen Maudland in Antarctica. Columbus had expected the shoreline to help guide him to India, but he had instead run into a continent buried in ice. Today, through satellite ice-penetrating imaging, the shoreline has been shown to be identical with the Piri Reis map. So now Antarctica has been added to the many locations thought to be the actual site of Atlantis. Could it be that this is where Atlantis was located? Some researchers today are suggesting that Atlantis exists under the ice of Antarctica as the result of a pole shift.

Though conventional science has brushed aside the idea that Earth's poles may have shifted long ago, the public has become increasingly interested in the concept of catastrophism, which is the idea that Earth has actually changed quickly and dramatically due to large-scale catastrophes, including pole shifts, earthquakes, floods, and meteor strikes from space, all of which could have wiped out civilizations like Atlantis. Much of this interest stems from the work of Charles Hapgood and Immanuel Velikovsky, who each observed different sets of evidence indicating the earth's quick changes. For instance, Velikovsky examined the electromagnetic effects of Earth's shifts and close encounters with space objects, specifically the planet Venus, while Hapgood has examined evidence from shifts in plate tectonics or Earth-crust displacement.

These men and their followers point to the fact that prehistoric animals have been found flash-frozen so quickly that their meat was still edible and undigested vegetation was still in their mouths. Tales of woolly mammoths abound, but one of the best documented of such accounts appeared in the 1990 book of Alaska zoology by Dale Guthrie entitled *Frozen Fauna of the Mammoth Steppe*. Guthrie described how his team of researchers discovered a thirty-six-thousand-year-old bison near Fairbanks, Alaska, in 1979. They proceeded to cook some of the meat in a pot of stock and vegetables. Guthrie said that "the meat was well aged but still a little tough, and it gave the stew a strong Pleistocene aroma."

Stories like Guthrie's support the idea that the Earth's freezing happened almost instantaneously, as well as the catastrophism argument that a once-great civilization disappeared virtually overnight.

Maurice Chatelain, who made a detailed mathematical study of ancient sites and legends, wrote, "Personally I am convinced that the story of Atlantis, as Solon heard it from Sonchis and as Plato has given it to us, is true from beginning to end and that someday the ruins of Atlantis will be found, just as one after another we found the once legendary Troy, Mycenae, Tiryns, and Knossos."

A WORLDWIDE CIVILIZATION

With Antarctica added to the list of places posited as the source of the Atlantis legend, the debate continued. It appears clear, however, that regardless of where it was located, the evidence indicates that a widespread and advanced civilization did indeed exist in prehistory. The evidence of Atlantis lies all about us, unrecognized for what it is because of narrow-minded thinking and conditioning.

In 1910, Oxford professor and Nobel laureate Frederick Soddy stated, "Some of the beliefs and legends bequeathed to us by antiquity are so universally and firmly established that we have become accustomed to consider them as being almost as ancient as humanity itself. Nevertheless we are tempted to inquire how far the fact that some of these beliefs and legends have so many features in common is due to chance, and whether the similarity between them may not point to the existence of an ancient, totally unknown and unsuspected civilization of which all other traces have disappeared."

Some have suggested that the search for this ancient civilization, whether it was called Atlantis, Mu, Lemuria, or anything else, can be compared to the Hindu fable of the blind men and the elephant. The basic story is that a group of blind men went to a zoo to experience an elephant. When asked to describe the elephant, each had a different version. The blind man who felt the elephant's head said it was like a large pot. The man who touched the elephant's ear said it was like a fan. One who touched the tusk said it was like a plowshare; the one touching its trunk described it as a hose, while the one touching the tail said it was like a rope. One who pushed against the elephant's side said it was like a wall, while the one who put his arms around the elephant's leg said it was like a pillar.

The point is that like the blind men and the elephant, none of the Atlantis researchers are right—but then again, none are wrong. They all have a piece of the truth, which is that at one time, long before our recorded history, there existed on Earth a global, highly technological civilization that fell into ruin due to natural catastrophes, war, or both.

Many, including Professor Hapgood, have reached this same conclusion. He wrote, "The evidence presented by ancient maps appears to suggest the existence in remote times, before the rise of any known cultures, of a true civilization, of an advanced kind, which either was localized in one area but had worldwide commerce, or was, in a real sense, a worldwide culture. This culture, at least in some respects, was more advanced than the civilizations of Greece and Rome."

Early in the twentieth century, Charles Fort extended this hypothesis to include speculation that this vanished culture was the product of extraterrestrials. Maurice Chatelain, who noted how the scientific knowledge of astronomy by ancient peoples, such as the Sumerians, was "far superior" to that of astronomers only three hundred years ago, went so far as to state that all terrestrial civilizations evolved from the same source and this was "some extraterrestrial source in human affairs many thousands of years ago." He added, "This theory is already generally accepted by the public and also is considered a possibility by part of the scientific establishment, but it is difficult to get the official scientific establishment to accept this theory because it would turn upside down all traditional scientific beliefs. Nevertheless, this theory is true and accurate, because there is none other that would better explain the sudden appearance of intelligent man and his very advanced scientific knowledge so long ago."

SUMER: THE FIRST KNOWN CIVILIZATION

WHILE THE VERY EXISTENCE OF ATLANTIS IS STILL BEING DEBATED, we find the first of the great recorded civilizations was ancient Sumer. Also known as Shinar and Chaldea, this civilization arose between the Tigris and Euphrates rivers in the area known today as Iraq, which derived its name from the ancient Sumerian city of Uruk. From Sumer came an amazing and fully evolved civilization that handed down the basics for all ensuing Western cultures, from written language and law to mathematics, agriculture, and astronomy.

According to conventional history, Sumer grew out of a collection of hunter-gatherer clans who banded together to form the first human civilization within the Tigris-Euphrates Valley about 4000 BC. Yet by 3300 BC, archaeological studies have shown that Sumerians had drained marshes, dug canals, constructed dams and dikes, and built a large-scale irrigation system next to gleaming cities containing huge pyramidal structures called ziggurats. What prompted this sudden spurt of civilization?

About 2400 BC, Sumer was invaded from the west and north by Semitic tribes, and by about 2350 BC was captive to the warrior king Sargon the Great, who founded the Semite Akkadian Dynasty, whose empire stretched from the Persian Gulf to the Mediterranean. After years of wars and population displacements, the lands of Sumer were united under Hammurabi of Babylon, who's famous code of laws may have been instituted to discipline the mass migrations of people taking place at that time due to wars and geophysical catastrophes. It is now clear that the Code of Hammurabi was drawn from laws set down by the Sumerians centuries earlier, particularly the earliest law code yet discovered, issued by the Sumerian king Ur-Nammu.

Virtually nothing was known about the Sumerians until about 150 years ago, when archaeologists, spurred by the seventeenth-century writings of Italian traveler Pietro della Valle, began to dig into the strange mounds that dotted the countryside in southern Iraq. In 1843, the Frenchman Paul-Émile Botta discovered Sargon II's palace near modern-day Khorsabad, and soon after, archaeologists found buried cities, broken palaces, artifacts, and thousands of clay tablets detailing every facet of Sumerian life. By the late 1800s, Sumerian was considered an original language and was being translated. Despite today's knowledge, the general public still has been taught little about this first great human civilization, which suddenly materialized in Mesopotamia.

Before it strangely vanished, it had greatly influenced life as far east as the Indus River and as far west as Palestine and Egypt. In fact, it would appear that civilizations such as those of the Akkadians, Phoenicians, Minoans, Assyrians, Babylonians, and even the Egyptians were merely devolved versions of ancient Sumer. Yet the public has long believed them to be separate entities, an assumption which has hindered a truthful understanding of human history.

CUNEIFORM TABLETS

Despite our superficial knowledge of the Sumerians, we have already been able to credit them with many world "firsts." Samuel Noah Kramer, author of *History Begins at Sumer* and *The Sumerians*, noted that these people developed the wheel, schools, medical science, the first written proverbs, history, the first bicameral congress, taxation, laws, social reforms, the first cosmogony and cosmology, and the first money (a weighed silver shekel), as well as the first writing system, cuneiform.

Sumerian cuneiform writing may reveal more to us about Sumerian culture than we know about the ancient Egyptians, Greeks, and Romans. The papyrus papers of other elder empires disintegrated over time or were destroyed by the fires of war, but cuneiform was etched onto wet clay tablets with a wedge-shaped stylus. These tablets were then dried, baked, and kept in large libraries. About five hundred thousand of these clay tablets have now been found, providing invaluable knowledge of ancient Sumer (which is not to be confused with the Biblical Samaria, the name of a mountain, city, and region north of Jerusalem).

The Sumerian tablets went undeciphered until 1802, when a German high school teacher named Georg Grotefend began systematically translating the trilingual Persian inscription of Darius the Great on the Behistun Rock, which included a version in Babylonian cuneiform. Today nearly eighty percent of cuneiform tablets have not yet been translated into English because the sheer quantity has overwhelmed the world's handful of translators.

The Sumerian alphabet was essentially shorthand for a much older original language made up of logograms (symbols representing concepts rather than words) similar to antique Chinese characters. Because this older language was not as detailed as English, many different translations may stem from a Sumerian sentence.

LONGEVITY AND NUMBERS

One ancient Sumerian document, known as the King List, described not their "gods" but the earliest Sumerian rulers and the lengths of their reigns. At first glance, the list seems preposterous, as it states, "After the kingship descended from heaven, the kingship was in Eridu. In Eridu, Alulim became king; he ruled for 28,800 years." Other kings served even longer, according to the list. For example, Alalngar reigned for 36,000 years, while En-men-lu-ana ruled for an amazing 43,200 years.

Such longevity is also recorded in the Bible, wherein Methuseleh, Noah, Seth, Enos, and others are reported to have lived more than nine hundred years. In China, rulers of the first dynasties each ruled more than seven hundred years, while the Hindu Vedas state that prior to 3000 BC, the life span was about a thousand years.

After the Great Flood, these numbers began to decrease until Gilgamesh ruled for a mere 126 years, followed by others whose reigns were in only the double-digit range. Either there was something very wrong with the ancient counting systems or there was something very unearthly about their rulers. Could extraterrestrial intervention in human evolution account for such longevity? Could the promise of a much longer life be used today to gain the allegiance of ranking politicians who otherwise would disdain bribes or other enticements?

Sumerians traveled frequently and widely and are thought to have brought their advanced shipbuilding technology and mapping abilities to the early Phoenicians, who settled along the eastern Mediterranean coast in what is now Lebanon and later traveled the world.

Sumerian knowledge of the heavens was both amazing and puzzling. "The whole concept of spherical astronomy, including the 360-degree circle, the zenith, the horizon, the celestial axis, the poles, the ecliptic, the equinoxes, etc., all arose suddenly in Sumer," noted Alan Alford. Sumerian knowledge of the movements of the sun and moon resulted in the world's first calendar, used for centuries afterward by the Semites, Egyptians, and Greeks.

Few people realize that we also owe our geometry and modern timekeeping systems to the Sumerians. "The origin of 60 minutes in an hour and 60 seconds in a minute is not arbitrary, but designed around a sexagesimal (based on the number 60) system," Alford reported. He added that the modern zodiac was a Sumerian creation based on their twelve "gods." They used it to chart a great precessional cycle that would take 25,920 years to fully complete, a period known as the Platonic year. "The uncomfortable question which the scientists have avoided is this: how could the Sumerians, whose civilization only lasted 2,000 years, possibly have observed and recorded a celestial cycle that took 25,920 years to complete? And why did their civilization begin in the middle of a zodiac period? Is this a clue that their astronomy was a legacy from the gods?" asked Alford.

His question could be enlarged to question how the early primitive humans of almost six thousand years ago suddenly transformed from small packs of hunter-gatherers into a full-blown—advanced even by today's standards—civilization?

MYTH OR HISTORY?

It is difficult to believe that primitive humans acquired so much knowledge on their own overnight. Through thousands of translated Sumerian tablets along with their inscribed cylinder seals, perhaps we should allow the Sumerians themselves to explain.

The answer, echoing claims from many other ancient peoples, is that all their knowledge came from their "gods." Scholars in the past believed the Sumerians were talking about ethereal and imagi-

nary beings in the sky. Today a growing number of researchers suspect they might well have been referring to physical beings who
would descend to earth, much like the gods of ancient Greece, such
as Zeus and Athena.

"All the ancient peoples believed in gods who had descended to
Earth from the heavens and who could at will soar heavenwards,"
explained Zecharia Sitchin in the prologue to the first book of a
series detailing his translations and interpretations of Sumerian accounts of their origin and history. "But these tales were never given
credibility, having been branded by scholars from the very beginning as myths."

Yet Sitchin and many others have questioned why ancient scribes
would have taken the time and energy to painstakingly write down
fables of absolute dreamlike fantasy. Wouldn't it be more reasonable
to conclude that they wrote such tales as fables to recount dimly
remembered history?

Understanding the Sumerian version of the human origin requires only a slight shift in mind-set. Sitchin and others simply believe that the ancient Sumerians may have just been putting down
on their clay tablets history as they understood it rather than fanciful myths.

The Sumerian descriptions of many ancient cities were believed
to be mere fables until their ruins were discovered and excavated. In
2003, scientists claimed to have found the tomb of Gilgamesh, previously thought by most to have been merely a mythological character. Why not also consider their written history as reality?

Regarding the ancient texts, author Paul Von Ward stated, "To
accept them only as fantasy or metaphor, we must first be able to
demonstrate that they do not refer to actual events. Until we have
proven their claims are false, we have no defensible justification for
not interpreting them as plausible scenarios in our still-evolving
knowledge." Ward added that while it is easy to find data on nonhuman beings in the historical record, "you will find—as I did—

that the toughest challenge lies in overcoming our institutionally implanted assumptions."

We also must remember that before the twentieth century and the advent of heavier-than-air flight, scholars would not have thought of spaceflight as possible. Thus, Sitchin reasoned, "Now that astronauts have landed on the Moon, and unmanned spacecraft explore other planets, it is no longer impossible to believe that a civilization on another planet more advanced than ours was capable of landing its astronauts on the planet Earth sometime in the past." Nor is it impossible now to consider the biological manipulation of a species in light of the modern sciences of cloning and in vitro fertilization.

The belief in ancient gods from the sky was not the sole province of Middle Eastern cults. In North America, the Blackfoot tribe awaited the promised return of Napi, said to be the son of the sun and the moon. In legend, Napi, also known as the Old Man, created humans from clay and taught them the skills to survive. Other Algonquians watched for Glooscap, the legendary figure who created humans and brought them knowledge. In Central America, when the Spanish conquistadors arrived, the Aztecs welcomed them as the return of their ancient god, Quetzalcoatl.

After researching numerous American legends of creation, Von Ward noted,

> Quetzalcoatl . . . reportedly sprinkled his blood with the bones of earlier creatures to create humans. In the American West, the Selish tribes' creator . . . Amotken used hair from his head to create the first five women. The Quinaults of the Pacific Northwest believe their "changer god Kwatee" created humans from his own sweat. All these methods could imply a contribution of the gods' DNA. And these gods, as did the Anunnaki, came from the sky.

In fact, mythologies from around the world appear to tell the same essential story—that in ancient times individuals with "god-like" powers arrived to restore civilization following a period of catastrophes.

Quetzalcoatl, the great teacher of the Mayans, was known as Viracocha to the Incas and as the sun god Ra to the Egyptians. Sargon, the first great leader of the Akkadian dynasty, which succeeded the Sumerians, attributed his knowledge to the god Anu, while the Babylonian king Hammurabi was said to have gained power through Marduk, again a reference to the accounts of the Anunnaki.

In India, it is believed that man is descended from gods who flew in fiery craft called *vimanas*. The Teutons point to ancestors in flying craft called *Wanen*. The ancient Mayans thought their predecessors came from the Pleiades, while the Incas said simply that they were the "sons of the sun." Chinese texts tell of long-lived rulers from the heavens who sailed through the skies in "fire-breathing dragons." The Dogon tribe in Mali, West Africa, tells of space travelers called Nommos, who came to Earth thousands of years ago from the Sirius star system and gave them detailed information about their world and our solar system. The Dogon described Sirius as having dual or binary suns, a fact not known until recent years. Debunkers, including the late Carl Sagan, tried to argue that recent Western visitors had given them such information, perhaps inadvertently. However, this theory failed to explain a four-hundred-year-old Dogon artifact that apparently correctly depicts the Sirius configuration or ceremonies conducted by the Dogons since the thirteenth century celebrating the cycle of Sirius A and B.

Most of these accounts lack any physical evidence to support them. However, at least one account of ancient visitors did provide such evidence, though the case ended tragically. In 1938, archaeologist Chi Pu Tei discovered regularly aligned rows of graves in the

Baian Kara Ula Mountains near the Sino-Tibetan border. Beneath cave drawings of beings wearing helmets along with depictions of the stars, sun, and moon, small frail skeletons with unusually large skulls were found. Chi Pu Tei theorized that the skeletons belonged to an extinct species of mountain ape and that the drawings were left in the caves later by human tribes. Since the graves were in systematic rows, his theory was laughed at and forgotten until 1962, when stone plates found among the graves were translated by Professor Tsum Um Nui of the Academy of Prehistoric Research in Beijing.

The translation told an eerie story of a group of beings who claimed to have come from star system Sirius and crash-landed on Earth about twelve thousand years ago. Unable to repair their craft, this group attempted to make friends with the mountain tribes but were hunted down and killed due to their nonhuman features. Locals buried them with circular holed stones strikingly identical to some UFO descriptions. Since this account was not compatible with the Western worldview, it, too, was dismissed, but curiously, the mountainous crash site remains off limits to foreigners.

THE ANUNNAKI: IMPROVING THE BREED?

IN SEVERAL ACCOUNTS ETCHED PERMANENTLY INTO THEIR CLAY tablets, the ancient Sumerian scribes gave more detail as to the source of their knowledge. They wrote that 432,000 years before the Great Flood, the Anunnaki arrived and taught them the basics of civilization.

According to the interpretations of Zecharia Sitchin and many others, the term *Anunnaki* means "those who came from the heavens to the Earth." In Sitchin's narrative, these were astronauts from the planet Nibiru who traveled through the Great Bracelet (the asteroid belt) and initially landed in the Persian Gulf. There they began to colonize and search for gold. But strikes broke out over the hard work, and it was decided to engineer a slave race by manipulating the DNA of primitives on Earth. Thereafter, kings and dynasties were established among the new hybrids, which led to conflicts, warfare, and widespread devastation.

Michael Tellinger noted that Zulu creation legends agree with Sitchin's interpretation of the Sumerian tablets.

> *Most of African mythology speaks about the same things, the sky gods the abelungu who came down from the sky. They created the people, to mine gold. The Zulu people, people from the sky. The abelungu have the same aspects as ascribed to the Anunnaki in the Sumerian tablets. Credo Mutwa [an African shaman] tells us Abantu in Zulu means the children of Antu. Antu is the Sumerian Goddess of the Abzu—where the gold came from. Lord Enki is also known as Enkei as the creator-god, the Sumerian medicine man. He cloned a species. His symbol is the medical symbol, caduceus. This is one of the oldest symbols on the earth encoded with so much knowledge and information we can spend a lecture on it alone.*

THE NEFILIM CHAIN OF COMMAND

According to Sitchin's interpretations of Sumerian texts, about 450,000 years ago, during Earth's Pleistocene ice age, the highly developed inhabitants of Nibiru—the Anunnaki—journeyed to Earth as the two planets came into proximity. Their initial landings were made in the Persian Gulf, just as our own astronauts at first splashed down in the ocean.

Logically, these ancient astronauts would have sought a base camp that could provide moderate weather and a good source of water and fuel. Only one location met all these criteria—the Fertile Crescent, which included the Tigris and Euphrates river valleys in Mesopotamia.

With the supreme Nibirian ruler, Anu—or An or El, depending on the source—supervising their effort from the home planet, the Anunnaki began a systematic colonization of Earth under the leadership of Anu's two sons, Enlil and Enki. All of the Anunnaki leaders were later to assume the role of "gods," or Nefilim, to their human subjects. *Nefilim* was translated by almost all ancient writers as those who had "fallen." In religious terms, they were thought to be angels who fell from the grace of God. But "fallen" can also be seen as those who came down, and in more recent times, the term has taken on the meaning of giants who were a hybrid of two species.

In the tablets' story, Enlil was the mission commander, while Enki served as executive and science officer. There was immediate and long-standing antagonism between the two half-brothers, due to Nibirian protocol. As in later Earth dynasties, the firstborn, Enki, was relegated to secondary status because his mother was not the official wife of Anu. This removed him from the royal line of succession. Yet it was Enki who led the first expedition to Earth.

Enki was both scientist and engineer. Under his leadership, the marshes on the northern shore of the Persian Gulf were drained, dikes were constructed, and irrigation systems were dug, as well as canals connecting the Tigris with the Euphrates. Reinforcements later arrived under the leadership of Enki's firstborn son, Marduk.

There is no doubt that the Anunnaki were real and important. The prologue to the *Lawcode of Hammurabi* refers to these same Anunnaki overlords, stating,

> *When exalted Anu, king of the divinities [the Anunnaki],*
> *and Enlil, lord of heaven and earth, the determiner of the*

destinies of the land, determined for Marduk, the first-born
of Enki, the dominion over the whole of humankind, made
him the greatest among the deities, called Babylon by its ex-
alted name, made it supreme in the world, and established
for him in its midst an eternal kingship, whose foundations
are as firm as heaven and earth, then it was that Anu and
Enlil named me, Hammurabi, the devout and god-fearing
prince, to promote the welfare of the people, to cause justice
to prevail in the land, to destroy the wicked and the evil,
that the strong might not oppress the weak, to rise like the
sun over the black-headed people, and to light up the land.

SITCHIN'S CRITICS

The translations by Sitchin and others have gathered many detrac-
tors, especially over the depiction of the Anunnaki as extraterrestrials. Michael Heiser, who earned degrees in the Hebrew Bible and
ancient Semitic languages and was one of Sitchin's most vocifer-
ous critics, stated on his website, SitchinIsWrong.com, "that what
Sitchin has written about Nibiru, the Anunnaki, the book of Genesis, the Nephilim, and a host of other things has absolutely no basis
in the real data of the ancient world."

In an open letter to Sitchin, now addressed to "Ancient Astronaut Enthusiast" following Sitchin's death in 2010, Heiser argued
that the name Anunnaki appears nowhere in the Electronic Text
Corpus of Sumerian Literature published on the Internet by the
University of Oxford.

While technically this may be true, the term *Anuna gods* appears numerous times in the literature and obviously could be col-
lectivized into the plural term *Anunnaki*. One example of this term
from the Oxford Sumerian texts recounts the boasts of Enki, who

proclaimed, "With An the king, on An's dais, I oversee justice. With Enlil, looking out over the lands, I decree good destinies. He has placed in my hands the decreeing of fates in the place where the sun rises. I am cherished by Nintur. I am named with a good name by Ninhursaga. I am the leader of the Anuna gods. I was born as the firstborn son of holy An."

Naturally, no reputable scientist who desires to protect conventional textbooks and his funding sources would publicly admit to subscribing to Sitchin's theories, yet many thousands have followed Sitchin's work, some researchers augmenting the details of his narrative. Author, psychologist, and minister Paul Von Ward spoke for many when he wrote, "Although I do not agree with his cosmology . . . his elucidation of historical details and connection of them to other fields of knowledge stand up under comparative review with the work of other scholars. His summary of information relating to the 'olden gods' known in Sumeria as the Anunnaki presents a cohesive and defensible mixture of textual material and judicious interpretation."

C. L. Turnage, an author who has studied more than three hundred translations of ancient Mesopotamian and Vedic writings, including the extrabiblical *Book of Enoch*, wrote, "After studying [Sitchin's] theory, I began my own contemplation of the pre-biblical Babylonian *Epic of Creation* or *Enuma Elish*. It was from a study of this narrative that Sitchin became aware of the planet Nibiru and its establishment within our own solar system. This tale was originally written on seven clay tablets, each corresponding to a 'day' of creation. . . . The creation of man was recorded on the sixth tablet, while the seventh was reserved for the exaltation of the Babylonian national deity Marduk, the 'creator god.' After my own study of these chronicles, I concurred with Sitchin's findings. It does appear that the first three chapters of Genesis, particularly the seven days of creation, were actually derived from the older creation epic, and other chronicles—then revamped to meet Hebrew theology. Why would the Hebrews borrow the creation story from older Mesopotamian texts? Was it because they worshipped one of the Mesopotamian deities themselves?"

AN EARLY GOLD RUSH

Over thousands of years Earth time, according to the Sumerian narrative, the Anunnaki continued to put a thriving colony in place, and their attention turned to their primary objective—gold.

Some researchers have composed elaborate metaphysical explanations for Anunnaki activities on Earth, many having to do with energy fields and spiritual planes disrupted by the passing of Nibiru and the creation of Earth. One theory was that the more highly evolved Anunnaki were attempting to rescue "lost souls" left behind after the planetary collision.

But more documented and acceptable is the idea of Sitchin and others that these colonists were after Earth's mineral wealth— particularly gold—for use on their home planet. "The Anunnaki sought gold to save their atmosphere, which had apparently sprung leaks similar to those we have created in ours by damaging the Earth's ozone layer with hydrofluorocarbons," explained author Lloyd Pye. "The Anunnaki solution was to disperse extremely tiny flakes of gold into their upper atmosphere to patch holes. . . . Ironically, modern scientists contend that if we are ever forced to repair our own damaged ozone layer, tiny particulates of gold shot into the upper atmosphere would be the best way to go about it."

This theory is not so far-fetched when one considers that in 1997 a research team led by the physicist Edward Teller, known as the father of the hydrogen bomb, proposed various methods for controlling solar radiation, including the seeding of heavy metals, such as gold particles, into the upper atmosphere. Also, it is known that gold is an excellent conductor of electromagnetic energy, and it never rusts. In fact, in April 2009, President Obama's science adviser, John P. Holdren, publicly suggested that heavy-metal "pollutants" be sprayed into the upper atmosphere to create a heat shield to retard perceived "global warming."

But when the Anunnaki attempted to retrieve gold from the Persian Gulf by an extraction process, it proved inefficient and time-consuming. Anu, along with his heir Enlil, visited the colony and assigned Enki to find more gold. Enlil was placed in overall command of the Earth colony while Enki led a foray to Africa and eventually to South America, where he set up gold-mining operations. Proof of such early gold mining has come from scientific studies conducted for the Anglo-American Corporation, a leading South African mining company, in the 1970s. According to South African author Michael Tellinger, company scientists discovered evidence of thousands of ancient mining operations, some dated as far back as 100,000 BC. Similar ancient mine excavations have been found in Central and South America. They indicate that the Anunnaki mining efforts were worldwide and may go far in explaining the early diffusion of humans.

Further substantiation of such wide-ranging travel may be found by comparing the names of ancient Mesopotamian cities and localities as recorded by the second-century AD geographer Ptolemy to counterparts for gold-mining sites in Central America:

MESOPOTAMIAN NAME	CENTRAL AMERICAN NAME
Chol	Chol-ula
Colua	Colua-can
Zuivana	Zuivan
Cholima	Colima
Zalissa	Xalisco

The raw mined ore was then carried from the far-flung mines by cargo craft back to Mesopotamia for smelting and processing into hourglass-shaped ingots called *zag*, or "purified precious." Engravings of such ingots are numerous, and some of the actual ingots have been found in archaeological excavations.

In an effort to ease the increasing rivalry between the half-brothers Enlil and Enki, their father, Anu, placed Enlil in charge of the Mesopotamian colony E-din—perhaps the basis for the biblical Eden—while assigning Enki to Ab-zu, or Africa, the "land of the mines."

OUT OF AFRICA

A number of writers believe that the Anunnaki mined gold on Earth for more than a hundred thousand years, until the rank-and-file Anunnaki, who were doing the backbreaking work in the mines, mutinied about three hundred thousand years ago. On top of the unrelenting drudgery of the mining operations, difficulties for these extraterrestrial colonists had increased due to climate changes.

Enlil, the commander in chief, wanted to punish the workers for their rebellion. He called an Assembly of the Great Anunnaki, which included his father, Anu, who was more sympathetic to the plight of the Anunnaki miners. He saw that the work of the mutineers was very hard and that their distress was considerable. One Sumerian text reported, "The load is excessive, it is killing us! Our work is too hard, the trouble too much! So every single one of us gods has agreed to complain to Ellil [Enlil]."

Enlil wondered aloud if there wasn't another way to obtain gold. At this point, Enki suggested that a primitive worker, called an Adamu, be created to take over the difficult work. Enki pointed out that a primitive humanoid—what we call *Homo erectus* or a closely related hominid—was quite prevalent in Abzu (Africa), where he maintained a laboratory.

Just as today we furiously debate animal experimentation, gene splicing, and cloning, the Anunnaki also debated the morality of tinkering with a species. Anunnaki leaders argued, "Creation in the hands of the Father of All Beginning alone is held!"

Enki counterargued that producing a hybrid—half Anunnaki and half primitive human—would not be an act of creation but merely improving the existing breed. Many people today believe that Sitchin and his followers are claiming that aliens created humans. Instead, the process as described in the Sumerian tablets was only a breeding program similar to what has been done with various animals by mankind to improve the stock.

And so Enki's plan to create a worker race in Africa was approved by the Anunnaki Assembly, and the Anunnaki created a race in their image. Sound like a familiar refrain? One of the most puzzling verses in the Bible, Genesis 1:26, assures readers that there is only one true God, but then quotes God in the plural, stating, "Let us make man in our image, after our likeness . . ." Could the plural gods here be the Anunnaki?

The Genesis verse may reveal two things about our history. The first is that the plural Elohim of the Old Testament, later interpreted as "God" by the monotheists who wrote Genesis, indeed may have referred to the Anunnaki Assembly. The second idea from this verse is that creating man "in our image" meant simply genetic manipulation of an existing species, not the creation of a new race. As Zecharia Sitchin explained, "As both Orientalists and Bible scholars now know . . . the editing and summarizing by the compilers of the Book of Genesis [was] of much earlier and considerably more detailed texts first written down in Sumer."

The Anunnaki Earth mission's medical officer was a female named Ninhursag, who had already been working with Enki in genetic experimentation. On at least one Sumerian cylinder seal, an illustration of Enki and Ninhursag depicted them surrounded by vials or vessels, a table, shelves, a plant, and a helper, looking very much like a laboratory. Enki and Ninhursag produced many mutated creatures, including animals, such as bulls and lions with human heads, winged animals and apes, and humanoids with the head and feet of goats. If true, it is obvious that these experiments may have been the source for the many legends of "mythological" creatures and superhumans, such as Atlas, Goliath, Polyphemus, and Typhon.

In addition to these fantastic creatures, the Sumerian tablets describe how Enki produced the first test-tube infant by combining DNA and producing a hybrid of human and alien origin in his laboratory. Could this be why recent studies of mitochondrial DNA indicate that all of Earth's humans can be traced back to one primitive female who lived in Africa?

Michael Tellinger and South African researcher Johan Heine have added considerable strength to the argument that modern humans are the offspring of the Anunnaki gods from space.

The pair has unearthed startling new evidence that human civilization is far older than believed by conventional history and that large human habitants were flourishing within huge communities in South Africa more than two hundred thousand years ago. In fact, they claim that they may have found the location of Enki's laboratory at the ruins called Adam's Calendar on the Transvaal Escarpment.

In *Temples of the African Gods*, Tellinger and Heine wrote, "The discoveries we have been making right here since 2003 are so astonishing that they will require a dramatic paradigm shift in our perception of human history. . . . A new understanding of the real history of humankind may just provide some of the answers we have been searching for and deliver a new sense of comfort for many who feel betrayed by our historians and especially by our religions."

Tellinger and Heine claim that even the Sumerian civilization may have been preceded by an African culture whose settlements covered most of South Africa and may have even known how to harness free energy from the Earth. An ancient petroglyph found in Africa, a circle containing a cross inside a sweeping boomerang shape, resembles the famous winged disc normally associated with Sumer, Babylonia, and Egypt. Another connection between Africa and Sumer may be found in the names of their gods, which bear a striking resemblance to the Sumerian overlords. "It is astonishing to discover that ancient Zulu culture and religion, including those of all other Bantu tribes, is directly linked to the Sumerians," noted Tellinger and Heine.

"Our proof comes in the form of large stone monolith statues, petroglyphs and symbols, discovered in Mpumalanga and other parts of South Africa, which were previously believed to be of Sumerian and Egyptian origins." Tellinger and Heine have also been careful to look at the Sumerian tablets to formulate their conclusions. "These tablets are the oldest written record of human history and the constant reference to southern Africa in these tablets leaves little doubt that there was a lot of activity here, long before Sumer or Egypt were established. It is now very clear that the first civilization merged many thousands of years ago in a land the Sumerians called the ABZU—the land of the FIRST [emphasis in the original] people in southern Africa—where the gold came from."

THE HYBRID

The Sumerian account of the creation of the first man—written as Lu-lu in the Sumerian or in Hebrew, Adama, literally translated as Man of Earth or simply Earthling—is quite clear in light of today's knowledge concerning cloning and in vitro fertilization. But up to twenty-five years ago or so, the whole concept would have been incomprehensible to even the most learned scholar.

It is written that Enki and Ninhursag took the reproductive cell or egg from a primitive African female hominid and fertilized it with the sperm of a young Anunnaki male. The fertilized ovum was then placed inside an Anunnaki woman—reportedly by one of Enki's own wives, Ninki—who carried the child to term.

Although a Cesarean section was required at birth, a healthy young male Adama hybrid was produced for the first time on Earth, bypassing natural evolution by millions of years. According to the ancient Sumerian reporters, "When Mankind was first created, they knew not the eating of bread, knew not the dressing with garments, ate plants with their mouth like sheep, drank water from the ditch. . . . "

Human antiquity lends much support to the legitimacy of the Sumerian accounts of humankind's beginnings. And consider that both the Dogon tribe in Africa and the aborigines of Australia—continents apart—both claim knowledge passed down for more than fifty thousand years of human creation by beings who came from the stars.

If this seems like a far stretch of the imagination, consider that the *Encyclopaedia Britannica* tells the same story, only it is under the heading of Mesopotamian mythology.

Until about 1996, when Dolly the sheep was cloned in Scotland, scholars reading the Sumerian texts regarding the hybridization and cloning of humans are excused for believing the stories were all fanciful myths. But today, cloning, gene splicing, and in vitro fertilization are commonplace procedures.

In July 2011, a modern parallel to the Sumerian story of humankind's creation became apparent when it was revealed that human-animal hybrids were secretly being created by scientists in Britain. According to reports, 155 embryos, containing both human and animal genetic material, had been created since the introduction of Britain's 2008 Human Fertilisation Embryology Act. This research, conducted in hopes of finding cures for disease, was carried out in labs at King's College in London, Newcastle University, and Warwick University.

Lord David Alton of Liverpool criticized the research, proclaiming, "I argued in Parliament against the creation of human-animal hybrids as a matter of principle. None of the scientists who appeared before us could give us any justification in terms of treatment." Although officials said the scientists were not concerned over the human-animal hybrid embryos, because legally they must be destroyed within fourteen days, the experiments were stopped, reportedly due to lack of funding.

Continuing the Anunnaki narrative, Enki and Ninhursag went on to produce a number of Adamas, both male and female, although at this time they were incapable of reproduction and lived very short lives compared to the Anunnaki. This was apparently done in a conscious effort to prevent any competition from the new human race. It is interesting to note that, according to Genesis 3:5, the very first order of the Elohim was that man—in the allegorical form of Adam and Eve—was to remain ignorant, lest "ye shall be as gods" (King James Version).

The "laboratory" which produced the first Adamas was called Shi-im-ti, or "the house where the wind of life is breathed in," by the Sumerians. Compare this phrase with Genesis 2:7, in which God, after forming man from "the dust of the ground" or *adamu*, meaning "earth," "breathed into his nostrils the breath of life."

"Adam was the first test-tube baby," proclaimed Sitchin after the birth of the first modern test-tube baby in 1978. He saw this modern birth as support for his Sumerian translations.

That the ancient Sumerians passed along symbols representing the long-forgotten science of cloning is suggested by the caduceus, the logo of physicians even today. This ancient symbol of life-giving medical treatment represented by entwined snakes along a winged staff bears a striking resemblance to the double spiral strings of DNA molecules. DNA, discovered only in 1946, is the compound within nucleated cells that stores that individual organism's genetic blueprint. It is the manipulation of DNA that can produce a duplicate (clone) or hybrid.

The first human workers were like mules and could not procreate. The Anunnaki had to constantly create new batches, a time-consuming procedure considering the span of time between in vitro fertilization and birth. So Enki and Ninhursag set about to create an Adama race that could reproduce itself.

Genesis 2:8–15 makes it clear that the Adamas were created elsewhere and then placed in the Garden of Eden, or that area of the original Anunnaki colony called E-din, described as the plain between the Tigris and Euphrates rivers. The Sumerian texts relate how an envious Enlil raided Enki's African lab and returned with captives to E-din, where they were put to work producing food and serving the Anunnaki. It has been theorized that in retaliation for Enlil's raid on his African lab, Enki traveled to Eden, where he created a human-reproduction lab for Enlil but secretly manipulated the genetic code to allow sexual reproduction.

Although the Sumerian texts describing the details of this process have been either lost or are as yet undiscovered, researchers have assumed that the procedure involved obtaining life-producing Adama DNA, possibly by extracting a rib while the subject was under anesthesia. This time the male Adama's DNA was combined with a female Adama rather than an Anunnaki, possibly with some accompanying DNA-sequence cutting and splicing, a procedure within the abilities of our technology today.

The result was a male Adama with the ability to reproduce through sex with an Adama female, or to "know" a woman, as the Bible euphemistically puts it. The man Adam had gained the "knowledge" of reproduction, a fact that many Elohim/Anunnaki, including Enlil, deplored. They complained that next the humans would want to live as long as they themselves. "The man has now become like one of us, knowing good and evil," reported Genesis 3:22 (New International Version). "He must not be allowed to reach out his hand and take also from the tree of life and eat, and live forever." Therefore, DNA manipulation drastically reduced the human life span along with the ability to make full use of human brain capacity.

Such manipulation may explain the telomeres, caps on the ends of the human chromosomes. These caps, something like the protective caps on shoelaces, after a certain length of time prevent cells from reproducing, leading to oxidation, aging, and eventually death. No one knows for certain how or why these caps were placed in the DNA, but they prevent extended life. Furthermore, in 2011, researchers at Johns Hopkins University announced that telomere shortening is linked to diabetes, cancer, lung disease, and other age-related illnesses.

With the ability to reproduce, the human population exploded, both in the far-flung Anunnaki mining operations and in Mesopotamia. Many Adamas were taken to work in the other cities growing up along the Tigris and Euphrates rivers. Some were returned to mining chores, and others may have escaped into the wild or may have been sent away for population control. In any case, the Adama were sent out of E-din.

The result of this human population growth and increasingly close human contact with the Anunnaki was perhaps predictable. Genesis 6:1–4 related, "When men began to increase in number on the earth and daughters were born to them, the sons of God [the Nefilim/Anunnaki] saw that the daughters of men were beautiful, and they married any of them they chose. . . . The Nefilim were on the earth in those days—and also afterward—when the sons of God went to the daughters of men and had children by them" (New International Version). Apparently, the term *Nefilim* was applied to both pure Anunnaki and their later hybrid offspring.

Over the centuries, the Adama race, in addition to such interbreeding, was the object of continued experimentation by the Anunnaki, which eventually resulted in changing Neanderthal to Cro-Magnon, or modern man. But some specific deficiencies remained, including a progressive decline in the human life span. Descendants of the early Adamas lived for thousands of Earth years, thanks to their Anunnaki genes. The extreme life spans of the more pure-blooded Anunnaki rulers made them appear as immortal. *The Epic of Gilgamesh* states, "Only the gods live forever under the sun. / As for mankind, numbered are their days: / Whatever they achieve is but the wind!"

In 2012, a group of genetic scientists, attempting to pinpoint telltale variants in the genetic code, found surprising evidence that supported the idea of ancient genetic manipulation of human DNA. They turned up 13.4 million genetic variants in three African groups—3 million of which had never before been seen in humans. They sequenced the genome of five individuals from three different African hunter-gatherer populations including pygmies from Cameroon and Khoesan-speaking Hadza and Sandawe from Tanzania. As expected, the scientists found that ninety percent of the gene flow from one species into the gene pool of another, by the repeated backcrossing of a hybrid with one of its parent species, traced back to the Neanderthal. But surprisingly, the other ten percent came from what they could only describe as an unknown "foreign group."

The three selected African groups represent some of the most ancient lineages in the world and the findings support the idea that modern humans evolved out of Africa. Such findings also lend support to the Sumerian account of human hybrids being bred by the spacefaring Anunnaki.

Joshua Akey, one of the science team, told Linda Moulton Howe, reporter and editor of the award-winning science and environment news website, www.Earthfiles.com, "[W]e can detect in the genomes and DNA of present-day Africans these bits of DNA that seem like they came from another (unknown) group. . . . We don't know anything really about this group. . . . If we collect more genome sequences from African individuals, we think we will be able to learn more about this unknown group. . . . The group that we think contributed this foreign DNA to these African populations was much more closely related to anatomically modern humans than *Homo erectus*. I think it is more appropriate to think of this foreign group as about as different as Neanderthals were to Cro-magnon *Homo sapiens sapiens*."

Akey said this foreign DNA is not found in non-Africans except for a few groups outside that continent. "And so what we think is the explanation for that is that as anatomically modern humans started dispersing out of Africa, those individuals that originally left Africa already contained some of that foreign DNA. And so the foreign DNA was taken out of Africa with those initial waves of migrations that peopled the world." Asked if such foreign DNA might imply breeding attempts by ancient astronauts, Akey laughed and replied, "I think the claim of extraterrestrial manipulation is such a high bar that as a scientist, you have to be skeptical about everything and that just strains the bar of credibility."

For early man, life was not pleasant. As bluntly stated in the Bible, Adam, Eve, and their progeny were not destined for a life of ease, but one of hard work and survival at the hands of their "Lords." Sitchin stated, "The term that is commonly translated as 'worship' was in fact *avod*—'work.' Ancient and biblical man did not 'worship' his god; he worked for him."

Researcher Arthur Horn stated that study of the Sumerian texts made it clear that "the Anunnaki treated their created slaves poorly, much like we treat domestic animals we are simply exploiting—like cattle. Overt slavery in human societies was common from the first known civilizations until quite recently. Perhaps it shouldn't surprise us to learn that the Anunnaki were vain, petty, cruel, incestuous, hateful—almost any negative adjective one can think of. The evidence indicates that they worked their slaves very hard and had little compassion for the plight of humans. Yet, the Anunnaki eventually decided to grant humankind their first civilization, the Sumerian civilization."

LONGEVITY AND ANOTHER NOAH

The Bible often describes the very long human lives of those who came before Noah, such as Adam, Seth, Enosh, Kenan, Enoch, and Methuselah. Alan Alford has pointed to the fossil record and the Sumerian texts placing the birth of humans at 450,000 years ago. In order to make the Bible's timeline make sense next to the Sumerian and fossil timeline, Alford multiplied biblical ages by 100; he found that the time between the birth of Adam's son Seth and the great Flood of Noah was 165,000 years. This number is more consistent with the Sumerian accounts. "The Jewish people spent an extremely long exile in Egypt for 400 years prior to the Exodus. Later they spent around 60 years exiled in Babylon," explained Alford. "The Jews were thus a long way from the Sumerian origin of their patriarch Abraham, and had lost the knowledge of the sexagesimal system in which their ancestry through to Abraham was recorded."

According to the new interpretations of Sumerian tales, the first humans—the Adama—were produced about three hundred thousand years ago. After further genetic manipulation allowed reproduction, human women found favor with Anunnaki males, and they began interbreeding about one hundred thousand years ago. Not long after this, a new Ice Age began, decimating the human population outside Anunnaki control. Neanderthals slowly disappeared, while Cro-Magnons survived only in the Middle East. By fifty thousand years ago, some Anunnaki leaders allowed humans fathered by Anunnaki to rule in selected cities. This angered Enlil, already incensed that some Anunnaki would mate with human women. In fact, mating in general seemed to bother Enlil—he complained that the sound of mating humans kept him awake at night. Enlil became determined to do something about the irritating humans.

About twelve thousand years ago, the Anunnaki leadership realized that severe climatic changes would occur with the imminent return of the planet Nibiru to the vicinity of Earth. Enlil made his move. In the Anunnaki's Great Assembly, Enlil convinced the majority to allow nature to take its course—to wipe out the humans while the Anunnaki waited out events in evacuation ships orbiting Earth.

But Enki had a plan of his own. Whether out of some affection for humans or simply to thwart Enlil's plans, Enki passed along the murderous "secret of the gods" to one of his most prized human assistants, the Sumerian Utnapishtim. In Babylonian legend, he was Atrahasis. The Bible called him Noah.

The Akkadian version stated Utnapishtim had lived in Shuruppak, the seventh city built by the Anunnaki, which has been identified as the Anunnaki medical center. It was also referred to as the city of Sud, who has been identified as Ninhursag—the one who assisted Enki with the genetic creation of the Lu-lu, the first Earthling.

Nearly all cultures have their own version of a Noah who survived the Great Flood. He was Ziusudra to the ancient Sumerians, Nuwah to the Chinese, Cox to Aztecs, Powaco to other Native Americans, Manu Yaivasata to the Hindus, Dwytach to the Celts, Noa to the natives of the Amazon, and Nu-u to the Hawaiians.

Utnapishtim has been called the Sumerian Noah, and the parallels between the biblical account of Noah and the *Gilgamesh* account of the Great Flood are both striking and obvious. Referring to the story of Noah, Sitchin stated that "the biblical account is an edited version of the original Sumerian account. As in the other instances, the monotheistic Bible has compressed into one Deity the roles played by several gods who were not always in accord."

According to the Sumerian texts, it was Enlil's rival half-brother, Enki, who instructed Utnapishtim/Noah how to construct an ark, using readily available bitumen to make it waterproof. The *Gilgamesh* version added some interesting details deleted from the Biblical account. For example, Enki provided Utnapishtim with an excuse to explain to his neighbors why he was building a boat—as a follower of Enki he was forced to leave the Enlil-controlled area and needed the boat to journey to Enki's territory in Africa.

It also states that Enki instructed Utnapishtim/Noah, "Aboard ship take thou the seed of all living things. . . ." This instruction is most fascinating: because Enki had been the science officer involved in the genetic engineering of humans, it makes plausible the idea that Utnapishtim/Noah took DNA samples of all living things rather than a boatload of animals, insects, and plants. A ship's cabin full of tiny samples would be much more reasonable than a floating zoological park.

Scattered archaeological excavations over many years indicate that what is regarded as the Great Flood was a planetwide catastrophe, though not every portion of the world went underwater. In fact, the Akkadian account stated that the Great Flood was not merely the result of heavy rains but also colossal winds that increased in intensity, destroying buildings and rupturing dikes. These are the kinds of conditions we might expect from a large planetary body passing by Earth.

One theory holds that the gravitational forces caused by the passing of Nibiru shook the Antarctic ice sheet—already unstable from the end of the last ice age—causing it to slide into the ocean and raise sea levels all over the planet. Even today, most of the original Anunnaki cities near the mouths of the Tigris and Euphrates rivers remain deep under water and silt.

Such a great catastrophe might explain why there were so few humans in the past on a planet that had housed so many great civilizations more than ten thousand years ago—most were lost in the Great Flood. This planetwide catastrophe might also explain the disappearance of Beringia, the thousand-mile-long land bridge between Siberia and North America. During the Pleistocene ice age more than ten thousand years ago, much of Earth's waters were contained in glaciers. Beringia had been a dry, grassy plain, drawing both animals and humans that connected Asia and North America across the Bering Strait. However, worldwide flooding may have melted great scores of ice, thus inundating Beringia.

After six days and nights, the storms receded. Yet most of the land had disappeared. Finally, as in the biblical account, the ark of Utnapishtim/Noah came to rest atop Mount Ararat. In one version of the story, wherein Utnapishtim/Noah actually brought animals aboard his boat, he sent a dove, a swallow, and a raven from the ark. Only the raven didn't return, indicating that more dry land was nearby. Noah and his family then left the ark and offered a burnt sacrifice, which drew the attention of the returning Anunnaki. An ancient text stated that the "gods crowded like flies" around the cooking flesh. Apparently, they had developed a hunger for fresh food during their long confinement in the ships orbiting Earth during the flood.

After he realized that the humans had survived the flood, Enlil had little choice but to relent and allow them to remain on Earth. With flood waters subsiding and Nibiru moving out of the solar system, the Anunnaki and the handful of surviving humans set about reconstructing the world. But this post-Flood world was to prove less peaceful than the previous one.

Prior to the Flood, any humans not working directly for the Anunnaki were roaming hunters or gatherers. But virtually overnight they became farmers. "Farming may be more work than hunting, judging by the available ethnographic data and [results] in an unstable man-modified ecosystem with low diversity index results," noted archaeologist Kent Flannery. "Since early farming represents a decision to work harder and eat more 'third-choice' food, I suspect that people did it because they felt they had to, not because they wanted to farm. Why they felt they had to, we may never know, in spite of the fact that their decision reshaped all the rest of human history."

SEPARATING THE HUMANS

The Sumerian tablets explained why humans had to cultivate the land and domesticate animals—because their gods demanded it. After the floods, men began to cultivate land not in the rich soil of the river valleys but in the mountain highlands of Mesopotamia and Palestine. Evidence of this exists even today. A Sumerian text fragment recounts the story: "Enlil went up to the peak and lifted his eyes; he looked down; there the waters filled as a sea. He looked up: there was the mountain of the aromatic cedars. He hauled up the barley, terraced it on the mountain. That which vegetates he hauled up, terraced the grain cereals on the mountain."

With farming came larger and more densely crowded cities than before the Flood. Each city was ruled by one of the Anunnaki overlords, who were now beginning to be considered gods by the humans, as they had not only survived the devastation but had returned with their knowledge and technology.

Like modern humans, certain food crops appeared to have no antecedent in Earth's evolutionary chain. They just suddenly appeared—fully cultured—about 13,000 years ago according to archaeological finds. "There is no explanation for this botanogenetic miracle, unless the process was not one of natural selection but of artificial manipulation," commented Sitchin. His point may have some merit, as three critical phases of human development—farming (circa 11,000 BC), higher culture (circa 7500 BC), and civilization (circa 3800 BC)—occurred at intervals of 3,600 years, the same period of time for a complete orbit by Nibiru.

KINGS AND CONFLICT

During a post-Flood assembly of the Anunnaki/Nefilim, it was decided to divide the Earth into four regions, with the captive human

population split up within three of these areas—lower Mesopotamia, the Nile Valley, and the Indus Valley. The Anunnaki reserved
the Sinai Peninsula—their new spaceflight center following the
Flood—as their private, or "holy," sanctuary.

Obviously, this divide-and-rule strategy for the scattered human
communities required separate leaders. Thus was born the concept
of kingship, human rulers specially chosen by the Anunnaki, or
"gods," to be intermediaries between themselves and the humans,
whom they still considered as little better than animals.

This practice began in the Sumerian city of Kish, which Sitchin
equates with the biblical Cush. Genesis 10:8–12 relates that Cush
was a grandson of Noah and father of the legendary Nimrod, who
ruled and built such cities as Babylon, Erech, and Akkad from
his base in Sumer, before constructing cities in Assyria, including
Nineveh. The practice of dynastic kingship based on a royal lineage
traceable to the gods has affected nations and governments up to
the present day, as evidenced by the fact that the Rothschilds of
today claim kinship to Nimrod.

It may have been Nimrod's attempt to thwart Enlil's dispersion
plan that led to the Old Testament story of the Tower of Babel. This
narrative began at Baalbek, believed to be a post-Flood center for
Anunnaki space-shuttle operations. The massiveness of the 1,100-
ton granite block of the Trilithon, and others weighing more than
300 tons each, buttresses the idea that this may have once been a
landing or launch pad.

One explanation for the trouble at Babel was that the humans
there attempted to construct their own launch tower, apparently
hoping to produce their own *shem*, or flying vehicle, with a view
toward arguing against the breakup of humanity with the off-world
ruler, An. "Come, let us build ourselves a city with a tower that
reaches to the heavens," they were quoted in Genesis 11:4 (New
International Version) as saying, "so that we may make a *shem* for
ourselves and not be scattered over the face of the whole earth."

An Arabic text found at Baalbek stated that Nimrod and his followers also tried to construct a *shem* there. "*Shem*, inadvertently misunderstood, was rendered by most translators as a sign for the word 'name.' However, it originally signified 'that which goes up,'" explained author Turnage. "Sitchin designates the origin of *shem* as Mesopotamian, originating from the word *mu* or the Semitic derivative *shu-mu*, or *sham* . . . 'that by which one is remembered,' evolving into 'name.' The original meaning of the words, however, was originally connected with the concept of something that flies."

"The realization that *mu* or *shem* in many Mesopotamian texts should be read not as 'name' but as 'sky vehicle' opens the way to the understanding of the true meaning of many ancient tales, including the biblical story of the Tower of Babel," wrote Sitchin. Even Sitchin's critics agree that *shem* or *shamaim* (heaven) stem from the word *shamah* translated as "that which is highward."

The activity at Baalbek only increased Enlil's fear of human competition and made him even more determined to break up the humans. His reaction may have been reflected in Genesis 11:5–8 (Revised Standard Version), "And the Lord came down to see the city and the tower, which the sons of men had built. And the Lord said, 'Behold, they are one people and they have all one language; and this is only the beginning of what they will do; and nothing that they propose to do will now be impossible for them. Come, let us go down, and there confuse their language, that they may not understand one another's speech.' So the Lord scattered them abroad from there over the face of all the Earth and they left off building the city."

Soon the three branches of humankind—all descendants of Noah's sons Shem, Ham, and Japheth—were transported to the preordained locations, where different languages indeed developed over time.

Alford theorized that Utnapishtim/Noah may have had wives representing separate racial groups. The offspring of these wives would have been of different races, offering an explanation for the presence of the Negroid race in Africa, Mongoloids in Asia, and Caucasoid in the Near East.

Both the Sumerian texts and the Bible agree that Shem and his descendants remained in the area encompassing Mesopotamia, Ham and his kin were taken to Africa—here including parts of Arabia—while Japheth's people were transported to the Indus Valley, possibly becoming the mysterious Aryans who suddenly appeared there in ancient times.

This dispersion, accompanied by the growth of new cities with their newly installed kings and increased food production, should have led to a congenial peace. But unfortunately it appeared that the ancient "gods" were no more able to produce lasting peace than humans.

Trouble began even as the Anunnaki began to relocate their spaceflight facilities from Sumer—now mostly underwater due to the flood—to the Sinai Peninsula at a place that came to be called El Paran (God's Glorious Place). Mount Ararat, in what is now eastern Turkey and is reportedly where the ark finally grounded, provided the northernmost landmark for a glide path to the Anunnaki's Sinai landing facility. This base was located on the thirtieth parallel in the geographic center of Sinai. The southern glide path landmark was the two highest peaks of Mount Sinai, the higher being Mount Catherine (8,652 feet above sea level) and the lower, Mount Moses (7,500 feet). What was lacking for this glide path was a matching landmark to the west. Because that area was flat, some researchers claim that tall markers were constructed—the great pyramids of Giza.

The editors of the *Holman Bible Dictionary* reported that Mount Sinai probably came from the word meaning "shining" and was likely derived from the Babylonian god Sin. However, Sin was simply the Semitic name for Nannar, the firstborn son of the Anunnaki leader Enlil and sovereign of Ur, the home city of Abraham.

Sin also was the Chaldean name for the moon, where the Sumerians claimed Enki first obtained the life-producing tissue cells or "seed" for his human hybrid experiments that remained from the clash between Nibiru and the planet Tiamat. "The enormity of this single name change on human history is beyond comprehension," declared author William Henry. "When the Christian interpreters came along, they repeated the story that we were born in sin. They were entirely accurate in their statement. However, they omitted the fact that Sin referred to the Moon, the source of our genetic material!" In the ensuing wars between the Anunnaki overlords, Sin was reported to have sided with the human benefactor Enki, which caused Enlil to declare those who opposed him as "sinners."

Because the Anunnaki mission control center at the Sumerian city of Nippur was destroyed during the Flood and because of the need for a location equidistant from the glide path lines, a new control center was needed. It was built at Mount Moriah, translated as "Mount of Directing." It was the site of the future holy city of Jerusalem, long considered a most sacred place by all major Western religions.

Eventually, new generations of the Anunnaki were on the Earth, and from their descendants came stories filled with intrigues, conspiracies, and outright wars pitting brother against brother and sister against sister. These conflicts, rebellions, and wars would eventually involve humankind, providing their first exposure to armed combat, which continues even today.

According to the Sumerian texts, Enki's firstborn son, Marduk, gained sovereignty over the lands of Egypt and became known as Ra. It was his children, Shu and Tefnut, who set an example for future pharaohs by wedding each other. Their offspring, Geb and Nut, also married and were the next royal couple as well as the parents of some of Egypt's most famous god/rulers—Osiris, his sister/wife Isis, Seth, and Nephthys, sister of Isis.

There may be a fascinating rationale for such interbreeding, as explained by researcher Bill Putnam. He said that this was a method for exactly reproducing the chromosomes of the pharaoh. Egyptian literature indicates that the pharaohs usually married a half sister. If a pharaoh's son bred with the daughter of an unrelated wife (the pharaohs had several wives), the resulting match of the X and Y chromosomes would result in reproducing an exact match of chromosomes of the original pharaoh. "The net effect was that the DNA of the 'god on Earth' would be reproduced every other generation," explained Putnam. Putnam said they were most likely following the example of their gods, the Anunnaki, to whom reproducing the bloodline was a most necessary deed. This could help explain this practice among humans, which continues until today within royal and bloodline families. "Princess Diana had more claim to the bloodline than Prince Charles," said Putnam.

All this interfamily marriage led to a succession problem, solved by dividing the country. Osiris was given Lower Egypt and Seth, mountainous Upper Egypt. Unsatisfied with his apportionment, Seth began to maneuver against Osiris, and thus began the legendary wars of ancient Egypt.

In a story reminiscent of Romeo and Juliet, the Sumerian stories tell of a granddaughter of Enlil named Inanna, who married the youngest son of Enki, Dumuzi, with the wary blessing of both feuding families. But when Dumuzi was killed after being taken into custody by Enki's firstborn son, Marduk, or Ra, for violating the Anunnaki moral code, Inanna attacked Marduk/Ra.

To stop this conflict, Marduk was tried for Dumuzi's death. As it could not be proven whether the death had been deliberate or accidental, and because Marduk/Ra was proclaimed a god, it was decided to sentence him to life imprisonment in a huge, impenetrable place whose walls reached the skies. Sitchin identified Marduk's prison as none other than the Great Pyramid. He wrote that his translations of the Sumerian texts explained that the curious well shaft within the Great Pyramid—a puzzling hand-hewed tunnel connecting the pyramid's Descending Passage to its Ascending

Passage—was dug to bypass the large granite stone that plugs the Ascending Passage in an attempt to rescue Marduk, who escaped but eventually returned. The capture and imprisonment of an Egyptian god are well recounted in ancient Egyptian hieroglyphics.

Despite Marduk's punishment, Inanna was far from satisfied, as she, too, wanted power. The Anunnaki could satisfy her only by giving her control over another area, now identified as the Indus Valley. Mounded ruins of Mohenjo-daro, the largest city of a civilization dating back to before 2500 BC, were first recognized on the Indus River in southern Pakistan in 1922. Although thoroughly— and strangely—devastated in some prehistoric time, the baked-brick construction of buildings and the preplanned layout of the city indicated to some researchers an obvious connection with Sumer. Author Alford said the city was inhabited by a people called the Harappans, who "worshipped a sole female deity, whose depiction bore an amazing similarity to other images of the goddess Inanna."

If this Indus goddess was indeed Inanna, she continued her quest for power, according to the Sumerian texts, eventually replacing Ninhursag among the major Anunnaki leaders. Using a human hybrid named Sharru-Kin, Inanna carved out a new empire. The man she picked is also known as Sargon the Great. Believed to be the offspring of a human mother and an Anunnaki father, Sargon claimed that he, like Moses later, was placed in a sealed basket of reeds by his mother and floated down a river to safety while a baby. Sargon went on to found the Semite Akkadian dynasty about 2200 BC, which finally encompassed all of Mesopotamia.

With the fall of Sargon and the Akkadian empire, Marduk slipped from exile and attempted to regain his sovereignty over Babylon sometime before the year 2000 BC. But alliances quickly shifted, and Enlil and Inanna aligned their forces against Marduk and his father Enki. Marduk also faced a crushing defection from his son Nergal, who joined Enlil. For the Anunnaki, a true civil war was taking place.

Many are familiar with the biblical patriarch Abraham, but few realize that he may have been involved with Anunnaki civil war. According to Zecharia Sitchin, a variety of texts clearly indicate that Abraham was far from just a wandering Hebrew, as often popularly believed, but was rather a ranking Sumerian from Ur. "Coming to Egypt, Abraham and Sarah were taken to the Pharaoh's court; in Canaan, Abraham made treaties with the local rulers," he noted. "This is not the image of a nomad pillaging others' settlements; it is the image of a personage of high standing skilled in negotiation and diplomacy."

Genesis 14:14–16 alludes to the fact that Abraham also commanded armed troops—according to the biblical text, he took 318 "trained men" to rescue his nephew Lot and his family from an invading coalition of armies under Marduk, as Marduk had been maneuvering to retake the Sinai space port from the north. Abraham's warriors turned him back before he could reach the Sinai space facilities at El Paran. This feat later brought praise and blessing from Melchizedek, king of Salem, as well as a covenant with Yahweh, identified as Enlil.

Instead of a full retreat, Marduk stopped to sack the cities of Sodom and Gomorrah in the Siddim Valley, which lies on the southern edge of the Dead Sea. Here, he defeated the kings of these cities, and took Lot prisoner before moving back north. After being rescued by Abraham, Lot returned to the area. As usually the case in so many wars, things got out of hand for the Anunnaki. It may have been at this time that the world felt the first blast of a nuclear explosion.

ATOMIC WAR?

Enlil and his sons, fearing Marduk's power, persuaded Anu to allow the use of seven mighty weapons, now believed by many to have been tantamount to tactical nuclear missiles, against Marduk/Ra. Meanwhile, the kings of Sodom and Gomorrah felt betrayed by their Enlilite "gods," who had failed to protect them from the invading coalition, so they switched their allegiance to Marduk, in essence, sealing their doom.

But in honor of Abraham's past service, Enlil decided to give him warning. Genesis 18 explains what happened next. Yahweh came to Abraham and warned him that the cities would be destroyed because they had turned away from him. This warning is evidence that the destruction of Sodom and Gomorrah was a planned event, not some unanticipated natural disaster.

Such foreknowledge is also evidenced by the warning of Lot in Sodom by two "angels," although the original Hebrew word, *mal'akhim*, actually only meant "emissaries," while *Webster's 3rd New International Dictionary* defines them as "messengers." Could this mean emissaries from Enlil? Following some trouble with the neighbors over the visitors, as recounted in Genesis 19:12–13, the pair told Lot, "Have you anyone else here? Sons-in-laws, sons, daughters, or any one you have in the city, bring them out of the place; for we are about to destroy this place, because the outcry against its people has become great before the Lord, and the Lord has sent us to destroy it" (Revised Standard Version).

Lot and his kindred fled to the mountains as instructed, but the fiery cataclysm reached out to his own family. According to Genesis 19:26, Lot's wife, who had lagged behind, was turned to "a pillar of salt." But Zecharia Sitchin noted that the original Sumerian word interpreted by Hebrew scribes as "salt" also meant "vapor." Lot's wife then was vaporized by the explosion that consumed Sodom and Gomorrah. Lot and the rest of his family survived. They may have been shielded by the crest of a hill or the like.

Abraham, standing miles away in the mountains, looked down and saw a column of dense smoke rising as if from a furnace. Could it have been mushroom shaped? Evidence that Sodom and Gomorrah were destroyed by a nuclear explosion has come from many sources. The nearby Dead Sea covered the bombed cities with salt water, perhaps under the shallow southern section of the sea below the Lisan Peninsula. Oddly enough, the bottom of the Dead Sea is almost 2,500 feet below the level of the Mediterranean, indicating it was created by something quite unusual and unnatural.

More evidence came from hydrology research on the west bank of the Dead Sea in the 1960s that revealed some springs in the area still register higher than normal background radioactivity. In addition, bones found at the Ain es-Sultan Spring, located on the site of ancient Jericho, contained alpha radiation, according to researchers I. M. Blake of Oxford University and J. Cynthia Weber of Harvard. Although they argued against an ancient explosion, they did note that surrounding settlements were suddenly abandoned for several centuries about 2040 BC. The Bible also hints that this radioactivity brought about sterility. In II Kings 2:19, a delegation from Jericho tells the prophet Elisha, " . . . the situation of this city is pleasant . . . but the water is bad and the ground barren."

In addition to the devastation of Sodom and Gomorrah, the ancient tablets recount how the Sinai spaceport also was targeted for nuclear destruction, apparently to prevent it from falling into Marduk's hands. According to Sitchin, Alford, and others, the Sinai detonation produced an unnatural scarring of the peninsula that can still be seen from space, as well as a multitude of scorched rocks in the area. "In the eastern Sinai, millions of blackened stones are found strewn for tens of miles. These stones are, without any doubt, unnatural," reported Alford, who asserts that "photographs clearly demonstrate that the rocks are blackened only on the surface."

Throughout the Middle East and beyond, there is evidence that other targets, unrecorded and as yet undiscovered, may also have experienced nuclear detonations. There are mysterious globules of fused glass and vitrified rocks at cities deep in the strata of archaeological digs at Pierrelatte in Gabon, Africa. Similar evidence attesting to the possible use of nuclear weapons in the distant past also has been found in the Euphrates Valley, the Sahara Desert, the Gobi Desert, the Mojave Desert, Scotland, Egypt (during the Old and Middle Kingdoms), and south-central Turkey.

Such globules, some referred to as tektites, are thought to come from meteorites. However, in most cases there are no visible impact craters in the vicinity. If not meteoric in origin, the problem is how they were created.

John O'Keefe, writing in *Scientific American*, noted, "If tektites are terrestrial, it means that some process exists by which soil or common rocks can be converted in an instant into homogeneous, water-free, bubble-free glass and be propelled thousands of miles above the atmosphere."

Such fused material today can be found only at test sites for nuclear weapons. Moreover, scientists have found a number of ancient mining operations near deposits of uranium.

One of the most convincing indications of ancient nuclear war can be found in the ruins of Harappa, in northeast Pakistan, and Mohenjo Daro, another major city of the same period, located in south-central Pakistan. Both were major cities of the Bronze Age Indus Valley civilization, and both seem to spring up suddenly with no clear traces of a primitive past. Curiously, the lowest strata at Mohenjo Daro seem to indicate that the civilization was *more* advanced earlier in its history than later. Soapstone was replaced by common clay; crude shapes replaced lifelike engravings, and finely glazed ceramics devolved to plain clumsy pots. "Even the bricks were inferior," said Jonathan Gray, Australian archaeologist and author of *Dead Men's Secrets*.

According to Gray, we know almost nothing about Harappa and Mohenjo Daro "except that both were destroyed suddenly. In Mohenjo-Daro, in an epicenter 150 feet wide, everything was crystallized, fused or melted; 180 feet from the center the bricks are melted on one side, indicating a blast. Excavations down to the street level revealed 44 scattered skeletons, as if doom had come so suddenly they could not get to their houses. All the skeletons were flattened to the ground. A father, mother and child were found flattened in the street, face down and still holding hands. It has been claimed that the skeletons, after thousands of years, are still among the most radioactive that have ever been found, on a par with those of Hiroshima and Nagasaki."

An ancient Indian text called the *Mahabharata* describes how war broke out between the early "Masters" of the cities of Harappa, Mohenjo Daro, and another city, Kot Diji. According to the text, flying machines called *vimanas*—apparently similar to the Anunnaki flying craft—launched a weapon that seemed to be as devastating as an atomic bomb. Although the language differences prohibit an absolute connection to the accounts of the Anunnaki craft and weapons, the similarities are provocative. The weapon was described thus:

> . . . *(it was) a single projectile*
> *Charged with all the power of the Universe.*
> *An incandescent column of smoke and flame*
> *As bright as the thousand suns*
> *Rose in all its splendor . . .*
> *. . . it was an unknown weapon,*
> *An iron thunderbolt,*
> *A gigantic messenger of death,*
> *Which reduced to ashes*
> *The entire race of the*
> *Vrishnis and the Andhakas*
> *. . . The corpses were so burned*
> *As to be unrecognizable.*
> *The hair and nails fell out;*
> *Pottery broke without apparent cause,*
> *. . . After a few hours*

> *All foodstuffs were infected . . .*
> *. . . to escape from this fire*
> *The soldiers threw themselves in streams*
> *To wash themselves and their equipment.*

There is surprising scientific support for this account of nuclear weapons used in India. A layer of radioactive ash was found covering a three-square-mile area in Rajasthan, ten miles west of Jodhpur, India. Archaeologist Francis Taylor, translating etchings at the site, remarked, "It's so mind-boggling to imagine that some civilization had nuclear technology before we did. The radioactive ash adds credibility to the ancient Indian records that describe atomic warfare."

Conventional history states that mighty Sumer simply vanished suddenly, absorbed by the new empires of Babylon and Assyria, though Sumerian texts tell a much more horrible story. Besides destroying a number of cities, tragic collateral damage came about as a result of the nuclear blasts on the Sinai Peninsula—in the fallout from the explosions, a radioactive cyclone formed and moved through Mesopotamia and on into the Indus Valley, obliterating all life and ending the Sumerian civilization.

According to various "lamentations" translated by the Sumerian scholar Samuel Noah Kramer, "On the land [Sumer] fell a calamity, one unknown to man; one that had never been seen before, one which could not be withstood. A great storm from heaven . . . A land-annihilating storm . . . An evil wind, like a rushing torrent . . . A battling storm joined by scorching heat . . . By day it deprived the land of the bright sun, in the evening the stars did not shine . . . The people, terrified, could hardly breathe; the evil wind clutched them, does not grant them another day . . . Mouths were drenched with blood, heads wallowed in blood . . . The face was made pale by the Evil Wind. It caused cities to be desolated, houses to become desolate; stalls to become desolate, the sheepfolds to be emptied . . . Sumer's rivers it made flow with water that is bitter; its cultivated fields grow weeds, its pastures grow withered plants . . . Thus all its gods evacuated Uruk; they kept away from it; they hid in the mountains, they escaped to the distant plains." This one great storm of radioactive fallout annihilated the world's first great civilization, leaving the bodies of the population "stacked up in heaps."

The final war in Mesopotamia was the Anunnaki's nuclear Armageddon. Their millennia-old colony of Eden was blown away. One theory was that the Anunnaki, shocked by what they had wrought, retreated to an enclave in the Sinai where most of them made the decision to return home, perhaps leaving behind only a caretaker force or perhaps abandoning the culprits who instigated the insurrection against the Anunnaki hierarchy.

To humans, all this occurred in ancient times, more than 4,000 years ago. If their time is counted by the 3,600-year revolution of their planet around our sun, then to the Anunnaki, all this would have taken place just a little more than a year ago. Some researchers feel an Anunnaki rescue mission may still be on the way to Earth. Only time will tell if there is any truth to this.

It was at this time, after the destruction of the Mesopotamian cities, that the detailed narratives of Sumer and its gods ceased. It would be centuries before civilization and writing once more flourished in parts of Mesopotamia as memory of the great cataclysm faded into vague stories of the nightmare.

HISTORY BECOMES MYTHOLOGY

In *Bloodline of the Holy Grail,* Laurence Gardner explained how these stories evolved into a twisted history "What actually transpired was that the original Mesopotamian writings were recorded as history. This history was later rewritten to form a base for foreign religious cults—first Judaism and then Christianity. The corrupted dogma—the new approved history—was so different from the original writings, the early first-hand reports were labeled 'mythology.'"

The term *mythology* stems from the Greek word *mythos*, simply meaning words or stories reflecting the basic values and attitudes of a people. In past ages, when the vast majority of humans were illiterate, easily understood parables were used to educate people about history, science, and technology. During the Dark Ages, when most people were taught that the Earth was flat, the word *mythology* was changed by the Roman Church to mean imaginative and fanciful tales veering far from any truthfulness. This small change in semantics has caused untold damage in current perceptions.

For example, the Mesopotamian saga of Gilgamesh, king of Uruk, is the world's earliest known epic poem. It tells of the offspring of a human mother and an Anunnaki father, who, along with his nonhuman companion, Enkidu, sets out on a journey to find the secret of immortality. The epic was thought to be merely a fable at the time of its discovery in 1872. However, in 2003, German archaeologists working at the site of ancient Uruk discovered what they believed to be the lost tomb of Gilgamesh. "I don't want to say definitely it was the grave of King Gilgamesh, but it looks very similar to that described in the epic," Jorg Fassbinder of the Bavarian Department of Historical Monuments in Munich told the BBC.

Once again, myth was turned into reality. Breakthroughs in astronomy, anthropology, archaeology, and Egyptology have only supported the theses of Erich von Däniken, Zecharia Sitchin, Alan Alford, Michael Tellinger, and many others. Outlandish as these concepts may appear to some, many people today believe strongly that soon the revised Sumerian version of history will become a widespread and legitimate subject of study in seminaries, universities, and science centers.

HAND-ME-DOWN CULTURES
AND CONTROL

SURVIVORS OF THIS EARLY NUCLEAR HOLOCAUST FACED A PERIOD OF regression and barbarism. The remaining humans made the best of things and began rebuilding their civilizations, a slow process without the overt aid of their "gods."

The humans longed for the gods' return, and they may have expressed this longing through art evoking flight. Those who participated in this art were part of something today called a cargo cult. Cargo cultists in certain areas of Melanesia in the Pacific believed for years that the sky gods would bring them goods—cargo—in "big birds." They especially believed such prophecies were coming true during World War II, when American and Japanese planes dropped food and matériel in the jungles for advancing troops. After the war, the natives built mock airstrips and even bamboo "radios" in an effort to prepare for a return of the "gods." Some of this practice continues even today.

Erich von Däniken saw a cargo cult behind the famous Nazca Lines in Peru. He speculated that in ancient times "unknown intelligences" landed at Nazca and laid down two runways before departing. Pre-Inca tribesmen witnessed their arrival and later extended the two runways and added several of their own to induce the "gods" to return. Similar etchings, which can only be discerned from the air, have been found in the Middle East.

Following the devastation north and east of Palestine, Abraham moved his people to the south, where he fathered Isaac when he was one hundred years old, thanks perhaps to his hybrid genes. Isaac's son Jacob became known as Israel, a name soon applied to his entire people. Some believe that the name Israel is nothing less than a combination of the Egyptian gods OsirIS and RA and the Mesopotamian god EL.

For about thirty-five generations, or more than 875 years, the Israelites passed along oral accounts of the stories of the Abraham and the Anunnaki until they finally wrote the stories down in Hebrew. Later, the life of Jesus Christ was added into the mix after the stories had been translated into Greek; the result was then "authorized" by a succession of rulers, including Britain's King James I. We now read these stories in the form of the Bible. It also must be understood that the narrative above is recounted, in one form or another, in the Sumerian texts uncovered only in the last 150 years, all of which predate the Bible by at least 2,000 years. Just consider what current events will sound like 2,000 years from now.

The evidence just covered only begins to scratch the surface of the wealth of data now available—both archaeological and in the cuneiform tablets—that supports this incredible narrative with its far-reaching implications. Even the authors and researchers studying this subject feel certain they do not have all the facts. And while these facts probably don't tell us the full truth of our history, they most likely are pointing us in the right direction. Dr. Horn summed it up by noting, "Let us make clear, once again, that we do not believe the ancient Sumerian and other Mesopotamian stories are 'absolutely true' history. These stories that have come to us through thousands of years of oral tradition and writing are bound to be somewhat distorted—probably in some cases deliberately distorted by the Anunnaki. But, I feel these ancient stories are probably as close as we'll come to the truth today. . . ."

Obviously, such revision of ancient history has had and will continue to have a profound impact on conventional science. Horn resigned as a professor of biological anthropology at Colorado State University in 1990 after he concluded that the conventional explanations for man's origins that he was teaching were "nonsense." After much study, he, too, came to believe that extraterrestrials were intricately involved in the origin and development of humans.

If some Anunnaki remained on the devastated Earth, they would have found themselves marooned on a primitive world, like the astronaut portrayed by Charleston Heston in the film *Planet of the Apes*. Without the infrastructure to manufacture the simplest items, they would have lost the use of their superior technology but not the knowledge of it, and they certainly would not have been satisfied with simply being another member of the ape horde.

But how could these ancient visitors control the much larger human population? How could one person, or even a handful of persons, control several billion people? Certainly not though physical control, but rather through deceit, secrecy, and the use of two historic institutions of power—first religion and later finance. Our visitors might have also tried to control us through fractious wars and slavery, which is practiced right up until today, although most forms of direct physical slavery were abandoned in First World nations by the mid-1800s.

GIVE ME THAT OLD-TIME RELIGION

Initially, our primitive ancestors most likely felt awe and reverence toward the technologically advanced visitors who came from the heavens. After all, what primitive human could fly and perform acts that must have seemed like magic? As author and scientist Arthur C. Clarke once stated, "Any sufficiently advanced technology is indistinguishable from magic." Despite our deference, the first humans thought of these visitors merely as watchers or messengers from the heavens. Only after Anunnaki leaders began to appoint rulers over humanity did the concept of religion come into play.

Rather than deal directly with the burgeoning human population, the ancient gods ordained an administrative body or priesthood to pass along edicts and instruction as well as interpret policy.

These clerics got a taste of wealth and power, a taste they were loath to relinquish. Religion soon evolved into a rigid structure of dogmas, catechisms, tithing, and obedience.

According to writers Peter Jiang and Jenny Li, some among those who study extraterrestrial phenomena—known as exoscientists—suggest that other extraterrestrials, who have come to Earth after the Anunnaki, have tried to manipulate humans genetically, technologically, and also through religious dogma and ritual. "Apparently, these extraterrestrials performed 'great feats' in order to be worshipped as 'gods.' The reported next step was to provide technology to these Earth humans so that these humans could create impressive looking 'rich' structures of religious worship, laid with gold and other mined mineral resources, of religious worship to these extraterrestrial 'gods.'"

By the time of the earliest recorded human civilizations, such as Assyria and Babylonia, religions were well established and had merged with the prevailing political structure. Certain civilizations had firmly established the idea that the clergy could be the only religious authority and that kingship was a divine right. Anointed priests who worshipped one god exhorted their followers to demonize the worshippers of the others. And anyone who failed to offer allegiance to their one true god was castigated as a blasphemer, heathen, Satan worshipper, or worse.

But as the physical gods—the earlier visitors—dropped from sight, the religions they created turned metaphysical. The concept of God evolved from a physical being to an omnipresent yet anthropomorphic supernatural entity. The elder conflicts between the ancient astronauts became a metaphor for ancient wars and a struggle between the new God and his evil counterpart, Satan. Baptist minister and author Paul Von Ward wrote about "the development of supernatural religion in what we call the cradle of civilization, beginning less than 3,000 years ago. Here religions that grew out of absentee-[Advanced Beings]-cults that described their gods as immortal, magical beings took the next step toward supernaturalism."

Religious expert, author, and Princeton professor of religion Elaine Pagels received both Rockefeller and Guggenheim fellowships and was a Mellon Fellow at the Aspen Institute, where she later served on the board of trustees. She noted, "The earliest mention of Satan occurs in a few scattered references in the Hebrew Bible. Jewish storytellers introduce a supernatural figure they call *ha satan*, which can be translated from Hebrew as 'the adversary,' or 'the opposer,' or 'the obstructer.' But this supernatural 'opposer' never dares to oppose *God*. On the contrary, he is one of God's obedient servants, his messengers, called in Hebrew *malakim*, members of the heavenly court. Translated into Greek, *malak* becomes *angelos*, from which we get the word 'angel.'"

The story of how one of God's trusted messengers turned against him came from various accounts of prebiblical Hebrew storytellers. One version was that Satan and his followers were thrown out of heaven after rebelling against orders from their commander in chief. Others stated they violated policy by mating with human women. Yet another was that the messenger Satan refused to bow down to a younger sibling, proclaiming, "Why do you press me? I will not worship one who is younger than I am, and inferior; I am older than he; he ought to worship me!"

Whatever the origin of Satan's rebellion, Pagels argued that Satan represented human hostility against other humans: "And it's no accident that the foundational texts of Christian tradition—the gospels of the New Testament, like the Dead Sea Scrolls—all begin with stories of Satan contending against God's spirit." Pagels explained that Christians later "turned the image of Satan against a far wider range of targets—against the Roman empire and its government, which persecuted Christians, and then against other 'intimate enemies'—other Christians, whom they called 'heretics.'

"What I've come to see is that when people invoke Satan—

whether in the first century or the twentieth—they have in mind not only some supernatural being, but also some very human beings. People who say, for example, 'Satan is trying to take over this country, but we are resisting him,' know exactly who they have in mind, and probably can name names!"

Von Ward elaborated on Pagels's viewpoint by stating that "history makes it clear that the Hebrews had simply followed the example of their patron god. They labeled their opponents, foreign or domestic, Satanic worshipers of Beelzebub, Belial, and the Princes of Darkness. In return, their opponents likely shouted their own epithets of 'infidel' (meaning 'unfaithful to the "true" god')."

According to Von Ward, a "confluence of historical events" provided the basis for Western supernaturalism during the Roman Empire. These events included the development of absentee non-human cult worship in the Middle East, the Hebrew worship of Yahweh, who was believed to be the leader of the olden gods, and the new and compelling reformation cult of Jesus of Nazareth. Von Ward also attributes the rise of supernaturalism to the simultaneous rise of powerful institutions—for instance, the development of Roman organizational skills and the creation of a Christ-centered church, the power of Rome to elevate Paul's Christian cult to the status of the state religion, and the Nicean council of bishops that "culled from competing texts a Bible that largely excludes references to the reality of other [Advanced Beings] and Jesus' humanity."

Von Ward said generations of humans slowly developed a defense mechanism once the ancient gods were no longer visible: "The Anunnaki had apparently decided to go about their own affairs, but humans felt bereft at being deserted. So supernatural theology was the defense mechanism created to help cope with the pain and anxiety of an obvious separation of humans from their gods. One of its purposes was to assure humans that the religious rituals would either bring the departed gods back to Earth or reconnect the humans to them in the supernatural realm."

With the rise of the Roman Empire, the keepers of ancient secrets moved their network from Mesopotamia to Rome. As the Roman Empire declined, Christianity became a major institution. With the founding of the Roman Church, the powers of the ruling elite skyrocketed. Even today, David Icke and others claim, "The Roman Catholic Church controlled by the Jesuit secret society remains at the heart of Illuminati operations."

SHOW ME THE MONEY

In early Eastern and Western cultures, rulers gained power and wealth from religion. Yet today, religion has waned, especially in highly developed nations. Now the favored method of control is through money.

The Hebrew Mogen David, or Star of David, is of Babylonian origin and is indicative of how Babylonian/Sumerian culture was blended with Hebrew religion during the Jews' captivity in Babylon. And it was in the Temple at Jerusalem that Jesus turned violent against the money changers.

Matthew 21:12–13 relates, "And Jesus went into the temple of God, and cast out all them that sold and bought in the temple, and overthrew the tables of the moneychangers, and the seats of those who sold doves, And said unto them, It is written, My house shall be called the house of prayer; but ye have made it a den of thieves" (KJV).

Author Joseph P. Farrell saw the development of the private issuance of bullion-based monies both in ancient times and in various later cultures as suggesting "the evident hand of a hidden international class of bullion-brokers, war merchants, slave traders, and mining operators, for almost invariably, the pattern is the same." The pattern involved blending finances with the prevailing religion as if money was ordained by God.

Farrell has argued that the methodology of aligning religion with money would go something like this: rulers could penetrate and ally with the temple, issue false receipts, substitute bullion for letters of credit as a measure against the false receipts, and thus create a facsimile of money.

> *Thus, we arrive back at the state of issuing false receipts, only in this instance, these receipts are neither false nor counterfeit, they are simply privately created notes or promises to pay a certain amount of bullion (which they also control). Thus, once again the money supply is not only expanded, but the use of such instruments actually served to allow the bullion brokers to circulate more of such notes than they had actual bullion to redeem. The key, once again, was the sanctifying probity that the temple association gave them. With this step their power and influence over the various states which they penetrated was almost complete, for it gave these ancient bankers, like their modern counterparts, the ability to expand or contract a state's money supply and to control their economies to create boom or bust.*

The power of exchanging money can be traced back to Palestine, where money changers were prevalent—people who exchanged the currencies of the various cities and nations into money acceptable to the temple priests. Money therefore became closely associated with the temples, which also doubled as centers for the study of astronomy and astrology.

Farrell presented the thesis that modern banking magnates are merely utilizing financial legerdemain learned from ancient practices. The earliest bankers, who originally dealt in gold and silver bullion, learned that great profits could be made by issuing written notes and credit vouchers.

Today, money is increasingly mere electronic blips in a computer accessed by plastic cards at ATMs. There is nothing to back it up. Yet this illusory currency is loaned at interest by great institutions. As the total amount of money grows, its worth decreases. This is called inflation, in effect a built-in tax on the use of money. And inflation can be manipulated upward or downward by those who control the flow of paper money or electronic blips.

"The result of this whole system is massive debt at every level of society today," wrote William Bramley, author of *The Gods of Eden*. "The banks are in debt to the depositors, and the depositors' money is loaned out and creates indebtedness to the banks. Making this system even more akin to something out of a maniac's delirium is the fact that banks, like other lenders, often have the right to seize physical property if its paper money is not repaid."

Both Bramley and Farrell saw that the strategy and practices of a banking elite in existence since ancient times involve war, slavery (whether physical or financial), usurpation of the money-creating power of the state, the invention of debt-as-money, and economic cycles coupled with astrology.

But in order to exert control over such a system, a banking elite would have required long-distance communication and the use of basic technology in order to construct a worldwide financial network. It has been well documented how early banking dynasties, such as the Medicis and Rothschilds, indeed were dependent on elaborate and effective communication systems. And both families exercised power over kings and monarchs, even selecting the pope.

There are examples of communication technology that could have been used in the past to simulate miracles and messages from divine beings. Konstantin Meyl, who teaches electronics and alternative energy technology at the University of Applied Sciences in Furtwangen, Germany, has built on the work of Nikola Tesla in describing how energy—including sound waves—can be transferred without wires via scalar waves, multidimensional standing-wave patterns that exist within the universal unified energy field.

G. Patrick Flanagan, author of *Pyramid Power*, has developed a device called a neurophone, which can carry sound to the brain without the use of the auditory system. Using "hyperspacial nested modulation" technology, this device takes a complex signal, such as the sound of an orchestra, and electrically processes it into square waves approximating human brain waves. After further processing, the waves are carried through zirconium titanate electrodes embedded in acrylic plastic tiles placed on the skin anywhere on the body. A person using a neurophone device can "hear" music and speech without the use of the ears. The neurophone has been used experimentally in communicating with dolphins, and further experimentation has shown that scalar-wave sound like radio waves may be discernible without the need for physical contact.

Such existing technology led Meyl to theorize that many ancient temples were constructed in such a way as to create a communication system. "The temples in antiquity were all shortwave broadcasting stations," bluntly stated Meyl in his 2003 book *Scalar Waves: From an Extended Vortex and Field Theory to a Technical, Biological, and Historical Use of Longitudinal Waves*. He said the temples were powered by ambient Earth electromagnetic energy as described by Michael Tellinger. Also they were constructed in such a manner as to harness energy from the sun, as well as neutrino radiation from the planets.

Studying the floor plans of the Greek temples of Zeus, Athena, Hera, and Apollo and even the Pantheon in Rome, Meyl presents a compelling argument that the dimensions of such sites show an uncanny geometric resemblance based on the golden ratio, an irrational (nonfractional) number, a mathematical constant used by many early artists and architects, who referred to such designs as sacred geometry. So by constructing edifices using certain rigid mathematical formulas and by utilizing ambient radiation, knowledgeable insiders within the banking elite were able to communicate at great distances via both aural and psychic means.

According to Meyl, old accounts have proved that this type of communication existed, yet those translating the accounts garbled the translations because they didn't understand the technology being discussed. For instance, those who have translated accounts of oracles, angelic voices, and prophecies may have actually meant that a receiver was in use. One old Latin text, for example, stated, "They sent by courier to the emperor in Rome and got for an answer . . . The answer of the emperor namely arrived at the squad at the latest in the following night." Meyl has posited that the correct translation should read, "They cabled" or "They broadcast to the emperor in Rome and got for an answer . . ." Meyl continued, "Such a big empire as the Roman Empire actually could only be reigned by means of efficient communication. Cicero coined the word: 'We have conquered the people of the Earth owing to our broadcasting technology.' . . . If engineers, however, rework the incorrect translations . . . much direct evidence exists concerning the practical use of this technology." Like many ancient philosophers, Cicero also wrote that the occult mysteries had more to do with natural science than with religion.

Bramley saw war as another important control mechanism. "War can be an effective tool for maintaining social and political control over a large population," he wrote. "A state of war [including an undeclared one, such as the War on Drugs or War on Terrorism] can also be used to encourage populations to think in ways that they would not otherwise do, and to accept the formation of institutions that they would normally reject. The longer a nation involves itself in wars, the more entrenched those institutions and ways of thinking will become."

With the control mechanisms of war, religion, and finance firmly in place and coupled with an effective communication system, the stage was set for subjugation of humanity by a relative handful of persons, all traceable to the original civilizations with their narratives of sky gods bringing knowledge and technology.

Much detail concerning the ancient Sumerians and their Anunnaki overlords has been kept from the general public, although in recent years some of this material has begun to break through into the corporate mass media. The History Channel's popular program *Ancient Aliens* broke many barriers in bringing the concept of extraterrestrials on Earth in the past to the public.

As the once great Sumerian culture disappeared into history, vestiges of this civilization rose and fell in the Near East. The empires of Akkad, Assyria, Phoenicia, Minoan Crete, and Egypt came to the fore. Their histories are both well documented and well known. Lesser known is that they were merely hand-me-down cultures based on the religion and technology of the much older civilization of Sumer. And behind their history lurked personages with a desire to rule humanity.

ANCIENT EGYPT

Egypt was ruled by pharaohs who, like other kings, jealously guarded their bloodline. The bloodlines of these Egyptian kings carried the DNA closest to that of the Anunnaki overlords, and it was this DNA that helped them claim their kingship. This custom had been passed down from generation to generation, even though the bloodline of the kings was probably diluted after wars or marriages took place or after the kings bred with commoners.

Although no one in the past had a clear understanding of extraterrestrial life, there are many tantalizing clues hinting at past visitations, found in engravings, jewelry, and statuary. In the small Egyptian village of Nazlet el-Samaan, located near the pyramids and the Giza Plateau, an ancient gate holds in its keystone a carving of a small alien "gray." The figure was carved from a two-and-a-half-ton block of marble, and the doorway's base was fashioned from blocks made from an aggregate of small, round crushed stones and sand, the stones in which have been dubbed "coins" by the villagers.

Few researchers have bothered to visit this poor neighborhood, nestled just beyond the paws of the Sphinx. Villagers claim that the diminutive figure on the gate has been there for as long as anyone remembers, yet they have no explanation or even an oral history concerning it. Lions or cats, long known as symbols of protection, were carved on both sides of the gate. Some say designs on the gate resemble those of the Mayans. Others say it appears to be Phoenician. Recently the doorway was demolished to be replaced by a modern entrance, but the ET carving was hidden away for safekeeping.

As the blocks comprising the doorway were of the same stone and craftsmanship as seen on the Great Pyramid, many others believe it dates back to the pyramid's construction. Until modern times, the area where the village is now located was covered with sand, which may explain why the doorway was so well preserved. This doorway was not an anomaly. There are other ancient doorways in Nazlet el-Samaan with keystones, as well as carved marble stairways and columns, most now broken into pieces. Many of these ancient pieces have been plastered over by the villagers who now live there and who seek to protect the pieces from those who wish to destroy anything that does not fit with official and conventional Egyptian history.

Some Egyptian locals claim that in many areas of Cairo there are entrances to a labyrinth of tunnels running beneath the Giza Plateau. Egyptian authorities continue to discount accounts of such tunnels. In 2009, six Egyptians died of suffocation while digging down to the tunnel system. They had visited the underground tunnels previously but died when their shaft collapsed. Annie DeRiso, news director of *The Common Sense Show* radio program, hosted by Dave Hodges, said she climbed down into the tunnels in 2006. In them, she and others found the same aggregate of sand and round, coinlike-stone that composed the "alien" gate, as well as fragments of glass and the bones of a giant humanoid.

Erhan Altunay, who said he, too, had visited the tunnels under the Giza Plateau, recalled,

> *During one of my visits to Egypt (in 1996, I think) I was guided by a local guide (although I hate to be disturbed by the guides around), and he said he would show something special if I gave him $20. We went to a special area near to the Pyramids but at the bottom of the plateau where the Pyramids are situated. We entered through a hole by paying $5 to the guard there and I was extremely surprised to see a lot of gates opening to endless tunnels. I saw also many statues, as you may see in the pictures. (It is strictly forbidden to take pictures, but you may take some if you pay the guard, as I did.) It seems to me that these tunnels are very old but also used in later times as I saw some sarcophagi which seem to be from very late periods. I've been in Egypt several times but this was the first and the last time I saw those tunnels, as it was forbidden to go there.*

In 1978, ground-penetrating radar was used to map what was described as "an extraordinary subterranean complex beneath the Egyptian pyramids." With the agreement of then president Anwar Sadat, secret excavations were conducted for the next three decades. The excavations were colloquially known as the Giza project. In a private screening many years after the project began, one of the scientists reportedly involved, James J. Hurtak, showed a film of the findings. According to one participant, Paul White, Hurtak's film depicted "a vast megalithic metropolis, 15,000 years old, reaching several levels below the Giza plateau." The film depicted underground waterways, massive chambers, and enormous statues carved in situ, the size of those in the Valley of the Nile. White has called this underground sprawl the City of the Gods, stating, "It is the legacy of a civilisation and a technology beyond our own."

Dr. Hurtak, who commands an international following, compared the discovery of the underground city with its miles of tunnels to contact with an advanced extraterrestrial culture. He said the sprawling city was the work of Atlanteans, which he described as the Fourth Root Culture. To Hurtak, this discovery was unequivocal evidence that all languages, cultures, and religions can be traced back to a single common source, which he called the Parent Civilization.

Adding to the mystery of the Giza underground labyrinth are many other disturbing oddities, which can still be found amid Egyptian ruins. In 2010, seventeen new pyramids were found through the use of NASA satellite imaging. Images found on the ceiling beams of the three-thousand-year-old New Kingdom Temple of Seti at Abydos appear to depict a modern helicopter, submarine, airplane, and hovercraft. The carvings were discovered only recently when a front piece fell from the beam. At Saqqara, Egypt, within the tomb of the sage and philosopher Ptahhotep, author of an extant book of advice to princes, hieroglyphics describe servants offering food to the deceased, who served Pharaoh Djedkare Isesi during his reign, part of the Fifth Dynasty, which lasted from 2494 until 2345 BC. Amazingly, at the bottom is a figure that resembles nothing less than a small alien "gray" as described by so many people who claim UFO contact experiences.

CLASSICAL GREECE

Egypt has long held the fascination of scientists, archaeologists, adventurers, moviemakers, and others, but ancient Greece has always been considered the foundation of Western culture. Greece was settled around 3500 BC. Its name comes from the Greek word *grai-*

koi, referring to the original inhabitants of Dodona, which held the oldest known shrine to the god of thunder, Zeus. Perhaps early inhabitants migrated from the decaying Minoan civilization on Crete.

By the sixth century BC, Greek power had become concentrated in the two city states of Athens and Sparta. After the Greeks twice defeated Persian invasions, Athens became the center of power and during the next few centuries led the nation's advancement in science, the arts, and philosophy.

Exhausted by war against each other, Athens and Sparta declined during the fourth century BC, and the power vacuum was filled by Philip of Macedon, whose son Alexander the Great, born in 356 BC, plundered Greece, then Persia, Syria, Phoenicia, Egypt, Babylonia, and parts of India before dying in Babylon at the age of thirty-three. During his rule of Egypt, he founded the city of Alexandria, which became the ancient world's most important center for scientific and literary studies, as well as for the transmission of esoteric traditions. Alexander was a student of the Greek philosopher Aristotle, who had been taught by Plato, who had learned from Socrates. By 146 BC, Greece was dominated by Rome. Centuries later, after the Roman Empire had been divided into eastern and western halves and the western empire had fallen, Greece became part of the Byzantine Empire.

GREEK GODS FROM EGYPT

A close study of mythology from around the world reveals striking similarities among many cultures and their beliefs in ancient gods. Legends from different peoples living in all corners of the Earth seem to tell essentially the same story—in the distant past, certain individuals with "godlike" powers molded mankind into a civilized state following a period of cataclysmic upheaval.

While there is no agreement on the specific connections among the "gods," due to the large amount of incidental material that has grown up around the stories, a general comparison of mythologies demonstrates common features that appear to go beyond coincidence and reveal the striking similarities among all versions of the ancient "gods." The names changed with different languages, but the characteristics remained the same.

ROLE	SUMERIAN	EGYPTIAN	GREEK	ROMAN
Heavenly Father	Anu	Amen-Ra	Cronos	Saturn
Heavenly Mother	Antu	Mut	Hera	Juno
Earth Lord	Enlil	Set	Zeus	Jupiter
Earth Mother	Ninhursag	Isis	Athena	Minerva
Earth Brother/Builder	Enki	Osiris	Apollo	Vulcan
Warrior Rival	Marduk	Horus	Ares	Mars
Underworld Lord	Nergal	Anubis	Hades	Pluto
Provider of Love	Inanna	Hathor	Aphrodite	Venus
Facilitator of the Gods	Ninurta	Thoth	Hermes	Mercury

It is important to understand that early on the Sumerians never considered, nor referred to, the beings who brought them knowledge as "gods." This was a later interpretation by the Romans and Greeks, who fashioned their own gods after the earlier traditions of the Egyptians and earlier civilizations.

All references to these gods carry similar attributes, which correspond to other worlds beyond the Earth and also convey the idea of influences over humanity as found in astrology, the origin of which is so ancient as to be unknown.

The Greek Herodotus, the "father of history," has been proven truthful in his accounts. The Scythian city Gelonus was a privileged trading partner to the Greeks until conquered by Alexander. Herodotus's description of this population center as being a thousand times larger than Troy was widely disbelieved until it was rediscovered in 1975.

Herodotus made it quite clear that the Greek gods, and the rites attributed to them, all came from Egypt, conquered by Alexander in 332 BC. The Egyptian gods simply assumed new names when translated into the Greek language. One clear example is the Greek term for their pantheon of gods, the Titans, who ruled the earth prior to an insurrection. The ruler of the Titans was Cronos, who has been identified as the Anunnaki Anu. He was succeeded by his son Zeus, who has been compared to the Sumerian overlord Enlil. Furthermore, the Titans have always been associated with the various planets, indicating a strong connection to the heavens, and in the Sumerian cuneiform tablets, the word for "those who live in the heavens" is Ti-ta-an.

Herodotus also noted the extreme longevity of ancient Egyptian rulers and also wrote that prior to eleven thousand years ago living "gods" had resided among the humans. "Thus far I have spoken on the authority of the Egyptians and their priests. They declare that from their first king to this last-mentioned monarch, the priest of Vulcan, was a period of three hundred and forty-one generations; such, at least, they say, was the number both of their kings, and of their high-priests, during this interval," wrote Herodotus in Book 2 of his *Histories*. "Now three hundred generations of men make ten thousand years, three generations filling up the century. . . . However, in the times anterior to [the human kings] it was otherwise; then Egypt had gods for its rulers, who dwelt upon the earth with men, one being always supreme above the rest. The last of these was Horus, the son of Osiris, called by the Greeks Apollo." As indicated in the comparison chart, Osiris was the Egyptian name for the Anunnaki god Enki, meaning that his son, Horus, would have been Marduk to the Sumerians and Ares to the Greeks, who was the god of war. Is it just coincidence that Marduk began the great civil war between the Anunnaki?

Close to twenty ancient buildings in southern Greece look like pyramids and show evidence of Egyptian influence. One impressive pyramid is located near the eastern Peloponnesian village of Hellenikon in Argolis, but for the most part, the structures are largely ruins. Some speculate that in the past the edifices were torn down and used as construction materials for churches and for lime production.

It appears that the Greek pyramids, like the Great Pyramid, were aligned with heavenly bodies. In the 1990s, archaeologists with the Archaeological Museum of Nauplion found the astronomical orientation of the long entrance corridor of the Hellenikon pyramid probably aligned with Orion's Belt between the years 2400–2000 BC. By measuring accumulated radiation using a method called thermoluminescence, archaeologists were able to date scrapings back past 3,000 BC, making them older than similar Egyptian structures.

Athletes and musicians gathered every few years in the Greek city of Delphi to compete in the Pythian Games, which may have begun even earlier than the Olympics, which according to tradition began in 776 BC. Delphi was also home to the Oracle of Delphi, a famed figure in classical Greek mythology. There are mysterious connections between this sacred site and other sites in Greece, such as the Acropolis of Athens, where the Parthenon is located.

In *Odyssey of the Gods*, an account of extraterrestrial contact in ancient Greece, Erich von Däniken writes of an experience with Theophanias Manias, a Greek Air Force officer who had studied topography at the National Technical University of Athens.

> He [Manias] took a pair of compasses, placed the point on Delphi and drew a circle through the Acropolis. Strange to say, the circumference of the circle also touched Argos and Olympia. These places were equal distances from each other. A strange coincidence, thought Colonel Manias, and then placed the compass point on Knossos at Crete. The circumference of this circle also touched Sparta and Epidaurus— strange! Colonel Manias continued. When the center was Delos, Thebes and Izmir lay on the circumference; when

the center was Paros, it was Knossos and Chalcis; when the
center was Sparta, Mycenae and the oracle site of Trofonion
were on the circumference.

Both Manias and von Daniken saw in these configurations a repetition of the previously described golden ratio indicating the influence of ancient knowledge. "In ancient Greece many such triangles can be drawn, and always with two proportions in regard to the length of their sides," noted von Daniken. "Such triangles joining cult sites cannot just arise by chance."

Maurice Chatelain has written of sacred sites connected with a perfection that could only have been accomplished from the vantage point of outer space. He described thirteen mystical sites within a 450-mile radius of the long-venerated Greek island of Delos connected by straight lines to produce a perfect Maltese Cross, later the emblem of the Knights Templar. Delos has always been considered one of ancient Greece's most holy sites, although no one has ever known exactly why. In *Our Ancestors Came from Outer Space*, Chatelain wrote, "What interests us now is how and why such a gigantic pattern was marked on the Aegean and surrounding lands. I do not believe that even today's land surveyors could so precisely mark such a gigantic figure of over 360 miles jumping from island to island and stretching over sea and mountains. Except from high up in the air this Maltese Cross would not be visible."

Hesiod, a Greek poet who lived about 700 BC, wrote extensively of the gods in his *Theogony*, a synthesis of stories concerning the Greek gods. He wrote of conflicts and wars, even between Zeus (Enlil in Sumerian) and his father Cronos (the sky god Anu in Sumerian). He may have been describing thunderous Anunnaki sky god Enlil and his more beneficent half-brother Enki when he wrote, "The glowing Sun never looks upon them with his beams, neither as he goes up into heaven, nor as he comes down from heaven. And the former of them roams peacefully over the earth and the sea's broad back and is kindly to men; but the other has a heart of iron, and his spirit within him is pitiless as bronze: whomsoever of men he has once seized he holds fast: and he is hateful even to the deathless gods."

In writing of the wars between the gods, Hesiod spoke of their flying chariots and may have even described ancient atomic weapons when he wrote, "And flame shot forth from the thunder-stricken lord in the dim rugged glens of the mount, when he was smitten. A great part of huge earth was scorched by the terrible vapour and melted as tin melts when heated by men's art in channeled crucibles; or as iron, which is hardest of all things, is softened by glowing fire in mountain glens and melts in the divine earth through the strength of Hephaestus. Even so, then, the earth melted in the glow of the blazing fire." Hesiod goes to some length to detail the many wives of Zeus and the spreading of his bloodline following the wars of the gods.

Many centuries after Hesiod, Plato wrote in the *Statesman* that Earth's poles shifted after the gods left the Earth.

> *In the fulness of time, when the change was to take place, and the earth-born race had all perished, and every soul had completed its proper cycle of births and been sown in the earth her appointed number of times, the pilot of the universe let the helm go, and retired to his place of view; and then Fate and innate desire reversed the motion of the world. Then also all the inferior deities who share the rule of the supreme power, being informed of what was happening, let go the parts of the world which were under their control. And the world turning round with a sudden shock, being impelled in an opposite direction from beginning to end, was shaken by a mighty earthquake, which wrought a new destruction of all manner of animals.*

The classical Greeks also wrote of leaders and rulers who, much like the Anunnaki, were the offspring of humans and gods. In the oldest telling of the story of Jason and the Argonauts, Pindar's Pythian Ode number 4, eleven adventurers, including Jason, all were said to have been descendants from the ancient gods.

Beyond the overlaps between Sumerian and Greek mythology and the influence the Greeks have had on our culture, it's possible that the Greeks and their gods are affecting us in ways we might never have imagined. Recently, a man known pseudonymously as Ted Connors, who worked with a Department of Defense subcontracting firm in Alabama, recounted how one morning in 2007 he saw a large metallic hubcap next to a tree with long wires stretching upward. Suddenly the object rose and disappeared in midair.

Connors was among several people who were reporting seeing such "spider drones." Later in the year, Connors found himself having disturbing dreams about his encounter. When he revisited the tree, he found that it had been cut down. As he sat nearby contemplating, he began to feel an electrostatic charge throughout his body and started to receive what he thought were telepathic messages from beings from another planet. They first explained that the object Connors saw was a drone probing Earth for information. They said they were from a planet called Oltissis, the twenty-third planet in their star system, one that has four moons. The probe came through a "tear" in time and space, which was repaired upon its return. Connors was told that our interpretation of time and space is incorrect. "All is infinite," they explained, adding that we would not understand their "ethos," a Greek word for the character or nature of a people.

As *ethos* is derived from the Greek and Oltissis sounds Greek, Connors wrote, "My feeling is these [telepathic beings] are the ancient Greeks. These [from Oltissis] are the ones who came here before Earth's historic timeline. They are the Greek gods."

Connors's tale might be written off as a delusion or fabrication, except for a further development. Because he connected his experience to the Greek gods, Connors visited a local library for a book on ancient Greece and stumbled across one entitled *Ancient Greek Gods and Lore Revisited*. It was copyrighted 1962 and was by an author whose name Connors remembers as Fredrico Ionnides. In this book he said he found three references to Oltissis. Apparently one reference mentioned Oltissis as a historic Greek pleasure palace. He said he left the book on his car seat, as he intended to read it when he had time.

Two days later, Connors said he was surprised to be called into his boss's office. He was even more surprised to find two men there who presented identification showing they were from the Department of Homeland Security (DHS) and the National Security Agency (NSA). The pair asked him about the library book he had obtained and said curtly, "We need to have that book." When asked why, the one from DHS replied it was a national security matter and asked if Connors was aware of the PATRIOT Act.

Connors's boss said brusquely, "Go get the book!" He immediately retrieved the book from his car and turned it over to the two men, asking, "How will I get the book back?"

"We will contact you," they replied.

Connors was flabbergasted and never thought to ask the men how they knew he had checked out this book from the library or why a book on ancient Greek gods would have any application to national security. Since he had mentioned the book's title in an e-mail to a friend, Connors suspected the agents learned of it through e-mail interception, and he suspected that the Greek god connection, whatever it may be, is a serious matter to certain federal authorities. "If there is one thing I'm sure of at this point in time [it] is that—and this is what I got from the first message I received—is that this is very important to mankind—not to governments—not to leaders—not to power brokers—but to mankind," he told journalist Linda Moulton Howe.

John Coleman, a veteran best-selling conspiracy author and a self-proclaimed former MI6 agent, provided connective tissue bringing the tales of Greek gods right up to date. In his book on the Tavistock Institute of Human Relations, Coleman said in modern America a "closely knit group of social psychologists, pollsters and media manipulators" is presided over by an elite group of powerful patrons, known as the Committee of 300 or, more significantly, "the Gods of Olympus."

POWER PASSES TO ROME

After the Greeks came the Romans. The Roman civilization is said to have been founded in 753 BC by Romulus and Remus, the twin sons of the Trojan leader Aeneas, who fled to Italy with other refugees following the fall of Troy in modern-day Turkey. It was said Aeneas was the son of the Greek goddess Aphrodite, and with his death, at his mother's request, he was deified as the god Jupiter Indiges. Venus, the goddess of beauty, sex, fertility, and victory, was the Roman counterpart of Aphrodite. Her Anunnaki counterpart would have been Inanna. Such connections indicate the ongoing cult worship that began in Sumer and then passed through Egypt and Greece.

About 80 BC, General Lucius Cornelius Sulla Felix, better known simply as Sulla, founded a college in Rome dedicated to the Egyptian goddess Isis. However, Isis worship was discouraged by the Roman consuls, who did not want to share control over the population. The worship of Isis at Rome continued to be suppressed by a succession of decrees until the reign of Caligula.

In 212 BC, a different man, Gaius Sulla, an ardent worshipper of Apollo, organized the first of the annual Ludi Apollinares, or Games of Apollo, honoring the Greek god whose counterparts were Osiris and Enki. The later warlord, Sulla Felix, was known to wear a small golden image of Apollo into battle. In many ways, Roman culture was merely the latest incarnation of Sumer, bringing with it many of the older centralized religious and political structures.

The Roman Empire was formed in 27 BC after Julius Caesar's nephew Octavian (Caesar Augustus) had emerged victorious from a series of ruinous civil wars, first primarily between Julius Caesar and his former ally Pompey, and then between Octavian and his former ally Mark Antony. Before his assassination in 44 BC by a group of senators hoping to restore the republic, Julius Caesar had seen to it that his name became so popular that it was used as a title for subsequent rulers; soon the title Caesar evolved from being a family name of the Julian clan of Rome to a title held by a Roman emperor. The name has lived on in the German word *kaiser* and the Russian title czar.

At the height of its power in about AD 117, the empire commanded most of the Western world. Like Greece and the United States, Rome began as a democratic republic but evolved into a voracious and aggressive empire ruled by a succession of tyrannical Caesars, its people distracted by bread and circuses—government-sponsored free food and weekly gladiatorial spectacles in the various coliseums.

However, after the death (possibly another assassination) of the last pagan emperor, Julian the Apostate, the true ruling power was the Roman Church, collector of tithes and lender of money to the government. As the power of the later Roman state rested on the power of the Church, it is instructive to review the rise of Christianity.

In the time of Jesus of Nazareth, Jews in Palestine were fragmented among the clerical and politically powerful Pharisees, the pious Sadducees, and the unconventional Essenes. Moreover, the interpretations of the Old Testament found in the Dead Sea Scrolls illuminate the ways in which the interpretations of James and the Jerusalem Christians devoted to the teachings of Jesus differed from those of Paul and his followers outside Palestine. It is interesting to note that in the Scriptures Jesus condemned both the Pharisees and Sadducees but pointedly ignored the Essenes, leading many to believe he favored the Essene philosophies.

As leaders of the Jerusalem church, Jesus's brother James and Mary Magdalene were at odds with Paul, who was bringing his version of Christianity to the gentiles to the north. There were immense squabbles over the most minute issues. In Galatians 5:12, Paul had become so exasperated with a continuing argument over circumcision that he expressed the hope that those initiating the controversy would emasculate themselves.

Bible scholar and former intelligence analyst Patricia G. Eddy wrote, "The first Jewish Christians believed that obeying all of the stringent Jewish religious laws, including circumcision and eating only Kosher food, were necessary for salvation." Yet according to Eddy, "Paul preached that salvation could be attained through faith and that the Jewish religious laws should not be allowed to impede people from becoming Christians. Paul's view eventually won out, as more and more gentiles converted to Christianity. By the third century, they outnumbered the Jewish Christians by a large margin, defined Christianity according to Paul's theology, and began castigating the original Jewish Christians as heretics."

By the middle of the second century, Irenaeus, the Bishop of Lyons, was condemning the followers of Jesus and James as heretics. These followers were known as Nazarenes, or the poor. The author Laurence Gardner noted that Irenaeus complained that these Nazarenes "reject the Pauline epistles and they reject the apostle Paul, calling him an apostate [rejecter] of the Law . . . the Nazarenes . . . denounced Paul as a 'renegade' and a 'false apostle,' claiming that his 'idolatrous writings' should be 'rejected altogether.'"

Elaine Pagels wrote that "diverse forms of Christianity flourished in the early years of the Christian movement. Hundreds of rival teachers all claimed to teach the 'true doctrine of Christ' and denounced one another as frauds. Christians in churches scattered from Asia Minor to Greece, Jerusalem, and Rome split into factions, arguing over church leadership. All claimed to represent 'the authentic tradition.' "

After becoming an established institution, the Roman Church quickly gained wealth and power. It derived a great deal of power from collecting tithes and lending money to the government. "Far above the wrangling in the local churches sat the Roman Church, unconcerned, untroubled, and probably, uncomprehending," Patricia Eddy wrote, adding that the Church at this time was primarily concentrating on missionary work in Europe, an activity which paid unexpected benefits. "Unwittingly, the Christianization of these heathen ultimately saved the Roman Church because the barbarians and their priests regarded the Roman Church as the authority for their religious beliefs. When the barbarians overran Rome, the Roman Church was spared. . . ."

Though spared by the barbarians, the Church still had to contend with a variety of sects, all with their own version of Christianity. Church control was maintained predominantly by fear of God's wrath as evoked by the priesthood. If that failed, there was always force.

And all of the Church's machinations were said to be supported by biblical scripture, which had been edited numerous times to eliminate certain messages that contradicted Church dogma. Editing, or redactions, as they are euphemistically called, over the years has led to errors in our translations of the Bible, which in turn have led some to misunderstandings over modern terms, such as *flight*, or when it came to secret codes hidden within its language. The Essenes of Jesus's time produced literature containing their own intricate codes and allegories to protect their knowledge from the uninitiated as well as from the Roman authorities. For example, when writing about the Romans, they used the term *Kittim*, but this word was often misinterpreted to refer to the ancient Chaldeans of Mesopotamia or some of the Greek islands.

In addition, according to C. L. Turnage, some Bible codes and symbols referred to multiple deities. "These coded references pointed the way toward an understanding that such beings were the gods, or Elohim, of the Bible, whose worship began in Sumer, and who ultimately originated on another world."

The conflicts both within and outside of Christianity were settled by the Roman emperor Constantine in a compromise to gain power. "Apart from various cultic beliefs, the Romans had worshipped the Emperors in their capacity as gods descended from others like Neptune and Jupiter," explained author Laurence Gardner. "At the Council of Arles in 314, Constantine retained his own divine status by introducing the omnipotent God of the Christians as his personal sponsor. He then dealt with the anomalies of doctrine by replacing certain aspects of Christian ritual with the familiar pagan traditions of sun worship, together with other teachings of Syrian and Persian origin. In short, the new religion of the Roman Church was constructed as a 'hybrid' to appease all influential factions. By this means, Constantine looked towards a common and unified 'world' religion—Catholic meaning *universal*—with himself at its head."

Once Christianity became the accepted religion of the empire, pagan holidays were expropriated. Saturnalia, for example, was the winter festival in honor of the god Saturn, the equivalent of the Sumerian god of the heavens, Anu, and the Egyptian god Amen-Ra (known to the Greeks as Cronos). Saturnalia was merely a latter-day extension of the Greek festival of Kronia, a remembrance of the "Golden Days" when Cronos ruled the world. By the end of the republic, it had evolved into a gay time of gift-giving, lighting candles, feasting, and general frivolities for the entire population, including slaves. But when Christianity arrived, the Roman rulers found it difficult to stamp out this holiday, so the Church simply announced that it was celebrating the birth of Jesus Christ, an observance that has been carried forward to this day as Christ Mass, or Christmas.

The church's co-optation of Christianity was sealed at the Council of Nicaea in AD 325. During the council, the priest Arius was beaten and tossed out because he and his followers believed that only God created everything and therefore Jesus was not God but simply a heavenly inspired teacher. His followers, the Arians, were banished from the Church, and the Nicene Creed was established, which formally defined God as a deity of three equal and coexisting parts—the Father, Son, and Holy Spirit, or Holy Ghost.

One year later, Constantine ordered the confiscation and destruction of all works that questioned the newly constructed orthodoxy and then opened the Lateran Palace, which was a precursor of the Vatican, to the Bishop of Rome. In 331, the emperor ordered new copies made of Christian texts, most of which had been lost or destroyed during the previous persecutions. The resulting editing included alterations that have become the foundation of modern Christianity.

BOOK BURNING

Although history lavishes praise on the Greek and Roman empires for the advances they brought in military strategies, construction, and sanitation, scant attention has been paid to the destruction of ancient sacred sites and indigenous cultures as these empires spread across the world.

Ancient knowledge and history were forgotten by the masses, often because the ruling classes destroyed libraries and historical records. Only a few of Homer's poems survived the destruction of his works by the Greek tyrant Pisistratus in Athens. Nothing survived the destruction of the Egyptian library in the Temple of Ptah in Memphis. Likewise, an estimated two hundred thousand volumes of priceless works disappeared with the destruction of the library of Pergamum in Asia Minor.

When the Romans leveled the city of Carthage in their drive for world conquest, they destroyed a library said to have contained more than five hundred thousand volumes. Then came Julius Caesar, whose war against Egypt resulted in the loss of the great library at Alexandria, considered the greatest collection of books in antiquity. With the loss of the Serapeum and the Bruchion branches of that library, a total of up to seven hundred thousand volumes of accumulated knowledge went up in flames.

European libraries also suffered under the Romans and later from zealous Christians. Between the sacking of Constantinople by Crusaders in 1204 and the Catholic Inquisition (1137–1825), an inestimable number of ancient works were irretrievably lost.

Collections in Asia fared little better, as Emperor Ch'in Shih Huang Ti ordered all histories of ancient China burned just before he died in 210 BC.

"Because of these tragedies we have to depend on disconnected fragments, casual passages and meager accounts," lamented Australian author Andrew Tomas. "Our distant past is a vacuum filled at random with tablets, parchments, statues, paintings, and various artifacts. The history of science would appear totally different were the book collection of Alexandria intact today."

Always this destruction was done in the name of God or the people. In Rome, the official slogan was *Senatus populus quis Romanus*, meaning the Senate (government) and the Roman people are one, or synonymous. It was an early and eerie forerunner of the German Nazi slogan *Ein Volk, Ein Reich, Ein Führer*, or One people, one Empire, one Leader.

The book burning of the Nazis is well known, but such destruction of knowledge did not stop with the end of World War II.

In Iraq, the central al-Awqaf Library, founded in 1920, contained 45,000 rare books and more than 6,000 documents from the Ottoman Empire. At the onset of the U.S. invasion, arsonists set fire to the building in April 2003. Although the staff managed to save 5,250 items, including a collection of older Korans, all else was lost. The fire spread, destroying all 175,000 books and manuscripts at the library of the University of Baghdad's College of Art. The entire library at the University of Basra was reduced to ash, and the Central Public Library in Basra lost 100 percent of its collection. Also lost in the invasion and subsequent occupation were volumes from the Iraqi National Library as well as those at Bayt al-Hikma, the Central Library of the University of Mosul, and others. According to Fernando Báez, director of Venezuela's National Library and author of *A Universal History of the Destruction of Books*, almost one million books and ten million priceless documents have been destroyed, lost, or stolen throughout Iraq since 2003. Báez described the losses as "the biggest cultural disaster since the descendants of Genghis Khan destroyed Baghdad in 1258."

LOST IN TRANSLATION

All this destruction of human origins and history has led to gaping holes in humankind's true history, leading in turn to confusion due to mistranslations, misinterpretations, and name changes within religious documents, which may be ascribed simply to the differences among languages and cultures or to deliberate obfuscation.

Rabbi Dovid Bendory, rabbinic director for Jews for the Preservation of Firearms Ownership (JPFO), is just one of the more recent researchers who have found major misunderstandings based on mistranslations of the Bible. In a 2012 commentary, Rabbi Bendory explained that one of the most commonly recognized lines of the Ten Commandments, "Thou shall not kill," is a mistranslation of the Hebrew *Lo tirtzach*, which actually means "Do not murder." He said this term has "a clear and unequivocal meaning," one that "forever changed the course of all human history," as both Jews and Christians have been plagued with guilt and remorse over killing in wars, by accident, or self-defense.

"There is a world of difference between killing and murder," he explained. "Can we possibly estimate the numbers of lives that have been lost by foolish pacifism rather than righteous defense in the face of evil?"

Mauro Biglino also has challenged interpretations and translations of the Bible. Biglino, formerly an Italian translator for the religious publishing house San Paolo Editors, has been a scholar of religious history and a student of ancient Hebrew for more than thirty years. Biglino was fired from his position as a translator of Vatican material after publishing a book in 2012 in which he claimed that extraterrestrials guided the development of humankind. He said this was confirmed by a careful and literal translation of the original Hebrew Bible.

In his original work, *The Book That Will Forever Change Our Ideas About the Bible*, now released as *There Is No God in the Bible*, Biglino pointed to the Old Testament book of Deuteronomy (1:28) in which scouts reported to Moses of encountering giants and great cities in the sky inhabited by the "sons of the Anakims." Current Bible dictionaries fail to explain the Anakims. Yet several researchers connect the Anakim to the Nephilim, the oversize hybrid offspring of the sons of gods and the daughters of men mentioned in Genesis 6:4. Large bones and tools found all over the world, though little publicized, attest to the existence once of a race of giants. The biblical story of David and Goliath comes to mind.

According to Biglino, like the Nephilim, angels in the Bible are described only by their function as messengers rather than their physical nature. He said this is because the ancient scribes were writing about physical beings whose nature was obvious to the people of that time who had encountered them. They ate, drank, slept, and even washed themselves, hardly the activities of nonphysical beings. Only in later centuries, when such face-to-face contact was lost, were these messengers transformed into metaphysical entities.

Biglino noted that the Israelites of the Old Testament obviously did not see their god as a transcendent and unique entity, and their relationship with him was not viewed as unavoidable. "The whole history of Israel is full of betrayals, abandonment, cults dedicated to other deities, also called *Elohìms*, all concrete, all present like the Elohìm leading Israel and with whom there had been this alliance: Jews would serve him and he would help them conquer the land and become a nation. This same Elohìm repeatedly calls himself jealous, and we wonder: how can one be jealous of a partner if there are no rivals in the relationship?" Biglino also compared the original Ten Commandments of Yahweh as written in Hebrew to the modern, sanitized, and Christianized version and found little in common.

In addition to the account of Ezekiel and his fiery flying saucer, well covered in other sources and found to accurately describe a subspace vehicle by a NASA scientist, Biglino described the experiences of other biblical figures. These include Elisha and the prophet Elijah, whose name, Eliyahu, means "My God is El." In II Kings 2:10–11, it is clear that Elijah has foreknowledge that he would be taken, and shortly he was pulled up into the heavens in a whirlwind by a "chariot of fire." For three days, his countrymen looked for him but failed to find any sign of him. Biglino has pointed out that: "This was an announced event, known in advance by the involved parties and therefore programmed by the *Elohìms* who had decided to take with them this representative of theirs. One does not search for three days, laboring over hills and dales, for someone who has been kidnapped just in a vision or a dream!" Enoch, the father of Methuselah, who reportedly lived 365 years, was also taken up to heaven by his god.

Could these accounts actually be of alien abductions? Biglino has said that the prophet Zechariah encountered an *efahm,* interpreted as a flying roll or cylinder, similar to some UFOs reported today. He compares such biblical experiences with the flying machines of the Sumerian Anunnaki.

The Bible's Psalm 82 describes God in assembly with other gods. Biglino viewed this as a description of a meeting between the ancient gods, or Elohims, and their superiors. Here they are warned about bringing arrogance to their positions over humans, as well as reminded that they, too, have finite, although lengthy, life spans. Biglino has pointed out that the connection is clear and simple: "The Elohims die like all ADAMS! It comes as no surprise to anyone who speculates that ANUNNAKI/ELOHIMS could have a long life—incredibly long for earthly beings, as it was measured on Nibiru's orbital cycles—but that, as people made of flesh and blood, they too were meant to die. Simply astonishing is the fact that the Bible itself says so![emphases in the original]." Mauro Biglino's conclusion was that we have worshipped the extraterrestrials who have come to our planet as gods, and the original recognition of these multiple gods has, over the years, been reduced to one god. This interpretation does not necessarily deny the existence of an omniscient universal creator God.

Biglino is not alone in believing that extraterrestrials are mentioned in the Bible. In 2003, Monsignor Corrado Balducci, a Vatican spokesman on the UFO issue, stated that not believing in "UFOs and the presence of other living beings is a sin. Their existence is not only proven by about a million witnesses, including those of many atheist scientists, but it is also confirmed by some passages of the Scripture that clarify some points about their presence."

This vision by the Catholic Church was supported by José Gabriel Funes, an Argentinean Jesuit and director of the Vatican Observatory. In a 2008 interview, Father Funes stated, "It is possible to believe in God and in extraterrestrials. The existence of other worlds and other life, even more evolved than ours, can be accepted without this interfering in the discussion of the faith of creation, the incarnation, the redemption. . . . As a multiplicity of creatures exist on earth, so there could be other beings, also intelligent, created by God. This does not contrast with our faith because we cannot put limits on the creative freedom of God."

The claims of José Funes and Mauro Biglino may seem outrageous to some. Yet their interpretation of the Bible is similar to the recent translations of Sumerian glyphs and ancient Hebrew. According to one reviewer of Biglino's work, "Many translators have come up with parallel results. Mr. Biglino brings validity to the former researchers by sharing it with us. These are the translations that come through when you use the correct database to transcribe from. Researchers that worked with Michael Heiser [that critic of Zecharia Sitchin] are government funded and they use a newer base to translate with, which is preposterous to do so, due to the changing meanings and subsets of civilizations over time. The originals were hundreds if not thousands of years older than the database that Heiser's group was translating with. Further, academics wouldn't be allowed to put their stamp of approval on any work they found that's related to extraterrestrials, due to the socioeconomic upheaval it could cause. That very thing must be avoided at all costs, as far as they are concerned. Our government and the people behind the scenes are not receptive to anything other than what they've mandated. History is written by the victors, and rarely does the truth match what the victors write about. If the government allowed the truth, then billions of history, medical, financial, etc. books would need to be corrected."

It is little wonder that learned men down through the ages have misunderstood the truths lying behind the gods of legend and myth? "Is it any wonder that 'science' can't find any evidence for ancient aliens, or lost knowledge?" asked author Philip Coppens, a prolific writer who has made a study of old legends and secret societies throughout his life. If historians have been misled concerning true history, then perhaps it is time we consider that much of modern man's entire worldview has been misguided.

PART III

THE MIDDLE AGES

The only thing new in the world is the history you don't know.

—HARRY S. TRUMAN

THE DARK AGES WAS A TIME OF GREAT INSTABILITY AND IGNO-rance in the Western world. It dragged on from approximately AD 500 until the Renaissance. Those living with the luxuries of the twenty-first century have largely forgotten that prior to the year 1900 the vast majority of people in the world were illiterate, had no indoor plumbing, and lived at the whim of their rulers.

Only remnants of Greece and Rome's knowledge had been preserved by a few Christian monks in Ireland, Italy, France, and Britain. If not for these monks, along with libraries in the Muslim countries, no knowledge whatsoever would have been preserved for us today.

The Roman Church controlled every aspect of life. To speak against the Church opened one to censorship, excommunication, or even death. The suffocation of free thinking led to the growth of secret societies and sects, many of which began in biblical times and vied with one another for control over ancient secrets. Much like the later Invisible College of Elizabethan times, these societies collec-tively were considered mystery schools, reservoirs of esoteric knowl-edge that was largely incomprehensible and thus fear-inspiring to the general public. Their literature was carefully constructed to both conceal and reveal some of their knowledge.

One such repository of ancient knowledge was the Sumerian "Table of Destiny," thought to be the same as the Tables of Testi-mony mentioned in Exodus 31:18, as other Bible verses—Exodus 24:12 and 25:16—make it clear that these tables are not the Ten Commandments. British author Laurence Gardner believed this ancient archive may be the legendary Emerald Tablet of Thoth-Hermes. This tablet, considered one of the most ancient and secret of writings, is claimed to be the work of Hermes Trismegistus

(Hermes the Thrice-Greatest), a composite character of the Greek god Hermes and the Egyptian god Thoth, called Ninurta in ancient Sumer. Thoth/Ninurta was said to be a survivor of Atlantis who passed along antediluvian knowledge to a son of Noah—Ham.

"He was the essential founder of the esoteric and arcane 'underground stream' which flowed through the ages," stated Gardner, "and his Greek name, Hermes, was directly related to the science of pyramid construction, deriving from the word *herma*, which relates to a 'pile of stones.' Indeed, the Great Pyramid is sometimes called 'the Sanctuary of Thoth.'"

This tablet of knowledge was passed from ancient Sumer to Egypt and on to Greek and Roman masters such as Homer, Virgil, Pythagoras, Plato, and Ovid. In the Middle Ages and onward, it was passed through such secret societies as the Rosicrucians and Knights Templar and on to the Freemasons.

But such ancient knowledge had to be kept secret in the ages following the collapse of the Roman Empire. Christianity had gained absolute supremacy in the Western world, and until the Great Schism and the fall of Constantinople to the Muslim Ottoman Empire in 1453, the Roman Church stood as the ultimate authority in the Western world. Through the lending of both its money and blessings, the Vatican dominated kings and queens and controlled the lives of ordinary citizens through fear of excommunication and its infamous Inquisition.

Only the clergy and aristocracy could read and write, and the smaller factions of Christianity were so fractious that they held little power. With the crusaders holding the Holy Land of the Middle East, the unchallenged power of the Church became further centralized and all-powerful. The fact that most kings and queens had borrowed money from the Vatican only added to their subservience. Only in Scotland, where King Robert the Bruce was excommunicated in 1306 and only when Martin Luther's Ninety-five Theses were made public in 1517 and Henry VIII established the breakaway Church of England in 1534 was the power of Catholicism challenged.

KNIGHTS TEMPLAR

Earlier, a gnostic group called Cathars, mostly located in southern France, had proved to be a problem for the Church, as they claimed to possess knowledge concerning Mary Magdalene and her descendants that ran counter to Rome's teachings. Known as the "pure ones" due to the conviction that their beliefs were purer than those of the Roman Church, the Cathars claimed that their knowledge had been passed along by refugees from Palestine who had fled the Roman invasion of AD 70. Beginning in 1209, French king Philip II, at the orders of Pope Innocent III, launched the Albigensian Crusade in an attempt to wipe out the Cathars, considered the most serious challenge to the Catholic Church to that date. Until very recently, little was known of the Cathars because the Roman Church had destroyed any material favorable to them.

To avoid annihilation, many Cathars simply blended into the populace. In later years, French leaders from Cathar families considered a religious crusade to take the Holy Land, and particularly Jerusalem, as a convenient excuse to search for verification of the Cathar traditions. Peter the Hermit—generally considered to be instrumental in promoting the First Crusade, along with Saint Bernard—was a personal tutor to the Crusade's leader, Godfrey de Bouillon, himself a member of a Cathar family and believed by some to be the founder of Freemasonry.

The First Crusade led to the creation of societies that used secrecy as protection from the Roman Church, which began protecting its theology by increasingly violent means. By many recent accounts, at least one group of Crusaders brought back more than just heresy—they also came back with hard evidence of error and

duplicity in Church dogma. In 1307, the Church tried to exter-
minate this group, proclaimed as heretics and blasphemers. They
were the Knights Templar, whose traditions live on today within
Freemasonry.

This religious-military knighthood, originally called The Order
of the Poor Knights of Christ and of the Temple of Solomon, was
formed in 1118 when nine French Crusaders appeared before King
Baldwin of Jerusalem and asked to be allowed to protect pilgrims
traveling to the Holy Land. They also asked permission to stay in
the ruins of Solomon's Temple, which had later been the palace of
King Herod. These knights were led by Hugh de Payens, a nobleman in the service of his cousin, Hughes, Count of Champagne,
and André de Montbard, the uncle of Bernard of Clairvaux, later
known as the Cistercian Saint Bernard. All were from families connected to the Cathars. Authors Lynn Picknett and Clive Prince,
experts on the Knights Templar, wrote, "Payens and his nine com-
panions all came from either Champagne or the Languedoc, and
included the Count of Provence, and it is quite apparent that they
went to the Holy Land with a specific mission in mind." Provence
lies adjacent to the Languedoc region of southern France and includes Marseilles, where by tradition Mary Magdalene arrived with
other Palestinian refugees following the crucifixion of Jesus Christ.
It was in Provence that the knights hid the treasure of both wealth
and knowledge they uncovered in Jerusalem.

Once in Jerusalem, King Baldwin, a brother of de Bouillon,
granted the knights' request, and the order was formed, becoming
known as the Knights of the Temple, soon shortened to Knights
Templar. For nine years, the Knights Templar excavated under the
palace of King Herod, which had been built on top of the ruins of
the temple built by King Solomon nearly a thousand years before
Christ. Some researchers state that Solomon's Temple was merely
a carbon copy of a Sumerian temple dedicated to the god Ninurta
and constructed almost a thousand years earlier.

Much of Solomon's treasure—which included not only much gold, silver, and precious gems but also texts, scrolls, and tablets bearing the ancient knowledge of the gods—had been buried there by Jews to protect it from looting Romans during the Jewish Revolt of AD 66. According to the *Histories*, a history of Rome written by Tacitus in AD 109, Pompey the Great was shocked when he entered Solomon's Temple in 63 BC only to find "the sanctuary was empty and the Holy of Holies untenanted."

However, after the fall of Jerusalem in AD 70, the Romans managed to cart off a portion of the treasure left behind to prevent further searching. They took it to Rome as war booty. The remainder, probably the most sacred tablets and scrolls, was secured in the catacombs under the temple and later forgotten by authorities when Herod's palace was built.

Knowledge of this undiscovered treasure passed into southern France in AD 410, when a former Roman commander, Alaric, led his Gothic army in sacking Rome. The secrets of Solomon's Treasure were taken to the homeland of the Goths, the Languedoc region in the foothills of the Pyrenees Mountains in southern France. It was from here that the French Cathars learned of the treasure still buried in Jerusalem. This information was passed through Cathari families and led to the fomenting of the First Crusade.

With the return of the Knights Templar, Solomon's Treasure was once again reunited with the portion taken from Rome by Alaric. It remained hidden, with only bits of the ancient knowledge being used by secret societies, such as the Rosicrucians, Freemasons, the Bavarian Illuminati, and the elusive Priory of Sion, until the entire treasure hoard was taken by the German Nazis in early 1944.

In addition to secrets involving architecture, medicine, and instruments such as magnetic compasses, the knights learned the management of money. Although conventional history traces the development of modern banking to early Jewish and Italian lending institutions, the Knights Templar predated the Rothschilds and the Medicis.

"They pioneered the concept of credit facilities, as well as the allocation of credit for commercial development and expansion. They performed, in fact, virtually all the functions of a 20th century merchant bank," wrote Baigent and Leigh. "At the peak of their power, the Templars handled much, if not most, of the available capital in Western Europe."

The Templars held long-term private trust funds, accessible only by the originators of the account, a practice that continues today in Swiss banks. It can also be argued that the Templars first introduced the credit card and packaged tours, as they developed fund transfers by note, a technique most probably obtained from their Muslim contacts in the Middle East.

ALCHEMY: SCIENCE, MAGIC, OR BOTH?

Pieces of the ancient knowledge handed down from the gods concerning chemistry were used during the Middle Ages as a basis for the science of that day, known as alchemy. During medieval times, one of the primary goals of alchemists was to turn base metals into valuable gold or silver.

There is some controversy over whether the word *alchemy* stems from ancient Egypt, earlier known as Khem or Chem, or if the name derived from the Medieval Latin *alkimia*, Islamic *kimya,* or perhaps from the Greek *khemeioa.*

According to English author E. J. Holmyard, adherents of alchemy have included the royal bloodlines of Europe as well as common folk. Among alchemists, he included everyone from "kings, popes, and emperors to minor clergy, parish clerks, smiths, dyers, and tinkers. Even such accomplished men as Roger Bacon, St. Thomas Aquinas, Sir Thomas Browne, John Evelyn, and Sir Isaac Newton were deeply interested in it, and Charles II had an alchemical laboratory built under the royal bedchamber with access by a private staircase. Other alchemical monarchs were Herakleios I of Byzantium, James IV of Scotland, and the Emperor Rudolf II."

Alchemy was the science of the times, and while it involved rudimentary chemistry, biology, geometry, numerology, and even physics, some practitioners gravitated toward the power of gold found in money.

The magic of money manipulation may have been perfected in more modern times, but its roots go far back into history, and there appears to be a correlation between control by money, gold, and the ancient gods. In his 2010 book, *Babylon's Banksters*, Joseph P. Farrell, as a doctoral graduate of Pembroke College, Oxford, who had unparalleled access to old books and manuscripts in Oxford University's library, said his thesis was both simple to state but difficult to understand. "Since ancient times and with more or less uninterrupted constancy, there has existed an international money power which seeks by a variety of means—including fraud, deception, assassination, and war—to usurp the money- and credit-creating power of the various states it has sought to dominate, and to obfuscate and occult the profound connection between that money-creating power and the deep 'alchemical physics' that such power implies."

In ancient times, the coinage of money was conducted and controlled by the priesthoods in obedience to their gods. In Babylon, descendant of the Sumerian culture, checks were in use as draws on deposits of valuables. But the gods demanded gold or silver, as noted in the Laws of Hammurabi. The monetary systems of Babylonia established branches on the coast of Greece and in the Mycenaean centers. The discovery of Babylonian seals in the Greek islands of the Cyclades showed that clay "promises to pay" in silver were written for loans against real goods. According to Farrell, such practices gave rise to an "international class of bullion brokers" or bankers. "Succinctly stated, the bullion trust and the temple are at the minimum allies, and at the maximum, the one has infiltrated and taken over the other."

The ancient rulers, whether aliens themselves or mere representatives, discovered that their religions required financial support.
Going back to at least the Babylonian civilization, the temples were
dependent on financial institutions.

The Hebrew Mogen David, or Star of David, is of Babylonian
origin and is indicative of how the Babylonian/Sumerian culture
was blended with Hebrew religion during the Jews' captivity in
Babylon. And it was in the Temple at Jerusalem that Jesus turned
violent against the money changers. Matthew 21:12–13 relates,
"And Jesus went into the temple of God, and cast out all them that
sold and bought in the temple, and overthrew the tables of the moneychangers, and the seats of those who sold doves, and said unto
them, 'it is written, My house shall be called the house of prayer, but
ye have made it a den of thieves.'

Gold remained at the top of the financial pyramid. As commonly known, gold was a basic of the ancient Egyptian culture,
being used for ornaments, statues, and coins. Gold, the objective
of the Anunnaki, was still considered sacred and divine in ancient
Egypt and was of special importance to the royal family, who themselves were considered gods. King Tutankhamen was buried with a
now-famous solid gold mask. Coins came in the form of rings of
gold, silver, and copper, each with a specific weight certified by the
priesthood. Coins were primarily used to pay foreign mercenaries,
who would take them to their home country to be exchanged for
goods and services.

The connection between church and state money management
continued through the Roman Empire. The Roman Constitution
decreed that the mining and coinage of gold was under the authority of the Roman pontiff. "Julius Caesar erected the coinage
of gold into a sacerdotal prerogative; this prerogative was attached
to the sovereign and his successors, not as the emperors, but as the
high priests of Rome," noted Alexander del Mar, the American
economist and historian who became the first director of the U.S.

Treasury's Bureau of Statistics in 1866. "It would have been sacrilege, punishable by torture, death, and anathema for any other prince than the sovereign-pontiff to strike coins of gold; it would have been sacrilege to give currency to any others; hence no other Christian prince, not even the pope of Rome, nor the sovereign of the Western or Medieval empire, attempted to coin gold while the ancient [Roman] Empire survived." It was only following the fall of Constantinople in 1204 that the legal authority to coin and regulate money became the prerogative of kings and national rulers.

Due to the reach of their empire, the Romans were able to mine more gold than the Egyptians. One example can be seen in their records, which noted that Spain shipped 1,400 tons of gold to Rome each year.

In 1717, the United Kingdom adopted the gold standard, renouncing it in 1931 due to market manipulation, which caused declining prices. The United States, which had prospered since abolishing a central bank in 1836, soon adopted the gold standard. Gold certificates circulated in the United States and could be converted to gold coins by visiting any bank. But in 1933, as the Great Depression deepened and bank runs became more and more common, an executive order by President Franklin Roosevelt mandated the confiscation of gold in an effort to inflate the dollar. The gold standard was formally abandoned under President Nixon in 1971, but private ownership of gold was again made legal in 1974.

In medieval Europe, only the most royal personages held gold. The common currency was copper coins. Thought to have healing powers, possibly due to secret knowledge passed down from the ancient civilizations, gold was consumed by the nobility in the form of leaf, flakes, or dust. This also was an overt display of wealth for some. Kings and queens wore crowns of gold, symbolizing the light of the sun, which bestowed divine authority.

The old alchemists apparently suspected the hidden magic of gold but had lost the specifics. It has been assumed that they wanted gold to become wealthy, but a close study of alchemy and occultism reveals that these men and women of the past were attempting to recover ancient knowledge long since lost in the mists of time. One such secret will be revealed later.

BACON'S INVISIBLE COLLEGE

Vestiges of the ancient science of energy manipulation were passed along through the Middle Ages via secret-society initiations, symbols, and coded language. In *The Shadow of Solomon*, Laurence Gardner traced this "underground stream of knowledge" from medieval alchemists through Sir Francis Bacon's Invisible College to more modern Masonic lodges, many of which were infiltrated by the mysterious Bavarian Illuminati. The brilliant Bacon, by several accounts the illegitimate son of England's Queen Elizabeth I, oversaw the editing of the King James Bible and is believed by many prominent persons to be the true author of William Shakespeare's plays and sonnets

Journalist A. E. Loosley wrote that "Francis Bacon was mainly, if not entirely, responsible for a threefold undertaking, (1st) the Shakespearian Plays; (2nd) the creation in its present form of Freemasonry, and (3rd) the translation of the Holy Bible into its present well-known Authorized Version. The three were undoubtedly intermingled." He also attributed an amazing coincidence of names in Psalms to a code of Bacon, known to have been a Rosicrucian grand master and described as a "founder of Freemasonry."

"I have been able, quite recently, to clear up one point of possible doubt and at the same time to establish a claim for its certainty. It was in connection with that 46th Psalm, in which, in the Authorized Version, the 46th word from the beginning is 'shake' and the 46th from the end is 'spear.' Such an arrangement—especially in the 46th Psalm—would be a most remarkable coincidence if it were not intentionally so arranged," noted Loosley. Tacked onto the end of Psalm 46 is the word *Selah,* which is not part of the psalm but a term of unknown meaning, though thought by scholars to signify a cue for the congregation to pause for a prayer or song.

"In order to satisfy myself on the question, I sought an opportunity of comparing the wording in the Authorized Version with that in one of the earlier versions. I have now been able to satisfy myself that it was not a coincidence at all, but was plainly the result of deliberate planning. I give below, side by side, the wording of the first three and last three verses in the 'Breeches' Bible and that in the Authorized Version. In the former the 47 words up to the word 'Shake' and the 44 words from 'Spear' to the end of the Psalm were altered to 46 in each case in the Authorized Version."

Loosley noted that forty-seven divines (clergymen) were entrusted by King James with the work of translating the Bible. If Francis Bacon was discounted as only the editor, that would leave forty-six, the number of the psalm in question. "If this be true, and I feel one is justified in believing it, a very interesting light is thrown on the keen working of Bacon's mind. The trick would be one in which he would take a keen delight."

Bacon's circle of friends included many Britons who undoubtedly had access to the elder secrets carried through the Knights Templar on into Freemasonry. These included Christopher Marlowe, Edmund Spenser, Ben Jonson, Edward de Vere, John Fletcher, and Philip Sidney, all of whom were connected to the national intelligence service created by Queen Elizabeth. There is good reason to believe that many, if not all, of these worthy men contributed to the writings of Shakespeare. They also were early Freemasons, members of that secret society created from stonemason guilds by the Knights Templar following their dissolution in 1307.

These Freemason secrets, through many generations of initiations, are intricately tied to King Solomon and the building of his great temple. What many don't know is that the name Solomon—as well as the name of King David before him—was initially just a title. His real name was Jedidiah. According to Gardner, the name of Solomon's father "is uncertain, since the titular style of David has predominated (although never recorded as a personal name before that time). Mesopotamian texts from the palace of Mari refer, however, to the *Davidum*, equivalent to caesar or emperor, and the title has stuck as a name to the present day. In reality, Solomon and his successors were all Davids (Davidums)."

Freemasonry's basic knowledge began with the secrets of King Solomon handed down from the ancient gods. These included money management, construction of arches using keystones, life-saving techniques, and even how to make a magnetic compass. Such hidden knowledge of the ancients then moved through the mystery schools of Egypt and via the Hebrew exodus into Palestine. From there, it was passed into Europe by the Knights Templar, who created Freemasonry from their stonemason guilds following the attacks by the Church in 1307.

The biblical Ark of the Covenant appears on the coat of arms of the United Grand Lodge of England, and a replica is featured in the Royal Arch Room in the George Washington Masonic National Memorial in Alexandria, Virginia. Clearly, the ark once was of the utmost significance to adherents of underground knowledge. This significance will be discussed later.

However, the secretive masons lost much of the ancient knowledge when the English Whig Revolution of 1688 exiled the Stuart dynasty. Many of the Stuart supporters, known as Jacobites, fled England, taking with them the original Masonic secrets. "When the new-style Georgian Freemasonry emerged from 1717 [when the Grand Lodge of England was founded], the best it could do was to endeavor to pick up some threads—but they were few," explained Gardner. With this break in the evolution of Freemasonry, much of the ancient knowledge was forgotten.

Apparently, the biggest secret of Freemasonry today is that it has lost most, if not all, of its secrets, especially those from antiquity. Gardner declared, "The skills of the Master Craftsman on which the philosophy was founded were switched in emphasis from the practical [operative masonry] to the personal [speculative masonry], and became so veiled by confusing allegory that the original purpose was lost and forgotten. This is not to say that the benevolent ideals of today's fraternity are anything less than commendable, but they are not what Freemasonry was concerned with before the 18th century."

THE MAGIC OF GOLD

Bacon's Invisible College members and their alchemist contemporaries, practicing a blend of philosophy, mysticism, astrology, and chemical technology, sought the power to create gold. However, contrary to what moderns believe, this gold was not necessarily in the form of nuggets, coins, or bars. One prominent seventeenth-century alchemist was Thomas Vaughan, who called himself Eirenaeus Philalethes. Vaughan wrote that the fabled philosopher's stone was actually "nothing but gold digested to the highest degree of purity and subtle fixation . . . a very fine powder."

Support for the idea that alchemists were attempting to duplicate the processes that transformed gold into a white powder came from *Alchemy, The Ancient Science*, by Neil Powell, who wrote, "Alchemists used a bewildering variety of ingredients in their search for the Philosopher's Stone. Copper and lead, sulfur and arsenic, urine and bile were but a few of them. Substances were combined and separated, heated and cooled, vaporized and solidified, and sometimes even just left to rot. The processes carried out in the laboratory were often fairly complex. Calcination, sublimation, and distillation are three of the better known ones. In *calcination,* metals and minerals were reduced to a fine powder. In *sublimation,* a substance was heated until it vaporized, and then returned to its solid state by rap-idly cooling the vapor. In *distillation,* a liquid was converted into a vapor by boiling, and then condensed back into a liquid by cooling. These and many of the other processes required heat, so furnaces were the most important equipment in the alchemist's laboratory."

The connection between the gold powder of the alchemists and ancient legends has caught the attention of a growing number of scholars and researchers, who have concluded that the search for gold powder was inspired by ancient accounts of our ancestors in-gesting what seemed to be strange, life-granting substances.

Laurence Gardner noted that the oldest complete book in the world—the Egyptian *Book of the Dead*—tells of the pharaohs in-gesting "the bread of presence," also called "schefa food," while making the ritualistic journey to the afterlife. At each stage, the pharaoh would ask, "What is it?"

This has been compared to the Biblical account of Moses and the Israelites in the desert following the exodus from Egypt. To sus-tain themselves in the wilderness, Moses and his people ate a white, powdery substance they called manna. This manna was baked into small cakes or boiled. In Hebrew, *manna* literally means "What is it?" The duplication of the Egyptian cry of "What is it?" is not lost on researchers.

"They knew there were superconductors inherent in the human body," Gardner wrote. "They knew that both the physical body and the light body [the spirit or soul] had to be fed to increase hormonal production and the ultimate food for the latter was called *shem-an-na* by the Babylonians, *mfkzt* by the Egyptians and *manna* by the Israelites."

It is significant that despite today's costly and extensive research in the area of superconductors, such secrets were known many thou-sands of years ago by ancient mystics and priests. Gardner wrote, "It is clear, however, from the documentary evidence of ancient times, that the attributes of superconductors and gravity defiance were known, even if not understood, in a distant world of priestly levitation, godly communication, and the phenomenal power of the 'electrikus.' In Greek mythology the quest for the secret of this substance was at the heart of the Golden Fleece legend, while in biblical terms it was the mystical realm of the Ark of the Covenant—the golden coffer, which Moses brought out of Sinai, and was later housed in the Temple of Jerusalem."

Gardner explained how this knowledge was lost through time. "In ancient Sumer, PGMs [platinum group metals] called *adamas* were classified as *an-na* (firestone). Because of the bright silvery color described in old records, the mysteriously designated shining metal was long presumed to have been tin by misguided metallurgical adepts of the Middle Ages, while others who knew something of cupellation and parting, strove earnestly with salts, sulfurs, and mystical solutions, endeavoring to extrapolate gold from lead. This leaves us no doubt that, although PGMs were a part of ancient technology, they were (just like electricity) lost to us for many centuries until archeological and geological research caught up with them again."

The story of Exodus may provide evidence of this powdered gold in use. It tells how Moses became angered upon his return from the mountain where he was given tablets by his god. It seems in his absence the Israelites had taken most of the gold in their possession and melted it down to make a calf, which they then worshipped. Exodus 32:20 (New International Version) states, "And he [Moses] took the calf they had made and burned it in the fire; then he ground it to powder, scattered it on the water and made the Israelites drink it." Since swallowing molten metal would be lethal, obviously Moses, who had been well educated in esoteric knowledge passed from Sumer to Egypt, knew the secret of making what has come to be known as high-spin monatomic gold powder.

This idea is supported by the accounts of British archaeologist William Flinders Petrie, who in 1904 discovered a large smelting facility on Mount Horeb, located in the southern end of the Sinai Peninsula. Some scholars believe that Horeb is the actual location of the Mountain of Moses mentioned in the Bible.

It was on Horeb that Petrie discovered an enclosed temple composed of adjoining halls, shrines, and chambers, all filled with carvings, pillars, and stelae depicting Egyptian nobility and mentioning the mysterious *mfkzt*. Most surprising was the discovery of a metallurgist's crucible along with a considerable amount of pure white powder cleverly concealed under the flagstone. Unconcerned with the powder, Petrie allowed it to blow away in the Sinai winds.

Engravings in this ancient temple depict various Egyptian rulers, among these Tuthmosis IV and Amenhotep III along with the god Hathor. In these carvings various persons are offering the king a conical loaf, suspected to be the legendary white powder known as *mfkzt*. This suspicion is strongly supported by the fact that the figure offering the powder can be identified as an Egyptian treasurer named Sobekhotep, elsewhere described as the man who "brought the noble Precious Stone to his majesty."

The ancient gold powder today can be connected to the accidental discovery of single-atom (monatomic) elements in the 1970s by Phoenix-area cotton farmer David Hudson. His discovery was followed by several scientific papers exploring the mysteries of atomic structure, nucleus deformation, and electromagnetism. Hudson, trained in the sciences, spent millions on research before obtaining eleven worldwide patents on his "orbitally rearranged monatomic elements (ORME)." He found that the nuclei of such monatomic matter act in an unusual manner. Under certain circumstances, they begin spinning, becoming deformed, flatten, and enter a "highward" or high-spin state. When reaching this state, the electrons turn to pure white light, and the individual atoms separate, producing a white monatomic powder.

Using thermogravimetric analysis, it was found that a sample of Hudson's monatomic matter lost 44 percent of its original weight when reduced to this white powder state. By either heating or cooling the material, it would gain weight or lose weight and when heated, could achieve a gravitational attraction of less than zero. Some scientists have concluded that this newly discovered material is "exotic matter" capable of creating energy fields that bend time and space. The material's antigravitational properties were confirmed when it was shown that a weighing pan weighed less when the powder was placed in it than it did empty. The matter had passed its antigravitational properties to the pan.

In addition to this amazing conclusion, it was found that when the white powder was heated to a certain degree, not only did its weight disappear, but the powder itself vanished from sight. When a spatula was used to stir around in the pan, there apparently was nothing there. Yet as the material cooled, it reappeared in its original configuration. The material had not simply disappeared, it apparently had moved into another dimensional plane.

The fabled Ark of the Covenant may have played a role in the story of the mysterious monatomic gold, as some researchers believe it was a vessel filled with the white powder, causing it to levitate and act as a speaker for the voice of a god. According to Gardner, "The Ark of the Covenant was a powerful electronic arcing device—the provider of the 'fire' with which Moses burned the Golden Calf. As a storage facility for the [ORME] powder, it also became a superconductor in its own right, with the ability to ride on its own Meissner Field." German physicist Walter Meissner demonstrated the effect of manipulating magnetic energy fields by a superconductor in 1933.

Was the ark a supernatural manifestation or an alien artifact? Gardner suggested that the ark was filled with the white powder of gold, which allowed it to be moved by levitation. After all, descriptions of the ark's solid gold mercy seat would mean it weighed more than 2,700 pounds, an impossible weight for only a few men to carry.

Alan Alford argued that Abraham's god, Yahweh, was an Anunnaki who kept in communication with his chosen people through the Ark of the Covenant, in reality a radio transmitter/receiver. Rene A. Boulay, author of *Flying Serpents and Dragons: The Story of Mankind's Reptilian Past*, also saw the ark as a communication device and thought it significant that the ark had to be completed according to very precise instructions before the tablets containing the Ten Commandments were placed inside. "The tablets presumably contained the power source necessary to activate the receiver-transmitter," he wrote.

A verse in the Old Testament (Numbers 7:89) may even have described the location of the device's speaker: "When Moses entered the Tent of Meeting to speak with the Lord, he heard the voice speaking to him from between the two cherubim above the atonement cover on the ark of the Testimony. And he spoke with him" (New International Version).

Science is coming to understand that gravity and time are interconnected aspects of hyperspace energy and that this new monatomic technology allows manipulation and control at the subatomic level. Some scientists believe that such control might do much more than offer new propulsion technology. It may open the door to antigravity, limitless free energy, faster-than-light speeds, and much more, perhaps even interdimensional travel and time travel.

DISCOVERIES IN IRAQ

In addition to the amazing properties listed earlier, some believe that the white powder of gold might also provide a cure for diseases such as AIDS and cancer, even put an end to the aging process. This amazing substance may have even been a source of interest for certain U.S. leaders with secret-society connections who wanted to send troops into Iraq in 2003. Could this white powder have been a reason?

In 1999, ABC News reported that nearly four hundred ancient Sumerian artifacts had been discovered in the southern Iraqi town of Basmyiah, about one hundred miles south of Baghdad. The Iraqi News Agency said the objects ranged from animal and human-shaped "toys" to cuneiform tablets and even "ancient weapons." At least one cylinder seal depicted a tall person thought to represent King Gilgamesh. The antiquities were dated to before 2500 BC and were stored in the basement of the Iraqi National Museum in Baghdad.

Further discoveries in Iraq were made in 2002 and early 2003 by archaeologists from the Bavarian Department of Historical Monuments in Munich, Germany, using digital mapping technology. According to spokesman Jorg Fassbinder, a magnetometer was utilized to locate buried walls, gardens, palaces, and a surprising network of canals that would have made Uruk a "Venice in the desert."

This equipment also located a structure in the middle of the Euphrates River, which Fassbinder's team believed to be the tomb of Gilgamesh. The new discoveries were added to those stored in Baghdad's Iraqi National Museum, which had been closed to the public since the first Gulf War in 1991.

By mid-2002, President George W. Bush was clearly intent on invading Iraq, citing weapons of mass destruction hidden there. His well-publicized claim of such weapons came despite assurances from United Nations chief weapons inspector Hans Blix, officials of the International Atomic Energy Agency, and even Scott Ritter, a former U.S. weapons inspector, that Iraq had no nuclear or biological weapons of mass destruction. On March 20, 2003, U.S. forces crossed Iraq's borders. Unlike previous military campaigns, in which armies captured key cities before consolidating their forces and moving to the next objective, U.S. forces made a beeline for Baghdad, bypassing most of the country.

Once the capital was in American hands, by late April 2003, looters took at least fifty thousand priceless artifacts and tablets from the Iraqi National Museum. Despite prior attempts to alert American military officers of the danger of losing seven-thousand-year-old artifacts, American authorities failed to prevent the wholesale looting of humankind's most ancient treasures. "It was my impression that the Department of Defense had made provisions for the safeguarding of monuments and museums," lamented Maxwell Anderson, president of the Association of Art Museum Directors. Anderson was among a group that in January 2003 had alerted Pentagon and State Department officials to the importance of these antiquities.

When the looting began, one Iraqi archaeologist summoned U.S. troops to protect the National Museum. Five Marines accompanied the man to the museum and chased out the thieves by firing shots over their heads. However, after about thirty minutes, the soldiers were ordered to withdraw, and the looters soon returned. The only building in Baghdad to receive full American protection was the Ministry of Oil.

Western media portrayed the looting as a chaotic scramble created by common thieves. Yet evidence has emerged that some of these looters were highly organized and had an agenda. According to an Associated Press report, some thieves had keys to the Iraqi National Museum and its vaults. McGuire Gibson of The Oriental Institute of the University of Chicago said that "it looks as if part of the theft was a very, very deliberate, planned action," and noted that the thieves were able to target the best material in the museum." I have a suspicion it was organized outside the country. In fact, I'm pretty sure it was," he said. Dony George, head of the Baghdad National Museum, agreed. "I believe they were people who knew what they wanted. They had passed by the gypsum copy of the Black Obelisk. This means that they must have been specialists. They did not touch the copies." Christopher Bollyn of the *American*

Free Press also noted that the thieves used glasscutters unavailable in Iraq. Moreover, they were able to take away a huge bronze bust that would have required a forklift to move.

Such suspicions were later confirmed by Colonel Matthew Bogdanos, deputy director for the Joint Interagency Coordination Group, originally assigned to seek out weapons of mass destruction in Iraq. After gaining permission from General Tommy Franks, Bogdanos probed the museum looting.

In an interview published in the January–February 2004 issue of *Archaeology*, Bogdanos was asked what was still missing from the Iraqi National Museum. He replied, "You have the public gallery from which originally 40 exhibits were taken. We've recovered 11. Turning to the storage rooms, there were about 3,150 pieces taken from those, and that's almost certainly by random and indiscriminant looters. Of those, we've recovered 2,700. So there's about 400 of these pieces, excavated pieces, missing.

"The final group is from the basement," he added. "The basement is what we've been calling the inside job. And I will say it forever like a mantra: it is inconceivable to me that the basement was breached and the items stolen without an intimate insider's knowledge of the museum. From there about 10,000 pieces were taken. We've only recovered 650, approximately."

Who wanted these artifacts gone and why? Could it be possible that the occupation of Iraq had more to do with gaining control over artifacts and technology than with stopping weapons of mass destruction or bringing freedom and democracy to the region? Michael E. Salla, who has taught at the American University in Washington, D.C., the Australian National University in Canberra, and George Washington University, believes this is indeed the case. "Competing clandestine government organizations are struggling through proxy means to take control of ancient extraterrestrial (ET) technology that exists in Iraq," he wrote in a 2002 research study. Could Saddam Hussein have been working on unlocking the secrets of the monatomic gold? After all, it was widely reported that Hussein believed he was the reincarnated Nebuchadnezzar. If the United States believed that he would succeed, could that have contributed to the rush to war with Iraq?

And yet this cutting-edge science of today apparently was known to selected persons thousands of years ago, including King Nebuchadnezzar. The biblical Book of Daniel details an attempt to communicate with ancient Mesopotamian gods by Nebuchadnezzar, who built a tall narrow structure of gold near Babylon. This structure has been described as a furnace, suggesting that it was used to produce the mystical white powder of gold. However, the king's men were unable to make it work properly. When three Hebrew scholar/priests who had been appointed by the prophet Daniel to administrate Babylon—Shadrach, Meshach, and Abednego— refused to serve the king, they were thrown into the crucible. But after clothing themselves in hats, coats, and "other garments," the trio survived the fire.

Oddly enough, when Nebuchanezzar checked to see if the three were dead, he was amazed, saying, "Lo, I see four men loose, walking in the midst of the fire, and they have no hurt; and the form of the fourth is like the Son of God" (Daniel 3:25, King James Version). Although no further mention is made of this fourth, godlike person, the three Israelites were honored by the king and prospered under his kingship. Obviously there is something much more to gold than ornamental jewelry and wealth.

Could the millennia-long veneration of gold have more to do with ancient knowledge of its intrinsic power than with its monetary worth? Could Saddam Hussein have been working on unlocking the secrets of the white-powder gold? Was there somewhere someone more concerned with gaining control over recently discovered knowledge and perhaps even technology that might undo the modern monopolies in religion and technology than with gaining oil or regime change?

This is not sheer science fiction. As noted by Laurence Gardner, "In the field of quantum mechanics, scientists have recently confirmed that matter can indeed be in two places at once. It is now established that, through quantum entanglement, particles millions of light-years apart can be connected without physical contact. Space-time can now be manipulated; teleportation is becoming a reality; gravity-resistant material is heralded for air transport, and virtual science has led to a greater understanding of hyperdimensional environments."

But most people don't know any of this. As Stephen Hawking noted in *The Illustrated Brief History of Time*, "Only a few people can keep up with the rapidly advancing frontier of knowledge, and they have to devote their whole time to it and specialize in one small area. The rest of the population has little idea of the advances that are being made or the excitement they are generating." The same could be said about the advances in understanding true human origins and history.

KHAZARIA: MASTERING FINANCIAL CONTROL

The two basic human control mechanisms—religion and banking—were first formed in ancient Sumer, legacies of the Anunnaki gods, according to some. The people who learned well these mechanisms dispersed after calamity struck Sumer and re-formed as the nucleus of the later Babylonian and Egyptian civilizations as well as lesser nation-states.

If the art of turning base metals into gold or gold into powder was lost, the art of turning a profit by exchanging and lending money was not. The appearance of money on Earth is an amazing event and yet one that cannot be conventionally explained or documented. Most developments can be traced to some originating source, but money appeared in unconnected places across the world in remarkably similar fashion. Exchanging real goods and services for representations (today predominantly paper or electronic scrip) evolved into an art.

Nowhere was the art of mastering money more developed than in the Khazarian Empire. From Mesopotamia, the descendants of the Sumerian priesthood and leadership who fled the sudden and mysterious destruction of ancient Sumer spread southward into Palestine and Egypt and northward into the Caucasus Mountain region. Here they mingled with nomadic Mongols, and their progeny centuries later formed the Empire of Khazaria, whence sprang the wealthy banking families of Europe. A few of them carried the secrets of ancient Mesopotamia. It was in Khazaria that nomadic raider clans attacked caravan routes between the Black Sea and Caspian Sea, known historically as the Silk Road.

In the fifth century, the Khazars rode with Attila the Hun. As they grew wealthy and powerful, the Khazar warlords determined that exchanging and loaning money would be more profitable and less hazardous than raiding caravans. But they had one big problem. By the eighth century, Khazaria was almost evenly divided among Christians, Muslims, and Jews. At that time, both Christians and Muslims believed that charging interest on a loan, called usury, was a sin. Only Jews could openly charge interest on loans, especially to non-Jews.

In 740, Khazaria's king Bulan, who claimed to have had a heavenly vision, became the first to adopt the religion of Judaism. By custom, everyone was expected to adopt the religion of their king, so every Khazar became a professed Jew, whether out of pragmatism or genuine religiosity. In 969, after enduring years of attacks from surrounding clans and nations, Khazaria was overrun by Scandinavian migrants called the Rus and dissolved. The area came to be called Russia.

Arthur Koestler, a Jewish author and journalist who gained international fame with his history of the Jews, entitled *The Thir-*

teenth Tribe, fled Eastern Europe during World War II and after a stay in Palestine, settled in Britain in 1945. Koestler, writing in 1978, stated that his book "was written before the full extent of the holocaust was known, but that does not alter the fact that the large majority of surviving Jews in the world are of Eastern European— and thus perhaps mainly of Khazar—origin. If so, this would mean that their ancestors came not from the Jordan but from the Volga, not from Canaan but from the Caucasus, once believed to be the cradle of the Aryan race; and that genetically they are more closely related to the Hun, Uigur and Magyar tribes than to the seed of Abraham, Isaac and Jacob. Should this turn out to be the case, then the term 'anti-Semitism' would become void of meaning, based on a misapprehension shared by both the killers and their victims. The story of the Khazar Empire, as it slowly emerges from the past, begins to look like the most cruel hoax which history has ever perpetrated."

About AD 1000, many displaced descendants of the Khazars migrated into Spain but were ousted after a century or two. They then moved to Portugal, but after a century or so were forced to move again. In the Netherlands, the Khazars, or Ashkenazi Jews, as they came to call themselves, prospered and began to spread across Europe and then to America. These people were never connected to the Hebrews of Palestine, although they were the originators of Zionism, a political movement that began in nineteenth-century Russia for the purpose of securing a Jewish "homeland" in the Middle East. As Koestler explained, "In the twelfth century there arose in Khazaria a Messianic movement, a rudimentary attempt at a Jewish crusade, aimed at the conquest of Palestine by force of arms. The initiator of the movement was a Khazar Jew, one Solomon ben Duji (or Ruhi or Roy), aided by his son Menahem and a Palestinian scribe. They wrote letters to all the Jews, near and far, in all the lands around them. . . . They said that the time had come in which God would gather Israel, His people, from all lands to Jerusalem, the holy city, and that Solomon Ben Duji was Elijah, and his son the Messiah." Duji's movement later became known as Zionism.

Later in life, Koestler was diagnosed with both Parkinson's disease and cancer. Despite both having left notes of farewell, some conspiracy researchers claim the 1983 suicide of Koestler and his wife, Cynthia Jefferies, were clever assassinations by the Israeli Mossad in retaliation for his having revealed too much true history. It should be noted that the greatest opponents of Zionism were Orthodox Jews, who did not believe it their place to take other people's lands but rather to await their Messiah. Some even claim that the Nazi Holocaust was encouraged by some Zionists to eliminate Orthodox rabbinical leaders opposed to their movement.

If the Khazars are the progenitors of many Eastern European Jews, then this would include the renowned Rothschild family, who financially ruled Europe for more than a century. Conspiracy researchers contend they still dominate the world financial order and have been the financial backers of the Rockefellers and other wealthy families. The Rothschilds claim as an ancestor Nimrod, the giant Sumerian king who was said to be a direct descendant of Noah as well as a demigod. Nimrod has also been associated with Molech, a variation of the Hebrew word for king or ruler. The name Molech has been applied to Sumerian deities. The biblical patriarch Abraham confronted Nimrod about his blasphemous worship of Molech, simply a later name for the Anunnaki moon god Sin.

This family's cohesiveness, its power, its secrecy, and its wealth, all might explain why Mayer Rothschild believed his oft-repeated quote, "Permit me to control the money of a nation, and I care not who makes its laws."

When the founder of the Rothschild dynasty, Mayer Amschel Rothschild, wrote his will, he exerted the right of primogeniture, which means that only the eldest son in each generation can control the family wealth. By this method, not only has the Rothschild family been held tightly together but, as in the secret societies, those family members who aren't privy to the innermost control have little knowledge of its financial dealings. Former top executives of the Rothschilds complained that they often were kept "out of the loop" on important decisions, so it is erroneous to blame the entire Rothschild family for lack of ethics.

Rothschild biographer Derek Wilson described the staying power of the Rothschild family by stating, "Genetics, mythology, deliberate training, the opportunities provided by wealth and connections—all have played their part in producing one of the most remarkable—perhaps *the* [emphasis in the original] most remarkable—family of recent history." He concluded with admiration, "Few dynasties, with the exception of hereditary monarchies preserved from oblivion by the right of primogeniture, have maintained their influence in the world for seven generations."

Jewish or not, globalist financiers have emulated the Rothschilds for decades, using secrecy and bribery to help them conduct business. Researcher John Churchilly wrote that "Americans should know Khazar descendants secretly dominate every aspect of American life. They have infiltrated the upper levels of American government, industry, banking, finance, commerce, mass media, communications, real estate, merchandising, arts, education, sports, professional associations, etc. This is not by chance or merit but by design, a careful preference in selection over many, many decades." Churchilly has voiced the concerns of many. One key component of this management is secrecy. Utilizing bought-off politicians, who catch the public rage and scrutiny, major globalists are able to operate out of the public eye, with impunity. This impunity is due to their dominance in the field of communications, especially Hollywood, which has set cultural trends worldwide for decades. But is there any truth in it?

"I have never been so upset by a poll in my life," wrote Joel Stein in 2008. A columnist for the *Los Angeles Times*, Stein complained,

"Only 22 percent of Americans now believe 'the movie and television industries are pretty much run by Jews,' down from nearly 50 percent in 1964. The Anti-Defamation League, which released the poll results last month, sees in these numbers a victory against stereotyping. Actually, it just shows how dumb America has gotten. Jews totally run Hollywood."

Stein went on to point out, "How deeply Jewish is Hollywood? When the studio chiefs took out a full-page ad in the *Los Angeles Times* a few weeks ago to demand that the Screen Actors Guild settle its contract, the open letter was signed by: News Corp. President Peter Chernin (Jewish), Paramount Pictures Chairman Brad Grey (Jewish), Walt Disney Co. Chief Executive Robert Iger (Jewish), Sony Pictures Chairman Michael Lynton (surprise, Dutch Jew), Warner Bros. Chairman Barry Meyer (Jewish), CBS Corp. Chief Executive Leslie Moonves (so Jewish his great uncle was the first prime minister of Israel), MGM Chairman Harry Sloan (Jewish) and NBC Universal Chief Executive Jeff Zucker (mega-Jewish). If either of the Weinstein brothers had signed, this group would have not only the power to shut down all film production but to form a minyan with enough Fiji water on hand to fill a mikvah. The person they were yelling at in that ad was SAG [Screen Actors Guild] President Alan Rosenberg (take a guess). The scathing rebuttal to the ad was written by entertainment super-agent Ari Emanuel (Jew with Israeli parents) on the Huffington Post, which is owned by Arianna Huffington (not Jewish and has never worked in Hollywood.)

"As a proud Jew, I want America to know about our accomplishment," concluded Stein. "Yes, we control Hollywood. Without us, you'd be flipping between 'The 700 Club' and 'Davey and Goliath' on TV all day. . . . But I don't care if Americans think we're running the news media, Hollywood, Wall Street or the government. I just care that we get to keep running them."

Stein's words were echoed in an opinion piece published in July 2012, in the *Times of Israel* by Manny Friedman, admittedly an as-

sumed name. Friedman wrote that it is funny how statements like
"The Jews control the media" incite Jews to be up in arms. "We
create huge campaigns to take these people down. We do what we
can to put them out of work. We publish articles. We've created
entire organizations [such as AIPAC, the American Israel Public
Affairs Committee] that exist just to tell everyone that the Jews
don't control nothin'. No, we don't control the media, we don't have
any more sway in DC than anyone else. No, no, no, we swear:
We're just like everybody else!" he wrote. But Friedman concludes,
"The truth is, the anti-Semites got it right. We Jews have something
planted in each one of us that makes us completely different from
every group in the world. We're talking about a group of people that
just got put in death camps, endured pogroms, their whole families
decimated. And then they came to America, the one place that ever
really let them have as much power as they wanted, and suddenly
they're taking over. Please don't tell me that any other group in the
world has ever done that. Only the Jews. And we've done it before.
That's why the Jews were enslaved in Egypt. We were too successful.
Go look at the Torah—it's right there. And we did it in Germany
too. . . . We no longer have to change our names. We no longer
have to blend in like chameleons. We own a whole freaking country." But Friedman adds that with such power in the public media
comes grave responsibility, stating, "It means that they're suddenly
culpable when they create dirty TV shows that sully the spiritual
atmosphere of the world. It means that things can't just be created
for the sake of amusement or fun or even 'art.' . . . We'll have to start
thinking about the things we create and the way we act. It means
we'll have to start working together. It means we'll have to hold one
another, and ourselves, to a higher standard."

Screenwriter and actor Ben Stein wrote of receiving a call from
an editor at *60 Minutes*, who wanted his opinion on their research
indicating that 60 percent of the most important positions in Hollywood were held by Jews. "I managed to disqualify myself by saying

that while Hollywood was not really 'run' by anyone (it's far too chaotic for that), if Jews were about 2.5 percent of the population and were about 60 percent of Hollywood, they might well be said to be extremely predominant in that sector," said Stein. "That was far too logical and un-PC an answer, and I never heard from her again." Stein admitted, "Hollywood's current product occasionally repels and even sickens me. I am truly disgusted with its language, its violence, its endless attacks on businessmen and military offi- cers. (On the other hand, it never can attack the CIA enough for me.)" But he concluded, "For now, Hollywood, in many ways the most successful cultural enterprise of all time and the most potent messenger of American values of all time, is changing, but it is still largely Jewish. And a very angry voice in my curly head makes me add, 'What the hell of it?' "

It must be noted that all Jewish Semites, or even those profess- ing the religion of Judaism, are not the problem. The problem of at- tempts at overreaching control stem from the adherents of Zionism, a political movement embraced by many non-Semites, including the Rothschilds.

The Rothschild fortune began in the 1700s, when Mayer Am- schel adopted the practice of fractional-reserve banking, the prac- tice of lending out more money than one has in assets. According to G. Edward Griffin, author of *The Creature from Jekyll Island*, as the Rothschilds "matured and learned the magic of converting debt into money, they moved beyond the confines of Frankfurt, and es- tablished additional operations in the financial centers, not only of Europe, but of much of the civilized world."

But did they just discover the magic of converting debt into money, or had this practice been passed along from distant ances- tors? Like their proclaimed Anunnaki ancestor Nimrod and other Anunnaki, the Rothschilds have had a particular interest in gold. According to Rothschild biographer Derek Wilson, "They became the major importers of bullion from the newly-discovered goldfields." The Rothschilds also financed Cecil Rhodes, who became the gold and diamond magnate of South Africa and later formed a secret society called the Round Tables, forerunner of the Council on Foreign Relations.

Journalist William T. Still said the family's creation of American wealth was "profound." "Working through the Wall Street firms of Kuhn, Loeb & Co., and J.P. Morgan Co., the Rothschilds financed John D. Rockefeller so that he could create the Standard Oil empire." According to testimony in congressional hearings, the National City Bank of Cleveland provided John D. Rockefeller with the money to begin his monopolization of the oil refinery business, resulting in the formation of Standard Oil. This bank was one of three Rothschild banks in the United States, and by the late 1800s, Standard Oil totally dominated the world's petroleum industry.

Railroad magnate Edward Harriman and steel industrialist Andrew Carnegie also received funding from the Rothschilds. The Harrimans, aside from mentoring Prescott Bush, the grandfather of former president George W. Bush, also founded the eugenics movement in the United States. Together with the Carnegies, they funded some of the nation's most prestigious foundations.

The 1917 Balfour Declaration, a letter by British foreign secretary Alfred Balfour affirming Britain had no objection to a Jewish state in Palestine, was later approved as a mandate by the League of Nations. Many acknowledge this letter as the foundation for the creation of the state of Israel. Balfour's declaration originally was a reply to a leading Zionist, Baron Walter Rothschild, the first English nobleman peer to not convert from Judaism. Most affected by this declaration was the Semitic Arab population in Palestine.

Pete Papaherakles, writing in the *American Free Press*, wondered if bankers desiring control over the Central Bank of the Islamic Republic of Iran (CBI) might be one of the primary reasons Iran was being singled out as an enemy by the Western and Israeli powers? It has been noted that Iran is one of only three countries left in the world whose central bank is not under Rothschild control. Prior to the 9/11 attacks, Afghanistan, Iraq, Sudan, Libya, Cuba, North Korea, and Iran were free of Rothschild-dominated Western banks. By 2012, all were under a central bank with the exception of Cuba, North Korea, and Iran. In Libya, a Rothschild bank was established in Benghazi even before fighting ended within that country in 2011.

In addressing the banking aspect of the saber rattling against Iran, it was noted that the concern over Iran possibly building one nuclear weapon is misplaced in light of the nuclear arsenals in Israel, Pakistan, and India. "What then is the real reason?" asked Papaherakles. "Is it the trillions to be made in oil profits, or the trillions in war profits? Is it to bankrupt the U.S. economy, or is it to start World War III? Is it to destroy Israel's enemies or to destroy the Iranian central bank so that no one is left to defy Rothschild's money racket? It might be any one of those reasons or, worse—it might be all of them."

IT RUNS IN THE GENES

The Rothschilds are only the most visible of those who consider themselves ordained to serve as masters over ordinary humans. The blue bloods, as they see themselves, are born leaders due to their bloodline. Only within white blood cells can be found human DNA, the blueprint of life, and today, researchers have suggested that some genes within white-blood-cell DNA may be from extraterrestrials. Such alien genetics might confirm the Sumerian accounts of visitation and intervention in antiquity by nonhumans.

The evidence for nonhuman genes within the blood is strong. Mammalian red blood cells primarily carry oxygen to body tissue but not DNA, as these cells do not have nuclei and are expelled during the maturation process. However, the nuclei of human white blood cells do contain DNA. Not only does the human body rely on DNA, but so do most living things, including plants, animals, and bacteria. Blood can be typed because of the DNA contained in our white blood cells.

After reviewing the latest discoveries in DNA and gene sequencing, one science writer pointed out that humans are suspected to contain only about 32,000 genes, which is much less than science's first estimate of 100,000. Oddly, out of our gene pool, we share 223 genes with bacteria. These are genes that do not exist in other life-forms, such as worms, flies, or even yeast. Researchers thought some ancient vertebrate genome took on bacterial genes in the same way that certain types of bacteria take in genes in a response to their environment.

"What a comedown from the pinnacle of the genomic Tree of Life!" remarked Sitchin. "In other words: At a relatively recent time as evolution goes, modern humans acquired an extra 223 genes not through gradual evolution, not vertically on the Tree of Life, but horizontally, as a sideways insertion of genetic material from bacteria . . . 223 genes is more than two thirds of the difference between me, you and a chimpanzee!"

The mysterious appearance of these genes has vexed researchers who adhere to conventional theories of evolution. Steven Scherer, director for mapping of the Human Genome Sequencing Center at Baylor College of Medicine, acknowledged these extra genes are "a jump that does not follow current evolutionary theories."

Equally perplexing is rhesus or Rh-negative blood, a term that designates the absence of a certain protein on the surface of red blood cells, a rare circumstance in the thirty human blood types. The Rh-negative phenotype is passed through the DNA of both parents. Oddly, a person with type O-negative blood is considered a universal donor, who can donate blood to anyone, regardless of blood type, without causing a transfusion reaction.

The Rh-negative blood type is considered a mutation of unknown origin, though it is theorized to have somehow originated in Europe about twenty-five thousand to thirty thousand years ago. Roslyn M. Frank of the University of Iowa noted that the Basques, an ethnic group centered in the western Pyrenees, between Spain and France, have the highest recorded level of Rh-negative blood. Some suspect that they are the original source of the Rh-negative blood type, although other populations with small populations of Rh-negative individuals are found in the eastern half of Asia, Madagascar, Australia, and New Zealand. Here again is evidence that something was occurring worldwide in the distant past.

The Basques had advanced navigational skills and technology even before the rise of the Roman Empire. In addition, the Basque language cannot be connected to any other human tongue. Frank believed that the Basques might be the last remnants of the megalith builders, who left behind dolmens, standing stones, and other rock structures. They may even have foraged in North America, as recently discovered British customs records show large Basque imports of beaver pelts in the period 1380–1433, long before Columbus sailed. But the tale of human origins linked to extraterrestrials gains even more strength when one considers that many Rh-negative children are born with a tail. The *cauda equina* is a nerve bundle extending beyond the spinal column. Some babies are born with an extended *cauda equina*, in essence a tail, which must be surgically removed at birth. The word *cauda* is Latin for tail. In astrological terms, the *cauda draconis* means the "dragon's tail," the point at which the moon's orbit passes below the ecliptic, and signifies malefic aspects.

Researcher Patty Boyer, among those questioning the relatively sudden appearance of Rh-negative blood, wrote, "The introduction of the RH-negative blood type was not a naturally occurring part of human evolution. This would lend credence that the RH-negative factor was introduced from an outside source. Could the source be from human-like beings from another planet? Or maybe we are just as alien as they are, in that, we are a product of their manipulation and interference. Could they have come here and manipulated life forms already present on earth to create modern man?" she asked, adding, "I suggest that man is a creation of a highly technological race of human-like beings that From the Heavens to the Earth came. I suggest that these advanced beings are still among us today and are still very active in the affairs of man."

THE BLACK NOBILITY

With the fall of the great empires, the descendants of the early priests and money changers rose to power in Venice. These Venetians intermarried with existing European royalty, gained power, and became known as the Black Nobility, both because of their generally antisocial behavior and their usurpation of royal titles.

Prior to the rise of the Rothschild dynasty, the secrets of money manipulation passed down from Sumer and Babylon found a home within the infamous Medici family of Italy, who virtually ruled Venice from the 1420s to 1737. The Medicis provided the world with at least four popes—Leo X, Clement VII, Pius IV, and Leo XI—a number of cardinals, and two queens of France. Giovanni di Bicci de' Medici founded the Medici Bank, which grew into an early multinational corporation. To their credit, the Medicis also provided the financing for both Leonardo de Vinci and Christopher Columbus.

The Medicis, along with other oligarchic families of Venice and Genoa, gained power through their monopolies, or "privileged trading rights," and marriages with royalty. By the late twelfth century, this group had gained control over Venice and the commerce of most of the Western world.

The Illuminati News website states, "These people earned the title of 'Black' nobility from their ruthless lack of scruple. They employed murder, rape, kidnapping, assassination, robbery, and all manner of deceit on a grand scale, brooking no opposition to attaining their objectives. They all have immense wealth. And money is power. The most powerful of the Black Nobility families are located in Italy, Germany, Switzerland, Britain, Holland, and Greece in that order. Their roots may be traced back to the Venetian oligarchs [led by the Medicis], who are of Khazar extraction, and married into these royal houses in the early part of the twelfth century. Following a great Khazar victory over the Arabs, the future Emperor, Constantine V, married a Khazar princess and their son became Emperor Leo IV, also known as 'Leo the Khazar.' The Medicci popes, and Pius XII (Eugenio Pacelli) were Khazars, as is the present Pope, John Paul II. Not all Black Nobility are of royal houses, and many of the royal families no longer have kingdoms."

As with many of the secret societies discussed in this book, the Black Nobility also may trace their lineage back to ancient Sumer. These Venetians originally called themselves Sepharvaim, which is a term derived from the collective names of two Mesopotamian cities also known as the Sippara, or the "booktowns"—that is, repositories of knowledge. One was on the east bank of the Euphrates and the other was the capital of Sargon I, where a great library was established.

By the mid-1500s, the Medicis had added the arts and alchemy to their banking interests. Illustrating the interconnectedness of the bloodline families, Francesco I de Medici, the second Grand Duke of Tuscany, in 1565 wed Joanna of Austria, youngest daughter of Holy Roman Emperor Ferdinand I and Anna of Bohemia and Hungary. He supported artists; he built the Medici Theater and founded the Accademia della Crusca. Francesco also began practicing alchemy, an interest in which he was joined by his stepbrother Don Giovanni de Medici. In the early 1600s, Don Giovanni worked with his palace librarian, Jewish scholar Benedetto Blanis, in the forbidden areas of astrology, alchemy, and the kabbalah.

During the Middle Ages, the Black Nobility aligned with the

papacy—their traditional enemy—to stop a common foe. A family dynasty of German kings called the Hohenstaufens had arisen, and one Hohenstaufen in particular, Frederick I, was bent on conquest. Frederick, commonly known as Frederick Barbarossa, literally Red-beard in Italian, led his forces to Italy and eventually was crowned emperor in 1155. But after the Black Nobility and the papacy pushed Frederick out, he returned to Germany to fight his Welf cousin, Duke Heinrich (Henry the Lion) of Saxony and Bavaria in 1180.

The conflict between Frederick and the other German princes, led by the Welf family, resulted in a major rift. The supporters of the Welfs were called Guelphs, an Italianized version of Welf, while those who supported Frederick were called Ghibellines, a name derived from an old battle cry. With the death of Frederick while on crusade, his supporters lost the advantage and the Guelphs, with the backing of the Black Nobility and the pope, went on to support William of Orange when he took the throne of England. This eventually resulted in the formation of the Bank of England and the East India Company, the two major English financial powers of the eighteenth and nineteenth centuries.

Working through a number of trusts, or corporations, large banks, and a bewildering number of secret societies, the wealthy elite managed a long series of financial manipulations behind the booms and busts of the 1800s. They have been accused of creating the Federal Reserve System in the United States, fomenting World Wars I and II, the Great Depression, and the ups and downs of the U.S. economy leading to the meltdown of 2008.

PART IV

THE MODERN
ERA

For more than a century, ideological extrem-
ists at either end of the political spectrum have
seized upon well-publicized incidents such as my
encounter with Castro to attack the Rockefeller
family for the inordinate influence they claim
we wield over American political and economic
institutions. Some even believe we are part of
a secret cabal working against the best interests
of the United States, characterizing my family
and me as "internationalists" and of conspiring
with others around the world to build a more
integrated global and political structure—one
world, if you will. If that's the charge, I stand
guilty, and I am proud of it.

DAVID ROCKEFELLER, *MEMOIRS*

THE FOUNDATIONAL BELIEF OF THE RULING ELITE IS THAT THEY were born to rule, while the vast majority of the populace is born to slavery, in one form or another. They see this as a natural consequence of their bloodline, or their blue blood, as it has been called. The term refers to the blood flowing in the veins of old, aristocratic families and may be derived from the blue veins seen on people of light skin tone or from the old Hindu gods, who were always depicted as blue in color. Where did they get the idea that most humans are born to be serfs or slaves? From the tyranny of the Anunnaki gods to the philosophy of Aristotle, who saw slavery as a necessary institution, to the wealthy elite of today, who cling to the simplistic Darwinian belief in survival of the fittest, the inheritors of wealth and privilege view themselves as God-ordained rulers of humankind.

HITLER AND THE BLUE BLOODS

And according to a growing number of conspiracy researchers, those causing the problems can all be traced back to thirteen to fifteen families who are all interconnected by blood. Webster Griffin Tarpley, James Higham, John Coleman, Ralph Epperson, and others have identified the intermarried families connected to the Black Nobility. The old-line ruling families "believe that they have the right to rule the world because they are descended from the emperors of the ancient Roman and so-called 'holy' Roman Empires," wrote Tarpley and Higham. According to these authors, these families include the Rothschilds, the Rockefellers, the Warburgs, the Lazards, the Seafs, the Goldmans, the Morgans, the Schroeders, the Bushes, and the Harrimans.

Tarpley and Higham offered other names, rarely heard in the United States, including "the Giustiniani family, of Rome and Venice, who trace their lineage to the Emperor Justinian; Sir Jocelyn Hambro of Hambros (Merchant) Bank; Pierpaolo Luzzatti Fequiz, whose lineage dates back six centuries to the most ancient Luzzatos, of Venice, and Umberto Ortolani of the ancient Black Nobility family of the same name." They identified a number of other old Venetian Black Nobility names, tracing their lineages back to Roman senators and noblemen. Like many other wealthy families, these names are largely unknown to the public, including some family members, due to the inordinate secrecy used to cloak both their activities and their history. But occasionally there are glimpses of what really goes on within family circles.

It is shocking but possible that one unexpected member of this Black Nobility, and the Rothschild family in particular, was none other than the Nazi führer, Adolf Hitler. This astounding information came from Walter C. Langer, a psychologist who produced a wartime psychoanalysis of Hitler for the OSS. Langer reported that a secret prewar Austrian police report proved that Hitler's father was the illegitimate son of a young peasant cook named Maria Anna Schicklgruber, who at the time she conceived her child was "employed as a servant in the home of Baron [Salomon] Rothschild" in Vienna. Rothschild biographer Ferguson stated that the son of one of Salomon's senior clerks recalled that by the 1840s, Salomon Rothschild "had developed a somewhat reckless enthusiasm for young girls."

Upon learning of her pregnancy in 1837, Maria left Vienna and gave birth to Hitler's father of record, Alois. Five years later, she reportedly married an itinerant miller named Johann Georg Hiedler. Yet Alois carried his mother's name of Schicklgruber until nearly forty years of age, when Hiedler's brother, Johann Nepomuk Hiedler, offered him legitimacy. Due to the illegible writing of a parish priest in changing the birth register, the name Hiedler became Hitler, either by mistake or to confuse authorities. Alois Hitler, a government bureaucrat, married his second cousin, Klara Pölzl, in 1885, after obtaining special Episcopal dispensation. Adolf was born in Braunau, Austria, in 1889, when Alois was fifty-two years old.

In the late 1930s, Hitler's English nephew, William Patrick Hitler, hinted to newsmen about the German leader's Jewish background. Hitler's personal attorney, Hans Frank, confirmed this scandalous information but reported that the father of Alois had the last name Frankenberger instead of Rothschild. When no record of a Frankenberger could be found in Vienna, the matter was quietly dropped by all but Hitler. Historians have long noted that the question of possible Jewish ancestry haunted Hitler throughout his life. "It is possible that Hitler discovered his Jewish background and his relation to the Rothschilds, and aware of their enormous power to make or break European governments, re-established contact with the family," wrote Ralph Epperson. "This would partially explain the enormous support he received from the international banking fraternity, closely entwined with the Rothschild family, as he rose to power."

This incredible story might be written off as wartime propaganda except for the fact that the OSS never made this story public, indicating that the tale may have been considered too sensitive to make public, even as propaganda.

A UNIQUE GOLD BOOK

If Hitler indeed carried Rothschild blood, he also may have been part of the royal Habsburg line. At the turn of the twentieth century, Emperor Franz Josef of Austria self-published an extraordinary book, bound in green leather with a gold-tipped binding, engraved and embossed from plates of copper, steel, and zinc. It was titled

An ehren und an siegen Reich, which in translation means "Toward an Honorable and Victorious Reich." It was a handmade, one-of-a-kind book, and apparently no more than five copies were printed. Readership was limited to Habsburg family members.

The volume provided a detailed history of the Habsburgs and the Holy Roman Empire, and it predicted the coming of an Austrian-German superstate. Each chapter had a different design and topic, covering the various aspects of the nation's history. One of these copies ended up in the hands of Adolf Hitler, who kept it secured during World War II, perhaps in deference to his own family history.

At the end of the war, a British soldier found the book in the ruins of Hitler's chancellery and took it as a souvenir. In the late 1980s, this fellow died, and the book was passed to the man's son. The son did not know the full worth of the book, but he realized that it was expensive. He explained the book's history and gave it to Jim Delittoso of Phoenix, Arizona, to repay a loan he had used to return to Ireland and bury his father.

Delittoso had the book appraised by Abe Feder, a Phoenix book appraiser who once worked for the Museum of Natural History in New York City. In 1997, Feder studied the book for several months. At least two persons participated in its translation. Feder told this author, "I have never seen a book like this." Feder's appraisal of the book essentially was that it was "priceless."

In March 1999, the book disappeared. A business associate of Delittoso had borrowed it to use as collateral for a loan, and then the person who made the loan allowed a business partner to borrow the book. This fellow sold the book to another man for an undisclosed price. This man, in turn, sold it to another person, whose name has never become known, and the book was gone, although several persons had handled it and photographs of some pages remain. Some have speculated that someone during this process realized the importance of the book and secreted it away. The amazing story recounted in this uncommon book is how the Habsburg line was joined with a Jewish bloodline during the time of the Third Crusade.

The book recorded that Frederick I Barbarossa, crowned emperor of the Holy Roman Empire in 1155, had a sickly son named Albrecht I by his wife Margaret, daughter of King Gustav of Sweden. Frederick took his family with him to the Holy Land while on crusade and there took a Jewish wife named Rebeccah, who bore him a son, whom he named Albrecht II. Frederick Barbarossa died before returning home, and Albrecht I was killed by assassins. Eventually his wife Margaret and Albrecht II returned to Germany, where Albrecht started a lineage that included Albrecht III and IV. Eventually, Albrecht's lineage led to the Emperor Maximillian and the later Habsburg line.

Franz Joseph's book indicates that the Rothschild family is a part of the bloodline stemming from Albrecht II, meaning that the Habsburgs and the Rothschilds shared a common Jewish ancestor. This part of the Habsburg history was carefully hidden during the years that anti-Semitism grew in Europe. Apparently, in commissioning this extraordinary book, Emperor Franz Josef had decided it was time that the entire family learned of their heritage. Some suspect that this untold history may have been known within the Rothschild family, which could go far in explaining their support for later German regimes.

Blue bloods believe that, due to their ancestry, they have a right to control others. Perhaps it has been the attempts at such control that kept the human race constantly on the move. After leaving the cradle of civilization in ancient Sumer, humans moved into the Caucasus Mountains and spread throughout Europe, while others moved into Egypt and Palestine. What drove people to leave established homes and travel to strange and distant lands?

Historians have been clear that people migrated to escape political and religious tyranny. It is unarguable that throughout human history, tyrants have attempted to corral and subjugate the human population. Throughout our history, rulers from the pharaohs and caesars to European royals and even the German Nazis have filled the roles of these tyrants. What made them so confident that their role was to rule others? And why were these tyrants so concerned about the sanctity of their bloodline? Could it be that they were genetically connected to the early sky gods and that they wanted to maintain this connection?

NOBODY EXPECTS THE SPANISH INQUISITION

From time immemorial, religion has been the first-choice method of control of populations by the blue blood elite. "God ordained me to tell you how to live and what to tithe" was the word from religious authorities from ancient Sumer to the present day. Since its formation, the Roman Church has perpetrated a number of crimes—including the massacres of the Cathars and Native Americans, the Crusades, the Inquisition and the killing of those deemed "witches" and "heretics," and the church's cozy relationship with Hitler's Third Reich and its attendant Holocaust. The Church has also been quite good at covering its tracks.

Barbara G. Walker, award-winning author of the *Women's Encyclopedia of Myths and Secrets*, has pointed to Henry Charles Lea's 1888 study of the Inquisition, *A History of the Inquisition of the Middle Ages*, as being illustrative of Church practices. "Even in his time, Lea said, Vatican authorities were already beginning secretly to destroy most of these damning records. The Inquisition was the worst holocaust in European history; it lasted nearly five centuries; and yet the church was succeeding in misrepresenting its extent and its impact in their official histories. This was my earliest realization of patriarchy's propensity to lie itself into respectability."

Adding to Walker's insight, New Zealand researcher Martin

Doutré stated, "We're deluding ourselves if we think we live in some kind of 'bright new age' of enlightenment and that the 'Dark Ages' passed into memory centuries ago. The powerbase that ran the Inquisitions was never dismantled and remains more strongly in place today than ever, controlling, directing, misleading, deceiving, suppressing, propagandizing, war mongering, persecuting, dominating and exploiting, etc., etc."

Doutré pointed to the church's persecution of Galileo as a classic example of religious perfidy. The aging astronomer-mathematician simply tried to explain that the Earth revolved around the sun and not vice versa as presented in church dogma, but was finally forced to recant before the court of Inquisition rather than end his days in the torturer's dungeon.

During the time of the Inquisition, church authorities taught the ignorant masses that the Earth was flat. The educated aristocrats of the time knew better, but a flat Earth suited their purposes, because it kept the population from straying too far from their grasp. The educated also knew that something was amiss with conventional history, but they didn't want to probe this subject too far. After all, the Inquisition's racks were always ready for new victims. It's not all that much better today.

YOU CAN BANK ON THIS

Since at least the time of the Babylonians, religious institutions have relied on financial institutions. The pattern involved blending the finances of money changers with the prevailing religion as if money was God-ordained.

The Roman Empire, especially after Christianity became the official state religion, accelerated the spread of the money changers, whose reach extended into the highest levels of Roman society. "The result," according to Joseph P. Farrell, "was that the

Mesopotamian and Syrian money changers and merchants effectively colonized Rome's provinces bordering the Mediterranean Sea, Roman banking was all but monopolized in their hands as the influence of Mesopotamian mystery cults extended throughout the Empire, and the activities of the temple continued to be associated with commerce."

Following the fall of the Roman Empire, the money changers moved into northern Europe. In 1602, the Dutch chartered the Dutch East India Company, and they began to settle South Africa. William of Orange, scion of one of the elite Dutch bloodlines, in 1688 invaded England and became King William III. In 1691, William initiated the growth of the global banking system by creating the Bank of England, which led to the growth of the British Empire. By 1820, the Rothschild banking dynasty had gained control of the Bank of England, thanks to loans made to Prince Regent George Augustus Frederick (note the historical nature of these names), later King George IV, by Nathan Rothschild.

"[The] expansion of the British and other European empires to all parts of the world exported the bloodlines to every continent, including, most importantly today, North America," commented David Icke.

The advent of the printing press led to the Renaissance and the Age of Enlightenment and thus the decline of the Roman Church, as it also allowed for the printing of the Bible, as well as paper money. Before printed paper money, gold, silver, and copper coins, beads, shells, and even sticks of wood were used as currency. After the invention of printing, paper money began to replace religion as the primary control mechanism of the elite.

During the reign of England's King Henry I, people used tally sticks, notches carved into wood or bone, to represent numbers or quantities. Wooden tally sticks were split in half. The piece that bore the notches was kept by the king as protection against counterfeiting; the other half circulated as money. Talley sticks were accepted in payment for taxes, and not only were they used by the public, but they were in great demand.

The tally system worked well for 726 years, but any currency aside from silver and gold is only as good as the faith people place in it. Today no one remembers the stick system. When the Bank of England was formed in 1694, its shareholders, the money changers of their day, whose names were kept secret, realized that tally sticks represented money outside their power, which is exactly what King Henry had intended.

Unbelievable as it sounds, these shareholders bought stock in the bank with the notched pieces of wood, then proceeded to slowly eliminate that system in favor of Bank of England notes. The use of tally sticks continued until 1826. In 1834, the remaining sticks were ordered burned. Ironically, the stove used to burn the sticks in the Houses of Parliament went out of control, gutting the Palace of Westminster. It was the largest blaze in London since the Great Fire of 1666.

Thanks to fractional-reserve banking, the shareholders of the bank lent out much more money than they had on hand, and by backing wars and revolutions, such as Oliver Cromwell's overthrow of King Charles, they became so wealthy that they took over a square mile of property still known as the City of London. The City (as opposed to London proper), Wall Street in New York City, and Zurich remain the three dominant financial centers of the world today.

One example of manipulating a money system, which paralleled the recent economic scandals in the United States yet predated the founding of the nation, was known as the Great South Sea Bubble of 1721. The South Sea Company, a British joint stock company founded in 1711, was granted a monopoly to trade with Spain's South American colonies. Speculators ran up the price of stock from about £100 to more than £1,000 per share. The government encouraged such speculation by eliminating taxes on dividends and allowing women to own stock, one of the few forms of property that women could possess in their own right.

In 1719, the company proposed to purchase half the public debt of Britain with the promise to lower the interest rate. It was said that everyone would benefit. Speculation led to a gigantic economic bubble that finally burst in 1721, ruining most investors and crashing the company's stock. In the ensuing investigation, fraud by the company's directors was found, as well as corruption within the British cabinet.

Despite popular myth, the American colonial revolt against England occurred more over concern for its own currency than a small tax on tea. During a visit to Britain in 1763, Benjamin Franklin was asked about the prosperity of the American colonists by officials of the Bank of England. Franklin explained, "That is simple. In the colonies, we issue our own money. It is called Colonial Scrip. We issue it in proper proportion to the demands of trade and industry to make the products pass easily from the producers to the consumers. In this manner, creating for ourselves our own paper money, we control its purchasing power, and we have no interest to pay to no one."

Franklin later stated, "The colonies would gladly have borne the little tax on tea and other matters had it not been that England took away from the colonies their money, which created unemployment and dissatisfaction. The inability of colonists to get power to issue their own money permanently out of the hands of George III and the international bankers was the prime reason for the Revolutionary War." The American revolutionists knew that to gain true freedom, they had to break the power of the Rothschild-dominated Bank of England, which had outlawed their money—colonial script based on goods and services—in favor of interest-bearing Bank of England notes.

By the mid-1800s, the bankers of Europe had gone worldwide, despite their setback in North America due to the American Revolution. But they didn't give up in their attempts to regain control of the United States and may in fact have been instrumental in influencing the course of events leading to the Civil War.

German chancellor Otto von Bismarck once stated, "The division of the United States into federations of equal force was decided long before the Civil War by the high financial powers of Europe. These bankers were afraid that the United States, if they remained in one block and as one nation, would attain economic and financial independence, which would upset their financial domination over the world. The voice of the Rothschilds prevailed. . . . Therefore they sent their emissaries into the field to exploit the question of slavery and to open an abyss between the two sections of the Union."

For some years, the Rothschilds financed major projects in the United States on both sides of the Mason-Dixon Line. Nathan Rothschild, who owned a large Manchester textile plant, bought his cotton from Southern interests and financed the importation of Southern cotton prior to the war. At the same time, wrote Rothschild biographer Wilson, "He had made loans to various states of the Union, and had been, for a time, the official European banker for the US government and was a pledged supporter of the Bank of the United States."

The War Between the States was more over economics than slavery, despite how modern political correctness aims to convince otherwise. And it was encouraged through secret societies, especially the Knights of the Gold Circle, of which John Wilkes Booth, the assassin of President Abraham Lincoln, was a member.

Abraham Lincoln was more concerned with preserving the federal union than freeing slaves. In late 1862, he proclaimed, "My paramount object in this struggle is to save the Union, and is not either to save or to destroy slavery. If I could save the Union without freeing any slave, I would do it; and if I could save it by freeing all the slaves, I would do it; and if I could save it by freeing some and leaving others alone, I would also do that. What I do about slavery and the colored race, I do because I believe it helps to save the Union. . . ."

Lincoln understood that the true reason for sectional friction in the United States was not slavery, but the fact that the South desired to buy less-costly imported European products even though the powerful Northern manufacturers had imposed stiff import tariffs. These tariffs were raised even higher after Southern congressmen left Washington in 1861. The industrial North, filling rapidly with immigrants willing to work for a pittance, had no need for slaves, while the major planters of the agrarian South were totally dependent on human labor. Although antislavery advocates in both North and South realized that technological advances meant the demise of slavery was only a matter of time, extremists on both sides, encouraged by agents of the European financiers, continually fanned the fires of discontent, and war became inevitable. Many of the famous American wealthy families enriched themselves from Lincoln's Great War.

Lincoln may have failed to recall that the first assassination attempt on an American president was against Andrew Jackson, who incurred the wrath of the international bankers by abolishing the country's central bank. In need of money to fund the war effort, Lincoln turned from those lenders and, instead of borrowing from the European banks as expected, in 1862 issued about $450 million in currency printed with green ink and thus called greenbacks. This paper money, legalized by an act of Congress with nothing to back it, was debt-free fiat money. Lincoln saw the debt-free creation of money as government's greatest creative opportunity. But he also found that it was fatal to cross the international bankers. He was shot by John Wilkes Booth while attending Ford's Theatre on April 14, 1865, and died the next morning.

The money changers of Europe gained even greater power during World War I, when many of Europe's royal houses lost their leadership positions. Their greatest fear came with the rise of communism in Russia. Although the Bolsheviks were aided in their revolution against the czar by Western bankers, the bankers' control slipped when Stalin ascended to dictatorial power following Lenin's death in 1924. With the success of the Bolshevik Revolution, wealthy and titled Russians fled to Western nations, warning of the dangers to capitalism from international communism. Great fear was engendered among the wealthy. The cry of "Workers of the world, unite!" reverberated within Communist parties from Berlin and Paris to London and New York.

It may well have been the post–World War I plan of the banker elite to create a socialist East and pit it against the capitalist West, but the fear of the spread of communism caused a change in plans. Something had to be done to halt the spread of communist socialism, and Germany was in a central position to act as a barrier.

However, something first had to be done with the democratic Weimar Republic in Germany. One solution was to combine American capitalism with German corporations in the 1920s under the Dawes Plan and the Young Plan, which ostensibly were plans to help Germany repay its debt after World War I. These plans used American loans to create and consolidate the German steel and chemical giants, Vereinigte Stahlwerke and IG Farben, both major supporters of the fledgling Nazi Party. Both plans were described by historian Carroll Quigley as "largely a J.P. Morgan production."

FOLLOW THE LEADER

The final solution was to finance an Austrian Army corporal who was drawing pay as an undercover agent for his military superiors after his failed attempts as an artist. This, of course, was Adolf Hitler, who gained power through the backing of both the occult Thule Society, composed of German aristocrats and wealthy industrialists, as well as Western banking interests. Over the course of several years, the former corporal brought his National Socialist German Workers Party (the Nazis) from a handful of members to a national organization of millions.

In early 1933, Hitler was elected chancellor of Germany. In 1934, with the death of President Paul von Hindenburg, Hitler consolidated his office with that of president and assumed the title of führer, or leader of the entire nation.

But then Hitler made a fatal error—the same one that may have cost the life of Lincoln. He failed to follow the wishes of the moneyed elite to borrow money from the international bankers. Instead, he issued his own debt-free money, reichsmarks, and put the Germans back to work on public projects such as the autobahn highway system and the production of war materials.

In early Nazi meetings, Hitler had listened to the views of German economist Gottfried Feder, who advocated monetary control through a nationalized central bank rather than private banks and believed that financial interests had enslaved the population by controlling the money supply. One of the platforms of the Nazi Party was the breaking of "debt-slavery"—in other words, interest payments.

"When listening to Gottfried Feder's first lecture about the 'Breaking of the Tyranny of Interest,' I knew immediately that the question involved was a theoretical truth which would reach enormous importance for the German people's future," wrote Hitler in *Mein Kampf.* " . . . Germany's development already stood before my eyes too clearly for me not to know that the hardest battle had to be fought, not against hostile nations, but rather against international capital. . . . The fight against international finance and loan capital has become the most important point in the program of the German nation's fight for its independence and freedom." Unfortunately, Hitler's view narrowed from all international finance to only internal Jewish finance.

In 1933, Germany, like America, was in the depths of the Great Depression. A large segment of the population was out of work, and the money hyperinflated. Many recall the stories of Germans needing a wheelbarrow loaded with paper money to buy a single loaf of bread. By the time of the 1936 Berlin Olympics—a mere three years later—Germany had become an economic powerhouse, with nearly full employment and stable money, thanks to its freedom from the international bankers. However, the wealthy elite, whose secrets came from ancient Sumer, could not afford to have the rest of the world see the benefits of the interest-free money sought by Benjamin Franklin, Thomas Jefferson, and many others throughout history.

Winston Churchill, a member of the aristocratic and wealthy elite, summed up their reaction to Hitler's actions during World War II when he stated, "You must understand that this war is not against Hitler or National Socialism but against the [economic] strength of the German people, which must be smashed once and for all, regardless whether it is in the hands of Hitler or a Jesuit priest."

One may ask, if Lincoln was assassinated for bypassing the international bankers, weren't there assassination attempts on Hitler, who did the same? Only about two dozen. But unlike Lincoln, Hitler was surrounded by loyalists who kept him protected even from his own generals. It took the strength of more than two dozen nations combined in a world war to stop Hitler and his plans for a thousand-year Reich.

The Germans lost the war, but the wealthy elite, who had funded Hitler and the Nazis, did not. In fact, in many ways, they won. The Nazis experimented with new technology in nuclear science, energy manipulation, psychiatric drugs, and innovative techniques of propaganda and mind control, all of which helped the elite. They learned the best ways to overthrow nations, dumb down populations with fluoride and other chemical agents, and how to insinuate fear, torture, and assassination into a civilized society. They brought all this, along with thousands of unrepentant Nazis, to

America under a variety of programs, including Operation Paperclip, which recruited former Nazi scientists and brought them to the United States. All of this helped them create their new police state.

A number of events in America during the first part of the twenty-first century eerily paralleled the National Socialist takeover of Germany in the 1930s. In both nations, an attack on a prominent building led to rushed legislation reducing civil liberties, followed by the gradual erosion of civil law, the militarization of the police, torture, indefinite detention, and war. In Berlin, the Reichstag, Germany's parliament building, was set ablaze in early 1933. A half-wit named Marinus van der Lubbe was arrested and, after torture, confessed to setting the fire alone. After the disaster, the German president von Hindenberg blamed the communists for a conspiracy and declared many key civil liberties of German citizens nullified. The legislature then passed the Enabling Act, which allowed Hitler in his role as chancellor to consolidate all of the country's legislative powers in his hands, effectively making Germany's constitution moot. Hitler also consolidated all of Germany's police agencies under the pretext of fatherland security. Similarly, in the United States in the first years of the twenty-first century, the World Trade Center towers were destroyed, blame was placed on terrorists—this time they were Middle Eastern fanatics—and the PATRIOT Act was passed by Congress, effectively limiting civil liberties in the United States and allowing the government greater license to monitor its citizens. This was followed by the creation of the Department of Homeland Security.

BREAKS IN THE COLD WAR

In the aftermath of World War II, the banking elite returned to their original plan of pitting the socialist East against the capitalist

West. It was called the Cold War, and it was built on secrecy. Leaders on both sides, most unaware of the machinations in play, did not know the capabilities or the intentions of their adversary.

The Cold War created an arms race between the superpowers of the United States and the Soviet Union. Naturally, banks prospered during this time, especially during actual conflict, such as the "police action" known as the Korean War, which took place between 1950 and 1953 and cost almost thirty-four thousand American and about four million Korean lives. Even here can be seen hidden manipulation from the top level of control. Never a declared war, the Korean conflict was run by the United Nations, a supranational organization created during the distraction of world war in October 1944. The UN was merely a replacement for the old League of Nations, a failed attempt at world government instigated by Woodrow Wilson and members of the Round Table secret society, which created the Council on Foreign Relations in 1921.

American Korean War veterans would be flabbergasted to learn that the Russians were running both sides of the conflict. During the war, the Soviets were supplying the North Koreans with military hardware, technology, and advisers. Soviet military officers were largely in control of the war on the North Korean side. Author Ralph Epperson cited a Pentagon press release that identified two Soviet officers as being in charge of movements across the 38th parallel, the action that precipitated the fighting. One officer, General Stefan Vasilev, actually was overheard giving the order to launch the attack against the south.

General Vasilev's chain of command reached from Korea to Moscow to the UN undersecretary general for political and Security Council affairs. At this same time, Allied general Douglas MacArthur's chain of command went through President Truman and thence also to the UN undersecretary general for political and Security Council affairs, an office held at that time by Russian general Constantine Zinchenko. This meant that the Soviet officers overseeing the North Korean war strategy were reporting to a fellow Soviet officer in the UN who was coordinating the Allied war effort.

But the money changers were not satisfied with the Cold War, even though the war in Vietnam made defense contractors billions while costing fifty-eight thousand American and at least five million Southeast Asian lives. The bankers failed to fully profit from the Cold War due to the fact that historically Russia had disdained the formation of a privately owned central bank. Neither the czars nor the communists had allowed the private management of the Russian economy.

This all changed with the collapse of communism, usually marked by the destruction of the Berlin Wall on November 9, 1989. The end of the Cold War came about due to economic strains on the Russian economy, causing widespread discontent, but also perhaps due to the loss of all secrecy, thanks to psychic remote viewing by both sides, as mentioned previously.

On July 13, 1990, less than a year after the Berlin Wall fell, the international bankers were gratified by the creation of the Central Bank of the Russian Federation. Like the Federal Reserve System, this bank is an independent entity that controls the Russian economy through the exclusive right to issue coins and banknotes.

With the economies of the two world superpowers now within their hands and with the creation of the European Union, the money changers were able to concentrate on the last remaining major obstacle to their quest for one-world control—freedom within the United States.

As far back as 1865, the international banking elite recognized the danger represented by a free and prosperous United States. An editorial that year in *The Times* of London, which, according to many, speaks for the British establishment, warned, "If that mischievous financial policy which had its origin in the North American Republic [debt-free money] should become indurated down to a fixture, then that government will furnish its own money without cost. It will pay off its debts and be without a debt. It will become prosperous beyond precedent in the history of the civilized governments of the world. The brains and wealth of all countries will go to North America. That government must be destroyed or it will destroy every monarchy on the globe."

Since the *Times* article was published, events in the United States have certainly followed a course of destruction for individual freedom and liberty as well as for the economy. And anyone who tried to obstruct this plan to destroy the economic strength and social cohesion of the American people was demoted, fired, blackmailed, ridiculed as a "conspiracy theorist" and "paranoid," or as a last resort, especially if he or she held some important office or commanded a public platform, simply eliminated.

Intimidation in business was a last resort, the first being mergers and forced consolidation. Which is further intensified by interlocking directorships.

MASTERS OF CONTROL

President John F. Kennedy, like Lincoln, attempted to curtail the bankers by diminishing the power of the Federal Reserve. In June 1963, he issued $4.2 billion in United States Notes through the U.S. Treasury rather than the Federal Reserve System and also took steps to shift power away from the wealthy corporate elite. According to University of Pittsburgh professor Donald Gibson in his well-researched 1994 book *Battling Wall Street: The Kennedy Presidency*, these steps included: tax proposals to redirect the foreign investments of U.S. companies, making distinctions in tax reform between productive and nonproductive investment, eliminating the tax privileges of U.S-based global investment companies, cracking down on foreign tax havens, rejecting proposals to eliminate tax privileges for the wealthy, proposing increased taxes for large oil and mineral companies, and revising the investment tax credit.

For such attempts to equalize the economy, Kennedy was killed in a military-style ambush while riding in a motorcade through Dallas in November 1963 in circumstances still unsettled. Many conspiracy researchers do not believe it is sheer coincidence that Lincoln and Kennedy—the only two U.S. presidents to issue debt-free money—were both shot in the head in public.

The assassinations of John F. Kennedy, Robert Kennedy, and Martin Luther King Jr.—still unresolved in the minds of most of the public—along with the drug revolution of the Sixties, with continuous escalation of the War on Drugs in reaction, heralded a continuing degradation of culture, civility, and common sense in America. The Great Depression, two world wars, and subsequent "brushfire" wars in Korea, Vietnam, Kuwait, Iraq, Afghanistan, and Libya have depleted public self-confidence as well as the U.S. Treasury.

James G. Watt, former interior secretary in the Reagan administration, saw the money manipulation of insiders firsthand. "For years I had been irritated by 'right wingers' who came to whisper about Council on Foreign Relationers and The Trilateral Commission. . . . Now, after sitting in the cabinet room of the White House in meeting after meeting listening to President Reagan's advisors, I am of a different opinion," Watt related.

"A most telling incident happened one morning in the spring of 1982. As President Reagan sat down with us cabinet officers, he announced that Don Regan (then treasury secretary) would share an economic report and that David Stockman (then budget director) would have some comments to make. Secretary Regan led off the cabinet meeting by reporting that several American banks were owed alarming sums of money by some third world countries. So destitute were these nations, he said, that not even the interest on these loans could be paid back to the Bank of America, Chase Manhattan, Citibank, and others. Secretary Regan urged sending tax-payers' dollars through the International Monetary Fund to these nations, enabling them to make interest payments to U.S. banks. . . . I asked if anyone believed these countries could ever pay back any of the principal. Silence! Did anyone believe these loans for the payment of interest would ever be paid back? When most of my col-leagues just stared at the table, I pressed on. Then why, at our tax-payers' expense, do we keep bailing out these countries? Annoyance erupted around the table: 'Jim, these American banks will be in jeopardy if those loans are in default by lack of interest payments.' I countered, 'Does that mean American bank customers would lose money?' 'No,' they hotly responded, 'but investors might lose some dividends.' Incredulous, I leaned back from the cabinet table and watched the president, seated only two chairs away. Absolutely nothing was going to stop those cabinet officers from bailing out a few powerful U.S. banks. President Reagan was given no other option.

"Was there a conspiracy by members of the trilats and CFR, first, to control the economies of other nations and now to 'save their own hides'? No. I still don't believe the liberals are capable of getting together to plan a conspiracy. Yet, that was the end result. How could it have happened? I believe there is a conspiracy of shared values, a commonality in the thoughts and objectives of these liberals. These internationalists don't want to trust their eco-nomic fortunes to the free market. They want stronger government controls to secure their economic fortunes and political clout. . . ."

Watt still believed in the dichotomy of "liberal" versus "conser-vative" and did not realize that the power behind such un-American decisions was not due simply to "shared values" or "liberal ideals," but rather to the power of the international money changers operat-ing behind the scenes who manage both major parties.

Another person who not only saw global financial manipula-tion but actively participated in it was John Perkins, author of the

New York Times best-seller *Confessions of an Economic Hit Man.* In the book, Perkins describes the activities of economic hit men as "highly-paid professionals who cheat countries around the globe out of trillions of dollars. They funnel money from the World Bank, the U.S. Agency for International Development (USAID), and other foreign 'aid' organizations into the coffers of huge corporations and the pockets of a few wealthy families who control the planet's natural resources. Their tools included fraudulent financial reports, rigged elections, payoffs, extortion, sex, and murder. They play a game as old as empire, but one that has taken on new and terrifying dimensions during this time of globalization."

Perkins's consulting firm sent him around the world. He said his job was "to enslave nations that had resources our corporations coveted by burdening them with debts they could never repay. We then demanded that they sell those resources cheap, without social or environmental regulations, to our corporations. It was an incredibly successful strategy. In essence it created the world's first truly global empire and the first one that was not built primarily through military occupations. It also transformed geo-politics. The power of elected officials was usurped by those who sit at the top of the multinational corporations (the 'corporatocracy')." Perkins said the corporatocracy soon realized that similar strategies could be used in the United States to prevent the population from exercising democratic rights that might threaten its wars and other interests.

"By 1980, the [corporatocracy] understood that its most effective weapon to protect corporations against labor movements was debt. Borrowers were deceived into believing that they were paying low interest rates when in fact balloon payments, adjustable rate mortgages, and other technically complex packages resulted in higher overall rates that made it increasingly difficult to break the shackles of debt. This story continued. Regulations that protected our rights were demolished. New wars erupted. Family businesses were wiped out by the unfair practices of huge chains. The media was commandeered by a handful of giant conglomerates. Unemployment, poverty and foreclosures escalated. The upward trend line of a growing and prospering middle class plummeted."

Perkins saw "a mutant, viral and extremely dangerous form of capitalism has thrived under the ever-increasing powers of Wall St., Big Business, and governments that support them. . . . The global economic crisis is a symptom and a messenger. It has exposed our darkest secrets. The most materialistic and wealthiest nation in the history of the world, the U.S., also has the highest rates of suicide, drug abuse, murder, incarcerations, and other negative social factors. Our economy is based on fighting wars—killing people and ravaging the planet—trading paper (mergers, derivatives, etc.), and selling each other things most of us don't need. Meanwhile our planet is drowning in pollution, people are starving, our resources are dissipating, and our animals and plants are disappearing at shocking rates."

Such forthright statements prompted vicious attacks from the corporate mass media. *Washington Post* columnist Sebastian Mallaby described Perkins as "a frothing conspiracy theorist, a vainglorious peddler of nonsense," while a *New York Times* writer referred to Perkins's work as "cloak-and-dagger atmospherics."

Yet Perkins's words echo those of Marine major general Smedley Butler, who in his 1935 book *War Is a Racket* explained, "Bankers lend money to foreign countries and when they cannot pay, the President sends Marines to get it." Butler also explained that the racket of war is "something that is not what it seems to the majority of the people. Only a small 'inside' group knows what it is about. It is conducted for the benefit of the very few, at the expense of the very many. Out of war a few people make huge fortunes."

But the money changers overextended themselves. Their ballooning economy began to lose air in the meltdown of 2008. Many commentators have attributed the financial crisis and the Great Recession that followed to conscious planning by the elite money changers of today with help by government hacks. After all, many members of Congress held investments with the Wall Street companies behind the mortgage-backed securities fraud that broke in 2008.

Internet commentator Michael Rivero called the collapse "the biggest financial swindle since the Great South Seas Bubble of 1721." Rivero groused, "In short the US Government took your jobs, so the banks could take your homes, to cover the losses from this gigantic swindle they were caught playing on the whole world. Tens of millions of Americans have had their homes confiscated to keep the Wall Street crooks out of jail. It is wealth confiscation to protect the banks, just like FDR did in 1933 with the gold, only this time done with houses and in such a way as to trick Americans into thinking it was their own fault they lost their homes."

In the years before the crisis, Congress passed laws reducing government oversight and regulation, while banks were encouraged to make questionable loans and offer an $8,000 first-time home buyer credit in order to lure more buyers. Many bad mortgages were "bundled" with a few good ones to produce packages called derivatives. These were marked A-1 by rating agencies receiving bank money, then sold and resold to banks and other institutions. Then the whole scam came unraveled. Sold on the canard that some banks are "too big to fail," Congress voted to bail them out. This was nothing more than using public money borrowed from the Federal Reserve to cover the bad loans and credit swaps. It was a classic example of "taxation without representation," as the vast majority of the American public did not want to save the bankers from their own misdeeds. To add insult to injury, there have been no prosecutions of the Wall Street insiders or bank officials involved.

Why was no one prosecuted? In mid-October 2008, the president of the Federal Reserve Bank of New York, Timothy Geithner, met with Andrew Cuomo, then the New York attorney general. Before he became the governor of New York, Cuomo was looking into banking and rating irregularities and also looking into questionable bonuses during the bailout of the now-defunct American International Group (AIG). According to persons with knowledge of the meeting, Geithner argued that he was concerned about the "fragility of the financial system" and requested that there be no prosecutions. Previously it had been Geithner, acting as undersecretary of the treasury, along with Henry Paulson, who had sent $5 billion of U.S. taxpayer money through AIG to the giant Swiss bank UBS. In defense of Cuomo's inaction, William K. Black, a professor of economics and law at the University of Missouri, wrote, "This is not some evil conspiracy of two guys sitting in a room saying we should let people create crony capitalism and steal with impunity. But their policies have created an exceptional criminogenic environment. There were no criminal referrals from the regulators. No fraud working groups. No national task force. There has been no effective punishment of the elites here." Black should know. In the 1980s, he served as the federal government's director of litigation during the savings-and-loan crisis. This lack of punishment stands in stark contrast to that scandal, in which special government task forces referred one thousand cases to prosecutors, resulting in more than eight hundred bank officials going to jail.

President James A. Garfield, just two weeks before he was assassinated in 1881, stated, "Whoever controls the volume of money in our country is absolute master of all industry and commerce . . . and when you realize that the entire system is very easily controlled, one way or another, by a few powerful men at the top, you will not have to be told how periods of inflation and depression originate."

THE EXCHANGE STABILIZATION FUND

One of the hidden tools of financial control may come from the Exchange Stabilization Fund (ESF) of the United States Treasury.

This little-known agency is one of those government constructs that has morphed into a gigantic money-moving operation with absolutely no oversight by the U.S. government, the states, or the American people. Yet the ESF uses tax money and its profits to fund operations both inside and outside the country. Texas congressman Henry B. Gonzalez, a vocal opponent of the Fed, while chairman of the House Banking Committee, criticized the ESF for "back-door financing" and "a complete lack of public accountability."

The ESF was created and originally financed by the Gold Reserve Act of 1934. Its purpose, according to an official description, was "to contribute to exchange rate stability and counter disorderly conditions in the foreign exchange market." The act authorized the secretary of the treasury to exclusively deal in gold, foreign exchange, securities, and instruments of credit subject to the approval of the president. While ownership of gold was outlawed for Americans in 1933, the ESF transferred gold out of the country to foreigners in exchange for dollars, draining our gold reserves for years to come. Today, when people blame the Federal Reserve for stealing America's gold reserves, they should know that it was actually the ESF, never scrutinized or questioned by Congress, that drained the Federal Reserve many years ago.

Under agreements with the International Monetary Fund (IMF), in 1978 Congress amended the Gold Reserve Act to provide short-term credit to foreign governments and monetary authorities. Such ESF "bridge loans" are financed through swaps, which means that dollars held by the ESF are made available to a country through its central bank in exchange for the same value in that country's currency.

The ESF also administers special drawing rights (SDRs), assets created by the IMF and then loaned to countries requiring help in financing balance-of-payment deficits. SDRs are permanent resources of the ESF, whose operations are conducted through the Federal Reserve Bank of New York. The New York Fed acts as an intermediary between the ESF and those foreign governments seeking short-term financing.

This all sounds fine until one learns that it allows the U.S. Treasury secretary to operate outside U.S. laws. According to minority members of the House Committee on Coinage, Weights, and Measures who reviewed this law in its preparation, "This [law] in fact, means that the Secretary of the Treasury shall be under no obligation to comply with general laws of the United States in the handling of this fund. . . . We believe that [this] places autocratic and dictatorial power in the hands of one man directly over the control of the value of money and credit and indirectly over prices. . . . We believe that this is too great a power to place in the hands of any one man. We believe that it is contrary to every true principle of American Government."

After serving as the president of the Federal Reserve Bank of New York, Timothy Geithner was appointed treasury secretary when Barack Obama took office. After being appointed by the president, a Senate panel must confirm the treasury secretary. Much like a corporate president or CEO, the secretary is merely the top administrative executive, who makes certain that things run smoothly. The real power comes from above. Sunset provisions in the 1934 law provided that the ESF would expire after two years, but President Roosevelt extended its life by declaring that the economic emergency of the Great Depression was continuing. The ESF, like so many other government instrumentalities, is still with us.

During World War II, the ESF was headed by Harry Dexter White, who was not on the regular Treasury payroll but rather was paid from the ESF budget. He was given vast authority in and full responsibility for all Treasury matters related to foreign relations as well as all Treasury economic and financial matters related to U.S. Army, U.S. Navy, and civilian-affairs operations anywhere overseas. At the same time, White sat on the Office of Strategic Services (OSS) Advisory Committee. The OSS was the counterespionage and counterpropaganda agency of the government, a large organization of more than twelve thousand people who created wartime propaganda and planted false rumors, including the manufacture and propagation of scandals, as well as other activities designed to sow confusion and distrust. All this was financed by the ESF.

After the war, the ESF helped design the world's new monetary system, including its best-known creations—the International Monetary Fund (IMF) and the World Bank. The ESF also has been charged with providing unaccountable funds to the CIA. According to Lawrence Houston, the first general counsel of the CIA, "The heart and soul of covert operations is . . . the provisions of un-vouchered funds, and the inviolability of such funds from outside inspection."

Now the ESF has copycat agencies in many states and itself has become nothing more than a slush fund to bankroll CIA black operations. There are even accusations of laundering drug money. The slush funds operate without legislative oversight or public scrutiny and, while technically legal, outside of the intentions of the U. S. Constitution and Bill of Rights. To pinpoint the movement of tax money to questionable recipients would require a full audit of all the economic stabilization funds and the legislation that regulates transfers of public tax monies to innumerable clandestine and questionable, though technically "legalized," funds.

Internet commentator Eric deCarbonnel has documented an immense amount of information on the ESF and has concluded that the agency "controls the New York Fed, runs the CIA's black budget, and is the architect of the world's monetary system (IMF, World Bank, etc). ESF financing (through the OSS and then the CIA) built up the worldwide propaganda network which has so badly distorted history today (including erasing awareness of its existence from popular consciousness). It has been directly involved in virtually every major US fraud/scandal since its creation in 1934: the London gold pool, the Kennedy assassinations, Iran-Contra, CIA drug trafficking, HIV, and worse. . . ."

It is inner connections like the ESF that lead to the creation of economic hit men like John Perkins, who strong-arm and even oust the leaders of foreign nations. Because these covert agencies operate largely in secret and because their corporate masters own the mass media, most Americans are unaware of the high crimes perpetrated in their name.

Though the ESF began during the age of the Great Depression, the history of conspiratorial banking control goes much further back. Mujahid Kamran, vice chancellor of the University of Punjab and an expert on corporate America, has concluded that the American banking system is ultimately pernicious. "The advent of the industrial revolution, the invention of a banking system based on usury, and scientific and technological advancements during the past three centuries have had three major consequences," he wrote in *The Grand Deception: Corporate America and Perpetual War*. "These have made the incredible concentration of wealth in a few hands possible, have led to the construction of increasingly deadly weapons culminating in weapons of mass destruction, and have made it possible to mold the minds of vast populations by application of scientific techniques through the media and control of the educational system. The wealthiest families on planet earth call the shots in every major upheaval that they cause. Their sphere of activity extends over the entire globe, and even beyond, their ambition and greed for wealth and power knows no bounds, and for them, most of mankind is garbage—'human garbage.' It is also their target to depopulate the globe and maintain a much lower population compared to what we have now." Dr. Kamran also noted that universities in developing countries operate in close partnership with the large private foundations and that the only way to truly understand the operation of the world is "to realize the U.S. Government is owned by those who own these foundations."

PROOF OF THE PLOT

IF THE IDEA THAT A SMALL GROUP OF INTERNATIONAL YET INTER-
connected individuals control the worlds of finance and commerce
seems like a paranoid conspiracy theory, consider a 2011 study
by three scientists at the Swiss Federal Institute of Technology in
Zurich. Combining mathematics used to model natural systems
with comprehensive corporate data, they traced the ownership
of the transnational corporations. From a database of 37 million
companies and investors, the Swiss team constructed a model of
which companies controlled others through shareholding networks,
coupled with each company's operating revenues, to map the structure of economic power.

The study shockingly confirmed the worst fears of conspiracy
theorists and the Occupy protestors, as the analysis of the relationships among forty-three thousand transnational corporations identified a relatively small group of companies—primarily banks—with
disproportionate power over the global economy.

One of the authors of the study, James B. Glattfelder of the
Swiss Federal Institute of Technology, hesitated to draw conclusions
or support anyone's theories, but he said, "Reality is so complex, we
must move away from dogma, whether it's conspiracy theories or
free-market. Our analysis is reality-based."

According to an article in *New Scientist*, the study

> *revealed a core of 1,318 companies with interlocking owner-
> ships. Each of the 1,318 had ties to two or more other com-
> panies, and on average they were connected to 20. What's
> more, although they represented 20 per cent of global operat-
> ing revenues, the 1,318 appeared to collectively own through
> their shares the majority of the world's large blue chip and*

manufacturing firms—the "real" economy—representing a further 60 per cent of global revenues.

When the team further untangled the web of ownership, it found much of it tracked back to a "super-entity" of 147 even more tightly knit companies—all of their ownership was held by other members of the super-entity—that controlled 40 per cent of the total wealth in the network. . . . Most were financial institutions. The top 20 included Barclays Bank, JPMorgan Chase & Co, and The Goldman Sachs Group.

"In effect, less than one per cent of the companies were able to control 40 per cent of the entire network," explained Glattfelder.

Although study members and commentators disparaged talk of conspiratorial control, they did admit that such interconnectedness was worrisome, as it might bring on instability in world markets. "If one [company] suffers distress, this propagates," said Glattfelder, who added that perhaps there should be global antitrust rules to limit such centralized control. One suggestion offered was a tax on corporations that display excessive interconnectivity.

The Swiss researchers limited their study to corporations and never sought to analyze the family, social, and business relationships among owners and stockholders. Yet personal relationships *do* matter, especially in matters of business and politics.

One classic example of individuals guiding corporate decisions may be found in the 1985 acquisition by Capital Cities Communications of the ABC television network, a company about two thirds larger than the acquiring company. In late 1984, William J. "Bill" Casey, then President Reagan's CIA director, demanded that the Federal Communications Commission (FCC) revoke ABC's licenses because it had reported repeatedly on CIA scandals. The FCC was so unimpressed by the request that it never asked the network to respond. But Casey's demand prompted ABC News president Roone Arledge to state, "The CIA's complaint constitutes an unprecedented effort by a government agency to involve the power of government to suppress vigorous reporting about its activities. It raises serious and disturbing First Amendment concerns." Rebuffed by the FCC, Casey turned to Capital Cities, of which he was a founder. He owned 34,755 shares of the company, and his wife owned a comparable number, giving the pair a controlling interest. Thus with the purchase of ABC, the head of the CIA took control of one of the major TV networks with little reporting of this fact outside the financial pages of a few newspapers. The Cap Cities–ABC deal, the biggest broadcasting merger in U.S. history, started an avalanche of media mergers and takeovers. It also ended any deep investigative reporting on the CIA by ABC.

As always, behind the flow of money necessary for such mergers and acquisitions were the banks. Once there were hundreds of banks in America, owned by individuals and local families. But due to government regulations put into place during the Reagan-Bush years, these banks either faded away or consolidated. In 1990, there were thirty-seven major banks in the U.S. By 2009, buy-outs, mergers, and bankruptcies had reduced this number to four. Those left standing were Citigroup, JPMorgan Chase, Bank of America, and Wells Fargo, according to the General Accounting Office. Ominously, in June 2012, the giant global rating agency Moody's downgraded the ratings of Bank of America, Goldman Sachs, and JP Morgan, citing concerns for the stability of the world's financial system.

Gerald Celente, founder of the Trends Research Institute and author of best-sellers *Trend Tracking* and *Trends 2000*, pointed out that even Jesus became an activist when he confronted the money powers. "When you think about the Prince of Peace, when's the only time he became violent? It was when he picked up a whip and drove the moneychangers out of the temple. The moneychangers have taken over the temples—the temples of Athens, the temples of Rome, the temples of Berlin and the City of London. They've taken over Washington. They've taken over every capital of every major city in the world. So where's it going? It's very simple to see where it's going. It's called class warfare."

Stephen Moore, senior economic writer for the *Wall Street Journal* editorial page, said Americans have become a nation of takers, not makers. "Today in America there are nearly twice as many people working for the government (22.5 million in 2011) than in all of manufacturing (11.5 million). This is an almost exact reversal of the situation in 1960, when there were 15 million workers in manufacturing and 8.7 million collecting a paycheck from the government. It gets worse. More Americans work for the government than work in construction, farming, fishing, forestry, manufacturing, mining, and utilities combined."

Big banks, big government, mortgage firms, ratings agencies, derivatives, credit swaps . . . they all sound too complicated for the average person. But are they really? Greed is still greed. Corruption is still corruption, and criminality is still criminality, no matter the cover of law, regulations, corporate policy, or legal technicalities.

This was not all due to accident and coincidence. It was all the plan of a handful of insiders, many operating within the secret societies, who provide a disproportionate number of government leaders and officials. Who's behind it all? According to a growing number of conspiracy researchers looking to answer that question, it can be traced back to thirteen families, all interconnected by blood.

VOICES OF THE ELITE

Various individuals have publicly claimed to be a part of the Illuminati, the inner elite, or whatever name one would like. While most are of dubious character with few or no real credentials, their stories tend to support the accounts of various conspiracy researchers. Their stories are surprisingly consistent and offer fascinating insights into the workings of such an elite.

Bill Ryan, who worked on a famous social sciences project called Project Camelot, interviewed one of these self-proclaimed elite members. "In the summer of 2010, I was approached by a very unusual man," Ryan explained. "I've called him 'Charles.' He's spent many years working for the elite group that considers it their responsibility to run the planet. He's not an academic, a historian, or a scientist. But he wanted to communicate some important information about the worldview and philosophy of this group. Ryan reported,

> They are a controlling group of 33 individuals who meet frequently to make strategic decisions about humanity and the planet. They are not the "Illuminati," which is a lower-level secret society—of which there are many, like the Knights of Malta, the Rosicrucians, Skull and Bones, the Priory of Sion, numerous Masonic groups, and more. The 33 can be compared to a Board of Directors of a very large global corporation. Like a real Board, there is a "Number One Man" who makes final policy decisions, having consulted his colleagues, all of whom have expertise and who have earned a right to participate. There are differences of opinion sometimes—and different personalities, as in any group of people—but basically they are very much aligned with the overall purpose, which is (using this analogy) to ensure that Corporation Plant Earth continues to expand and prosper. All in line with the Corporation's "mission statement"—which is about optimizing the human genome.
>
> Charles explained that each of these people, each representating one of thirty-three bloodlines, is so powerful

and controls so much wealth and assets that each could be
regarded almost as a nation-state in his (or occasionally
her) own right. They all regard it as their responsibility to
"manage" planet Earth. He said they are party to a great
deal of hidden history through their private possession of an-
cient documents and artifacts, many located in the Vatican
Library.

The history and lineage of the human race is not—at
all—what the public has been told. It has been decided a
long time ago that the human race could not handle these
truths. This information is regarded as a kind of "sacred
knowledge." Safeguarding this knowledge is taken extremely
seriously, and, as Charles explained, there is a great deal
of tradition and historical culture—going back thousands
of years—which is almost inextricably interwoven with the
way the group functions. As Charles also tried to explain,
they do not see time as you and I do. Delaying something by
a year, or a decade, or a hundred years, means very little.
They do not operate to a calendar. Only to unfolding events.

One woman, who goes by the pseudonym of Svali, claimed to
have escaped the Illuminati after working for years as a high-level
programmer and trainer. She said that while she was growing up, her
mother and stepfather were Illuminati members. According to Svali,
the Illuminati have six chairs on their "ascended masters council"—
representing the sciences, government, leadership, scholarship, spiritual affairs, and military affairs—and she claimed that her mother
sat on a Washington, D.C., area regional council and served as spiritual chair. A German philosopher named Adam Weishaupt is often
credited with founding the Illuminati in 1776 in Germany, but Svali
said that this was untrue. "They chose him as a figurehead and told
him what to write about. The financiers, dating back to the bank-

ers during the times of the Templar Knights who financed the early kings in Europe, created the Illuminati. Weishaupt was their 'gofer,' who did their bidding," she said. Svali explained:

> The Illuminati is a group that practices a form of faith known as "enlightenment." It is Luciferian, and they teach their followers that their roots go back to the ancient mystery religions of Babylon, Egypt, and Celtic druidism. They have taken what they consider the "best" of each, the foundational practices, and joined them together into a strongly occult discipline. Many groups at the local level worship ancient deities such as "El," "Baal," and "Ashtarte," as well as "Isis and Osiris" and "Set." This said, the leadership councils at times scoff at the more "primitive" practices of the anarchical, or lower levels. I remember when I was on council in San Diego, they called the high priests and priestesses the "slicers and dicers," who kept the "lower levels happy." This is not to offend anyone, it only shows that at the leadership levels, they often believe they are more scientifically and cognitively driven. But they still practice the principles of enlightenment.
>
> There are 12 steps to this, also known as "the 12 steps of discipline," and they also teach traveling astral planes, time travel, and other metaphysical phenomena. Do people really do this, or is it a drug induced hallucination? I cannot judge. I saw things that I believe cannot be rationally explained when in this group, things that frightened me, but I can only say that it could be a combination of cult mind control, drug inductions, hypnosis, and some true demonic activity. How much of each, I cannot begin to guess. I do know that these people teach and practice evil.
>
> At the higher levels, the group is no longer people in robes chanting in front of bonfires. Leadership councils have ad-

ministrators who handle finances (and trust me, this group makes money. That alone would keep it going even if the rest were just religious hog wash). The leadership levels include businessmen, bankers, and local community leaders. They are intelligent, well educated, and active in their churches. Above local leadership councils are the regional councils, who give dictates to the groups below them, help form the policies and agendas for each region, and who interact with the local leadership councils.

At the national level, there are extremely wealthy people who finance these goals and interact with the leaders of other countries. The Illuminati are international. Secret? By all means. The first thing a child learns from "family, or the Order" as they are called, is "The first rule of the Order is secrecy." This is why you don't hear from more survivors who get out. The lengths that this group goes to, to terrify its members into not disclosing, is unbelievable. . . . Try being buried in a wooden box for a period of time (it may have been minutes, but to a four year old it is an eternity), and then when the lid is lifted, being told, "if you ever tell, we'll put you back in forever." The child will scream hysterically that they will NEVER EVER [emphasis in the original] tell. I was that child, and now I am breaking that vow made under psychological duress. Because I don't want any other children to go through what I did, or have seen done to others.

The Illuminati are present in every major metropolitan center in the United States. They have divided the United States up into seven major regions, and each has a regional council over it, with the heads of the local councils reporting to them. They meet once every two months, and on special occasions. . . . They also have excellent lawyers who are well paid to help cover their tracks. There are also people in the *media paid to help keep stories from coming out. I know of three people in San Diego who worked for the* Union Tribune *who were faithful Illuminists, and who also wrote frequent articles attacking local therapists who worked with RA [Ritual Abuse] survivors. I remember leadership boasting they had "run so-and-so out of town" because of a media blitz, and being quite happy about it.*

The Illuminati believe in controlling an area through its banks and financial institutions (guess how many sit on banking boards? You'd be surprised). Local government: guess how many get elected to local city councils? Law: children are encouraged to go to law school and medical school. Media: others are encouraged to go to journalism school, and members help fund local papers.

Another proclaimed whistle-blower from within the elite entered the AboveTopSecret Forum in the fall of 2008 using the avatar Hidden Hand. This insider described experiencing life within The Family, a group of elitists aligned with extraterrestrials. They are alternately termed the Illuminati, Nephilim, Custodians, Watchers, and Advanced Beings, and they are the product of distinct bloodlines that have passed along wealth and power from one generation to another. "I am a generational member of a Ruling Bloodline Family," Hidden Hand proclaimed. "Our lineage can be traced back beyond antiquity. From the earliest times of your recorded 'history,' and beyond, our Family has been 'directing' the 'play' from behind the scenes, in one way or another. . . . There are 13 'base' or 'core' original bloodlines. Yet there are many, many other lines that spring from these, as do rivers from the oceans. If you imagine the 13 original lines as primary colors, that can be mixed to create a vast array of other colors, then you will have some comprehension. Again, no competition, just Family."

Hidden Hand contradicted David Icke's belief that this family was filled with reptilian creatures. "We are most certainly not Reptilian," Hidden Hand stated. "And there is nothing remotely reptilian about the True Power Bloodlines."

Hidden Hand's posts were compiled and presented by Michael E. Salla, who is the founder of the Exopolitics Institute, which studies the politics of the impact of extraterrestrial life on humanity. In 2004, Salla was dismissed from his position with the Center for Global Peace in Washington's American University for his research on UFOs. Salla interpreted Hidden Hand as suggesting that there is a "Luciferian group soul that is working in our Galaxy that has established power not only on our planet, but on other worlds. Reptilian worlds under the influence of the Family, or Luciferian entity, would be as highly manipulated as our own by off-world bloodlines.

"This appears uncannily similar to the Star Wars saga where a group of dark spiritual entities called the Sith secretly infiltrate and take over political and spiritual organizations in the Galaxy," said Salla. "If the Hidden Hand and his Luciferian peers belong to something similar to the Sith, is there a positive counterpart similar to the Jedi Knights? This is how the Hidden Hand describes the modern equivalent of the Jedi Knights—a positive polarity 'Family.' "

After Hidden Hand's posts, the AboveTopSecret website was soon filled with cries of "Hoax!" and "disinformation." But after studying the lengthy dialogs with Hidden Hand, Salla concluded, "In my opinion, it is a genuine revelation by an insider belonging to an organization called 'The Family' that has both Earthly human and extraterrestrial membership. The Family has been secretly involved in ruling both the Earth and other planets through highly placed elites in key social and political institutions."

PRESIDENTIAL BLUE BLOODS

Though times have changed since the ages of the Habsburgs and the Rothschilds, it appears that the person closest to the ancient bloodlines carries the day in United States national elections. It has been noted that in every election the candidate with the most royal genes always wins.

Mainstream news reports in 2000 quoted researchers at *Burke's Peerage* who predicted that George W. Bush would win the presidency over Al Gore because "the presidential candidate with the most royal genes and chromosomes has, up to now, always won the White House." They said that while both Bush and Gore were related to the elite families and of royal blood, the Bush family was more closely connected. "[Bush] is closely related to every European Monarch both on and off the throne," said *Burke's* publishing director, Harold Brooks-Baker. He noted that both the Bush and Pierce families were members of high society going back a thousand years at least. "Not one member of his [Bush's] family was working class, middle class, or even middle, middle class," he added.

"You can't just write off 200 years of accurate predictions," stated Brooks-Baker, noting that Michael Dukakis, the 1988 Democratic nominee, was the son of Greek immigrants who had no connections to any European throne, and he lost in a landslide.

David Icke, citing information from *Burke's Peerage*, wrote, "Every presidential election in America, since and including George Washington in 1789 to Bill Clinton, has been won by the candidate with the most British and French royal genes. Of the 42 presidents to Clinton, 33 have been related to two people: Alfred the Great, King of England, and Charlemagne, the most famous monarch of France. So it goes on: 19 of them are related to England's Edward III, who has 2000 blood connections to Prince Charles. The same goes with the banking families in America. George Bush and Barbara Bush are from the same bloodline—the Pierce bloodline, which changed its name from Percy, when it crossed the Atlantic. Percy is one of the aristocratic families of Britain, to this day. They were involved in the Gunpowder Plot to blow up Parliament at the time of Guy Fawkes."

If anyone should think that Barack Hussein Obama must be an exception to these bloodline connections, that person would be wrong. According to Lynne Cheney, wife of Dick Cheney, Obama is an eighth cousin to the former vice president. She discovered this familial connection while researching her ancestry for a book. According to a Cheney spokesperson, Obama is a descendant of Mareen Duvall, a French Huguenot whose son married the grand-daughter of a Richard Cheney, who had arrived in Maryland in the late 1650s from England.

Moreover, the *Chicago Sun-Times* reported that both Obama and Cheney are blood relations to the Bush family. According to the paper, George W. Bush and Obama are tenth cousins once removed. They are linked through a seventeenth-century Massa-chusetts couple, Samuel Hinckley and Sarah Soole. Hinckley is a distant relative of George Herbert Walker Bush's friend John War-nock Hinckley Sr., whose son, John Warnock Hinckley Jr., was the man accused of shooting President Ronald Reagan in 1981. According to a Reuters news story in late 2011, presidential candidate Mitt Romney also is related to the Bush family.

Gary Boyd Roberts, a former senior research scholar at the New England Historic Genealogical Society, has traced George W. Bush's family tree to sixteen U.S. presidents besides his father: George Washington, Millard Fillmore, Franklin Pierce, Abraham Lincoln, Ulysses Grant, Rutherford B. Hayes, James Garfield, Grover Cleve-land, Teddy Roosevelt, William H. Taft, Calvin Coolidge, Herbert Hoover, Franklin D. Roosevelt, Richard Nixon, and Gerald Ford. Moreover, the Bush family, according to several sources, is closely related to the king of Albania and has kinship with every member of the British royal family and the House of Windsor. They are related to twenty British dukes, and George W. Bush is a thirteenth cousin of Britain's queen mother, and of her daughter, Queen Elizabeth II. George W. is thirteenth cousin once removed from Prince Charles and has direct descent from King Henry III, Charles II, and Edward I of England. According to *Burke's Peerage*, even former president Bill Clinton is genetically related to the House of Windsor.

Many are unaware that the Windsors, the royal family of England, originally were known by their German name, Sachsen-Coburg und Gotha, a German dynasty, often shortened to Saxe-Coburg-Gotha. The change to Windsor came during World War I, when England was at war with Germany and there was considerable anti-German sentiment. To distance themselves from their German heritage, on July 17, 1917, Queen Victoria's grandson King George V officially declared that all male descendants of Queen Victoria would bear the name Windsor. The name Windsor came from a castle owned by the family. Six British monarchs, including Queen Victoria and King George III, who ruled during the American Revolution, were members of the German House of Hanover.

In 1947, England's Elizabeth II married Prince Philip, her third cousin, the son of Alice of Battenburg and a member of the House of Schleswig-Holstein-Sonderburg-Glücksburg. Philip was an offspring of Greek and Danish royal families, born in Greece. After serving in the Royal Navy after World War II, Philip became a British citizen and adopted the name Mountbatten. With Elizabeth's ascension to the throne in 1952, it was assumed she would take her husband's name, Mountbatten, but her family and Winston Churchill insisted she retain the name Windsor. Through an Order in Council in 1960, the name Mountbatten-Windsor was adopted for Philip and Elizabeth's male-line descendants.

Phillip Eugene de Rothschild, a Rothschild descendant now living in America, explained to David Icke that the German Battenberg bloodline is joined with the Bauer-Rothschild bloodline in a "Rothsburg dynasty" that traces its ancestry back to Aeneas. In

Greek and Roman mythology, Aeneas was a Trojan soldier who was said to be a human hybrid, son of the goddess Venus, as well as the father of Romulus and Remus, the founders of Rome.

The claim that both European and American rulers are related to the ancient bloodlines has been disputed. It has been said that nearly everyone can be genetically connected to everyone else. One genealogist calculated that as of 2001 there were 657 living legitimate descendants of England's King George III and 4,982 living descendants of George I. "There are probably more illegitimate descendants than legitimate ones. George I is 11 generations from Prince William (via senior line). But Edward of Windsor is another 12 generations back from George I. He could have 20 million living descendants. And Charlemagne is another 19 generations back from Edward. The majority of people in Europe and northern America are descended from him," stated the unnamed genealogist in Yahoo's Answers section.

The idea that any person can be genealogically linked to any other came into being with a university study indicating that any individual is only about six steps of acquaintance away from any person on Earth. Actor Kevin Bacon, who once commented that he had worked with everyone in Hollywood or someone who had worked with everyone, even became the object of a trivia game entitled Six Degrees of Kevin Bacon, in which participants try to connect any person in Hollywood to Bacon as quickly as possible. Of course, being genealogically connected and being merely an acquaintance are two entirely separate things. While games and statistics seem to disparage the idea that certain bloodlines have passed down knowledge, rule, and royalty throughout human history, many still feel disquieted that so many world leaders, including U.S. presidents, have been connected to the royal bloodlines of Europe, people who trace their line back to the dynasties of Egypt, Babylon, and Sumer. Apparently the sons and daughters of miners, cooks, and laborers somehow are disqualified from high public office.

According to several researchers, the ancient bloodlines of the Anunnaki spread from Sumer, Babylon, Egypt, and even China to encompass the entire world. While conventional history has concentrated on the male descendants of these bloodlines, through the centuries the bloodlines have also been passed through the mitochondrial DNA of the females. While the passing of the "true" bloodline often has been done by incest and intermarriage, practiced by most of history's rulers, an extended network of relations has been created through concubines, mistresses, slaves, and hired help, often by rape.

A growing number of researchers and writers are building the case against a handful of people who seem intent on creating a New World Order, one in which elites rule through financial institutions so as to maintain their hereditary privileges instead of helping the world's people develop individual worth, creativity, and productivity.

According to David Icke, these bloodlines have been "the force behind many of the major Empires of history." Since its inception, this force has spread throughout the world as an informal organization with members at the top of corporate and political hierarchies. Credo Muta, official historian of the Zulu nation, has described how the colonial powers, after proclaiming independence for African countries, continued their control by selecting African leaders who came from the bloodlines of former kings and queens claiming to have descended from ancient sky gods.

Icke described how the chain of command works within this family network, termed by some the Illuminati, as follows:

> The Illuminati structure can be symbolized as a web or as a pyramid in which the few at the top dictate to the many at the bottom. The many are kept in ignorance of what is really going on. The pyramid structure of secret societies is mirrored in government, banking, business and every other organiza-

*tion and institution. . . . They are "compartmentalized"
and the only people who know how it all fits together are
the very few sitting at the top—the bloodline families and
their lackeys.*

*The smaller pyramids, like the local branch of a bank, fit
into bigger and bigger pyramids, until eventually you have
the pyramid that encompasses all of the banks. It is the same
with the transnational corporations, political parties, secret
societies, media empires, and the military. If you go high
enough in this structure all the transnational corporations
(like the oil cartel), major political parties, secret societies,
media empires and the military (via NATO, for instance),
are controlled by the same families who sit atop the biggest
pyramids. . . . All roads lead eventually to them—everything
from the food we eat; the water we drink; the "medical care"
we receive, including vaccines; the "news" we watch, hear
and read; the "entertainment" we are given; the governments that dictate to us; the military that enforces the will of
the governments; and the drug-running network aimed at
destroying young people. The same families and their gofers
control all these areas and much more.*

BAD FOOD AND WATER

If there is a ruling elite, the best way to keep its subjects under control would be through bad water and bad food that made people
unhealthy, obese, and depressed. One of the ways to make the water
bad would be through the use of fluoride, which, despite much positive publicity, is only used in public water supplies by eleven nations.

Concern over fluoride in the nation's water supply was once de-
rided as right-wing paranoia, but recently the public has become

privy to studies suggesting the dangers of fluoride toxicity. International author and medical writer Mary Sparrowdancer noted that, since the 1930s, German and Austrian scientists knew how to treat overactive thyroids by bathing a person in fluoride. This was effective because fluoride blocked thyroid function. "For the US government, long partnered with the pharmaceutical industry, to then force this same treatment on a nation of people with healthy thyroids under the lie that fluoride 'prevents cavities in children,' is unconscionable. The Nuremberg Code of ethics pertaining to human experimentation labels it an act of crime, stating, 'The voluntary consent of the human subject is absolutely essential.' Today, 70 percent of the US is being forced to receive this thyroid-blocking chemical via their water without consent or medical monitoring for overdose, allergic reaction or blocked thyroid function."

Symptoms of thyroid damage and fluoride poisoning include weight gain, edema, kidney disease, kidney failure, hair loss, depression, aggression, aches, pains, skin problems, bone deformities including arthritis, sexual/erectile dysfunction, memory loss, weakness, fatigue, heart disease, irritability, digestive disorders, and cancer. As the dangers of fluoride reach more of the public, an increasing number of cities and communities have abandoned the fluoridation of their water supply, a practice initiated in the past with little or no debate. This is due to the fact that many of these cities didn't even have a choice on fluoride in the first place. According to the former head of the Harvard School of Dental Medicine, James M. Dunning, "The big cities in the United States were mostly fluoridated by executive action in such a way as to avoid public referenda."

And fluoride might be in more than just our drinking water. A 2005 study at the Washington University School of Medicine in St. Louis found some commercial iced tea mixes contain up to 6.5 parts per million (ppm) of fluoride, which is well above the 4 ppm maximum allowed by the EPA in drinking water and the 2.4 ppm permitted by the FDA in bottled water and beverages. Researcher Michael Whyte said, "When fluoride gets into your bones, it stays there for years, and there is no established treatment for skeletal fluorosis. No one knows if you can fully recover from it." Yet fluoridation has been an agenda item of the elite's giant chemical corporations for many years.

Who will ultimately control the state of the nation's water supply apparently was decided by an executive order signed in March 2012 by President Obama. Under section 201 (5), National Defense Resources Preparedness Order (NDRPO), the secretary of defense will be in charge of water resources, which seems odd in that under this order, the secretary of energy is in charge of energy and the secretary of transportation in charge of transportation. But defense? According to this NDRPO, virtually everything in the United States will come under the total control of the National Security Council and Homeland Security Council, in conjunction with the National Economic Council, all of which serve the president.

One firm at the center of worldwide controversy over the use of both chemicals and genetically modified organisms (GMOs) is Monsanto. As the world's leading chemical company (it partnered with the global Nazi chemical firm IG Farben prior to Farben's dissolution in 2003), Monsanto has been involved in several scandals involving toxic chemicals. For forty years, it produced industrial coolants known as PCBs (polychlorinated biphenyls), which were dumped by the millions of pounds into open-pit landfills and rivers. These coolants are now banned. Monsanto also helped manufacture a number of harmful dioxins that pollute the environment and can afflict humans who come into contact with them. The most famous of these was Agent Orange, a defoliant that caused many U.S. Vietnam War veterans, as well as several hundred thousand Vietnamese, to suffer debilitating problems after the war, such as skin, nerve, and respiratory disorders, cancer, birth defects in offspring, and many other problems.

An investigation in the early 1990s by the EPA concluded that the chemical giant had misrepresented data concerning the hazards of dioxins and Agent Orange, which led to the government denying compensation to Vietnam veterans exposed to Agent Orange and their children suffering birth defects.

In 2011, despite widespread opposition in the light of studies indicating harmful effects from genetically modified seeds and despite a Supreme Court decision banning the planting of such seeds pending environmental impact studies by the United States Department of Agriculture (USDA), Obama and the USDA decided to deregulate two of Monsanto's GMO seed varieties—alfalfa and sugar beets.

To legitimize such action, in 2012 riders were attached to both the 2012 Federal Agriculture Reform and Risk Management Act, known simply as the Farm Bill (HR 6083), and section 733 of the 2013 Agriculture Appropriations Bill (HR 5973) that would require the secretary of agriculture to "immediately" grant temporary approval or deregulation to GMO crops even if the crop's safety is in question or under legal review. "In other words, if this single line in the 90-page Agricultural Appropriations bill slips through, it's Independence Day for the biotech industry," warned Alexis Baden-Mayer and Ronnie Cummins on the AlterNet website. They noted that under this provision, the "Monsanto rider," all that any farmer or biotech firm need to do is ask, and "the questionable crops could be released into the environment where they could potentially contaminate conventional or organic crops and, ultimately, the nation's food supply."

To understand the purposes of such deregulation, one should look at who stands to gain from it. Anthony Gucciardi, writing on the Natural Society website, noted that Bill Gates, cofounder and chairman of Microsoft, was urging that GMO seeds be used to meet the world's demand for food and that his Bill and Melinda Gates Foundation had funded experiments with the seeds in five African nations. "Monsanto's drought-resistant corn seeds were given to African farmers facing drought conditions, replacing traditional and sustainable farming with Monsanto's GMO crops," reported Gucciardi.

At a meeting of the International Fund for Agricultural Development (IFAD) in early 2012, Gates touted the use of GMO seeds and announced that his foundation would provide $200 million in new grants to research new GMO corn. As of August 2010, Bill Gates's foundation had purchased five hundred thousand shares of Monsanto stocks.

Despite Gates's endorsement, some studies suggest that GMO crops may create more problems than they solve. John Vidal, the environment editor of London's *Guardian*, has written, "Genetic engineering has failed to increase the yield of any food crop but has vastly increased the use of chemicals and the growth of 'super-weeds,' according to a report by 20 Indian, south-east Asian, African and Latin American food and conservation groups representing millions of people."

Even more disturbing, a recent study reported in *Reproductive Toxicology*, showed Bt (*Bacillus thuringiensis*) toxins engineered into genetically modified foods were found in the blood of twenty-eight of thirty pregnant women tested and in 80 percent of the tested women's umbilical cords. In a nonpregnant group, traces were found in the blood of 69 percent. It was believed that the toxins entered the human body as a result of eating meat, milk, and eggs from farm livestock fed GM corn. Pete Riley, director of GM Freeze, a consumer group opposed to GMO farming, said, "This research is a major surprise as it shows that the Bt proteins have survived the human digestive system and passed into the blood supply— something that regulators said could not happen."

Despite a lack of reporting in the corporate news media in America, the public should know that Monsanto's plans for its GMO crops and seed, often referred to as Frankenfood, have been beaten back in more than two dozen nations. According to a February

2012 item in *European Biotechnology Science & Industry News*, "The exodus of plant biotechnology out of Europe seems to have accelerated. Just three weeks ago, BASF Plant Science announced it would leave Europe as an R&D location for developing its GM plants. But now, it looks like US-based Monsanto is following the example of its German R&D partner and turning away from Europe for good. First, the company announced that it does not plan to sell its genetically modified maize MON810 in France despite the highest court recently overturning a three-year ban on its sale. Now United Press International reported that Monsanto is closing its wheat growing operation, based in Cambridge, which employed 125 people, and selling off crop-breeding centers in France, Germany and the Czech Republic." The article also mentioned that many in Denmark were opposed to European governments approving GM plants. Apparently the European Union came to an agreement that companies seeking EU approval for a GM crop would agree not to market the product in those countries that wish to restrict cultivation, in return for those countries not blocking EU authorization to grow the crops elsewhere in Europe.

The fact that GMO products are taking a beating in Europe was acknowledged by BASF Plant Science president and CEO Peter Eckes, who wrote, "The socio-political climate and the regulatory conditions do not give us any indication that genetically modified plants can be successfully commercialized in Europe in the years to come."

This is not the case in America. Anthony Gucciardi reported that "The USDA has allowed Monsanto to run rampant, modifying staple crops, food items, and even milk. Monsanto's rBGH is a synthetic hormone created using molecules and DNA sequences that are a result of molecular cloning, which has been linked to breast and gastrointestinal cancer. In the United States, this synthetic hormone is present in 1/3 of all milk. Meanwhile, it is banned in 27 countries around the globe. Marketed under the name Posilac, Monsanto has since sold the brand to a division of Eli Lilly and Company, Elanco Animal Health."

Apparently even some Monsanto employees are wary of the company's products. In early 2012, according to Britain's *Independent*, Sutcliffe Catering Group, which caters to a Monsanto plant in High Wycombe, Buckinghamshire, banned GMO soybeans and corn from its menu so that "you, the customer, can feel confident in the food we serve." Monsanto executives confirmed the notice, but company spokesman Tony Coombes said the reason for the GMO-free food was because the company "believes in choice." This statement seemed ironic to many as Monsanto has for some time fought to prevent the clear labeling of GMO foods and threatened ruinous litigation against those who would investigate the firm.

Many researchers and scientists believe that Monsanto's GMO crops may be responsible for the die-off of bees, a critical pollinator in the environmental food chain. In addition to adding fluoride to our drinking water and allowing questionable companies to produce food using unsafe chemicals, the U.S. government also allows thousands of questionable additives to be used in the food supplies, such as aspartame and monosodium glutamate (MSG). During the Reagan administration in the 1980s, Donald Rumsfeld pushed the sugar substitute aspartame through a recalcitrant Food and Drug Administration (FDA) even though studies linked this chemical to various cancers. Aspartame, composed of 50 percent phenylalanine, 40 percent aspartic acid, and 10 percent methanol (wood alcohol), has been banned from children's food products by the European Union. In our bodies, methanol breaks down into formaldehyde, the main ingredient in embalming fluid, and formic acid. Aspartame is found in more than six thousand food products in the United States and Canada today, especially in the commercial sweeteners NutraSweet, Splenda, and Equal, but due to the controversy over its effects on the human body, the sugar substitute is being relabeled as AminoSweet.

MSG is the sodium salt of glutamic acid, a nonessential amino acid, and is used as a flavor enhancer. According to former food-processing engineer and food scientist Carol Hoernlein, mainstream media are now acting surprised that MSG has been linked to obesity, even though scientists have for forty years routinely used MSG or glutamate to induce obesity in lab animals. In the 1960s, John Olney found that MSG damaged cells of the hypothalamus in the brain and made lab mice morbidly obese. MSG also is a cumulative excitotoxin, a compound that overstimulates the brain, leading to migraines and hyperactivity, especially in children.

If it's not bad enough that our food is filled with these chemicals, some are now saying that substantial amounts of the poison arsenic can be found in fruit juices. Dr. Mehmet Oz sparked this debate when he told TV viewers that tests showed some samples of commercial apple juices contained total arsenic levels exceeding 10 parts per billion (ppb), the legal limit for bottled and public water. Furthermore, an investigation of apple and grape juice by *Consumer Reports* showed that roughly 10 percent of juice samples, from five brands, had total arsenic levels that exceeded federal drinking-water standards. Most of that arsenic was inorganic arsenic, a known carcinogen. One in four samples contained levels of lead higher than the FDA's bottled-water limit of 5 ppb. As with arsenic, no federal limit exists for lead in juice. The *Consumer Reports* research revealed that inorganic arsenic has been detected at disturbing levels in other foods and that a growing amount of scientific evidence suggests that chronic exposure to arsenic and lead, even at levels below water standards, can result in serious health problems. Special concern was given to children under age five, who research found drink juice in quantities exceeding pediatricians' recommendations. Joshua Hamilton, a toxicologist specializing in arsenic research, stated, "People sometimes say, 'If arsenic exposure is so bad, why don't you see more people sick or dying from it?' But the many diseases likely to be increased by exposure even at relatively low levels are so common already that its effects are overlooked simply because no one has looked carefully for the connection."

Health advocate Mike Adams, on his popular website, pointed to a number of problems in our food. He noted that two thirds of all fresh chicken meat sold in grocery stores today is contaminated with salmonella; diet soda is laced with aspartame; "natural" corn chips are made from genetically modified corn plants linked to widespread infertility; processed meats are laced with cancer-causing sodium nitrite; and everything from soups to salad dressings is "enhanced" with MSG. Supporting his allegations with many studies and news reports, Adams also pointed out that the high-fructose corn syrup used to sweeten sodas and thousands of other products causes diabetes and is often contaminated with mercury. He also noted that Chicken McNuggets are made with a chemical used in silly putty and the soy protein used in most protein bars is extracted using a highly toxic explosive chemical called hexane. "The FDA says nothing about all this," he added. "Instead, the agency wants you to believe that the real danger in the food supply is found exclusively in raw dairy products which contain no additives or synthetic chemicals, by the way." Those who attempt to deal in farm-fresh and organic food and milk now are finding themselves at the end of government guns as the number of armed arrests targeting real food continues to rise, even including the pacifist Amish.

Adams's concern may be well placed: male sperm counts have been dropping throughout the world for several years. A paper published in the *Internet Journal of Urology* stated, "There have been a number of studies over the past 15–20 years which suggest that sperm counts in men are on the decline. Since these changes are recent and appear to have occurred internationally, it has been presumed that they reflect adverse effects of environmental or lifestyle factors on the male rather than, for example, genetic changes in

susceptibility. If the decrease in sperm counts were to continue at
the rate that it is then in a few years we will witness widespread
male infertility."

Two recent studies published in the journal *Fertility and Sterility* concluded that men taking drugs, such as the anti-impotence
drug Viagra, could be damaging their sperm and lowering their
ability to conceive. Another study, published in an environmental
journal, the *Ends Report*, point to chemicals like dioxin as culprits
in lower male sperm count.

If we're not getting chemicals from our food and water, then
there's a good chance we're getting them from pills. Nearly half the
population of the United States today is taking some kind of drug,
according to studies—and we're not talking about illegal drugs.
One recent analysis by the *Los Angeles Times* based on government statistics showed that prescription-drug-induced deaths have
become so prevalent that their average yearly total now exceeds the
number of deaths caused by traffic accidents. This number does not
include illegal drug overdoses.

Despite the ever rising cost of health care in America and despite the fact that Americans score better than most other nations
in major measurements of health—such as lower percentage of tobacco smokers, lower alcohol consumption, and lower cholesterol
levels—health-care-induced fatalities are the third leading cause of
death, just after heart disease and cancer. These deaths occur from
unnecessary surgery, overmedication, and other mistakes in hospi-
tals, and from adverse effects of prescription drugs.

If one of our most prized institutions—medicine—is so great,
how do we explain the use of armed SWAT teams to force people
to take its pharmaceuticals, as happened to Maryanne Godboldo
in 2011. Godboldo is a Michigan mother who was surrounded in
her home by armed police—with a tank outside!—after refusing to allow her thirteen-year-old daughter to be injected with

Risperdal (risperidone), a controversial schizophrenia drug that had already caused severe adverse reactions in her daughter. Three courts finally ruled that her refusal was legal and ordered her daughter returned to her after the girl had been taken by the state. Godboldo had joined a growing number of persons concerned over the increasing number of inoculations, questionable therapies, and psychiatric drugs being forced on a gullible and ignorant population.

Poisonous food and water? When such issues are linked with the publicly expressed support for population reduction by the wealthy elite, it would appear that such activities are part of an agenda to reduce the human population.

As far back as 1977, notable academics Paul R. Ehrlich, Anne Ehrlich, and John Holden were advocating reducing the world's population through unsavory means. In their book *Ecoscience*, these authors promote involuntary abortions and sterilization by infertility chemicals placed in food and drinking water to rid society of those they believed contributed to "social deterioration." They also advocated an armed international police force to enforce a "planetary regime" over a global economy and social activities.

Holden, in April 2009, then serving as director of the White House Office of Science and Technology Policy and co-chair of the President's Council of Advisors on Science and Technology, suggested spraying heavy metal "pollutants" into the upper atmosphere to retard perceived "global warming," lending strong support to those researchers who claim that such a program, involving the globally observed chemtrails, has already been under way for years. Barium oxide and aluminum oxide, both harmful to the human respiratory system, have been identified among other substances as composing the chemtrails.

PEOPLE ARE THE PROBLEM

Could all the above be a ploy to kill off "undesirables"? In years past, the pseudoscience of eugenics was used to excuse murderous depopulation schemes. Few today realize that the theological and scientific basis for the Nazis' eugenics beliefs originated in the United States, particularly in California, long before the Nazis came to power in Germany. By 1900, thirty states had laws providing for the sterilization of mental patients and imbeciles. At least sixty thousand such "defectives" were legally sterilized.

Soon after the Nazis rose to power in Germany, they adopted similar techniques against those they considered unworthy of life. These programs and attitudes eventually led to the Holocaust. Edwin Black, author of *War Against the Weak: Eugenics and America's Campaign to Create a Master Race*, described how the Rockefeller Foundation helped create the German eugenics movement and even funded the program that included "research" by the infamous Josef Mengele before he became the "Angel of Death" at Auschwitz. "Eugenics would have been so much bizarre parlor talk had it not been for extensive financing by corporate philanthropies, specifically the Carnegie Institution, the Rockefeller Foundation and the Harriman railroad fortune," wrote Black. "They were all in league with some of America's most respected scientists hailing from such prestigious universities as Stamford [*sic*], Yale, Harvard, and Princeton. These academicians espoused race theory and race science, and then faked and twisted data to serve eugenics' racist aims." Many of these same families and firms helped finance Adolf Hitler and his rise to power.

It seems clear that the leadership of the new world order wants a good portion of humanity dead. When Henry Kissinger was the secretary of state, he directed the 1974 National Security Study Memorandum 200, which surveyed the populations of the world. This report, as well as the Global 2000 Report drafted during the

Jimmy Carter administration, and the royalty-supported Club of Rome study, all call for population reduction. Thomas Ferguson, a former Latin American case officer for the State Department's Office of Population Affairs, once stated, "There is a single theme behind all our work—we must reduce population levels."

In a 1981 interview, Maxwell Taylor, former chairman of the Joint Chiefs of Staff and a prominent member of the Council on Foreign Relations, advocated population reduction through limited wars, disease, and starvation. He blithely concluded, "I have already written off more than a billion people. These people are in places in Africa, Asia, and Latin America. We can't save them. The population crisis and the food-supply question dictate that we should not even try. It's a waste of time."

As if reading from Taylor's script, England's Prince Philip was quoted in *People* magazine as saying, "Human population growth is probably the single most serious long-term threat to survival. We're in for a major disaster if it isn't curbed—not just for the natural world, but for the human world. The more people there are, the more resources they'll consume, the more pollution they'll create, the more fighting they will do. We have no option. If it isn't controlled voluntarily, it will be controlled involuntarily by an increase in disease, starvation and war." Years later, Philip showed that this was not simply wishful thinking but a call to action, when he mused, "In the event that I am reincarnated, I would like to return as a deadly virus, in order to contribute something to solve overpopulation."

Such views correspond to those expressed on the mysterious Georgia Guidestones—the authorship of which is unknown—located in Elbert County, Georgia. The very first admonition on these stones is "Maintain humanity under 500,000,000 in perpetual balance with nature."

A POLICE STATE

Because the public cannot be counted on to voluntarily give up its freedoms and privacy, a complex and tangled set of laws must be put in place to regulate citizens. A police state must be created to force compliance with ever extending and sometimes overreaching laws.

An effective police state requires constant and intense surveillance. New vehicles are being equipped with in-car tracking devices like OnStar. Intersections, even in rural areas, are being equipped with traffic lights in place of stop signs. While this change may seem like a public service, it is being funded by the new Department of Homeland Security, and many lights now come with cameras that include radio frequency identification (RFID) chip readers and even facial identification software. Police, who once wore blue uniforms with patches bearing the motto To Serve and Protect, now wear black combat suits and are increasingly becoming militarized. The trend toward a militarized police force began many years ago, when President Richard Nixon declared a "War on Drugs" in 1968. Then in 1981, President Ronald Reagan signed the Military Cooperation with Law Enforcement Act, allowing the military to give local, state, and federal police access to military bases, research, and equipment. By 1988, the National Guard was conducting drug raids on city streets and using military helicopters to search for marijuana crops. In 1989, when President George H. W. Bush assigned the Department of Defense a larger role in the drug war, Secretary of Defense Dick Cheney declared, "The detection and countering of the production, trafficking and use of illegal drugs is a high priority national security mission of the Department of Defense." Such use of the military, which caused little criticism when linked to the Drug War, nevertheless began a movement in government to disregard the Posse Comitatus Act, a law passed in 1878 preventing the U.S. military from policing the civilian population. The law was passed following the shameful experience with martial law under Reconstruction.

A 1994 law authorized the military to donate surplus equipment to local police forces. Since that time, millions of pieces of equipment—from weapons and grenade launchers to armored personnel carriers and helicopters—have been handed over for use against the civilian population. These actions flagrantly disregard the Posse Comitatus Act. In the Huffington Post, Radley Balko noted that "the problem with this mingling of domestic policing with military operations is that the two institutions have starkly different missions. The military's job is to annihilate a foreign enemy. Cops are charged with keeping the peace, and with protecting the constitutional rights of American citizens and residents. It's dangerous to conflate the two."

Such arming of the police engendered a rise in Special Weapons and Tactics (SWAT) teams, whose forces more than doubled in the years between 1980 and 2000 in cities with fifty thousand or more people. "In 2002," Balko reported, "the seven police officers who serve the town of Jasper, Florida—which had all of 2,000 people and hadn't had a murder in more than a decade—were each given a military-grade M-16 machine gun from the Pentagon transfer program, leading one Florida paper to run the headline, 'Three Stoplights, Seven M-16s.'"

Recent legislation has only furthered this trend. "In the 10 years since the terror attacks of September 11, 2001, the government has claimed a number of new policing powers in the name of protecting the country from terrorism, often at the expense of civil liberties," Balko wrote. "But once claimed, those powers are overwhelmingly used in the war on drugs. Nowhere is this more clear than in the continuing militarization of America's police departments." Balko noted that delayed-notice search warrants, commonly called "sneak-and-peek" warrants that were part of the PATRIOT Act passed strictly as antiterrorism legislation, have been used in a terror investigation only fifteen times between 2006 and 2009. Yet during that same time period, such warrants have been issued more than sixteen hundred times in drug investigations.

Following the attacks of 9/11, the new Department of Homeland Security began adding funding for more military equipment to police arsenals. On the website AntiWar.com, Stephan Salisbury and Nick Turse pointed out,

> So much money has gone into armoring and arming local law-enforcement since 9/11 that the federal government could have rebuilt post-Katrina New Orleans five times over and had enough money left in the kitty to provide job training and housing for every one of the record 41,000-plus homeless people in New York City. It could have added in the growing population of 15,000 homeless in Philadelphia, my hometown, and still have had money to spare. Add disintegrating Detroit, Newark, and Camden to the list. Throw in some crumbling bridges and roads, too.
>
> We all know that addressing acute social and economic issues here in the homeland was the road not taken. Since 9/11, the Department of Homeland Security alone has doled out somewhere between $30 billion and $40 billion in direct grants to state and local law enforcement, as well as other first responders. At the same time, defense contractors have proven endlessly inventive in adapting sales pitches originally honed for the military on the battlefields of Iraq and Afghanistan to the desires of police on the streets of San Francisco and lower Manhattan.

But instead of rebuilding America's infrastructure, tax money has been spent on armored vehicles, SWAT armor, machine guns, helicopters, tactical gear and equipment, and even surveillance drones like those used against enemies in the Middle East. "We needed local police to play a legitimate, continuing role in furthering homeland security back in 2001," explained former Seattle police chief Norm Stamper, now a member of Law Enforcement Against Prohibition, a group of police and criminal-justice professionals advocating drug regulation rather than prohibition. "After all, the 9/11 terrorist attacks took place on specific police beats in specific police precincts. Instead, we got a 10-year campaign of increasing militarization, constitution-abusing tactics, needless violence and heartache as the police used federal funds, equipment, and training to ramp up the drug war. It's just tragic." Is it merely tragic or is this part of a plan by the elite to corral citizens and keep them under control even if it means using battlefield technology to do it?

In early 2012, the Federal Aviation Administration (FAA) was tasked to develop regulations for the testing and licensing of drones, making it easier for police agencies and private companies to put unmanned craft in the air. The FAA predicted that by 2020, there could be as many as thirty thousand drones in the air over America, some equipped with weapons, including wireless Tasers, and infrared, RFID, and facial recognition scanners.

Some drones are already in use. In late 2011, the sheriff's office of Montgomery County, north of Houston, announced that it was preparing to launch an unmanned Shadowhawk helicopter, which could potentially carry weapons. The $300,000 drone craft was acquired through a Department of Homeland Security grant. The craft will carry a powerful camera and a heat-seeking device. Sheriff Tommy Gage said the unmanned aerial vehicle (UAV) could be used in hunting criminals running from police as well as in drug investigations. Critics of drone technology warned that, privacy issues aside, unmanned drones might prove a hazard to both air traffic and the public on the ground. "We're not going to use it to be invading somebody's privacy. It'll be used for situations we have with criminals," assured Gage. In early 2012, critics' worst fears were realized when attendees of a private police-only test in Montgomery County witnessed the drone lose control and crash into the sheriff's SWAT team's armored vehicle, called the Bearcat.

In 2007, Houston mayor Annise Parker canceled plans to use these drones after the public became aware that Houston Police had secretly tested one there. The revelation of secret testing sparked a national debate over such measures and attracted the attention of civil libertarians concerned over issues of police searches without a warrant, spying into backyards, and issuing routine traffic tickets by surveillance from above.

Two news stories in 2012 were more ominous. On June 11, a 25,600-pound Navy RQ-4A Global Hawk unmanned drone costing $176 million went out of control during a routine training exercise and crashed into a tributary of the Nanticoke River near Salisbury, Maryland. There were no reported injuries or property damage, but the accident intensified critics' fears that a sky full of pilotless drones might represent a threat to the civilian population, as well as air traffic.

An even stranger story came out of the University of Texas at Austin, where a group of computer researchers, using $1,000 worth of computer parts, claimed they could hack into a government drone. Challenged by officials of the Homeland Security Department to prove their claim, a team under Professor Todd Humphreys did just that. By mimicking the drone's control signal, they were able to take control of the craft, much to the chagrin of the DHS officials. "Spoofing a GPS [Global Positioning System] receiver on a UAV [unmanned aerial vehicle] is just another way of hijacking a plane," explained Humphreys. His demonstration lent significant support to those who have theorized that such computer takeovers were employed in the hijacking of the four airliners on September 11, 2001.

Steven Aftergood, director of the Project on Government Secrecy for the Federation of American Scientists, said, "There are serious policy questions on the horizon about privacy and surveillance, by both government agencies and commercial entities. . . . It's not all about surveillance."

One would think with all this new high-tech, potentially lethal gadgetry for surveillance and control, local police forces would be hiring the most intelligent people available. Unfortunately, this does not seem to be the case. In 2000, the Second U.S. Circuit Court of Appeals in New York upheld the city's rejection of forty-nine-year-old Robert Jordan after he applied to be a police officer in New London, Connecticut. Jordan's application was rejected because he scored too high on an intelligence test. He sued the city, alleging discrimination and claiming that he doesn't have any more control over his basic intelligence than over his eye color, gender, or any other inherent attributes.

The average score nationally for police officers is 21 to 22, the equivalent of an IQ of 104, or just a little above average. New London police said they accepted only candidates who scored 20 to 27, on the theory that those who scored too high could get bored with police work and might soon leave the force after costly training. However, some believed that the lower IQ criterion was more about employing officers who would not question unconstitutional orders or policies than about losing the cost of training. Both the original court and the appeals court rejected Jordan's claim, stating that there was no discrimination, because the same standards were applied to everyone who took the test.

BIG BROTHER IS LISTENING

Long gone are the days of government agents snapping alligator clips to a suspect's phone lines. Today everything is electronics. Besides monitoring our daily activity outside the house, the government is monitoring what we say over phones, cell phones, and even online. According to the Associated Press, the CIA daily monitors more than five million tweets and Facebook messages from the agency's Open Source Center, located in a nondescript Virginia industrial park. Within the center, a team of several hundred linguists and analysts, many with library science degrees and thus called "vengeful librarians," pore over Facebook posts, newspapers, TV news channels, local radio stations, and Internet chat rooms around the world. Center director Doug Naquin said the group operates like the computer hacker heroine of the popular crime novel *The Girl with the Dragon Tattoo,* as they know "how to find stuff other people don't know exists."

Not only is the government listening to what we say; it's also storing our communications as well. Although some have accused Facebook of being a CIA-backed operation, they have failed to notice that the National Security Agency (NSA) is three times larger than the CIA and has been constructing a $2 billion compound in the desert of Utah one third larger than the U.S. Capitol to store all forms of communication among citizens—a yottabyte's worth.

A yottabyte? You might already be familiar with gigabytes, the most commonly used unit for computer hard disk storage space. A thousand gigabytes equal a terabyte. A thousand terabytes equal a petabyte. A thousand petabytes equal an exabyte. A thousand exabytes equal a zettabyte, and a thousand zettabytes equal a yottabyte. In other words, a yottabyte is 1,000,000,000,000,000 (one quadrillion) gigabytes. The average household computer holds about 200 gigabytes.

Devin Coldewey, writing on the computer site TechCrunch.com, asked,

> *What are they storing that, by some estimates, is going to take up thousands of times more space than all the world's known computers combined? Don't think they're going to say; they didn't grow to their current level of shadowy omniscience by disclosing things like that to the public. However,*

speculation isn't too hard on this topic. Now more than ever, surveillance is a data game. What with millions of phones being tapped and all data duplicated, constant recording of all radio traffic, 24-hour high definition video surveillance by satellite, there's terabytes at least of data coming in every day. And who knows when you'll have to sift through August 2007's overhead footage of Baghdad for heat signatures in order to confirm some other intelligence? Storage capacity of this magnitude implies a truly unprecedented amount of subjects for monitoring.

James Bamford, author of *The Puzzle Palace*, an exposé of the NSA, has noted,

Unlike the British government, which, to its great credit, allowed public debate on the idea of a central data bank, the NSA obtained the full cooperation of much of the American telecom industry in utmost secrecy after September 11 [2001]. For example, the agency built secret rooms in AT&T's major switching facilities where duplicate copies of all data are diverted, screened for key names and words by computers, and then transmitted on to the agency for analysis. Thus, these new centers in Utah, Texas, and possibly elsewhere will likely become the centralized repositories for the data intercepted by the NSA in America's version of the "big brother database" rejected by the British.

MEDIA CONTROL

Even with ubiquitous surveillance, there could be no real control of populations without top-down media control. After all, we define our democracy as rule by the majority, and the majority is manipulated by the corporate mass media, which by 2012 had devolved down to a mere five predominant international corporations.

At a Bilderberg meeting held in 1991 at Baden-Baden, Germany, David Rockefeller reportedly summed up the cozy relationship between the wealthy elite and the corporate news media when he told participants, "We are grateful to the *Washington Post*, the *New York Times*, *Time* magazine, and other great publications whose directors have attended our meetings and respected their promises of discretion for almost forty years. . . . It would have been impossible for us to develop our plan for the world if we had been subject to the bright lights of publicity during these years. But, the world is more sophisticated and prepared to march towards a world government. The supranational sovereignty of an intellectual elite and world bankers is surely preferable to the national auto determination practiced in the past centuries."

The control of these elites over the mass media has led to a degradation of our nation's news. Many stories of great importance to a free society are dropped or lost among trivial accounts of sports figures, celebrities, and inconsequential political blathering.

For example, with air, water, and food pollution causing an unprecedented rise in cancer rates and considering the billions of dollars that have been thrown at finding a cure, one would think that the media would have given more attention to new cancer treatments being developed. However, when one prodigious young girl possibly discovered an amazing cure, her work was only covered briefly by CBS News in early 2012.

Seventeen-year-old Angela Zhang, the daughter of Chinese immigrants living in Cupertino, California, received a check for $100,000 after winning the national Siemens science contest for her research paper detailing no less than a cure for cancer. As a high school freshman, Zhang began reading doctorate-level papers on bioengineering. In her sophomore year, she talked her way into a Stanford University laboratory and was conducting her own research. Her concept was to mix cancer medicine in a polymer that would attach to nanoparticles. The nanoparticles then would attach to cancer cells and show up in magnetic resonance imaging (MRI). Doctors could see exactly where the tumors were located. Zhang then determined that an infrared light aimed at the tumors would melt the polymer and release the medicine, killing the cancer cells while leaving healthy cells completely unharmed.

CBS reporter Steve Hartman noted, "It'll take years to know if it works in humans—but in mice—the tumors almost completely disappeared." Some questioned why this technique, which appears to successfully cure cancers, would take years to develop for humans when there is already so much money in cancer research. Others wondered if this hopeful story would even get repeated in corporate-controlled media addicted to pharmaceutical advertising.

There are also concerns over what's not in the news. Censorship works as well by omission as by commission. Many people are concerned over the fact that so many websites and pages of information on the Internet seem to disappear at an increasing rate, creating a nightmare for journalists and researchers, who suddenly find their sources changed or missing.

Is it simply irresponsibility, or is there method in the madness of corporate media control? Fairness and Accuracy in Reporting (FAIR), a nonprofit media watchdog group, reported that media corporations share board members with directors of a variety of other large corporations, including banks, investment companies, oil companies, health-care and pharmaceutical companies, and technology companies. The FAIR list showed interlocking board members in major media interests, including ABC/Disney, NBC/GE, CBS/Viacom, CNN/Time Warner, Fox/News Corporation, New York Times Co., Washington Post/Newsweek, Wall Street Journal/Dow Jones, Tribune Co., Gannett, and Knight-Ridder.

FAIR's findings were supported by a 2005 study by Project

Censored, an organization that examines news to find out what is left out of the national conversation because of political, economic, or legal pressure. The study determined that within ten large media corporations, there were 118 individuals who sat on 288 different national and international corporate boards. Project Censored reported a revolving-door relationship between big media and U.S. government agencies, as well as a close ongoing interlock between big media and corporate America. "We found media directors who also were former Senators or Representatives in the House such as Sam Nunn (Disney) and William Cohen (Viacom). Board members served at the FCC such as William Kennard (*New York Times*) and Dennis FitzSimmons (Tribune Company)."

The power of these media companies flows upward to the handful of globalists who own the banks that facilitate the corporate finances. Considering that these media organizations serve as the main sources of information for most Americans, corporate connections like the ones listed should require close and continuous public scrutiny for evidence of bias.

"Disney owns ABC, so we wonder how the board of Disney reacts to negative news about their board of director friends such as Halliburton or Boeing. We see board members with connections to Ford, Kraft, and Kimberly-Clark who employ tens of thousands of Americans. Is it possible that the US workforce receives only the corporate news private companies want them to hear?" asked the Project Censored research team. "If these companies control the media, they control the dissemination of news turning the First Amendment on its head by protecting corporate interests over people."

The national news media are not only linked by directorships to corporate business but also to higher education. The Project Censored team also found overlap between the boards of major media companies and prestigious U.S. universities. For instance, there was overlap between the *Washington Post* and the University of Southern California and New York University, between Gannett and Columbia University, between Disney and Georgetown University, and between Knight-Ridder and Wharton, the business school of the University of Pennsylvania. In the report, Project Censored team members Bridget Thornton, Brit Walters, and Lori Rouse wrote, "With the decreasing state and federal funding to universities, will we see our higher learning institutions tie themselves more to corporations than the government for their funding? . . . Will the universities eventually focus education around the production of workers or thinkers?"

The team also noted how history was repeating itself with media corporations. "As the Roman Empire declined, feudalism took the place of the government. The feudal lord was one of the few sources of jobs in the fourth and fifth centuries. These lords owned most of the land and resources. Today, we replace feudalism with corporatism. The mass population has few choices for their news, information and education. As corporate media applauds an ownership society, we must realize who gets to own. In corporate-dominated capitalism, wealth concentration is the goal and the corporate media are the cheerleaders."

While information on the control of news is readily available from public sources, it is never repeatedly and plainly presented to the millions of affected Americans by the corporate-controlled mass media. Mike Adams, on his widely read NaturalNews.com site, summed up the feelings of many when he wrote, "Much of the mainstream news is now utterly and completely fabricated these days . . . it's all so utterly false and unbelievable that an intelligent person watching the news can't help but explode with laughter . . . the information sources relied upon by the masses are unable to report the truth anymore and must resort to weaving politically expedient fictions on everything from health care and medicine to the fate of the U.S. dollar itself."

MORE EFFICIENT SERVITUDE

Some believe that a great deal of the control over our society comes from an organization called the Tavistock Institute of Human Relations. Originally the Tavistock Clinic, established in Sussex, England, in 1921 by royal command, it had been a research center for the British Special Intelligence Services (SIS). The clinic's founder, Brigadier General John Rawlings Reese, had been working on devising ways to manipulate political campaigns and public perceptions. In 1947, key members of the clinic formed the Tavistock Institute of Human Relations, which was funded by a grant from the Rockefeller Foundation. In 2006, the Institute merged with the Portman Clinic, a psychotherapy services clinic in London, to become the Tavistock and Portman National Health Service Foundation Trust.

In a book on the institute, John Coleman noted that it took shape prior to World War I for wartime public relations. Tavistock's leadership was given to two brothers—the Harmsworth brothers—who were also known as Lord Rothermere and Lord Northcliffe. "Tavistock began as a propaganda creating and disseminating organization centered at Wellington House, where the original organization was put together, with the intent of shaping a propaganda center that would break down the stiff public resistance being encountered to the looming war between Britain and Germany." Coleman added,

> *Funding was provided by the British royal family, and later by the Rothschilds to whom Lord Northcliffe was related through marriage. Arnold Toynbee was later selected as Director of Future Studies at the Royal Institute of International Affairs (RIIA). Two Americans, [journalist and media commentator] Walter Lippmann and Edward Bernays ["the father of public relations"], were appointed to handle the manipulation of British and American public*

opinion in preparation for the entry of the United States into World War I and to brief and direct President Woodrow Wilson, while Toynbee concentrated on changing British public opinion.

When John Rawlings Reese came in later on, he took the original mission of the organization one step further. Reese wanted to control political campaigns and develop certain types of public mind-control techniques. According to Coleman, "It was Reese who launched the method of controlling political campaigns, as well as mind control techniques, which continue to this very day, and it was Reese and Tavistock who taught the USSR, North Vietnam, China and Vietnam how to apply his techniques—all they ever wanted to know about how to brainwash individuals or a mass people," wrote Coleman.

Researchers at Tavistock found that the same psychotherapy techniques used to cure a mentally ill person could be reversed and used against a normal one. Coleman stated, "The modus operandi developed by Reese and his gurus of tampering with minds proved highly effective, and is still in wide use in America today. . . . We are tampered with, our opinions manufactured for us, all without our permission. What was the purpose of these behavior modifications? It was to bring about forced changes to our way of life, without our agreement and without even being aware of what was taking place."

Coleman said that Tavistock's tactics have been adopted by many organizations, from the global think tank the Club of Rome, the United Nations, the Rockefeller Foundation, and the Council on Foreign Relations to such disparate entities as Microsoft, Citibank, the New York Stock Exchange, the World Bank, the International Monetary Fund, and many others. "This is by no means a complete list of institutions in the hands of Tavistock planners," he added.

Today, major corporations and ultrawealthy individuals fund

organizations such as Tavistock. They utilize these organizations' secrets in the mass media to push just the right emotional buttons on social and cultural issues in order to manipulate both working-class and middle-class people into voting against their own economic interests. Edward Bernays, one of the pioneers of public relations and advertising, was named one of the hundred most influential Americans of the twentieth century by *Life* magazine and continued to serve as a government consultant through the Bush I administration. As far back as 1928, in his book *Propaganda*, Bernays wrote about the control of citizens in a democratic society, stating,

> *The conscious and intelligent manipulation of the organized habits and opinions of the masses is an important element in democratic society. Those who manipulate this unseen mechanism of society constitute an invisible government which is the true ruling power of our country. We are governed, our minds are molded, our tastes formed, our ideas suggested, largely by men we have never heard of. This is a logical result of the way in which our democratic society is organized. Vast numbers of human beings must cooperate in this manner if they are to live together as a smoothly functioning society. . . . In almost every act of our daily lives, whether in the sphere of politics or business, in our social conduct or our ethical thinking, we are dominated by the relatively small number of persons . . . who understand the mental processes and social patterns of the masses. It is they who pull the wires which control the public mind, who harness old social forces and contrive new ways to bind and guide the world.*

Such mind manipulation in the past was accomplished though conventional psychological methods combined with subliminal programming, thought by many to have been outlawed years ago. But the old techniques may seem mild compared to a new technology the Pentagon calls silent sound spread spectrum (SSSS), which delivers subliminal programming directly to the human brain via the auditory sense at frequencies imperceptible by humans. It is rumored that SSSS technology was used in the First Gulf War, causing thousands of battle-hardened Iraqi soldiers to surrender without a fight. "Why would eight-year veterans of Middle Eastern warfare (with Iran 1980–1988) behave this way? Simple. They were subjected to a technology that was so extreme and incomprehensible that they were suddenly reduced to the level of compliant children and felt grateful to still be alive in the wake of their mind-wrenching experience," stated A. True Ott, a Peabody Award–winning radio commentator and author.

Ott warned, "This technology is about to be used, albeit in a more subtle fashion, against American citizens in a highly classified and covert operation *to mind control and manipulate the entire population into 'compliance' with our New World order overlords* [emphasis in the original]. The technology will utilize a combination of HAARP [High-frequency Active Auroral Research Program] transmitters, GWEN [Ground Wave Emergency Network] towers, microwave cell-phone towers, and the soon-to-be-mandatory High Definition Digital TV that will enter your home via: a) cable, b) satellite, c) HD TVs, or d) those oh-so-easy-to-obtain 'digital converter boxes' that the government is so anxious to help you obtain and underwrite most of the cost on your behalf." Because of surreptitious programming broadcast at high or low frequencies outside the range of conscious perception, parents should no longer feel secure by simply monitoring the content of TV programming or video games. All content aside, the television has become a dangerous mind-control device.

Why the need for such control? The would-be masters of the world desire an undisciplined public, ignorant of the basic principles of individual liberty. They wish to keep them confused, disorganized, and absorbed with unimportant or distracting issues.

They wish to discourage critical thinking and technical creativity by means of low-quality public education in mathematics, logic, systems design, economics, and even the humanities while providing unrelenting emotional trauma through stories of self-indulgence, exploitive sex, and gratuitious violence in the corporate mass media. Such distractions lead the public away from serious consideration of their personal needs to inconsequential outside priorities.

More important, rewriting law and history changes the entire fabric of a society. Tavistock programming has been masterful with these techniques, as well as with the use of the Hegelian dialectic, or problem, reaction, solution. This method basically involves fabricating or intensify a problem, offering a draconian solution, then settling for a "compromise" that nevertheless furthers the intended goal.

Many are now seeing the centralization of such public control. Catherine Austin Fitts, who served as assistant secretary of housing and federal housing commissioner under George H. W. Bush, believes that technology concentrates power in fewer and fewer hands. In a 2011 interview, Fitts said that this power can "end up being extremely destructive of individual rights, extremely destructive of the environment, extremely destructive of all the things that create a healthy economy."

Fitts illustrated her point with a metaphoric character she called Mr. Global. "Mr. Global essentially thinks he's in charge of governing planet earth," she explained. "I think what Mr. Global would say is that you can't trust the average person to make intelligent decisions, that popular opinion will never turn the aircraft carrier in time, that democracy was a great experiment but it doesn't work because the average person can't see or relate to the whole and can't make critical decisions soon enough to turn the aircraft carrier, and so you have to do things like 9/11 to build the kind of consensus and global picture you need to act."

She also pointed to the growing distrust and disrespect between the citizenry and the developed world's leadership. This cycle of antipathy, she stated, is a part of centralization, "because centralization ultimately makes the body politic stupid, and so you need more and more tyranny to force things—and that's what we're really watching globally as very invasive technology makes now the kind of tyranny that Orwell once wrote about in fiction very plausible. That is what we see happening."

TO WHAT END?

What is the goal of the wealthy elite?

The agenda may have been revealed by Nick Rockefeller, a participant in the World Economic Forum and a member of the Council on Foreign Relations and the International Institute for Strategic Studies. According to Hollywood producer Aaron Russo, Rockefeller told him, "The end goal is to get everybody chipped, to control the whole society, to have the bankers and the elite people control the world."

It should be clear by now that the elite want to control the world, but the bigger question is why? Author Joseph P. Farrell wrote that while a final answer is not known to the uninitiated, one answer does suggest itself. "They are indeed trying to reconstruct a lost mythical past: a global 'golden age' with a supremely sophisticated science with which they can dominate and subjugate the Earth." But he added, "To reconstruct it, on the scale required and implied by their enterprise itself, will require that virtually the entire planet and its resources must be at their disposal."

Thoughtful persons outside the influence of the corporate mass media of America see more clearly the concentration of money and power for the aims of the ruling families. In early 2012, Mujahid Kamran of Punjab University wrote in the *Nation*,

The term New World Order (NWO) was first used, and actual plans laid out for achieving this goal over the next few centuries, in the year 1773, at a meeting of the 13 richest men of Prussia held in Frankfurt by the 33-year-old banker Mayer Amschel Rothschild. . . . Rothschild turned to a manuscript during the meeting and read his points, which outlined a plan of action for taking control of the entire globe . . . he emphasized: "The qualification for this aristocracy is 'wealth,' which is dependent on us." He laid down: "Candidates in public office should be servile and obedient to our commands, so that they may readily be used." He also laid down that their "combined wealth would control all outlets of public information." And finally came the most inhuman axiom of their policy: "Panics and financial depressions would ultimately result in world government, a new order of one world government." Modern day USA illustrates all these features with chilling clarity to anyone who cares to read the relevant literature.

Kamran said that the banking families have continued their relentless pursuit of the NWO and that hundreds of millions of deaths in maneuvered wars and conflicts "have not led to an iota of remorse in their hearts, minds and souls. . . . Like a parasite these families settle themselves or their agents in a healthy host, and having nourished themselves destroy the host. Germany was their host and now the US is their host." According to Kamran,

The think-tanks that present to the public the goal of global occupation and control by the international bankers in palatable terms include academics who are on their payroll and, among other things, formulate doctrines to give an air of respectability to the program of conquering and controlling mankind like slaves. In 1997, Zbigniew Brzezinski, founding member of the Trilateral Commission and member [of the] Council on Foreign Relations . . . in his book, The Grand Chessboard *. . . stated that in order to rule the world the US must occupy Central Asia. This reveals the continuity of goal, design and effort of the elite—its agents have maintained the same language over a 100-year period. The achievement of this goal will require a major war, a world war, starting most likely from the impending US-Israel attack on Iran. But to wage this war the US must be transformed into a genuine dictatorship. Legislation carried out in the wake of [the] Oklahoma bombing and 9/11 has ensured that the US public lives in constant fear of being arrested.*

Kamran pointed to three recent laws laying the groundwork for a virtual police state. One is the John Warner Defense Authorization Act, signed by Bush in 2007, which allows the use of the military against civilians without permission of the governor of a state. The second is the National Defense Authorization Act (NDAA), signed by Obama in late 2011, which does away with habeas corpus by allowing the president to detain indefinitely anyone suspected of terrorism—no proof required and no appeal permitted. Third, on March 8, 2012, Obama signed into law the Federal Restricted Buildings and Grounds Improvement Act of 2011 which criminalized protest. A response to the Occupy movement, this law provides for fines and imprisonment of up to ten years for anyone engaging in "disruptive" conduct near "restricted" areas.

"Taken together, the three laws indicate that the elite is well prepared to quell any civil unrest ruthlessly. The destruction of the middle class is also being pursued so that it is rendered homeless and hungry and its ability to protest destroyed. All this is part of the final push towards the NWO through a great war," wrote Kamran.

Kamran is not the only one to see an encroaching police state. Internet commentator Mac Slavo, after noting that gang-related crime in the major cities is on the rise while police personnel and social programs are declining, wrote, "As more cities cut services and hundreds of thousands continue to lose their jobs, the situation across the entire nation will become untenable. Social safety nets will fall apart and crime will become more violent and random as a new paradigm takes hold. Local law enforcement will be unable to control it using traditional policing. The people will not only accept assistance from the federal government in the form of tanks and soldiers on the streets of their neighborhoods—they'll demand it. Lucky for them—all of the executive orders for declaring a state of emergency are already in place and ready for implementation."

Led by the United States, the world's economy is tottering on the brink of collapse. A food and water shortage looms on the horizon. The Mediterranean Sea and the Gulf of Mexico are becoming bodies of dead water due to human misuse. At the time of this writing, deadly radiation continues to spew worldwide from damaged nuclear plants in Japan, with no end in sight. The world's wealth flows constantly into fewer and fewer hands as the so-called industrialized nations witness strikes, growing unemployment, and widespread social disorder. Governments, desperate to maintain the old social order, are cracking down on civil liberties and freedom.

The track record of world leaders today is shameful. They no longer listen to their populations but rather to their corporate backers. Corporate leaders, mindful of their precarious position beneath the real controllers, no longer seem to care for anything past their profit line. Their decisions are not about what's good for the public, the environment, or even any humane concept of morality.

When corporate leaders and their hired politicians speak of the "greater good," they are actually only talking about their own well-being, not that of the public. In fact, many of the actions taken by the corporate and political leaders of today seem to follow the millennia-long agenda of attempting to subjugate the human population. Their decisions are often contrary to any notion of public health and well-being.

And it may be worse than this. Many see their activities as yet another attempt to reduce the human population. Concern over population reduction and control by a wealthy ruling elite today is taking center stage in the public's mind, especially after witnessing the bailout of the plutocrats who were the cause of the financial crisis beginning in 2008.

Many, like Internet commentator Alex Jones, believe the New World Order agenda is to "thin the population leaving only an enslaved underclass who are forced to live on the poverty line in control grid cities while the overlords enjoy the bountiful paradise of the earth and evolve into super-beings with the aid of advanced life-extension technologies." Jones added that this long-term dream of the wealthy elite will become "a nightmare for the rest of humanity unless we rise up now and fight back against the systems of control that are being locked down to transform the earth into a prison planet."

Economic systems are failing all over the planet, and the only solution seriously considered by lawmakers is to borrow and print more money, leading to a never-ending spiral of inflation. Such "solutions" serve only to accelerate the economic collapse. "It's not a new world order; it's the bankers' order," observed Gerald Celente, author of *Trend Tracking*. He said control by private bankers has been a "major issue of this country since its founding up until 1913. . . . They're moneychangers and loan sharks. Get rid of them."

In addition to the economic problems of humanity, industrialization is taking a toll on the environment. The weather is becoming erratic. Recent years have witnessed unprecedented tornadoes, hurricanes, earthquakes, and tsunamis. Flooding and droughts are increasing, creating crop failures, food shortages, and higher costs at the grocery stores.

326 OUR OCCULTED HISTORY

Whole populations of bees, birds, and other creatures are being wiped out. Many think this is due to the variability of nature, but others, with some scientific support, blame it on the overuse of pesticides or the use of genetically modified organisms (GMOs).

Reporting on the lethal failure of nuclear energy has been placed on a back burner by the corporate mass media. The nuclear plants in Fukushima, Japan, damaged from a tsunami created by an offshore earthquake, continue to spew silent and invisible poison into the atmosphere. Right after the disaster, in March 2011, rainwater in Calgary, Canada, had an average of 8.18 becquerels (a unit for measuring radioactivity) per liter of radioactive iodine, easily exceeding the Canadian guideline of 6 becquerels per liter for drinking water. In late 2011, rainwater captured in St. Louis, Missouri, measured a radiation level of 13.3 microsieverts per hour, 130 times normal background radiation.

While the public is told that the radiation seeping from the Fukushima reactors is only at "low" levels and not immediately harmful, they fail to understand that the food supply has also been irradiated and that radioactive isotopes of cesium and other elements may persist for centuries. The cumulative effects of increasing exposure to ionizing radiation over the course of our lives have been noted by many people, like Mike Adams on his Natural News website. He asked, "How is the human race going to survive its exposure to CT scans, radioactive food, chest X-rays, TSA body scanners and even the secret DHS mobile X-ray vans that can penetrate your body with X-rays as you're walking into a football stadium? The total radiation burden on the human race is now reaching a point of mass infertility. That may be the whole idea, actually." Recalling the decrease in male sperm count throughout the world today, one may conclude that Adams's concern is well justified.

A DISASTER IN THE MAKING

Not long before the Fukushima disaster, another maritime catastrophe caused so much pollution that it is considered one of the worst environmental disasters of all time. On April 20, 2010, an explosion at the offshore Deepwater Horizon drilling platform caused untold millions of gallons of petroleum to leak into the Gulf of Mexico. Operated by British Petroleum (BP), the drilling platform disaster caused a number of human deaths and illnesses and eradicated huge swaths of Gulf wildlife. Was this simply a mishap or a plot created by a sinister agenda? If nothing else, it is a classic example of the blending of elitist corporate control and its unceasing demand for profits with a lack of government accountability, leading to tragedy for millions of people.

By the fall of 2010, after the cleanup, the Environmental Protection Agency (EPA) declared that air quality on the Gulf coastline was "normal," and President Obama proclaimed the area safe and "open for business." But the EPA had made a similar mistake in September 2001, when director Christine Todd Whitman announced in the wake of the 9/11 attacks, "I am glad to reassure the people of New York . . . that their air is safe to breathe and the water is safe to drink."

The EPA was wrong in 2001, and it was probably wrong after the Gulf oil spill. According to several published reports, nearly a thousand 9/11 first responders have now died from a variety of unidentified causes, and many New Yorkers claim a variety of illnesses due to bad air that emanated from the wreckage. Similarly, Gulf Coast residents continue to report serious illnesses that they blame on toxic water and air caused by the oil blowout and subsequent cleanup activities. Kim Anderson, professor of environmental and molecular toxicology in the College of Agricultural Sciences at Oregon State University (OSU), confirmed that toxins were being released into the Gulf. The oil pipe was reportedly sealed on July 15, 2010, but by then massive damage had been done. A study of waters off the Louisiana coast showed a fortyfold increase in carcinogens, such as polycyclic aromatic hydrocarbons (PAHs), between May and June 2010.

Even more disturbing, in late 2011, fresh oil was reported surfacing all over the northern quadrant of the Gulf of Mexico, with reports of huge expanses of oil sheen. Francis Beinecke, president of the Natural Resources Defense Council, who served on President Obama's National Oil Spill Commission, reported that "tar balls were continuing to wash up on shore, and that oil sheen trails were being seen in the wake of fishing boats. Wetlands and marshlands were still in decline and dying; crude oil lay offshore in deep water, as well as fine silts and sands onshore."

He added, "I have traveled throughout the Gulf Coast, and people routinely tell me that their communities have not recovered economically or psychologically. They are struggling to get their lives back to where they were on April 19—before the oil spill took their livelihoods, clean beaches, productive shrimp and oyster fisheries, and family traditions away from them."

Many families have also complained recently about the spraying of toxic oil dispersants, such as Corexit. Usually oil floats to the surface of a body of liquid, but Corexit, a product of the Nalco Holding Company, causes the oil to break into small globules that sink to the bottom. One would think that Corexit wouldn't have been needed after the initial spill, but nearly two years after the explosion, Corexit continues to be sprayed in the Gulf states, according to residents.

Darryl Malek-Wiley, an environmental justice organizer with the Sierra Club, has claimed that the fishing and environmental community agree that the use of the dispersants was not a smart idea for the long-term health of the region.

One point eight million gallons of dispersants into the Gulf of Mexico—nobody's ever put that amount of dispersant anywhere in the world, so we don't know what the impact of that is going to be. Some of the people who are sick, they're taking samples of their blood and they're finding the chemicals that make up the dispersants in their blood, as well as Louisiana sweet crude, and having serious health impacts . . . [like] loss of memory, rashes, sinus [problems]. Some folks we've talked with, they forget where they're going. They forget who you are. And these are men, all of them were fishermen in relatively good physical shape. And we don't know about long-term health impacts, but there's no immediate health care for folks who need it right now. And that's a big concern—people have been losing their health insurance because they're not able to work, and they don't have money to pay for independent health care . . . a whole range of things are happening. A number of them have lost their homes because they weren't able to work and they didn't get paid by BP like they said they were gonna be, and so, it's a serious impact on people's lives.

In a recent *Business Insider* article, Michael Snyder noted that almost every person who worked to clean up the 1989 Exxon Valdez oil spill in Alaska had died. He added, "The truth is that what we have out in the Gulf of Mexico is a 'toxic soup' of oil, methane, benzene, hydrogen sulfide, other toxic gases and very poisonous chemical dispersants such as Corexit 9500. Breathing all of this stuff is not good for your health, but the reality is that the true health toll of this oil spill is not going to be known for decades."

Any truthful investigation of the oil spill must "follow the money." The company that owned the Deepwater Horizon was Transocean, a firm saddled with legal problems, one that had been charged with bribery of foreign governmental officials, tax fraud, tax evasion, and falsifying records. In 2007, Transocean's financial advisers, Goldman Sachs and Lehman Brothers, helped the company merge with GlobalSantaFe. This merger brought in a staggering $15 billion to shareholders.

Frances Beinecke, the president of the Natural Resources Defense Council, stopped short of calling the BP oil spill a conspiracy. Yet she did state that "the blowout was not the product of a series of aberrational decisions made by rogue industry or government officials that could not have been anticipated or expected to occur again. Rather, the root causes are systemic and, absent significant reform in both industry practices and government policies, might well recur."

Radio commentator Dave Hodges, who wrote a series of articles titled *The Great Gulf Coast Holocaust*, was not so hesitant in pointing the finger of calculated neglect at BP, Transocean, Goldman Sachs, and Halliburton. According to Hodges, these companies, described as the Four Horsemen, have "repeatedly lied about the ecological damage done to the Gulf, lied about the damage done to the people and their health, lied about the damage done to the economic health of the Gulf, and continue to lie about the failure to properly compensate the victims in the Gulf while the continuing and unfolding holocaust is still growing in scope."

It does appear that everyone in the Gulf lost money on the oil spill except BP and its corporate partners. According to the BBC, BP and its Gulf Coast partners—Goldman Sachs, Transocean, and Halliburton—all experienced major gains in corporate profits as a result of the spill. Transocean rewarded its top officials with bonuses for achieving the "best year in safety performance in our company's history." Transocean CEO Steve Newman received a bonus payout of $374,062, part of his total compensation package of $5.8 million.

Worse yet, internal e-mails revealed that Goldman Sachs profited from the Gulf disaster by making "a substantial financial bet against the Gulf of Mexico" by short-selling Transocean stock *one day* before the explosion. Goldman insiders bet that the stock would go down, which it did in the wake of the explosion, so they profited. Federal investigators found an e-mail from Goldman employee Fabrice "Fabulous Fab" Tourre in which he bragged to a girlfriend, "One oil rig goes down and we're going to be rolling in dough. Suck it, fishies and birdies." Outraged, Sterling Allan wrote on the worldwide blog Examiner.com, "It turns out that Goldman Sachs really did place shorts on Transocean stock days before the explosions rocked the rig in the Gulf of Mexico sending stocks plunging while GS profits soared—benefitting once again from a huge disaster, having done the same with airline stocks prior to 9/11 then again with the housing bubble."

Goldman Sachs lies at the heart of a money-managing empire that ranges from the Exchange Stabilization Fund to Facebook. Former Goldman executives include Robert Rubin and Henry Paulson, both of whom served as U.S. Treasury secretaries. A former Goldman Sachs lobbyist named Mark Patterson was named chief of staff to Treasury Secretary Timothy Geithner even though President Obama pledged during his presidential campaign that he would limit the influence of lobbyists in his administration. Although Timothy Geithner has never worked directly for Goldman Sachs, as a former member of the New York Federal Reserve Bank, his connections in banking are extensive. In a 2009 interview, former assistant secretary of the treasury Paul Craig Roberts was asked if Geithner works for the people or for the banking system on Wall Street. Roberts replied, "He works for Goldman Sachs."

Aside from its political connections, Goldman Sachs is involved with a number of different projects and organizations. In the 1990s, Goldman partnered with David Rockefeller and his associates in ownership of Rockefeller Center. The multinational investment firm also conducts business with a number of banks, including Citi

Investment Research, T. Rowe Price Associates, J.P. Morgan Asset
Management, and Capital World Investors. In 2009, Goldman was
investigated for receiving $12 billion in the bailout of American
International Group (AIG) by the Federal Reserve.

Now Goldman Sachs has its hands in one of the largest growing industries—social media. In early 2012, Goldman announced
that it was investing $450 million in the privately owned social net-
work Facebook, valued then at $50 billion. The deal came with an
additional $50 million investment from Digital Sky Technologies
(DST), a Russian investment firm that also invested in Groupon
and Zynga, and it will allow Facebook to challenge Google as the
most prominent site on the Internet. Some saw this move as the
latest attempt by the banking elite to control the Internet.

FREEMAN OR SERF?

Goldman Sachs is large and powerful, yet, it is only one of the
global corporations that control Congress and generally run the
government. Years ago, one American president acknowledged as
much. In a letter dated November 23, 1933, newly elected president
Franklin D. Roosevelt admitted, "The real truth of the matter is,
as you and I know, that a financial element in the large centers
has owned the government ever since the days of Andrew Jackson."
In light of Roosevelt's admission, careful notice should be given to
what is happening in modern America and always under the excuse
of protecting the public. And serious questions should be asked.
These include:

- Why, in the name of protecting freedom of speech, are
  more and more laws being considered to curtail and
  censor the Internet and hinder free expression in public?
- Why do city governments, aided by federal funds, video-

tape citizens in public places 24/7 for purposes of "public safety," yet if citizens attempt to videotape police in those same public places, they are subject to threats, beatings, and arrest despite court decisions supporting the First Amendment?

- Why does the government claim that every single air traveler must be intimately searched and confirmed harmless in order to protect the safety of a few hundred passengers on the plane, when that very same government conducts no safety testing whatsoever on fluoride chemicals dumped into municipal water supplies, threatening the health of tens of millions?

- Why are commercial airline passengers required to submit to X-rays, strip off belts, coats, and shoes, and carry no more than two ounces of liquid, while private aircraft are free to come and go without scrutiny? Can potential terrorists not rent or hire private aircraft? And if there is such a dire threat of terrorists slipping into the United States with chemical or nuclear weapons, why has nothing substantial been done to secure the nation's borders?

- Why do armed government agents raid and arrest farmers for selling fresh milk yet do nothing to protect the public from corporate additives such as MSG, a common food additive linked to obesity. Why does the government continue to allow aspartame in diet soft drinks when it has been shown to cause seizures? Where is the public's protection from high fructose corn syrup, which increases the risk of diabetes? Why is processed grain used for making bread being cut with bromide, a known tumor-causing agent with "zombifying potential," instead of using essential iodine, necessary for the normal metabolism of cells, as was done up until the 1980s? Why is sodium nitrite, implicated as a cause of cancer, still found in processed meat? Why is there no prohibition on artificial food colors, many of which are suspected by the FDA as being linked to behavioral and health problems? Millions more Americans consume such problematic additives each day than drink raw milk.

• Why is the FDA proposing that traditional nutritional supplements like vitamin C, gingerroot, and echinacea be outlawed pending lengthy new safety reviews and approval processes, while the USDA has approved the widespread experimental planting of genetically modified crops with no safety testing whatsoever under the bizarre reasoning that GMOs are essentially "identical" to non-GMO crops? If they are identical, why are they patented and termed *modified*? And why have dozens of other nations banned GMO seeds?

• Why does the Federal Emergency Management Agency advise citizens to store food and water for a mere three-day emergency, such as a hurricane, while this same federal government has spent billions building massive underground bunker networks where it has stockpiled enough food, water, guns, ammunition, medical supplies, communications equipment, nonhybrid seeds, and much more to last decades?

• Why, in the wake of the 2011 Japan earthquake and tsunami that wrecked four nuclear power plants and spewed radiation all the way to the United States, did the U.S. Environmental Protection Agency actually downplay the disaster, stop reporting air quality on the West Coast, and propose increasing the allowable level of radioactive contamination in water, food, and soil?

• Why do government health officials claim the right to forcibly vaccinate all children to protect society when,

if such vaccinations were effective, all voluntarily vacci-
nated children would be protected against unvaccinated
children?

These and many other actions that diminish freedom and actually harm the public, committed regularly over long periods of
time, cannot be ascribed simply to accident, stupidity, individual
malfeasance, or bureaucratic incompetence. As Thomas Jefferson
once noted, "Single acts of tyranny may be ascribed to the accidental opinion of the day; but a series of oppressions, begun at a distin-
guished period, and pursued unalterably through every change of
ministers too plainly proves a deliberate, systematic plan of reducing us to slavery." Another quote, widely attributed to Jefferson,
indicates that we face the same problem as the people in his time:
"The issue today is the same as it has been throughout all history,
whether man shall be allowed to govern himself or be ruled by a
small elite."

Two authors who clearly foresaw the events and policies of today
were George Orwell in his famous book *1984* and Aldous Huxley
in *Brave New World*. In a 1949 letter to Orwell, Huxley wrote,

> *Within the next generation I believe that the world's rulers
> will discover that infant conditioning [dumbed-down edu-
> cation] and narco-hypnosis [drugging] are more efficient,
> as instruments of government, than clubs and prisons, and
> that the lust for power can be just as completely satisfied
> by suggesting people into loving their servitude as by flog-
> ging and kicking them into obedience. In other words, I
> feel that the nightmare of 1984 is destined to modulate into
> the nightmare of a world having more resemblance to that
> which I imagined in* Brave New World. *The change will
> be brought about as a result of a felt need for increased ef-
> ficiency. Meanwhile, of course, there may be a large scale*

> *biological and atomic war—in which case we shall have*
> *nightmares of other and scarcely imaginable kinds.*

Orwell, especially, may have been in a position to know whereof he wrote. Orwell was a pen name. His real name was Eric Arthur Blair. Although his family was not wealthy, they were nevertheless members of the British gentry, and Blair managed to study at Eton, where he met Aldous Huxley. Eton has long been accused of being a central education center for Britain's elite families. Nineteen prime ministers, including David Cameron, were educated there. It was at Eton that Blair was introduced to the Fabian Society, reputed to be a secret society of those desiring worldwide socialism. Blair eventually left the society, provoking some to speculate that his 1948 book, *1984*, actually is an exposé of the plans of the wealthy elite rulers. Whether this is true or not, *1984* is amazingly prescient in its account of a future global totalitarian socialist state. In the book, the world had been divided into three economic blocs called Oceania, Eurasia, and Eastasia. Today, we witness the existing European Union, the much-mentioned North American Union, and a future Asian union. Blair's neologisms—doublethink, Newspeak, and Thought Police—reflect current trends and now are being used widely by conspiracy writers.

Concerns over what many see as a move toward a totalitarian police state have revived the age-old queries: Who are we? Why are we here? Where are we going? A growing number of people are questioning the nature of our "reality." Why are all paths and aids to self-discovery continually denied us by religious and secular authorities? Why are the air, water, and food of our world being filled with toxins that hinder both physical and spiritual development? Why is almost everything humans naturally enjoy discouraged, restricted, controlled, or outlawed?

Will it be only a handful of youthful protesters who stand against the concentrated power of the banks and corporations? "The only word these corporations know is more," wrote Chris Hedges, former correspondent for the *Christian Science Monitor,* National Public Radio, and the *New York Times.*

> *They are disemboweling every last social service program funded by the taxpayers, from education to Social Security, because they want that money themselves. Let the sick die. Let the poor go hungry. Let families be tossed in the street. Let the unemployed rot. Let children in the inner city or rural wastelands learn nothing and live in misery and fear. Let the students finish school with no jobs and no prospects of jobs. Let the prison system, the largest in the industrial world, expand to swallow up all potential dissenters. Let torture continue. Let teachers, police, firefighters, postal employees and social workers join the ranks of the unemployed. Let the roads, bridges, dams, levees, power grids, rail lines, subways, bus services, schools and libraries crumble or close. Let the rising temperatures of the planet, the freak weather patterns, the hurricanes, the droughts, the flooding, the tornadoes, the melting polar ice caps, the poisoned water systems, the polluted air increase until the species dies.*
>
> *There are no excuses left. Either you join the revolt taking place on Wall Street and in the financial districts of other cities across the country or you stand on the wrong side of history. Either you obstruct, in the only form left to us, which is civil disobedience, the plundering by the criminal class on Wall Street and accelerated destruction of the ecosystem that sustains the human species, or become the passive enabler of a monstrous evil. Either you taste, feel and smell the intoxication of freedom and revolt or sink into the miasma of despair and apathy. Either you are a rebel or a slave.*
>
> *To be declared innocent in a country where the rule of law means nothing, where we have undergone a corporate*

coup, where the poor and working men and women are re-
duced to joblessness and hunger, where war, financial specu-
lation and internal surveillance are the only real business of
the state, where even habeas corpus no longer exists, where
you, as a citizen, are nothing more than a commodity to
corporate systems of power, one to be used and discarded, is
to be complicit in this radical evil. To stand on the sidelines
and say "I am innocent" is to bear the mark of Cain; it is
to do nothing to reach out and help the weak, the oppressed
and the suffering, to save the planet. To be innocent in times
like these is to be a criminal.

When Hedges rails against the "criminal class on Wall Street,"
he is speaking of the global super-rich, the bloodlines who, as we
have seen, can be traced back to our earliest history.

Recent news concerning financial meltdowns, polluted air, degradation of the environment, covert aerial spraying, faulty products,
untested drugs, adulterated vaccines, and contaminated food and
water raises these questions: Why are these corporate and political
elites making decisions that are harmful to the planet and its population? What humans in their right mind would want to destroy the
Earth, killing the source and sustenance of life? Would they really
kill the goose that lays golden eggs? Can such concerted efforts be
explained away as psychopathic behavior or mere corporate igno-
rance and greed?

Only through persistent study, curiosity, and critical thinking
will individuals become aware that our history has been corrupted
and suppressed. Such hiding of truth raises many unanswered questions. But the primary ones are: Who has directed our occulted
history? And to what end? Humanity appears to be in a footrace
to see whether we will gain true freedom and liberty or submit to
the technological and totalitarian world envisioned by Huxley and
Orwell and promoted by Perkins's corporatocracy.

And other questions remain. The evidence of ancient nonhuman visitation is compelling, almost overwhelming. Cave drawings, cuneiform tablets of clay, biblical descriptions, and existing anomalous artifacts attest to the reality of such a presence down through history. Assuming the ancient Sumerian tablets are based on truth, extraterrestrials were on Earth millennia ago. Did they all leave at some point, or are some still here?

The answer may be found by simply reviewing human history. We are taught that humans slowly evolved from hunter-gatherers to farmers who gathered in city-states, which became nations and empires. Yet a close scrutiny of history also tells of legends of marvelous lost civilizations, amazing artifacts, and reports from around the world of gods flying in ancient times—the flying dragons of the Chinese, the *vimanas* of the Hindus, the soaring boats of the Egyptians, the flying shields of Alexander, the airships of 1896–97 and the UFOs of today. Someone has been with us all through recorded history.

It also can be demonstrated that a mere handful of bloodline-fixated individuals hiding behind corporate fronts, foundations, and government bureaucracies are seeking to control the wealth and knowledge of the planet. Here there seem to be but three possibilities: members of the ruling elite are using modern technology in an effort to contact the ancient gods; they already have contacted the ancient gods and are being guided or controlled by them; or they *are* the ancient gods, the Anunnaki, the shining ones of antiquity.

It may well be time to ask in all seriousness: Are they even us? Do they want us out of the way? Should we be mobilizing for a concerted defense of Earth? And is there any nonhuman counteracting force to which we may look for hope and assistance? Or is it time for the average person to get off the couch and do something to counteract the control freaks bent on ruling the world?

The answer to the last question is up to you.

Sources

Introduction

Howard Phillips Lovecraft, *The Call of Cthulhu and Other Weird Stories* (New York: Penguin, 1999), 139.

Interbreeding bloodlines: David Icke, *The Biggest Secret: The Book That Will Change the World* (Scottsdale, AZ: Bridge of Love Publications, 1999), 1.

Carl Sagan on the reptilian complex: "Order of Melchizedek," www.thehermetica.com/thereptilianbrain.htm.

"I think we're property": Charles Fort, *The Complete Books of Charles Fort* (New York: Dover, 1974), 163 (in *The Book of the Damned*).

"Not pseudoscientific speculation": "Ancient Astronauts," www.skepdic.com/vondanik.html.

We were not alone: Philip Coppens, *The Ancient Alien Question: A New Inquiry into the Existence, Evidence, and Influence of Ancient Visitors* (Pompton Plains, NJ: New Page Books, 2012), 287.

Human race as source of labor: William Bramley, *The Gods of Eden* (San Jose, CA: Dahlin Family Press, 1990), 37.

Enough evidence of AB involvement: Paul Von Ward, *We've Never Been Alone: A History of Extraterrestrial Intervention* (Charlottesville, VA: Hampton Roads, 2011), 367.

Paul White on patriarchs: "Subterranean Tunnels, Underground Alien Bases," www.burlingtonnews.net/tunnels.

Part I: Origins of the Solar System

Rupert Sheldrake: www.holoscience.com/wp/links.

Big Bang Questioned

Paul J. Steinhardt, "Quantum Gaps in Big Bang Theory: Why Our Best Explanation of How the Universe Evolved Must Be Fixed—or Replaced," *Scientific American*, Apr. 2011.

Search for the Tenth Planet

A tenth planet theorized: Hugh McCann, "10th Planet? Pluto's Orbit Says 'Yes,'" *Detroit News*, Jan. 16, 1981.

Mysterious object reported: Thomas O'Toole, "Possibly as Large as Jupiter: Mystery Heavenly Body Discovered," *Washington Post*, Dec. 30, 1983, A1.

Planet X bunkum: Ian O'Neill, "2012: No Planet X," www.universetoday.com/14486/2012-No-Planet-X.

THE SUMERIAN ACCOUNT—MINGLING OF THE WATERS

Take epic at face value: Zecharia Sitchin, *The 12th Planet* (New York: Avon, 1976), 211.

MARTIAN LIFE

Viking scientist Patricia Straat: http://dsc.discovery.com/News/2009/09/28/Viking-Lander-Mars.html.

Mike Wall, Chris McKay, and Chris Carr on life from Mars: Mike Wall, "Are Earthlings from Mars? New Tool May Reveal Your Alien Ancestry," Mar. 23, 2011, www.space.com/11209-mars-earth-life-origins-evolution.html.

Francis Crick on advanced civilization: "Francis Crick on DNA: Intelligent Design," http://exopermaculture.com/2011/04/14/Francis-Crick-On-Dna-Intelligent-Design.

Fred Hoyle: *The Canadian*, www.agoracosmopolitan.com/Home/Frontpage/2007/01/26/01340.html.

STRANGE MOONS

Shklovsky, Singer, and Wilson: "Eisenhower White House on Mars' Moon Phobos Being Artificial," www.rense.com/General20/Eisenhowerwh.htm, from www.presidentialufo.8m.com.

Visits by galactic civilizations: Iosif Samuilovich Shklovsky and Carl Sagan, *Intelligent Life in the Universe* (San Francisco: Holden-Day, 1966), 461.

Phobos: Dirk Vander Ploeg, "Scientist Claims Mars Moon Phobos Is Hollow!" www.ufodigest.com/Article/Scientist-Claims-Mars-Moon-Phobos-Hollow.

IAPETUS

Richard Hoagland on artificial wall: www.enterprisemission.com/Moon1.htm.

Owen and Goldsmith on alien signpost: Thomas Horn, *Stargates, Ancient Ritual, and Those Invited Through the Portal*, part 4, www.bibliotecapleyades.net/Stargate/Stargate06_04.htm; quote from Tobias Owen and Donald Goldsmith, *The Search for Life in the Universe*, 3d ed. (Sausalito, CA: University Science Books, 2001), 383.

Iapetus/Japheth: Robert Graves, *The Greek Myths*, 2d ed. (Harmondsworth, UK: Penguin, 1960), 39.2, vol. 1, 146.

MOON ANOMALIES

Mascons as artificial objects: Don Wilson, *Secrets of Our Spaceship Moon* (New York: Dell, 1979), 156.

Nikolai A. Kozyrev: *The New Encyclopaedia Britannica*, 15th ed. (Chicago: Encyclopaedia Britannica, 1991), vol. 1, p. 294.

Lowell Observatory views reddish glows: Ibid., vol. 27, p. 546.

Gordon MacDonald on hollow sphere: Wilson, *Secrets*, 95.

Sean C. Solomon: Ibid., 97.

Maurice Ewing and Frank Press: Ibid., 101–2.

Isaac Asimov, capture theory not credible: www.agoracosmopolitan.com/News/Ufo_
Extraterrestrials/2011/08/10/494.html.

THE BIG WHACK

Hartmann and Davis on planetary collision: Alan Butler and Christopher Knight, *Who
Built the Moon?* (London: Watkins, 2005), 52.
Something had to put the moon at its altitude: William R. Shelton, *Winning the Moon*
(New York: Little, Brown, 1970), 58.
No astronomical reason: Don Wilson, *Secrets of Our Spaceship Moon* (New York: Dell,
1975), 87.

SPACESHIP MOON

Things explainable by new hypothesis: http://thedirtylowdown.wordpress.
com/2011/02/13/The-Case-For-The-Moon-As-A-Spaceship.

NONHUMANS ON THE MOON

Mare Crisium bridge: Don Ecker, "Long Saga of Lunar Anomalies," *UFO* 10, no. 2
(Mar.–Apr. 1995): 23.
H. P. Wilkens: Don Wilson, *Our Mysterious Spaceship Moon* (New York: Dell, 1975), 151.
Statuesque shadows photographed: Don Wilson, *Secrets of Our Spaceship Moon* (New
York: Dell, 1979), 23.
Blair and Abramov: Ibid., 20–21.
The Shard: Ecker, "Long Saga," 24.
"The Tower": Ibid.
Shadow resembling Washington Monument: Thomas O'Toole, "Six Mysterious Statuesque
Shadows Photographed on the Moon by Orbiter" *Washington Post*, Nov. 23, 1966, 1.
Statuesque shadows photographed: Wilson, *Secrets*, 23.
Alexander Abramov: Ibid., 21.
Similarity of Martian and Egyptian structures: Richard C. Hoagland, *The Monuments
of Mars* (Berkeley, CA: North Atlantic Books, 1987), 267–68.
Intelligent races on the moon: George Leonard, *Somebody Else Is on the Moon* (New
York: Pocket Books, 1977), 23.
Professionals ignore signs: Ibid., 27.

LOST PROBES

Jack Vlots, "Soviet Photo of a UFO near Mars," *San Francisco Chronicle*, Dec. 7, 1991.

HUMANKIND: THE ANOMOLIES CONTINUE

DARWINISM UNDER FIRE

Easier to explain to schoolchildren: J. Douglas Kenyon, ed., *Forbidden History: Prehistoric Technologies, Extraterrestrial Intervention, and the Suppressed Origins of Civilization* (Rochester, VT: Bear & Co., 2005), 9.
Hart and Gould on lack of confirmation: Ibid.

HUMAN CHRONOLOGY REVISED

Sue O'Connor on forty-two-thousand-year-old fishhooks: www.rawstory.com/ Rs/2012/01/15/Study-Shows-Humans-Were-Skilled-Fishermen-42000-Years-Ago.

Genetic differences three million years old: Alan Butler and Christopher Knight, *Who Built the Moon?* (London: Watkins, 2005), 111.

Gavin Menzies on DNA at Lake Superior: Gavin Menzies, *The Lost Empire of Atlantis: History's Greatest Mystery Revealed* (New York: HarperCollins, 2011), 303–8.

Maurice Chatelain on mummies and the mummification process: Maurice Chatelain, *Our Ancestors Came from Outer Space: A NASA Expert Confirms Mankind's Extraterrestrial Origins*, trans. Orest Berlings (Garden City, NY: Doubleday, 1978), 182.

Darren Curnoe and the Red Deer People: Charles Choi, "New Human Species? 'Red Deer Cave' Fossils May Be Neither *Homo sapiens* nor Neanderthal," www.huffing tonpost.com/2012/03/14/New-Human-Species-Red-Deer-Cave_N_1345216. html#S581873.

Buttermilk Creek, Texas: John Noble Wilford, "Spear Points Found in Texas Dial Back Arrival of Humans in America," *New York Times*, Mar. 24, 2011, www.nytimes. com/2011/03/25/Science/25archeo.html.

MAVERICK SCIENTISTS QUELLED

Ice Age "Holy Trinity": Kurt Johmann, "Debunking the Ice Age," www.johmann.net/ essays/ice-age.html; and D. S. Allan and J. B. Delair, *Cataclysm! Compelling Evidence of a Cosmic Catastrophe in 9500 B.C.* (Rochester, VT: Bear & Co., 1997).

Extremely wise experts: Giorgio de Santillana and Hertha von Dechend, *Hamlet's Mill: An Essay Investigating the Origins of Human Knowledge and Its Transmission through Myth*, rev. ed. (Boston: Gambit, 1969; Godine, 1992), 1977 ed. available at www. bibliotecapleyades.net/Hamlets_Mill/hamletmill.htm#top.

Anomalous dates and Virginia Steen-McIntyre: Michael A. Cremo and Richard L. Thompson, "Hidden History of the Human Race," available at http://preterhuman.net/texts/history/Michael%20A.%20Cremo%20and%20Richard%20L.%20 Thompson%20-%20Hidden%20History%20of%20the%20Human%20Race.pdf and www.earlyworld.de/forbidden_archeology.html.

Virginia Steen-McIntyre interview: "What's Wrong with Science?" *Midwestern Epigraphic Journal* 16, no. 1 (2002), www.S8int.com/wrong-science.html.

SUPPRESSION BY THE SMITHSONIAN

Martin Doutré and Park Service experience: "The Cahokia Mounds Complex: Ancient Open-Air University of North America—for Teaching Navigation & Cyclic Astronomy," www.celticnz.co.nz/Cahokia/Cahokia1.htm; e-mail to author, Jan. 8, 2012.

Smithsonian as great interloper: "Holocaust of Giants: The Great Smithsonian Cover-Up," www.xpeditionsmagazine.com/magazine/articles/giants/holocaust.html.

Horned human skulls: "Human Skulls with Horns," www.disclose.tv/forum/human-skulls-with-horns-t6293.html.w

Red-haired Nevada giants: www.helium.com/Items/1814848-Nevadas-Mysterious-Cave-Of-The-Red-Haired-Giants/Print.

Ivan T. Sanderson on giant skulls in the Aleutians: "Giants," www.6000years.org/ frame.php?page=giants.

Dennis Swift on Waldemar's book and ridicule: www.dinosaursandman.com/research/ THE_DINOSAURS_OF_ACAMBARO.pdf.

Phoenix Gazette article: "Lost Cave City in the Grand Canyon," www.crystalinks.com/ gc_egyptconnection.html.

Egyptian names in the Grand Canyon: http://www.crystalinks.com/gc_egyptconnec tion.html.

Grand Canyon cover-up: David Hatcher Childress, "Archeological Cover-Ups: Are the World's Top Scientific Institutions Covering Up Proof of High-Tech Ancient Civilizations?" *Nexus*, Apr.–May 1993.

HOAXES AND FORGERIES

Eugene Dubois and Java Man: "Eugene DuBois," The Robinson Library, www.robin sonlibrary.com/geography/anthropology/biography/bubois.htm.

Neanderthals as a separate lineage: "Ancient DNA and Neanderthals," Smithsonian National Museum of Natural History, http://humanorigins.si.edu/evidence/genet ics/ancient-dna-and-neanderthals.

THE WEALTHY CONTROL RESEARCH

Michael Cremo on knowledge filter: Michael A. Cremo and Richard L. Thompson, *Forbidden Archeology: The Hidden History of the Human Race*, introduction, www. mcremo.com/chapter.html.

Young paleontologist: J. Douglas Kenyon, www.ancient-hebrew.org/Ancientman/1008. html.

Rockefeller Foundation and control: Ibid.

J. Douglas Kenyon on scientists as priest class: Ibid.

Origins of Man game: www.agoracosmopolitan.com/Home/Frontpage/2007/12/21/02021. html.

Dr. Kevin Jones-Kern on the Rockefellers: http://Aabss.Org/Perspectives1999/ F20jones.html.

Presidents of the National Science Board: "Former Members," www.nsf.gov/nsb/mem bers/former.jsp.

Pat Eddy on Dead Sea Scrolls: Patricia G. Eddy, *Who Tampered with the Bible?* (Nashville, TN: Winston-Derek, 1993), 222–23.

Ann Getty and the Lucy research: Jon Kalb, *Adventures in the Bone Trade: The Race to Discover Human Ancestors in Ethiopia's Afar Depression* (New York: Copernicus Books, 2001), 298.

Scientists fearful for jobs over global warming: http://Online.Wsj.com/Article/Sb10001 424052970204301404577171531838421366.html.

CIA INVOLVEMENT

Accusations of CIA involvement: Kalb, *Bone Trade*, 146.

Donald Johanson questioned by government: author's interview, Dec. 23, 2011.

Church Committee conclusions on CIA: "The Church Committee on the CIA in Academia," excerpts from *The Final Report of the Select Committee to Study Governmental Operations with Respect to Intelligence Activities*, book 1, *Foreign and Military Intelligence*, U.S. Senate, Apr. 26, 1976, www.Cia-On-Campus.Org/Church.html.

Recent NSF and CIA collusion: "Epic Uncovers MOU between National Science Foundation and CIA on Scientific Support for Web Monitoring," http://epic.org/privacy/wiretap/nsf_release.html.

HUMAN ORIGINS CONTROVERSY

Mark Stoneking on scientific attacks and reconciliation: Mark Stoneking, "Human Origins: The Molecular Perspective," *EMBO* [European Molecular Biology Association] *Reports* (published by *Nature*), vol. 9, 2008, S46–S50, www.nature.com/Embor/Journal/V9/N1s/Full/Embor200864.html.

REMOTE VIEWING HUMAN ORIGINS

Small hairy creatures seeded: Joseph McMoneagle and Charles T. Tart, *The Ultimate Time Machine: A Remote Viewer's Perception of Time, and Predictions for the New Millennium* (Charlottesville, VA: Hampton Roads Pub. Co., 1998), 90–100.

Enoch on the Watchers: Richard Laurence, *The Book of Enoch the Prophet* (1821; Glasgow: John Thompson, 1882; repr. Muskogee, OK: Artisan Publishers, 1999) 13.

Outside civilizations visited Mu and Atlantis: Maurice Chatelain, *Our Ancestors Came from Outer Space: A NASA Expert Confirms Mankind's Extraterrestrial Origins*, trans. Orest Berlings (Garden City, NY: Doubleday, 1978), 20.

ANCIENT EVIDENCE—WORLDWIDE ANOMOLIES

Chinese characters on Olmec figures: Charles Fenyvesi, "A Tale of Two Cultures," *U.S. News & World Report* 121, no. 18 (Nov. 4, 1996)

Crystal skulls modern: Paul Rincon, "Crystal Skulls 'Are Modern Fakes,'" May 23, 2008, http://news.bbc.co.uk/2/hi/science/nature/7414637.stm, based on paper in *Journal of Archaeological Science*, May 2008.

High-speed drill in Peru: www.youtube.com/Watch?V=Duyf1ol31bs&Feature=Related.

Machined spirals in Urals: Jonathan Gray, "A Sampling of Some Original Sources for Ancient Technology," Archaeology Answers, www.beforeus.com/some_original.html.

Professor Michael Edmunds on Antikythera mechanism: Ian Sample, "Mysteries of Computer from 65 BC Are Solved," *Guardian*, Nov. 29, 2006, www.guardian.co.uk/science/2006/nov/30/uknews.

Dr. Craddock and Dr. Senechal: Arran Frood, "Riddle of 'Baghdad's Batteries,'" http://news.bbc.co.uk/2/hi/science/nature/2804257.stm.

Sitchin and space capsule: Laura Lee, "Evidence of Ancient ETs on Earth: Is This Artifact a Sculpted Scale Model of a Rocket Ship?" Dec. 1998, www.bibliotecapleyades.net/Sitchin/Esp_Sitchin_13.htm.

Philip Coppens on Goldflyer II: Philip Coppens, "Prehistoric 'Plane' Flies!" www.philipcoppens.com/bbl_plane.html.

Chinese X-ray machine and vaccinations: ancientstuff.maxforum.org/2011/05/29/ancient-x-rays/.

Aerial photographs of South America: Erich von Däniken, *Chariots of the Gods?* (New York: Bantam, 1971), 15.

HOARY STRUCTURES

Robert Schoch on Okinawan structure: Robert Schoch, "An Enigmatic Ancient Underwater Structure off the Coast of Yonaguni Island, Japan," 1999, Circular Times, www.robertschoch.net/Enigmatic%20yonaguni%20underwater%20rms%20ct.htm.

Richard Atkinson unconvinced by Gerald Hawkins: Gavin Menzies, *The Lost Empire of Atlantis: History's Greatest Mystery Revealed* (New York: William Morrow, 2011), 235.

Brazilian Stonehenge: Steve Kingstone, "'Brazilian Stonehenge' Discovered," http://news.bbc.co.uk/2/hi/americas/4767717.stm.

Robert Mason on Deir Mar Musa: "Mysterious 10,000-Year-Old Ruins Found in Syrian Desert," Fox News, June 25, 2012, www.foxnews.com/scitech/2012/06/25/10000-year-old-ruins-found-in-syrian-desert.

David Kennedy on stone wheels: Owen Janus, "Visible Only from Above, Mystifying 'Nazca Lines' Discovered in Mideast," Sept. 16, 2011, LiveScience.com, repr. www.foxnews.com/scitech/2011/09/16/visible-only-from-above-mystifying-nazca-lines-discovered-in-mideast/#Ixzz1z5j2bqfb.

Energy infinitely higher inside stone circles: author's interview, Feb. 3, 2012.

Nonpolar energy channeled: Michael Tellinger and Johan Heine, *Temples of the African Gods: Revealing the Ancient Hidden Ruins of Southern Africa* (Waterval Boven, South Africa: Zulu Planet, 2010), 131.

THE CORAL CASTLE

The secret of the pyramids: "Coral Castle," www.crystalinks.com/coralcastle.html.

Tellinger on ice-cream-cone phenomenon: "Michael of the Family Tellinger," Spirit Reality: Book of Transcriptures, www.afribeat.com/Journey/Nature/Spiritreality/Researcher_Michaeltellinger.htm.

Bruce Cathie and Tibetan monks: "Tibetan Sound Levitation of Large Stones Witnessed by Scientist," www.amazingabilities.com/amaze10c.html, in D. H. Childress, *Anti-Gravity and the World Grid*, ch. 8, pp. 213–17.

Basalt cone tools on Easter Island: Jo Anne Van Tilberg, "Field Season IV," July–Aug. 2011, Easter Island Statue Project, www.eisp.org/3879.

STRANGE ARTIFACTS

Paul Heinrich on pseudomorphs: Paul V. Heinrich, "The Mysterious 'Spheres' of Ottosdal, South Africa," *Reports of the National Center for Science Education* 28, no. 1 (Jan.–Feb. 2008): 28, http://ncse.com/Rncse/28/1/Mysterious-Spheres-Ottosdal-South-Africa.

Roelf Marx on sphere mystery: "Klerksdorp Spheres" (site search required to get to article), Forbidden History: A Central Repository for Problematic and Out of Place Artifacts, https://www.forbiddenhistory.info/?Q=Node/26.

Douglas James Cottrell: www.Youtube.com/Watch?V=Obgrwtju904&Feature=Share.

Sitchin and space capsule: Laura Lee, "Evidence of Ancient ETs on Earth: Is This Artifact a Sculpted Scale Model of a Rocket Ship?" Dec. 1998, www.bibliotecapleyades.net/Sitchin/Esp_Sitchin_13.htm.

Klaus Dona's exhibits: Richard Habeck, *Unsolved Mysteries: Die Welt des Unerklärlichen*

[The World of the Inexplicable] (Vienna: Vienna Art Center Schottenstift, 2001), www.Youtube.com/Watch?V=Q_B3xivtkam&Feature=Related.

ELONGATED SKULLS AND THE STARCHILD

Brien Foerster on Elongated Skulls: http://hiddenincatours.com/photo-sets/global-phenomenon-of-elongated-skulls.
Lloyd Pye and the Starchild skull: www.starchildproject.com.
No significant similarity to human DNA: www.starchildproject.com/Starchild_Ebook.htm; www.starchildproject.com/Dna2012.htm; and author's interview, Jan. 18, 2012.
Dr. Margaret Clegg on no DNA analysis: Zecharia Sitchin, *There Were Giants upon the Earth* (Rochester, VT: Bear & Co., 2010), 345.

SACRED SITES

THE OSIRION

Margaret Alice Murray on the Osirion: William Flinders Petrie and Margaret Alice Murray, "The Osirion at Abydos (Abtu)," 1904, Ascending Passage, http://ascending-passage.com/Osirion-at-Abydos.htm.
The Djed Pillar as metaphysical object: "Abydos: Abtu or Abdju—the City of the Djed," SanGraal: Sacred Geometry—Alchemy, www.sangraal.com/Abydos.
Egypt went downhill: J. Douglas Kenyon, ed., *Forbidden History: Prehistoric Technologies, Extraterrestrial Intervention, and the Suppressed Origins of Civilization* (Rochester, VT: Bear & Co., 2005), 89.

CARNAC

Carnac builders not given credit: Philip Coppens, *The Ancient Alien Question: A New Inquiry into the Existence, Evidence, and Influence of Ancient Visitors* (Pompton Plains, NJ: New Page Books, 2012), 112.

GÖBEKLI TEPE

Sean Thomas and Göbekli Tepe as funerary complex: Sean Thomas, "Göbekli Tepe—Paradise Regained?" *Fortean Times*, Mar. 2007, www.forteantimes.com/Features/Articles/449/Gobekli_Tepe_Paradise_Regained.html.
Ted Banning on residents at structures: "Archaeologist Argues World's Oldest Temples Were Not Temples at All," Phys, Oct. 6, 2011, http://phys.org/News/2011-10-Archaeologist-World-Oldest-Temples.html#Nrlv.
No meaning from the site: Linda Moulton Howe, *Mysterious 12,000-Year-Old Göbekli Tepe*, EarthFiles, June 16–July 2, 2012, www.earthfiles.com/news-print.php?ID=1984&category=Science.
Hassan Karabulut and Sandra Scham: Sandra Scham, "The World's First Temple," www.archaeology.org/0811/abstracts/turkey.html.
Andrew Collins on a suspected ruling elite: Adriano Forgione, interview of Andrew Collins, "Göbekli Tepe—Eden, Home of the Watchers," www.andrewcollins.com/page/articles/Gobekli_Tepe_interview.htm.

Layout plan decoded: www.Youtube.com/Watch?V=Idountm2e28&Feature=Player_Embedded.

Wayne Herschel on Easter Island similarities: Wayne Herschel, "Easter Island Deciphered," The Hidden Records: The Star of the Gods, www.thehiddenrecords.com/Easter-Island-Rapanui-Moai-Orion-Perseus.php.

BAALBEK

Michel Alouf on accurately placed blocks: www.eridu.co.uk/Author/Mysteries_Of_The_World/Baalbek/Baalbek6/Baalbek6.html.

Alan F. Alford on Baldwin's moving plans and superhumans: Ibid.

PYRAMID POWER

Christopher Dunn, "Evidence of Ancient Electrical Devices Found in the Great Pyramid?" June 2, 2011, Giza Power, www.gizapower.com/Anotherrobot.htm.

Rob Richardson on hieroglyphs: Rowan Hooper, "First Images from the Great Pyramid's Chamber of Secrets, *New Scientist*, May 25, 2011, www.newscientist.com/article/mg21028144.500-first-images-from-great-pyramids-chamber-of-secrets.html.

COSMIC WAR

Weapons of power and real interplanetary war: Joseph P. Farrell, *The Cosmic War: Interplanetary Warfare, Modern Physics, and Ancient Texts* (Kempton, IL: Adventures Unlimited Press, 2007), 191–92.

Tom Van Flandern speaks of intervention: Oil Is Mastery, Dec. 31, 2009, http://oilismastery.blogspot.com/2009_12_01_archive.html.

Ancient texts support this model: Farrell, *Cosmic War*, 25.

PYRAMIDS AS STAR MAPS

Pyramids reflect Orion: Robert Bauval and Adrian Gilbert, *The Orion Mystery: Unlocking the Secrets of the Pyramids* (New York: Crown, 1994), 122.

Prehistoric date for Great Pyramid: Ibid., 192–93.

Collin Andrews and Kevin Smith's comments: "What Does NASA Know?" KSS Report: News and Views from Kevin Smith, 2010, http://kevinsmithshow.com/kssblog/what_does_nasa_know.htm.

Pyramids match star systems: Wayne Herschel, *Hidden Records I* (self-published, 2003, order at: www.thehiddenrecords.com/book.htm), 284.

Celebration of the human species: Ibid., 20–21.

A sunlike star: Wayne Herschel, "Ancient Star Map Egypt and the Human Origin Blueprint Code," www.thehiddenrecords.com/sphinx.htm.

FORGOTTEN PYRAMIDS

Semir Osmanagić on energy beam and advanced builders: "World History and Bosnian Pyramids 2011, Dec. 15, 2011, www.piramidasunca.ba/eng/latest-news/item/7778-world-history-and-bosnian-pyramids-2011.html.

Anthony Harding debunks Bosnian pyramid: Anthony Harding, "The Great Bosnian

Pyramid Scheme," *British Archaeology*, no. 92 (Jan.–Feb. 2007), www.britarch.ac.uk/ba/ba92/feat3.shtml.

George Filer and the Xianyang pyramid: "China's Hidden Pyramids Were Built by ET," National UFO Center: Filer's Research Institute, Nov. 16, 2011, www.nationalufocenter.com/artman/publish/article_424.php.

Arkansas pyramid mounds: "Toltec Mounds Archaeological State Park," http://littlerock.about.com/cs/stateparks/p/aatoltecmounds.

Also See: "About the Pyramids," Ara's Art and News, www.arasartgallery.com/about-the-pyramids.html.

City of Cahokia: "The 'Origins' of Cahokia Mounds," Cahokia Mounds State Historic Site, www.cahokiamounds.org/explore/archaeology/origins.

PART II: THE ANCIENTS

A shadowy prehistory: Alan F. Alford, *Gods of the New Millennium: Scientific Proof of Flesh & Blood Gods* (Walsall, UK: Eridu Books, 1996), 1.

He who possesses Ram: Laurence Gardner, *Genesis of the Grail Kings* (London: Bantam Press, 1999), p. 100.

Paracelsus on wisdom carried to Egypt: Joseph P. Farrell, *The Philosopher's Stone: Alchemy and the Secret Research for Exotic Matter* (Port Townsend, WA: Feral House, 2009), 52–53.

WHERE WAS ATLANTIS?

Atlantis in *Timaeus*: Ignatius Donnelly, *Atlantis: The Antediluvian World* (New York: Gramercy Pub. Co., 1949), 9.

Gods begat children by mortal woman: Plato, *Critias*, trans. Benjamin Jowett, http://classics.mit.edu/Plato/critias.html.

Gods and goddesses simply kings and queens: Donnelly, *Atlantis*, 1.

Nicky White and submerged landscape: Wynne Parry, "A Lost World? Atlantis-like Landscape Discovered," Live Science, www.livescience.com/14974-geologists-remains-landscape-rose-north-atlantic-ocean-56-million-years-sinking.html.

THE BIMINI ROAD

R. Cedric Leonard, J. Manson Valentine, John Gifford, and Dimitri Rebikoff: R. Cedric Leonard, "The Bahama Island Underwater Ruins: Ignored by Main-stream Archeology," www.atlantisquest.com/Bahama.html.

THE MINOAN EMPIRE AND SANTORINI

Gavin Menzies on copper at Lake Superior: Gavin Menzies, *The Lost Empire of Atlantis: History's Greatest Mystery Revealed* (New York: HarperCollins Publishers, 2011), 303–8.

R. Cedric Leonard on objections to Minoan Empire as Atlantis: R. Cedric Leonard, "The Minoan Hypothesis: Could Santorini Have Been Atlantis?" www.atlantisquest.com/Minoan.html.

THE SOUTH CHINA SEA

McCanney on Santos, South China Sea, and Mars: Rick Martin, "The Sun-Earth Connection: Solar Winds & Planetary Bombardment, Bizarre Weather & Earth Changes, www.jmccanneyscience.com/Spectrumsept2003.htm.

OUT OF THIS WORLD

Rich Anders on parallel worlds: Rich Anders, "Atlantis, Dinosaurs, and the Parallel World," www.world-mysteries.com/Mpl_10ra.htm.

POLE SHIFT AND ANTARCTICA

Columbus had expected the shoreline: "New Analysis Hints Ancient Explorers Mapped Antarctic," *New York Times,* Sept. 25, 1984.
Thirty-six-thousand-year-old bison meat: Cecil Adams, "Prehistoric, It's What's for Dinner: Have Explorers Had Feasts of Woolly Mammoth?" www.straightdope.com/columns/read/2725/prehistoric-its-whats-for-dinner.
Atlantis will be found: Maurice Chatelain, *Our Ancestors Came from Outer Space: A NASA Expert Confirms Mankind's Extraterrestrial Origins,* trans. Orest Berlings (Garden City, NY: Doubleday, 1978), 175.

A WORLDWIDE CIVILIZATION

Frederick Soddy on disappeared civilizations: Louis Pauwels and Jacques Bergier, *The Morning of the Magicians* (New York: Avon, 1963), 181.
Charles Hapgood on worldwide civilization: Charles H. Hapgood, *Maps of the Ancient Sea Kings: Evidence of Advanced Civilization in the Ice Ages* (New York: Chilton, 1966), 193.
Extraterrestrial theory is true and accurate: Maurice Chatelain, *Our Ancestors Came from Outer Space: A NASA Expert Confirms Mankind's Extraterrestrial Origins,* trans. Orest Berlings (Garden City, NY: Doubleday, 1978), 200.

SUMER: THE FIRST KNOWN CIVILIZATION

CUNEIFORM TABLETS

Samuel Noah Kramer on Sumerian firsts: Zecharia Sitchin, *The 12th Planet* (New York: Avon Books, 1976), 120–21; see also Samuel Noah Kramer, *The Sumerians: Their History, Culture, and Character* (Chicago: University of Chicago Press, 1963); and Samuel Noah Kramer, *History Begins at Sumer,* 2d ed. (London: Thames & Hudson, 1961).

LONGEVITY AND NUMBERS

Geometry, time system, and celestial cycle: Alan F. Alford, *Gods of the New Millennium: Scientific Proof of Flesh & Blood Gods* (Walsall, UK: Eridu Books, 1996), 124.

MYTH OR HISTORY?

Tales branded as myth: Zecharia Sitchin, *The 12th Planet* (New York: Avon Books, 1976), viii.
Still-evolving knowledge: Paul Von Ward, *We've Never Been Alone: A History of Extraterrestrial Intervention* (Charlottesville, VA: Hampton Roads, 2011), xv, xxix–xxx.
Ancient astronauts capable of landing on Earth: Sitchin, *12th Planet*, viii.
Gods came from the sky: Von Ward, *We've Never Been Alone*, 31.
Cave graves: Jim Marrs, *Alien Agenda: Investigating the Extraterrestrial Presence among Us* (New York: HarperCollins, 1997), 33.

THE ANUNNAKI: IMPROVING THE BREED?

Zulu legends compare to Sumerian: "Michael of the Family Tellinger," Spirit Reality: Book of Transcriptures, www.afribeat.com/Journey/Nature/Spiritreality/Researcher_Michaeltellinger.htm.

THE NEFILIM CHAIN OF COMMAND

Hammurabi's prologue: Brian Edric Colless, "Hammurabi: The Empire of Hammurabi, The Lawcode of Hammurabi, Prologue," Collesseum: A Museum-Theatre for Scripts, http://sites.google.com/Site/Collesseum/Hammurabi.

SITCHIN'S CRITICS

Open letter to Sitchin: "Open Letter," Sitchin Is Wrong, http://sitchiniswrong.com/letter/letter.htm.
Enki in Sumerian texts: Oxford University Faculty of Oriental Studies, Electronic Text Corpus of Sumerian Literature, ETCSL translation search: Enki, http://etcsl.orinst.ox.ac.uk/cgi-bin/etcsl.cgi?simplesearchword=enki&simplesearch=translation&searchword=&charenc=gcirc&Lists=
A cohesive and defensible mixture: Paul Von Ward, *We've Never Been Alone: A History of Extraterrestrial Intervention* (Charlottesville, VA: Hampton Roads, 2011), 33.
Seven Tablets of Creation and support for Sitchin: C. L. Turnage, *War in Heaven: The Case for a Solar System War* (Santa Barbara, CA: Timeless Voyager Press, 1998), 7–8.

AN EARLY GOLD RUSH

Gold to repair upper atmosphere: Lloyd Pye, *Everything You Know Is Wrong: Human Origins* (Madeira Beach, FL: Adamu Press, 1997), 231–32.
Comparison of names: Ignatius Donnelly, *Atlantis: The Antediluvian World* (New York: Gramercy Pub. Co., 1949), 138.

OUT OF AFRICA

Complaints to Enlil: Stephanie Dalley, ed., *Myths from Mesopotamia: Creation, the Flood, Gilgamesh, and Others* (Oxford, UK: Oxford University Press, 2000), 12.
Creation alone in the hands of the Father: Zecharia Sitchin, *The Lost Book of Enki: Memoirs and Prophecies of an Extraterrestrial God* (Rochester, VT: Bear & Co., 2002), 130.
More detailed texts in Sumer: "UFOs and the Bible, Part 1," Spiritual, www.spiritual.com.au/2011/07/Ufos-And-The-Bible-Part-1.

The African connection to Sumer: Michael Tellinger and Johan Heine, *Temples of the African Gods: Revealing the Ancient Hidden Ruins of Southern Africa* (Waterval Boven, South Africa: Zulu Planet, 2010), 124.

Abzu where the gold came from: Ibid., 5.

THE HYBRID

Human-animal hybrids created: Daniel Martin and Simon Caldwell, "150 Human Animal Hybrids Grown in UK Labs: Embryos Have Been Produced Secretively for the Past Three Years," *London Daily Mail*, July 22, 2011, www.dailymail.co.uk/Sciencetech/Article-2017818/Embryos-Involving-Genes-Animals-Mixed-Humans-Produced-Secretively-Past-Years.html#Ixzz1iu3wyqjr.

Gilgamesh translation: E. A. Speiser, *The Epic of Gilgamesh*, in *The Ancient Near East: An Anthology of Texts and Pictures*, ed. James B. Pritchard (Princeton, NJ: Princeton University Press, 1958), 51.

Ancient man worked for his God: Zecharia Sitchin, *The 12th Planet* (New York: Avon, 1976), 337.

Foreign DNA in African groups: Joseph Lachance, Benjamin Vernot, Clara C. Elbers, Bart Ferwerda, Alain Froment, Jean-Marie Bodo, Godfrey Lema, Wenqing Fu, Thomas B. Nyambo, Timothy R. Rebbeck, Kun Zhang, Sarah A. Tishkoff, Joshua M. Akey, "Evolutionary History and Adaptation from High-Coverage Whole-Genome Sequences of Diverse African Hunter-Gatherers," *Cell* (July 26, 2012); Joshua Akey interview with Linda Moulton Howe, September 12, 2012.

Slaves treated poorly: Arthur David Horn with Lynette Anne Mallory-Horn, *Humanity's Extraterrestrial Origins: ET Influences on Humanities Biological and Cultural Evolution* (Mount Shasta, CA: A & L Horn, 1994), 65.

LONGEVITY AND ANOTHER NOAH

Sexagesimal system knowledge lost: Alan F. Alford, *Gods of the New Millennium: Scientific Proof of Flesh & Blood Gods* (Walsall, UK: Eridu Books, 1996), 297.

Several gods not always in accord: Zecharia Sitchin, *The 12th Planet* (New York: Avon, 1976), 380.

Kent Flannery on cause of farming: Arthur David Horn with Lynette Anne Mallory-Horn, *Humanity's Extraterrestrial Origins: ET Influences on Humanities Biological and Cultural Evolution* (Mount Shasta, CA: A & L Horn, 1994), 101.

SEPARATING THE HUMANS

Enlil institutes mountain farming: Zecharia Sitchin, *The Wars of Gods and Men* (New York: Avon, 1985), 121.

No explanation for botanogenetic miracle and three phases: Zecharia Sitchin, *The 12th Planet* (New York: Avon, 1976), 414–15.

KINGS AND CONFLICT

Shem as something that flies: C. L. Turnage, *War in Heaven: The Case for a Solar System War* (Santa Barbara, CA: Timeless Voyager Press, 1998), 12.

Sky Vehicle: Sitchin, *12th Planet*, 148.

William Henry, *One Foot in Atlantis: The Secret Occult History of World War II and Its Impact on New Age Politics* (Anchorage, AK: Earthpulse Press, 1998), 113.

Reproducing an exact match: Bill Putnam's letter to author, June 13, 2012.

Abraham as personage of high standing: Sitchin, *Wars of Gods and Men*, 292.

ATOMIC WAR?

Vapor translated as salt: Sitchen *Wars of Gods and Men*, 313–14n.

Radioactive Jericho bones: I. M. Blake and J. Cynthia Jones, "Radioactivity of Jericho Bones," *Archaeometry* 10, no. 1 (Aug. 23, 2007), http://onlinelibrary.wiley.com/doi/10.1111/j.1475-4754.1967.tb00623.x/pdf.

Stones blackened on surface: Alan F. Alford, *Gods of the New Millennium: Scientific Proof of Flesh & Blood Gods* (Walsall, UK: Eridu Books, 1996), 227.

If tektites are terrestrial: John O'Keefe, "The Tektite Problem," *Scientific American*, Aug. 1978.

Jonathan Gray on radioactive skeletons: "Ancient City Found, Irradiated from Atomic Blast," www.beforeus.com/Indusa.htm.

Mahabharata described weapon: David Hatcher Childress, *Technology of the Gods: The Incredible Science of the Ancients* (Kempton, IL: Adventures Unlimited Press, 2000), 237; excerpt is from Vyasa et al., *Mahabharata*, trans. Pratapachandra Raya and Kisari Mohan Ganguli (Calcutta: Bharata Press, 1889).

Francis Taylor on radioactive ash: "Ancient City Found in India, Irradiated from Atomic Blast," Veda: Vedic Knowledge Online, http://veda.wikidot.com/Ancient-City-Found-In-India-Irradiated-From-Atomic-Blast.

Kramer's translated "Lamentations": Alford, *Gods of the New Millennium*, 220–21.

HISTORY BECOMES MYTHOLOGY

Corrupted dogma: Laurence Gardner, *Bloodline of the Holy Grail: The Hidden Lineage of Jesus Revealed* (Rockport, MA: Element Books, 1996), 60.

Jorg Fassbinder and tomb of Gilgamesh: "Gilgamesh Tomb Believed Found," BBC News, Apr. 29, 2003, http://news.bbc.co.uk/2/Hi/Science/Nature/2982891.stm.

HAND-ME-DOWN CULTURES AND CONTROL

Nazca Lines as a cargo cult: Erich von Däniken, *Gods from Outer Space*, trans. Michael Heron (New York: Bantam, 1972), 105.

As close as we'll come to the truth: Arthur David Horn with Lynette Anne Mallory-Horn, *Humanity's Extraterrestrial Origins: ET Influences on Humanities Biological and Cultural Evolution* (Mount Shasta, CA: A & L Horn, 1994), 104.

GIVE ME THAT OLD-TIME RELIGION

Peter Jiang and Jenny Li, "Scientists Confirm Extraterrestrial Genes in Human DNA," www.agoracosmopolitan.com/home/Frontpage/2007/01/26/01340.html.

Step toward supernaturalism: Paul Von Ward, *We've Never Been Alone: A History of Extraterrestrial Intervention* (Charlottesville, VA: Hampton Roads, 2011), 285.

Elaine Pagels on Satan as a messenger: Elaine Pagel, "The Origin of Satan in Christian

Tradition," Tanner Lecture on Human Values, University of Utah, May 14, 1997, www.tannerlectures.utah.edu/lectures/documents/Pagels99.pdf.

Satan's quote: Ibid.

Invoking Satan: Ibid.

Princes of Darkness: Von Ward, *We've Never Been Alone*, 47.

Confluence of historical events: Ibid., 286.

Supernatural theology as defense mechanism: Ibid., 287.

SHOW ME THE MONEY

The pattern of bullion-based monies is the same: Joseph P. Farrell, *Babylon's Banksters: The Alchemy of Deep Physics, High Finance and Ancient Religion* (Port Townsend, WA: Feral House, 2010), 202–4.

A maniac's delirium: William Bramley, *The Gods of Eden* (San Jose, CA: Dahlin Family Press, 1990), 432.

Dr. G. Patrick Flanagan and neurophone: G. Patrick Flanagan, "About Dr. G. Patrick Flanagan," http://phisciences.com/About-Dr-G-Patrick-Flanagan.

Konstantin Meyl on ancient communication: Joseph P. Farrell, *The Cosmic War: Interplanetary Warfare, Modern Physics, and Ancient Texts* (Kempton, IL: Adventures Unlimited Press, 2007), 251–60.

War for Social and Political Control: Bramley, *Gods of Eden*, 3.

ANCIENT EGYPT

Giant humanoid found in tunnel: author's interview with Annie DeRiso, Jan. 10, 2012.

Visitors to underground tunnels: "Photos of Giza Tunnels," The Hermetics Resource Site, www.hermetics.org/Giza-tunnels.html. The photos were later removed.

James Hurtak and ground-penetrating radar: Paul White, "Ground Penetrating Radar Showing Ancient Civilizations," www.hiddenmysteries.org/mysteries/history/radar.html.

GREEK GODS FROM EGYPT

Herodotus on Egyptian kings and gods: Herodotus, *Histories*, trans. George Rawlinson, book 2, Iran Chamber Society, www.iranchamber.com/history/herodotus/herodotus_history_book2.php.

Argolis pyramids predate Egyptian ones: en.wikipedia.org/wiki/greek_pyramids.

Theophanias Manias and golden ratio: Erich von Däniken, *Odyssey of the Gods: The Alien History of Ancient Greece* (Pompton Plains, NJ: New Page Books, 2012), 105–10.

Mystical sites around Delos: Maurice Chatelain, *Our Ancestors Came from Outer Space: A NASA Expert Confirms Mankind's Extraterrestrial Origins*, trans. Orest Berlings (New York: Doubleday, 1978), 72–74.

Hesiod's chronology of gods and goddesses: Hesiod, *Theogony*, trans. Hugh G. Evelyn-White (Cambridge, MA: Loeb Classical Library, 1914), www.sacred-texts.com/cla/hesiod/theogony.htm.

Plato on polar shift: Fulton Oursler, "Why the Sun Stood Still: A Preview of Dr. Immanuel Velikovsky's Sensational New Book, *Worlds in Collision*," http://tmgnow.com/Repository/Secret/Velikovsky2.html; from Plato, *Statesman*, trans. Benjamin Jowett, http://classics.mit.edu/Plato/stateman.html.

"Ted Connors" and his drone and book experience: www.earthfiles.com/News.Php?Id =1870&Category=Environment; www.earthfiles.com/News.Php?Id=1871&Categor y=Environment.

John Coleman on the Olympians: John Coleman, *The Tavistock Institute of Human Relations: Shaping the Moral, Spiritual, Cultural, Political and Economic Decline of the United States of America* (Las Vegas, NV: World Intelligence Review, 2006), 47–48.

POWER PASSES TO ROME

Paul's view won out: Patricia G. Eddy, *Who Tampered with the Bible?* (Nashville, TN: Winston-Derek, 1993), 202.

Irenaeus, bishop of Lyon: Laurence Gardner, *Bloodline of the Holy Grail: The Hidden Lineage of Jesus Revealed* (Rockport, MA: Element Books, 1996), 154.

Diverse forms of Christianity: Elaine Pagels, *The Gnostic Gospels* (New York: Vintage Books, 1981), 7–8.

The Roman Church: Eddy, *Who Tampered with the Bible?'* 219–20.

Gods or Elohim: C. L. Turnage, *New Evidence the Holy Bible Is an Extraterrestrial Transmission* (Santa Barbara, CA: Timeless Voyager Press, 1998), 105.

Buyout by Constantine: "Religion of a Lie," Hidden Mysteries: Religion's Fraud, Lies, Control, www.hiddenmysteries.org/religion/christianity/religionlie.shtml.

BOOK BURNING

Distant past is a vacuum: Andrew Tomas, *We Are Not the First: Riddles of Ancient Science* (New York: Bantam Books, 1973), 8–9.

Fernando Báez and book destruction in Iraq: Humberto Marquez, "The Plunder of Iraq's Treasures," *Asia Times*, Feb. 17, 2005, www.atimes.com/atimes/Middle_East/GB17ak01.html.

LOST IN TRANSLATION

Rabbi Dovid Bendory on killing versus murder: Dovid Bendory, "The Ten Commandments, Killing and Murder: A Detailed Commentary," Jews for the Preservation of Firearms Ownership, http://jpfo.org/rabbi/6th-commandment.htm.

Biglino questioned Elohim jealousy: Mauro Biglino, *The Book That Will Forever Change Our Ideas About the Bible: The Gods Coming from Space* (Italy: Uno Editori, 2012), 90–91, www.holy-bible-aliens.com/?Page_Id=2.

No Search for a vision or dream: Ibid., 140.

The Elohims also must die: Ibid., 153.

Plurality reduced to a single God: Ibid., 169.

Monsignor Corrado Balducci: Ibid., 157.

Father José Funes on extraterrestrials: Francesco M. Valiante, "The Extraterrestrial Is My Brother," interview of Father José Funes, *L'Osservatore Romano*, May 14, 2008, http://padrefunes.blogspot.com/2008/05/extraterrestrial-is-my-brother.html; in original Italian: www.vatican.va/News_Services/Or/Or_Quo/Interviste/2008/112q08a1.html.

Biglino reviewer's comments: Biglino, *Book That Will Forever Change*, www.holy-bible-aliens.com/?Page_Id=6.

Science can't find evidence: Philip Coppens, *The Ancient Alien Question: A New Inquiry into the Existence, Evidence, and Influence of Ancient Visitors* (Pompton Plains, NJ: New Page Books, 2012), 285.

PART III: THE MIDDLE AGES

Underground stream of knowledge: Laurence Gardner, *Genesis of the Grail Kings: The Astonishing Story of the Ancient Bloodline of Christ and the True Heritage of the Holy Grail* (London: Bantam Press, 1999), 219–20.

KNIGHTS TEMPLAR

A specific mission in mind: Lynn Picknett and Clive Prince, *The Templar Revelation: Secret Guardians of the True Identity of Christ* (New York: Touchstone, 1997), 100.

Templars handled most European capital: Michael Baigent and Richard Leigh, *The Temple and the Lodge* (New York: Arcade, 1989), 47–48.

ALCHEMY: SCIENCE, MAGIC, OR BOTH?

Adherents of alchemy: E. J. Holmyard, *Alchemy* (1957; Mineola, NY: Dover, 1990), 15.

International money power seeks to usurp money-creating power: Joseph P. Farrell, *Babylon's Banksters: The Alchemy of Deep Physics, High Finance and Ancient Religion* (Port Townsend, WA: Feral House, 2010), 20.

Allies or Infiltrated: Ibid., 163.

Alexander del Mar on the high priests of Rome: Alexander del Mar, *History of Monetary Systems* (London: Effingham Wilson, Royal Exchange, 1895) www.archive.org/stream/historyofmonetar00delmrich/historyofmonetar00delmrich_djvu.txt.

BACON'S INVISIBLE COLLEGE

Francis Bacon's 46 code in Psalms: A. E. Loosley, "Francis Bacon and the James 1st Bible," Sir Francis Bacon's New Advancement of Learning, www.sirbacon.org/Links/Bible.html.

Solomon as a *davidum*: Laurence Gardner, *Lost Secrets of the Sacred Ark: Amazing Revelations of the Incredible Power of Gold* (London: HarperCollins/Element, 2003; New York: Barnes & Noble, 2005), 137.

Freemasonry picking up the threads: Laurence Gardner, *The Shadow of Solomon: The Lost Secret of the Freemasons Revealed* (London: HarperElement, 2005; York Beach, ME, Weiser, 2007), 349.

THE MAGIC OF GOLD

Eirenaeus Philalethes and powder: Laurence Gardner, *The Shadow of Solomon: The Lost Secret of the Freemasons Revealed* (London: HarperElement, 2005; York Beach, ME, Weiser, 2007), 43.

Furnaces were the most important equipment: www.alchemy-books.com/ebook_library/alchemy_the_ancient_science.pdf, 19.

Schefa food: Laurence Gardner, *Lost Secrets of the Sacred Ark: Amazing Revelations of the Incredible Power of Gold* (London: HarperCollins/Element, 2003; New York: Barnes & Noble, 2005), 25.

Human body superconductors: Laurence Gardner, "Lost Secrets of the Sacred Ark—

Lecture: Revelations of the Phenomenal Power of Gold," http://graal.co.uk/lostsecrets lecture.php.

Platinum Group Metals: Laurence Gardner, *Lost Secrets of the Sacred Ark*, 112.

Material moved to another plane: Ibid., 163–71.

Ark rides on Meissner field: Gardner, *Shadow of Solomon*, 348.

Weight of Mercy Seat: Gardner, *Lost Secrets of the Sacred Ark*, 76.

Tablets activated transmitter: R. A. Boulay, *Flying Serpents and Dragons: The Story of Mankind's Reptilian Past* (Escondido, CA: Book Tree, 1997), 292.

DISCOVERIES IN IRAQ

Artifacts in Iraq: "Artifacts Uncovered in Iraq," ABC News, Dec. 28, 1999.

Pentagon alerted to museum importance: Andrew Curry, "History's Loss," *US News & World Report*, Apr. 28, 2003.

McGuire Gibson and Dony George: Jocelyn Gecker, "Experts: Looters Had Keys to Iraq Museum," Associated Press, Apr. 17, 2003.

Bogdanos on inside Job: "Conversations: Building Trust in Iraq," interview of Matthew Bogdanos, *Archaeology* 57, no. 1 (Jan.–Feb. 2004), www.archaeology.org/0401/etc/conversations.html.

Competing clandestine government organizations: Michael E. Salla, "An Exopolitical Perspective on the Preemptive War Against Iraq," Exopolitics: Political Implications of the Extra-terrestrial Presence, Feb. 3, 2003, www.exopolitics.org/Study-Paper2.htm.

Quantum Mechanics and Hyper-Dimensional Environments: "Lost Secrets of the Sacred Ark," Laurence Gardner, http://graal.co.uk/lostsecrets.php.

Few people keep up: Stephen Hawking, *The Illustrated Brief History of Time* (New York: Bantam Books, 1998), 185.

KHAZARIA: MASTERING FINANCIAL CONTROL

Most cruel hoax: Arthur Koestler, *The Thirteenth Tribe: The Khazar Empire and Its Heritage* (New York: Random House, 1976), 17.

A messianic movement in Khazaria: Ibid., 136.

Rothschilds and primogeniture: Derek Wilson, *Rothschild: The Wealth and Power of a Dynasty* (New York: Scribner's, 1988), 455.

Khazars dominate American life: "A Brief History of Khazars in the 'Goldene Medin,'" The Vatic Project, July 13, 2011, http://vaticproject.blogspot.com/2010/07/brief-history-of-khazars-in-goldene.html.

Joel Stein on Jews in Hollywood: Joel Stein, "Who Runs Hollywood? C'mon," *Los Angeles Times*, Dec. 19, 2008, http://articles.latimes.com/2008/dec/19/opinion/oe-stein19.

Jews own a freaking country: Manny Friedman, "Jews *Do* Control the Media," *Times of Israel*, July 1, 2012, http://blogs.timesofisrael.com/Jews-Do-Control-The-Media.

Ben Stein on call from *60 Minutes*: Joel Stein, "Who Runs Hollywood? C'mon," *Los Angeles Times*, Dec. 19, 2008, posted to 800 Pound Gorilla, http://ehpg.wordpress.com/2009/01/22/Who-Runs-Hollywood-C%E2%80%99mon-Jews-Totally-Run-Hollywood.

Magic of converting debt into money: G. Edward Griffin, *The Creature from Jekyll Island: A Second Look at the Federal Reserve* (Westlake Village, CA: American Media, 1994), 219.

Rothschilds as major gold importers: Wilson, *Rothschild*, 178.

The real reason behind the threats to Iran: Pete Papaherakles, "Rothschilds Want Iran's Banks," *American Free Press*, Feb. 10, 2012.

IT RUNS IN THE GENES

DNA within white blood cells: Donald E. Riley, "DNA Testing: An Introduction for Non-scientists," Scientific Testimony: An Online Journal, www.scientific.org/tutorials/articles/riley/riley.html.

Humbling gene discoveries: Elizabeth Pennisi, "The Human Genome," Chinese Medical and Biological Information, http://cmbi.bjmu.edu.cn/News/0102/97.htm.

Difference among me, you, and a chimpanzee: "Human Genome," Science Mysteries, World Mysteries, http://www.world-mysteries.com/sci_1.htm.

Steven Scherer on a jump: Zecharia Sitchin, "The Case of Adam's Alien Genes," Rense, http://rense.com/General9/Adam.htm.

Basques were far advanced: Roslyn Frank, Recovering European Ritual Bear Hunts: A Comparative Study of Basque and Sardinian Ursine Carnival Performances, *Insula* 3, June 2008, 41–97, http://uiowa.academia.edu/RoslynMFrank/Papers/471942/A_single_document_containing_three_published_articles_1_Recovering_European_ritual_bear_hunts_A_comparative_study_of_Basque_and_Sardinian_ursine_carnival_performances_2_Evidence_in_Favor_of_the_Palaeolithic_Continuity_Refugium_Theory_PCRT_Hamalau_and_its_linguistic_and_cultural_rela tives_Part_1_3_Evidence_in_Favor_of_the_Palaeolithic_Continuity_Refugium_Theory_PCRT_Hamalau_and_its_linguistic_and_cultural_relatives_Part._2._

Cauda draconis: "Cauda Draconis," Astrology Dictionary, Astrology Weekly, www.astrologyweekly.com/dictionary/cauda-draconis.php.

Patty Boyer on Rh-negative blood: "Abductee Bloodtypes," What's New, UFO Meme, http://ufomeme.iwarp.com/whats_new_4.html.

THE BLACK NOBILITY

Medici popes as Khazars: "The Black Nobility," Illuminati News, www.illuminati-news.com/black-nobility.htm, from http://groups.yahoo.com/group/TheNeuschwa benlandTimes/message/54.

PART IV: THE MODERN ERA

HITLER AND THE BLUE BLOODS

Intermarried families connected to the black nobility: John Coleman, "The Committee of 300: A Brief History of World Power . . . Venetian Black Nobility, Roots of Today's Ruling Oligarchy, http://investigate911.org/Oligarchy.htm.

Enthusiasm for young girls: Niall Ferguson, *The House of Rothschild*, vol. 1, *Money's Prophets: 1798–1848* (New York: Viking, 1998), 186.

Hitler's ancestry: Walter C. Langer, *The Mind of Adolf Hitler: The Secret Wartime Report* (New York: Basic Books, 1972), 112.

Hitler's support from banking fraternity: A. Ralph Epperson, *The Unseen Hand: An Introduction to the Conspiratorial View of History* (Tucson, AZ: Publius Press, 1985), 266.

A UNIQUE GOLD BOOK

Abe Feder and the contents of the Habsburg book: Author's interviews with Abe Feder and Jim Delittoso, Mar. 1999.

The pyramid structure of the Illuminati: David Icke, *Tales from the Time Loop: The Most Comprehensive Exposé of the Global Conspiracy Ever Written and All You Need to Know to Be Truly Free* (Wildwood, MO: Bridge of Love Publications, 2003), 45–46.

Bloodlines work through secret-society network: Ibid., 43–44.

NOBODY EXPECTS THE SPANISH INQUISITION

Inquisition the Worst Holocaust: freethoughtnation.com/contributing-writers/63-acharya-s/521-womb-envy-an-interview-with-barbara-g-walker.html.

Deluded about the Dark Ages: Martin Doutré, e-mail to author, Jan. 23, 2012.

YOU CAN BANK ON THIS

Mesopotamian merchants monopolized Roman banking: Joseph P. Farrell, *Babylon's Banksters: The Alchemy of Deep Physics, High Finance and Ancient Religion* (Port Townsend, WA: Feral House, 2010), 272.

Bloodlines work through secret-society network: David Icke, *Tales from the Time Loop: The Most Comprehensive Exposé of the Global Conspiracy Ever Written and All You Need to Know to Be Truly Free* (Wildwood, MO: Bridge of Love Publications, 2003), 43–44.

Colonial scrip prime reason for Revolutionary War, described by Ben Franklin: Mike Kirchubel, "How Benjamin Franklin Caused the Revolutionary War," OpEd News, www.opednews.com/Articles/How-Benjamin-Franklin-Caus-By-Mike-Kirchubel-110711-773.html.

Otto von Bismarck: G. Edward Griffin, *The Creature from Jekyll Island: A Second Look at the Federal Reserve* (Westlake Village, CA: American Media, 1994), 374.

Nathan Rothschild official European banker: Derek Wilson, *Rothschild: The Wealth and Power of a Dynasty* (New York: Scribner's, 1988), 178.

Abraham Lincoln on preserving the Union: "I Would Save the Union," Abraham Lincoln: From His Own Words and Contemporary Accounts, National Park Service, www.nps.gov/history/history/online_books/source/sb2/sb2t.htm.

A J. P. Morgan production: Antony C. Sutton, *Wall Street and the Rise of Hitler* (Seal Beach, CA: '76 Press, 1976), 24.

FOLLOW THE LEADER

The fight against international finance: Adolf Hitler, *Mein Kampf* (New York: Houghton Mifflin, 1940), 287–88.

Winston Churchill quote: Emrys Hughes, *Winston Churchill: British Bulldog—His Career in War and Peace* (New York: Exposition Press, 1955), 145.

BREAKS IN THE COLD WAR

Soviet generals and UN undersecretary: A. Ralph Epperson, *The Unseen Hand: An Introduction to the Conspiratorial View of History* (Tucson, AZ: Publius Press, 1985), 319–20.

Times of London editorial: David Allen Rivera, *Final Warning: A History of the New World Order*, http://modernhistoryproject.org/mhp?Article=Finalwarning&C=2.1.

MASTERS OF CONTROL

James G. Watt and cabinet experience: *News Watch Magazine* (July 2010); also see James G. Watt, *The Courage of a Conservative* (New York: Simon and Schuster, 1985), 124–25.

Perkins's critics: Sebastian Mallaby, "The Facts Behind the 'Confessions,'" *Washington Post*, Feb. 26, 2006; and Landon Thomas Jr., *New York Times*, Feb. 19, 2006.

War Is a Racket: www.archive.org/Stream/Warisaracket#Page/N1/Mode/2up.

Michael Rivero on bubble swindle: Michael Collins, "Beyond ForeclosureGate: It Gets Uglier," Daily Censored: Underreported News and Commentary, http://dailycensored.com/2011/04/20/Beyond-Foreclosuregate-It-Gets-Uglier.

Private meeting between Timothy Geithner and Andrew Cuomo: Gretchen Morgenson and Louise Story, "In Financial Crisis, No Prosecutions of Top Figures," *New York Times*, Apr. 14, 2011, www.nytimes.com/2011/04/14/business/14prosecute.html?_r=1&_R=1&pagewanted=all.

William K. Black on criminogenic environment: Ibid.

President James A. Garfield: www.Goodreads.com/Quotes/Show/288058.

THE EXCHANGE STABILIZATION FUND

Exchange Stabilization Fund description: "Exchange Stabilization Fund," Federal Reserve Bank of New York, www.newyorkfed.org/Aboutthefed/Fedpoint/Fed14.html.

Treasury secretary need not comply with U.S. laws: C. Randall Henning, *The Exchange Stabilization Fund: Slush Money or War Chest?* (Washington, DC, Institute for International Economics, 1999), 12.

Lawrence Houston on unvouchered funds: Eric deCarbonnel, "The Exchange Stabilization Fund Role in Financing CIA Covert Operations," Market Skeptics, Sept. 4, 2010, www.marketskeptics.com/2010/09/Exchange-Stabilization-Fund-Role-In.html.

ESF: Eric deCarbonnel, "The ESF and Its History," Market Skeptics, June 3, 2011, www.Marketskeptics.com/2011/06/The-Esf-And-Its-History.html.

Mujahid Kamran on wealthiest families and foundations: Mujahid Kamran, "Who Really Controls the World?" New Dawn, www.newdawnmagazine.com/Articles/Who-Really-Controls-The-World.

PROOF OF THE PLOT

James Glattfelder and Swiss study: Andy Coghlan and Debora MacKenzie, "Revealed—the Capitalist Network That Runs the World," *New Scientist*, Oct. 24, 2011, www.newscientist.com/article/mg21228354.500-Revealed--The-Capitalist-Network-That-Runs-The-World.html.

William Casey and his acquisition of ABC: Jim Marrs, "A Look at William Casey, the CIA & ABC," *Freedom*, Dec. 1986–Jan. 1987.

Money changers have taken over temples: Anthony Wile, interview of Gerald Celente, "Gerald Celente on Trend Forecasting and the Crisis of Western Civilization," Daily Bell, Jan. 22, 2012, www.thedailybell.com/3526/Staff-Report-Celente-Interview.

Stephen Moore on takers, not makers: *Wall Street Journal*, http://online.wsj.com/Article/Sb10001424052748704050204576219073867182108.html#Articletabs%3darticle.

VOICES OF THE ELITE

Bill Ryan on insider "Charles" interview: Project Avalon, www.projectavalon.net, link to all "Charles" threads at 25 January 2011 heading.

Svali explains the Illuminati: "Part 2: Who and What Is the Illuminati?" Whale, www.whale.to/b/svali2.html.

Michael Salla and hidden hand: Michael E. Salla, "Hidden Hand Dialogue Reveals Extraterrestrial Factor in Illuminati Control of Earth," Exopolitics, Nov. 7, 2011, http://exopolitics.org/Exo-Comment-110.htm; and hidden hand dialogue: "Gray Area: Personal Stories—Window of Opportunity," www.abovetopsecret.com/forum/thread402958/pg1.

PRESIDENTIAL BLUE BLOODS

Harold Brooks-Baker on presidential royal connections: Tony Eufinger, "Royal Red Carpet Is Path to White House, ABC News, Oct. 25, 2000, http://abcnews.go.com/international/story?id=82279&page=1#.tzgcsff7r8e.

David Icke on every U.S. election won by royal genes: "American Presidential Bloodlines," Atlantean Conspiracy, Sept. 25, 2011, www.atlanteanconspiracy.com/2008/06/presidential-bloodlines.html.

Obama's family ties to Dick Cheney: "Lynne Cheney: VP, Obama Are Eighth Cousins," NBC News, Oct. 17, 2007, www.msnbc.msn.com/Id/21340764/Ns/Politics/T/Lynne-Cheney-Vp-Obama-Are-Eighth-Cousins/#.UEY9io2PXWH.

George W. Bush related to Obama: New York Post, www.nypost.com/P/News/Regional/Item_Kjxdkmwzqbghpdxxdgwnep.

David Icke quoted Phillip Eugene de Rothschild: David Icke, Tales from the Time Loop: The Most Comprehensive Exposé of the Global Conspiracy Ever Written and All You Need to Know to Be Truly Free (Wildwood, MO: Bridge of Love Publications, 2003), 262.

Majority descended from Charlemagne: http://answers.yahoo.com/Question/Index?Qid=20090119144925aaupqv0.

Credo Muta on African leaders: Icke, Tales from the Time Loop, 40.

BAD FOOD AND WATER

Fluoride blocks thyroid function: Mary Sparrowdancer, "Fluoride Poisoning: It's All Over," Apr. 9, 2011, Rense, http://rense.com/General93/Fluo.htm.

James M. Dunning on fluoridation: Editors, Social Science & Medicine 19 (1984), 1245; also see Fluoride Action Network, "Communities Which Have Rejected Fluoridation Since 1990," Anti Oligarch: This Is Not a Hate Site, Feb. 23, 2012, http://antioligarch.wordpress.com/2012/02/23/Communities-Which-Have-Rejected-Fluoridation-Since-1990.

Michael Whyte on skeletal flourosis: "Harmful Fluoride Levels Found in Instant Iced Tea," Fox News via WebMD, Jan. 25, 2005, www.foxnews.com/story/0,2933,145423,00.html#ixzz1ospu0pqz.

Water resources controlled by defense secretary: "Executive Order—National Defense Resources Preparedness," White House, Mar. 16, 2012, www.whitehouse.gov/The-Press-Office/2012/03/16/Executive-Order-National-Defense-Resources-Preparedness.

EPA investigation of Monsanto: www.lightparty.com/Economic/Monsantodioxinfraud.html; also see: ebookbrowse.com/a-beginners-guide-to-dioxins-pdf-d140490005.

Obama deregulates Monsanto GMO seeds: http://Truth-Out.Org/Index. Php?Option=com_K2&View=Item&Id=1400:Obama-Deregulates-Gmo-Crops-Despite-Supreme-Court-Injunction.

"Monsanto rider": Ronnie Cummins and Alexis Baden-Mayer, "The 'Monsanto Rider': Are Biotech Companies About to Gain Immunity from Federal Law?" AlterNet, July 6, 2012, www.alternet.org/story/156195/the_%27monsanto_rider%27%3A_are_biotech_companies_about_to_gain_immunity_from_federal_law.

Anthony Gucciardi on GMO seeds to African farmers: Anthony Gucciardi, "Bill Gates Foundation Buys 500,000 Shares of Monsanto," Natural Society, Aug. 30, 2010, http://naturalsociety.com/Bill-Gates-Foundation-Buys-500000-Shares-Of-Monsanto.

Bill Gates touting GMO seeds: "Bill Gates: We Need Genetically Modified Seeds," Common Dreams, Feb. 23, 2012, www.commondreams.org/headline/2012/02/23-2.

John Vidal on failure of GMO crops: www.guardian.co.uk/Environment/2011/Oct/19/Gm-Crops-Insecurity-Superweeds-Pesticides.

Pete Riley and Canadian study of pregnant women: Sean Poulter, "GM Food Toxins Found in the Blood of 93% of Unborn Babies," May 20, 2011, www.dailymail.co.uk/health/article-1388888/gm-food-toxins-blood-93-Unborn-Babies.html.

Monsanto genetically modified crops removed from Europe: http://www.viacampesina.org/downloads/pdf/en/Monsanto-Publication-EN-Final-Version.pdf.

Peter Eckes on lack of support for GMO plants in Europe: www.basf.com/Group/Corporate/En/Products-And-Industries/Biotechnology/Plant-Biotechnology/Index.

Anthony Gucciardi on GMO seeds: Anthony Gucciardi, "USDA Steps Back and Gives Monsanto More Power over GMO Seeds, Natural Society, Dec. 27, 2011, http://naturalsociety.com/Usda-Steps-Back-And-Gives-Monsanto-More-Power-Over/#Ixzz1mxksmnho.

Monsanto cafeteria bans GMO food: Crisis Boom, "Genetically Modified Foods Not Served in Monsanto Cafeteria and You Would Think After Investing 20M in GMOs You Would Know Something," Newsnet 14, www.newsnet14.com/?p=94326.

Carol Hoernlein on MSG link to obesity: Carol Hoernlein, MSG Truth, www.msgtruth.org.

Joshua Hamilton and arsenic in juice: "Arsenic in Your Juice: How Much Is Too Much? Federal Limits Don't Exist," *Consumer Reports*, Jan. 2012, www.consumerreports.org/cro/consumer-reports-magazine-january-2012/arsenic-in-your-juice/index.htm.

Mike Adams on problem food: Mike Adams, Proof That the FDA's Assault on Raw Milk Has Nothing to Do with Consumer Safety," Natural Society, Aug. 16, 2011, www.naturalnews.com/033339_Fda_Food_Safety.html#Ixzz1p2jc3yjf.

Sperm counts dropping around the world: Shiva Dindyai, "The Sperm Count Has Been Decreasing Steadily for Many Years in Western Industrialised Countries: Is There an Endocrine Basis for This Decrease?" *Internet Journal of Urology* 2, no. 1 (2004), www.ispub.com/journal/the-internet-journal-of-urology/volume-2-number-1/the-sperm-count-has-been-decreasing-steadily-for-many-years-in-western-industrialised-countries-is-there-an-endocrine-basis-for-this-decrease.html.

Factors lowering male sperm count: Charlotte Maden, "Concern over Decreasing Male Fertility Rates," IVF [In Vitro Fertilization], News, Mar. 10, 2008, www.ivf.net/ivf/concerns-over-decreasing-male-fertility-rates-o3264.html.

Drug deaths outnumber vehicle accident deaths: Lisa Girion, Scott Glover, and Doug Smith, "Drug Deaths Now Outnumber Traffic Fatalities in U.S., Data Show," *Los*

Angeles Times, Sept. 17, 2011, http://articles.latimes.com/2011/sep/17/local/la-me-drugs-epidemic-20110918.

Health care is third leading cause of death: Kah Ying Choo, "America's Healthcare System Is the Third Leading Cause of Death," World Health Education Initiative, www.health-care-reform.net/causedeath.htm, summary of Barbara Starfield, "Is US Health Really the Best in the World? *Journal of the American Medical Association* 284, no. 4 (July 26, 2000): 483–85.

Maryanne Godboldo: "CCHR Human Rights Awardee: Maryanne Godboldo," Citizens Commission on Human Rights International, www.cchrint.org/tag/maryanne-godboldo.

Arguments in ecoscience: Ben Johnson, "Obama's Biggest Radical," Front Page, Feb. 27, 2009, http://archive.frontpagemag.com/readarticle.aspx?artid=34198.

John Holdren and chemtrails: http://www.nypost.com/p/news/politics/bam_man_cool_idea_block_sun_2Opipflho393Yi7gYoJLXP.

PEOPLE ARE THE PROBLEM

Edwin Black and eugenics financing: Edwin Black, "The Horrifying American Roots of Nazi Eugenics," History News Network, Nov. 25, 2003, http://hnn.us/Articles/1796.html.

Thomas Ferguson on single theme: Lonnie Wolf, "The Haig-Kissinger Depopulation Policy," *Executive Intelligence Review*, Mar. 10, 1981, posted as "World Depopulation Is Top NSA Agenda: Club of Rome," Light Network, http://home.iae.nl/users/light-net/world/depopulation.htm.

Maxwell Taylor on a waste of time: Editors, "Maxwell Taylor: 'Write Off a Billion,'" *Executive Intelligence Review*, Sept. 22, 1981.

Prince Philip on population reduction: www.people.com/People/Archive/Article/0,,20080998,00.html.

Philip as a virus: Steve Watson and Alex Jones, "Modern British Royalty: Eugenicists, Nazis, and Neo-Feudalists," Prison Planet, http://www.prisonplanet.com/Pages/100604_prince_philip.html.

Georgia guidestones: "'Let These Be Guide Stones to an Age of Reason': The Message of the Georgia Guidestones," www.thegeorgiaguidestones.com/Message.htm.

A POLICE STATE

Military participation in Drug War increased: Montie Hess, *The Role of the Military in the War on Drugs*, www.dtic.mil/dtic/tr/fulltext/u2/a222302.pdf.

Dick Cheney on high-priority mission of DoD: Christopher M. Schnaubelt, "Can the Military's Effectiveness in the Drug War Be Measured?" *Cato Journal* 14, no. 2 (Fall 1994), www.cato.org/pubs/journal/cjv14n2-5.html.

Radley Balko on danger to conflate cops and soldiers: Radley Balko, "A Decade after 9/11, Police Departments Are Increasingly Militarized," Huffington Post, Nov. 12, 2011, www.Huffingtonpost.com/2011/09/12/Police-Militarization-9-11-September-11_N_955508.html.

Government could have rebuilt New Orleans: Stephan Salisbury and Nick Turse, "Weaponizing the Body Politic," Antiwar, Mar. 5, 2012, http://original.antiwar.com/Engelhardt/2012/03/04/Weaponizing-The-Body-Politic.

Norm Stamper on ten-year campaign: Balko, "Decade after 9/11."

Sheriff's drone crashed into Bearcat: gizmodo.com/5890507/Police-Drone-Crashes-Into-Police.

Houston area drones: www.Click2houston.com/News/New-Police-Drone-Near-Houston-Could-Carry-Weapons/-/1735978/4717922/-/59xnnez/-/Index.html.

Maryland drone crash: Chris Lawrence, "Navy Drone Crashes in Maryland," CNN U.S., http://articles.cnn.com/2012-06-11/us/us_maryland-drone-crash_1_drone-crash-site-routine-training?_s=PM:US.

Researchers hijack Global Hawk drone: "Texas College Hacks Drone in front of DHS," RT: Question More, June 28, 2012, http://rt.com/Usa/News/Texas-1000-Us-Government-906.

Steven Aftergood on drones and surveillance: S. Smithson, "Drones over U.S. Get OK by Congress," *Washington Times*, Feb. 7, 2012, www.washingtontimes.com/news/2012/Feb/7/coming-to-a-sky-near-you.

Cop applicant rejected for being too smart: "Court OKs Barring High IQs for Cops," ABC News, http://abcnews.go.com/us/story?id=95836&page=1#.t079_nl7r8h.

BIG BROTHER IS LISTENING

CIA monitors Facebook: Elizabeth Flock, "CIA Is Watching Tweets, Facebook," *Washington Post*, World, blog, Nov. 4, 2011, www.washingtonpost.com/blogs/blogpost/post/cia-is-watching-tweets-facebook/2011/11/04/gIQAvyylIM_blog.html.

Devin Coldewey questions what's being stored: "NSA to Store Yottabytes of Data in Utah Megarepository," TechCrunch, Nov. 1, 2009, http://techcrunch.com/2009/11/01/Nsa-To-Store-Yottabytes-Of-Surveillance-Data-In-Utah-Megarepository.

James Bamford on British refusal of central data bank: James Bamford, "Who's in Big Brother's Database?" review of Matthew M. Aid, *The Secret Sentry: The Untold Story of the National Security Agency* (New York: Bloomsbury, 2009), *New York Review of Books*, Nov. 5, 2009, www.nybooks.com/articles/archives/2009/nov/05/whos-in-big-brothers-database.

MEDIA CONTROL

David Rockefeller on march to world government: Daniel Estulin, *The True Story of the Bilderberg Group* (Walterville, OR: Trine Day, 2009), 92–93.

Angela Zhang and her cancer cure: Steve Hartman, "Calif. HS Student Devises Possible Cancer Cure," CBS Evening News, Jan 13, 2012, www.cbsnews.com/8301-18563_162-57358994/calif-hs-student-devises-possible-cancer-cure.

FAIR list of interlocking directors: "Interlocking Directorates," Fairness & Accuracy in Reporting, www.fair.org/index.php?page=2870.

Interlocking corporate directors: Bridget Thornton, Brit Walters, and Lori Rouse, *Censored*, ch. 6, "Corporate Media Is Corporate America," in Stephen Ostertag, ed., Online Library for Information on Media, Crime, and Imprisonment, http://employees.oneonta.edu/Ostertsf/Guide-Corporate-Media-Ownership.pdf.

Mike Adams on unbelievable news: Mike Adams, "14 Signs That the Collapse of Our Modern World Has Already Begun," Natural News, May 2, 2011, www.naturalnews.com/032258_Economic_Collapse_2012.html

MORE EFFICIENT SERVITUDE

Tavistock funding from royal family and Rothschilds: John Coleman, *The Tavistock Institute of Human Relations: Shaping the Moral, Spiritual Cultural, Political and*

Economic Decline of the United States of America (Las Vegas, NV: World Intelligence Review, 2006), i.

Tavistock taught the USSR: Ibid., 157.

Tampering with minds still done today: Ibid., 172.

By no means a complete list: Ibid., 130.

Bernays on domination by small number of persons: "Edward Bernays," http://en.wikiquote.org/wiki/Edward_Bernays.

True Ott on SSSS used on American citizens: True Ott, "Digital TV: Mind Control by the Sound of Silence," www.wariscrime.com/2008/12/15/News/Digital-Tv-Mind-Control-By-The-Sound-Of-Silence.

Catherine Austin Fitts and Mr. Global: Lars Schall, "9/11 Was a Fantastically Profitable Covert Operation," Sept. 3, 2011, www.larsschall.com/2011/09/03/911-Was-A-Fantastically-Profitable-Covert-Operation.

TO WHAT END?

Nick Rockefeller quote: Alex Jones, "Nick Rockefeller Revealed Elite Agenda to Aaron Russo During Friendship," Jones Report, Feb. 21, 2007, www.jonesreport.com/articles/210207_rockefeller_friendship.html.

Entire planet's resources at their disposal: Joseph P. Farrell, *Babylon's Banksters: The Alchemy of Deep Physics, High Finance and Ancient Religion* (Port Townsend, WA: Feral House, 2010), 296.

Mujahid Kamran on now: Mujahid Kamran, "Dictatorship at Home and War Abroad," *Nation* (English-language Pakistani daily), Sept. 5, 2012, www.nation.com.pk/pakistan-news-newspaper-daily-english-online/columns/20-mar-2012/dictatorship-at-home-and-war-abroad.

Emergency order already in place: Mac Slavo, "Domestic War Zone: 'Like Tribal Warfare in Iraq'; Cops Outnumbered 500-to-1, SHTFplan: When It Hits the Fan, Don't Say We Didn't Warn You," July 12, 2012, www.shtfplan.com/Headline-News/Domestic-Warzone-Like-Tribal-Warfare-In-Iraq-Cops-Outnumbered-500-To-1_07122012.

Alex Jones on overlords as superbeings: Paul Joseph Watson, "Endgame: Elite's Plan for Global Enslavement Exposed," Prison Planet, Oct. 25, 2007, www.prisonplanet.com/articles/october2007/251007_end_game.htm.

The bankers' order: Anthony Wile, interview of Gerald Celente, "Gerald Celente on Trend Forecasting and the Crisis of Western Civilization," Daily Bell, Jan. 22, 2012, www.thedailybell.com/3526/Staff-Report-Celente-Interview.

Radioactive iodine in Calgary water: Alex Roslin, "What Are Officials Hiding About Fukushima?" Straight, Oct. 20, 2011, www.straight.com/Article-491941/Vancouver/What-Are-Officials-Hiding-About-Fukushima.

St. Louis rainwater radiation: "Report: St. Louis Rainwater Shows Radiation Dose at 13.3 Microsieverts per Hour—130+ Times Background," ENENews: Energy News, Sept. 17, 2011, http://enenews.com/St-Louis-Rainwater-Shows-13-3-Microsieverts-Per-Hour-Video.

Mike Adams on exposure to X-ray radiation: Mike Adams, "14 Signs That the Collapse of Our Modern World Has Already Begun," Natural News, May 2, 2011, www.naturalnews.com/032258_Economic_Collapse_2012.html.

A DISASTER IN THE MAKING

Dead 9/11 first responders: Jerry Mazza, "9/11 First Responder Death Toll Nears 1,000," Intrepid Report, Apr. 7, 2011, www.intrepidreport.com/archives/1432.

OSU release on heightened carcinogens in gulf: "OSU Researchers Find Heightened Levels of Known Carcinogens in Gulf," Sept. 30, 2010, http://oregonstate.edu/ua/ncs/archives/2010/Sep/Osu-Researchers-Find-Heightened-Levels-Known-Carcinogens-Gulf.

Francis Beinecke on no recovery on Gulf Coast: Frances Beinecke, "On National Oil Spill Commission, We Concluded Systemic Problems Led to Gulf Blowout," Huffington Post, Jan. 11, 2011, www.huffingtonpost.com/frances-beinecke/on-national-oil-spill-com_b_807311.html.

Darryl Malek-Wiley on lack of health care: Melinda Tuhus, interview of Darryl Malek-Wiley, "One Year after BP Oil Spill Disaster, Environmental and Economic Destruction Difficult to Calculate," Between the Lines, Apr. 27, 2011, www.btlonline.org/2011/seg/110506bf-btl-malek-wiley.html.

Michael Snyder on oil cleanup deaths: Michael Snyder, "Warning to Gulf Volunteers: Almost Every Cleanup Worker from the 1989 Exxon Valdez Disaster Is Now Dead," Business Insider, June 30, 2010, www.businessinsider.com/warning-to-gulf-cleanup-workers-almost-every-crew-member-from-the-1989-exxon-valdez-disaster-is-now-dead-2010-6#ixzz1mzy0zzdd.

Frances Beinecke on root causes: Beinecke, "Systemic Problems Led to Gulf Blowout."

Dave Hodges and the great Gulf Coast holocaust: Dave Hodges, "The Great Gulf Coast Holocaust," part 1, June 29, 2011, http://gunnyg.wordpress.com/2011/06/29/Dave-Hodges-The-Great-Gulf-Coast-Holocaust-Part-1.

BBC reports on oil spill profits: "Halliburton Profits Up Despite Oil Spill," BBC News, Business, July 19, 2010, www.bbc.co.uk/news/business-10688301.

Transocean CEO and executive bonuses for safety: "Transocean Gives Safety Bonuses Despite Deaths in Gulf of Mexico Oil Rig Explosion," Associated Press, Apr. 2, 2011, www.nola.com/news/gulf-oil-spill/index.ssf/2011/04/transocean_gives_safety_bonuse.html.

Sterling Allan on Goldman Sachs short-selling: Sterling Allan, "No Joke: Goldman Sachs Shorted Gulf of Mexico," San Francisco Examiner, May 5, 2010, www.examiner.com/breakthrough-energy-in-national/no-joke-goldman-sachs-shorted-gulf-of-mexico.

Paul Craig Roberts on U.S. Treasury secretary: Barry Ritholtz, "Tim Geithner, Employee of Goldman Sachs?" The Big Picture, July 10, 2009, www.Ritholtz.com/Blog/2009/07/Tim-Geithner-Employee-Of-Goldman-Sachs.

Goldman Sachs invests in Facebook: Susanne Craig and Andrew Ross Sorkin, "Goldman Offering Clients a Chance to Invest in Facebook," New York Times, Dealbook, Jan. 2, 2011, http://dealbook.nytimes.com/2011/01/02/Goldman-Invests-In-Facebook-At-50-Billion-Valuation.

FREEMAN OR SERF?

Roosevelt's 1933 letter: Elliot Roosevelt, ed., F.D.R.: His Personal Letters 1928–1945, vol. 1 (New York: Duell, Sloan & Pearce, 1950), 371–73.

Iodine essential to human health: www.Optimox.com/Pics/Iodine/Iod-05/Iod_05.html

For more on overstepping government, see: Mike Adams, "The Great Government Hoax of Public Safety," Natural News, Mar. 1, 2012, www.naturalnews.com/035116_ Government_Public_Safety_Democide.html; and John Stossel, "Illegal Everything: Stunning Video Report About Government Completely Out of Control," Fox News, posted to Natural News, Mar. 28, 2012, http://tv.naturalnews.com/V.Asp?V=783b7c 44aa93208d325b26fbb54fe025.

Governed by self or a ruling elite: Neal Ross, "The Real Purpose of the Constitution," Tenth Amendment Center, Aug. 8, 2008, http://tenthamendmentcenter. com/2008/08/08/The-Real-Purpose-Of-The-Constitution.

Aldous Huxley letter: Aldous Huxley to George Orwell, Oct. 21, 1949, "1984 v. Brave New World," Letters of Note, Mar. 6, 2012, www.lettersofnote.com/2012/03/1984- v-brave-new-world.html.

Chris Hedges on the only word corporations know: Chris Hedges, "The Best Among Us," Truthout, Sept. 30, 2011, http://truth-out.org/index.php?option=com_ k2&view=item&id=3689:the-best-among-us.

INDEX

Uranus, 6, 8, 15
Ur Kaœdim, 93
Ur-Nammu, Sumerian king, 126
USAID (Agency for International Development), 268
U.S. Congress:
control of, 332
legislation of, 270
U.S. government:
electronic monitoring by, 309–11
employees of, 279
Exchange Stabilization Fund (ESF), 271–75
and food additives, 291–301, 333–34
lack of accountability, 327
media control by, 311–15
and mind manipulation, 318–21
as police state, 304–9, 332–36
and Smithsonian, 39–40
Ussher, James, *Annals of the World,* 4–5
Utnapishtim, 97, 151–53

V (TV), x
vaccination, 334–35
Valentine, J. Manson, 116
Vander Ploeg, Dirk, 13–14
Vasilev, Stefan, 263
Vasin, Michael, 21
Vatican:
power of, 208–9
works confiscated by, 197
Vatican Library, 281
Vaughan, Thomas, 219
Velikovsky, Immanuel, 122
Venice, money and power in, 241
Venus (goddess), 192, 289
Venus (planet), 8, 9, 69, 122
Viagra, 300
Victoria, queen of England, 288
Vidal, John, 295
Vietnam War, 264, 266, 293–94
Viking Lander, 9–10
Viracocha, xiii
Virgil, 208
Visoko, Sarajevo, 105
Von Ward, Paul, 130–31, 137, 172, 174
We Have Never Been Alone, xiii
Vyse, Howard, 99

Walker, Barbara G., 252
Walker, Sydnor, 52
Wall, Mike, 10
Walters, Brit, 315
war, as control mechanism, 179
Warburg family, 247

Warner, John, 323
War on Drugs, 266, 304, 305–7
Washington, George, 286, 287
Watchers, 63, 92–93, 284
water:
fluoride in, 291–93, 297
infertility chemicals in, 301
Waters, Michael R., 32
Watt, James G., 266–67
Weber, J. Cynthia, 163
Weird Science, xi
Weishaupt, Adam, 281–82
Welf family, 243
West, John Anthony, 88
Whig Revolution, 218
White, Harry Dexter, 273
White, Nicky, 116
White, Paul, xiii, 182–83
White, Tim, 55
Whitman, Christine, 327
Whyte, Michael, 293
Wilkens, H. P., 22
William of Orange, 243, 254
William, Prince (England), 289
Wilson, Allan, 58–60
Wilson, Derek, 233, 236, 257
Wilson, Don, 17
Wilson, Raymond H. Jr., 13
Wilson, Woodrow, 263, 317
Winnemucca, Nevada, museum, 41
Woolley, Leonard, 111
World Bank, 268, 274, 317
World Trade Center, New York, 262, 305
World War I:
and mind manipulation, 317
and money, 258–59
World War II, 273
postwar, 262–65

Yad Hanadiv, 53–54
Yadin, Yigael, 54
Yahweh, 161, 162, 174, 201, 224
Yang Ji, 107
Yonaguni Monument, 71–72
Young, Ray and Melanie, 81

Zawyet el-Aryan pyramid, 104
ZEP TEPI, xiii
Zhang, Angela, 312–13
ziggurats, 71–73, 125
Zinchenko, Constantine, 264
Zionism, 231–32, 236, 237
zodiac, 129
Zucker, Jeff, 234
Zulu, 134, 143, 290

BOOKS BY JIM MARRS

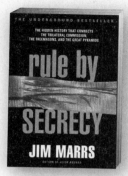

RULE BY SECRECY
**The Hidden History That
Connects the Trilateral Commission, the Freemasons,
and the Great Pyramids**

Available in Paperback

Jim Marrs examines the world's most closely guarded secrets, tracing the history of clandestine societies and the power they have wielded.

THE RISE OF THE FOURTH REICH
**The Secret Societies That
Threaten to Take Over America**

Available in Paperback and eBook

Throw out everything you think you know about history. *The Rise of the Fourth Reich* reveals the truth about American power.

OUR OCCULTED HISTORY
Do the Global Elite Conceal Ancient Aliens?

Available in Paperback, eBook, and Large Print

In *Our Occulted History*, Marrs goes beyond the revelations of his classic *Alien Agenda* and illustrates how human civilization may have originated with non-humans.

THE TRILLION-DOLLAR CONSPIRACY
**How the New World Order, Man-Made Diseases, and
Zombie Banks Are Destroying America**

Available in Paperback, eBook, and AudioCD

"Jim Marrs can't be ignored."
—*Dallas Observer*

ALIEN AGENDA
**Investigating the
Extraterrestrial
Presence Among Us**

Available in Paperback

"You may find yourself watching the skies a little more intently . . ." —*Ft. Worth Star-Telegram*